Palgrave Studies in A

MW01088512

Series Editors
Marc Brightman
Department of Anthropology
University College London
London, UK

Jerome Lewis
Department of Anthropology
University College London
London, UK

Our series aims to bring together research on the social, behavioral, and cultural dimensions of sustainability: on local and global understandings of the concept and on lived practices around the world. It publishes studies which use ethnography to help us understand emerging ways of living, acting, and thinking sustainably. The books in this series also investigate and shed light on the political dynamics of resource governance and various scientific cultures of sustainability.

More information about this series at
http://www.springer.com/series/14648

Marc Brightman • Jerome Lewis
Editors

The Anthropology of Sustainability

Beyond Development and Progress

palgrave
macmillan

Editors
Marc Brightman
Department of Anthropology
University College London
London, United Kingdom

Jerome Lewis
Department of Anthropology
University College London
London, United Kingdom

Palgrave Studies in Anthropology of Sustainability
ISBN 978-1-137-56635-5 (hardcover)   ISBN 978-1-137-56636-2   (eBook)
ISBN 978-1-349-93441-6 (softcover)
DOI 10.1057/978-1-137-56636-2

Library of Congress Control Number: 2017946895

Cover image © skhoward, iStock / Getty Images Plus
Cover design by Fatima Jamadar

Printed on acid-free paper

This Palgrave Macmillan imprint is published by Springer Nature
The registered company is Nature America Inc.
The registered company address is: 1 New York Plaza, New York, NY 10004, U.S.A.

PREFACE

The Centre for the Anthropology of Sustainability (CAoS), based in the Department of Anthropology at UCL, promotes research, discussion and publications that take the dream of sustainability seriously and, most importantly, that search and struggle for alternatives. CAoS was launched with a conference in 2015, 'Anthropological Visions of Sustainable Futures', that brought together a group of eminent colleagues to discuss the insights our discipline can contribute to the concept of 'sustainability', and conversely to consider the consequences of applying the idea of sustainability to our discipline and its distinctive core methodology: ethnography. In addition to two days of plenary presentations followed by lively commentary from invited discussants, the conference hosted Marcus Coates, an artist whose work offers a multispecies commentary on aspects of the human condition, and presented a sell-out performance of the play 'Gaia Global Circus' conceived by Bruno Latour, written by Pierre Daubigny, and directed by Frédérique Aït-Touati and Chloe Latour, contemplating what climate change and the Anthropocene mean for humanity.

The results of this gathering exceeded our expectations. The presentations and ensuing discussions offered profound insights into what the notoriously ambiguous and politically manipulated term 'sustainability' means; of what needs to be sustained to ensure future livability; of the value of ethnography for understanding what living sustainably means in practice for human societies, and what it does not; of the emerging academic significance of anthropology in the Anthropocene; and of the ethical-cum-political duty of anthropologists to fight more forcefully for diversity so as to secure a livable future for humans and non-humans in the ecologically nested systems we share. This volume makes these surprisingly convergent insights available to a wider audience.

We are immensely grateful to all of the discussants at the CAoS conference whose thoughtful and provocative reflections helped further inspire the editors and contributors to this volume: Olivia Angé, Laura Bear, Phil Burnham, Carolina Commandulli, Gill Conquest, Phillippe Descola, Pablo Dominguez, Keith Hart, Evan Killick, Hannah Knox, Ellen Potts, Anne-Christine Taylor, Cathryn Townsend, Olga Ulturgasheva and Cédric Yvinec. We wish to thank Haidy Geismar, Vanessa Grotti, Martin Holbraad, Katherine Homewood and Hannah Knox for their comments on the text. Special thanks are due to Paul Carter-Bowman, Hernando Echeverri, and Cathryn Townsend for their help organizing the event. We also gratefully acknowledge the generous support of the Faculty of Social and Historical Sciences and the Joint Faculty Institute of Graduate Studies at UCL, the Institut Français de Londres, the Royal Anthropological Institute, and the Association of Social Anthropologists. This book is dedicated to the memory of Gill Conquest, an extraordinary person, exceptional student and polymath who helped us to build CAoS from its earliest days.

London, UK
2017

Marc Brightman
Jerome Lewis

CONTENTS

NOTE ON CONTRIBUTORS

Bill Adams is Moran Professor of Conservation and Development in the Department of Geography at the University of Cambridge. He is currently working on a new edition of his book on sustainable development (*Green Development*, Routledge 2003), and a new project on *Future Natures*, focusing on ideas of naturalness, authenticity, and artificiality in nature conservation. This looks at the implications of novel technologies in conservation theory and practice, and the importance of ideas of place in conservation territorialization.

Frédérique Aït-Touati is the director of the Experimental Programme in Arts and Politics at Sciences Po Paris (SPEAP), a theatre director and a researcher at the CNRS and EHESS. The main focus of her research is the relationship between fiction and knowledge. She has directed plays and performances including *Gaia Global Circus* and *The Theatre of Negotiations/Make It Work*, a simulation of an international conference on climate change, in collaboration with Bruno Latour. She is the author of *Fictions of the Cosmos, Science and Literature in the Seventeenth Century* (Chicago, 2011). Her current book project, entitled *Performing knowledge*, explores the relationship between cultures of performance and cultures of knowledge from the early modern period to the present.

Mauro Almeida was born in Acre, Brazil, and obtained his PhD in Social Anthropology at the University of Cambridge. He is associate professor at the Campinas State University (retired), where he is a member of the Centre for Rural Studies (CERES). He has field experience in Amazonia (on rubber tappers, mixed-blood Amazonians) and does research on the boundaries between traditional knowledge and scientific knowledge. His publications include the *A enciclopédia da floresta. O Alto Juruá: prática e conhecimentos das populações* (The Forest Encyclopedia. Upper Jurua: practices and knowledge of inhabitants), co-authored with Manuela Carneiro da Cunha.

Marc Brightman is Lecturer in Social and Environmental Sustainability in the Department of Anthropology, University College London. He has carried out research among Carib-speaking peoples (Trio, Wayana and Akuriyo) of north-eastern Amazonia (Suriname and French Guiana) on leadership, property relations, and perspectives on environmental conservation, and has studied forest governance and the 'greening' of development, focusing on the UN-REDD 'readiness' programme. His current project explores the role of migrants in agriculture in southern Italy. His most recent book is *The Imbalance of Power: Leadership, Masculinity and Wealth in Amazonia* (Berghahn Books, 2016).

Manuela Carneiro da Cunha is professor emerita of Anthropology at the University of Chicago as well as the University of São Paulo. In 2011–2012, she was visiting chair at the Collège de France. She has carried out research on historical anthropology, on emancipated West African slaves and ethnicity, on indigenous history and land rights in Brazil, and on traditional people's knowledge and intellectual rights. She is a member of the Brazilian Academy of Sciences.

Marcus Coates was born in 1968 in London, UK. In 2008, he was the recipient of a Paul Hamlyn Award, and in 2009, he won the Daiwa Art Prize. His solo exhibitions include *The Trip*, Serpentine Gallery, London; *Implicit Sound*, Fundació Joan Miró, Barcelona; *Psychopomp*, Milton Keynes Gallery and *Marcus Coates*, Kunsthalle, Zurich, Switzerland. Group exhibitions include *Private Utopia*: Contemporary Art from the British Council Collection, Tokyo Station Gallery, Japan; *Station to Station*, Barbican Art Centre, London; *THE BEAUTY OF DISTANCE: Songs of Survival in a Precarious Age*, Sydney Biennale, Australia; *ALTERMODERN, Tate Triennial*, Tate Britain, London; *MANIFESTA 7*, Trento, Italy; *Transformation*, Museum of Contemporary Art, Tokyo; *Laughing in a Foreign Language*, Hayward Gallery, London; *Hamsterwheel*, Malmo Konsthall, Sweden and Venice Biennale. A retrospective book, *Marcus Coates*

(2016), commissioned by Kunsthalle Zurich and Milton Keynes Gallery, is published by Koenig. Marcus Coates lives and works in London.

Arturo Escobar is Professor of Anthropology at the University of North Carolina, Chapel Hill, and research associate with the Culture, Memory, and Nation group at Universidad del Valle, Cali. His main interests are political ecology, ontological design, and the anthropology of development, social movements, and technoscience. Over the past 25 years, he has worked closely with several Afro-Colombian social movements in the Colombian Pacific, in particular the Process of Black Communities (PCN). His most well-known book is *Encountering Development: The Making and Unmaking of the Third World* (1995, 2nd ed. 2011). His most recent book is *Sentipensar con la Tierra. Nuevas lecturas sobre desarrollo, territorio y diferencia* (2014).

James Fairhead is Professor of Social Anthropology at the University of Sussex. He has researched on environmental and medical questions in Central and West Africa since the 1980s, and more latterly on the history of the region and of anthropology itself. He is author of many works including *Misreading the African Landscape* (CUP 1996), *Reframing Deforestation* (Routledge 1998), *Science Society and Power* (CUP 2003), *Vaccine Anxieties* (Routledge 2007) and *The Captain and the Cannibal* (Yale, 2015). During the Ebola crisis he helped found the Ebola Response Anthropology Platform that provided social, cultural, and political analysis to the medical response.

Kirsten Hastrup is Professor of Anthropology at the University of Copenhagen. In recent years she has worked with a hunting community in Northwest Greenland, studying the changes in climate and community. Earlier, she worked in Iceland and published three monographs on its long-term history, natural and social. An overall thematic interest in her work is the co-constitution of nature and society, which points far beyond 'the local'. From 2009 to 2014, she held an ERC Advanced Grant; the project, Waterworlds, studied water-related challenges to diverse communities across the globe. Among her recent books are the edited volumes on *Anthropology and Nature* (2014), and *Waterworlds: Anthropology in Fluid Environments* (2016, co-edited with Frida Hastrup).

Katherine M. Homewood studied Zoology at Oxford University and gained her PhD in Anthropology at the University of London. After working at the University of Dar es Salaam in Tanzania, she joined UCL as Lecturer and Tutor in Human Sciences, an interdisciplinary and interdepartmental degree. She is now Professor in Anthropology at UCL. Her work centres on the interaction of conservation and development in sub-Saharan Africa, with a special focus on pastoralist peoples in drylands, among other groups and ecosystems. She researches the implications of natural resource policies and management for local people's livelihoods and welfare, and the implications of changing land use for environment and biodiversity. Her Human Ecology Research Group integrates natural and social sciences approaches to interactions of environment and development around the global South.

Alf Hornborg is Professor of Human Ecology, Lund University, Lund, Sweden. He is the author of *The Power of the Machine* (AltaMira, 2001), *Global Ecology and Unequal Exchange* (Routledge, 2013), and *Global Magic* (Palgrave Macmillan, 2016) and editor of *Rethinking Environmental History* (AltaMira, 2007), *The World System and the Earth System* (Left Coast Press, 2007), *Ethnicity in Ancient Amazonia* (University of Colorado Press, 2011), and *Ecology and Power* (Routledge, 2012). His research interests include economic anthropology, environmental history, political ecology, and ecological economics.

Signe Howell is Professor Emeritus of Social Anthropology at the University of Oslo. She has undertaken extensive field work with Chewong, a hunting-gathering, shifting-cultivating group in Peninsular Malaysia, and with Lio people in Eastern Indonesia. More recently, she has been engaged in a study of the implementation of the global REDD initiative (Reducing Emission from Deforestation and Forest Degradation) in tropical forest countries, especially in Indonesia. She has published extensively on topics ranging from cosmology, ritual, kinship, and gender, to environmental ideologies and practices.

Bruno Latour is Professor at Sciences Po Paris, Director of the Médialab, of the SPEAP master in political arts and of the FORCCAST project on mapping controversies. Most of his papers and all references may be accessed on his web site www.bruno-latour.fr.

Jerome Lewis is Reader in Social Anthropology at University College London. He researches egalitarianism among Central African hunter-gatherers and other hunter-gatherer societies across the world. After researching the impact of the genocide on Rwanda's Twa he worked with Mbendjele in Congo-Brazzaville on egalitarian politics, forest management, child socialisation, play, religion, language, music and dance. He also studies hunter-gatherers' relations with outsiders and the impact of logging and conservation initiatives on their lifeways. He collaborates with affected hunter-gatherers and other local people through the Extreme Citizen Science Research Group at UCL to support environmental justice (www.ucl.ac.uk/excites).

Dominique Millimouno is an independent social development researcher in the Republic of Guinea. He has published widely on medical and ecological practices in the context of a variety of assignments with UN and Aid organisations and European universities.

Henrietta L. Moore is the Director of the Institute for Global Prosperity and Chair in Culture, Philosophy and Design at UCL. As an anthropologist and cultural theorist, her recent work has focused on the notion of global sustainable futures. Her approach draws together ideas about institutional change, citizenship and social justice with diverse understandings of what it means to flourish. She is actively involved in the application of social science insights to policy at all levels and is committed to involving grassroots communities in the production of new types of knowledge through citizen science.

Laura Rival is associate professor at Oxford University, where she teaches various courses relating to the anthropology of nature, society, and development. Her research interests include anthropology and interdisciplinarity; Amerindian conceptualizations of nature and society; historical and political ecology; development, conservation and environmental policies in Latin America; sustainability in the Anthropocene; indigenous peoples and theories of human development.

Veronica Strang is the Director of Durham University's Institute of Advanced Study and a Professor of Anthropology. Her research focuses on human-environmental relationships, in particular engagements with water. Her publications include *The Meaning of Water* (2004); *Gardening* *the World: Agency, Identity and the Ownership of Water* (2009), *Ownership and Appropriation* (2010), and *Water: Nature and Culture* (2015). She was one of UNESCO's international *Les Lumières de L'Eau* in 2007, and since 2013 has served as Chair of the Association of Social Anthropologists of the UK and the Commonwealth. She also writes on interdisciplinarity, including *Evaluating Interdisciplinary Research: A Practical Guide* (2015), and *Transforming the Way We Think* (2016).

Anna Tsing teaches anthropology at the University of California, Santa Cruz. She is also a Niels Bohr Professor at Aarhus University, where she co-directs Aarhus University Research on the Anthropocene (AURA), an interdisciplinary program for fieldwork-based collaborations across the arts and sciences. Her most recent book is *The Mushroom at the End of the World: On the Possibility of Life in Capitalist Ruins* (Princeton University Press, 2015).

List of Figures

Introduction: The Anthropology of Sustainability: Beyond Development and Progress

Marc Brightman and Jerome Lewis

'Sustainability' is the dream of passing a livable earth to future generations, human and nonhuman. The term is also used to cover up destructive practices, and this use has become so prevalent that the word most often makes me laugh and cry.
Anna Tsing (Chap. 3)

Anthropologists are quick to point out the contradictions, abuses and politically motivated uses of the term 'sustainability'. But what happens if anthropologists apply their knowledge to understanding what sustainability *should* mean and what that entails? This book is the beginning of an answer. The answer takes many forms, some will inspire, others challenge, but all converge to suggest a radical shift and restructuring of what we imagine anthropology to be, and a greater appreciation of the importance of the role

M. Brightman (✉) • J. Lewis
Department of Anthropology, University College London, London, UK

© The Author(s) 2017

M. Brightman, J. Lewis (eds.), *The Anthropology of Sustainability*,
Palgrave Studies in Anthropology of Sustainability,
DOI 10.1057/978-1-137-56636-2_1

required of anthropologists in the twenty-first century to help ensure a liveable earth.

Our insights are distinctive, some even surprising, because anthropology is holistic and involves shifting temporal and spatial scales of analysis. It explores how values and practices, ontologies and epistemologies interact and change, paying attention to the details of the everyday as much as to the exotic, and to the powerful as well as to subalterns. By documenting the diversity of relationships between humans and non-humans, it provides unique insights on the present possibilities available for humanity and offers ways to rethink humanity's current trajectory in order to help pass on a liveable earth to future generations.

The anthropology of sustainability involves studying cultural processes from 'multiple perspectives, based on the interests and needs of particular societies, rather than the universalist interests of any single ideological, historical, or methodological tradition' (Maida 2007: 12). Yet anthropology is not just about the study of individual human societies and cultures, but crucially about their interaction and long-term co-constitution. Anthropologists have been translating between cultures since the birth of the discipline, and this skill is likely to have important new applications to support better communication between scientific disciplines as we seek to comprehend the Anthropocene. The challenge of sustainability demands much more than the protection or preservation of communities or nature reserves, and more than technical fixes for CO_2 production or resource limitations: it requires re-imagining and reworking communities, societies and landscapes, especially those dominated by industrial capitalism, to help us build a productive symbiosis with each other and the many nonhumans on whom we depend.

This is an ambitious project of change. It challenges the ideology of progress and development that continues to prevail across political and economic institutions. Anthropology is well placed to facilitate this shift by exchanging ideas, values and practices across cultural and disciplinary boundaries, by explaining the necessity of expanding our notion of community inclusively at both the micro and macro scales, and contemplating the constraints that should be placed on unsustainable practices. Sustainability, from this point of view, might best be understood as the process of facilitating conditions for change by building and supporting diversity— ontological, biological, economic and political diversity.

This is in direct contrast to the increasingly popular term 'resilience' that is touted by many as the best way of addressing climate change and the harm caused by the excesses of industrial capitalism. Increasingly international bodies, governments, bankers, development organizations, the military and other large corporations support approaches to sustainability in terms of resilience. This move is based on the belief that an ability to 'bounce back' after a shock, and return to whatever was the pre-crisis condition, is the best way of enduring into the future. However, as Neocleous (2013) argues, this focus diverts attention from seeking to address the forces causing the shocks, to the ability of the victims to cope with them and continue on as they did before. In contrast to how we propose sustainability to be understood, the focus on building resilience drives efforts into recovery and places blame on the individual for not being able to cope rather than on the structural issues causing the shocks.

For these reasons, we here argue the need to focus our approach to the future in terms of sustainability—on how to ensure a future liveable earth, but not in terms of maintaining what went before (as resilience thinking implies) but as a process that prepares us for an unpredictable future by supporting and encouraging diversity in all its forms, at the same time as confronting the causes of the situation head-on.

THE ORIGINS OF SUSTAINABILITY

The concept of sustainability is notoriously fuzzy and has been subject to dozens of different definitions, Latouche (1995) notes 60, but it has a specifically European heritage. The German cultural historian Ulrik Grober argues that the idea of sustainability begins to appear during the enlightenment. The first use of the German word for sustainability, *nachhaldigkeit*, appears in a treaty on forestry, called *Sylviculture oeconomica*, or 'A guide to the cultivation of native trees', by Hans Carl von Carlowitz, published in Leipzig in 1713. In the context of increasing demand for wood to fuel the furnaces of smelting plants and hammer mills in Saxony, Von Carlowitz criticized the short-term thinking that was allowing more and more woodland to be converted to fields and meadows. He advocated greater efficiency through the insulation of buildings, improved stoves, furnaces and hearths, and the use of alternative fuels such as peat. Above all, he called for systematic reforestation. He then asked, 'how such a conservation and cultivation of wood can be arranged so as to make possible a continuous, steady and *sustaining* use (*nachhaltende Nutzung*), as this is an indispensable necessity, without which the country cannot maintain its being' (Grober 2012: 83). As Grober writes, the term 'joins together the adjectival participle *nachhaltend* with *Nutzung* (use) in a construction which opens the door for the abstract noun *Nachhaltigkeit* ('sustainability', the state of being sustainable)' (ibid.). No other European language of the time had an equivalent term.

Already in the eighteenth century, the rise of ideas of sustainability was accompanied by a rise in managerialism, promoted by enlightenment methodologies for the rational management of natural resources. But this view of sustainability was grounded in a Cartesian belief in the right to subjugate nature to human needs, from which emerged a form of domination that relied on the governance of life, what Foucault called 'biopower' (2009). Ecology began as an alternative discourse, and Goethe was one of its earliest proponents. Like the later Romantics, he saw man as a part of nature, and inspired by Spinoza and Linnaeus, spoke of the 'economy of nature' as a foundation for all economic activity, placing ecological relations at the heart of a sustainable economy (Grober 2012: 95). The interrelatedness of all organisms is most powerfully articulated in modern discourse in the philosophy of deep ecology (Naess 1989), but globally better represented by diverse animistic ways of relating to the environment.

In the UK, the rise of managerialism was prompted by the Victorian passion for natural history alongside the extensive nineteenth-century commercial extraction of particular species such as birds of paradise for millinery, or entire landscapes such as wetlands being drained for cultivation. This combination led to the resulting species' declines being clearly documented, prompting the rise in managerial approaches to landscapes and the resources they contained. In the twentieth century, this developed into recognition of the importance of conservation and dedicated funding for it in the aftermath of World War II (Lowe 1983). Inspired by the 'economy of nature' and developments in Europe and USA, the environmentalist movement became more influential in the 1960s, but also a more institutionalized and a more managerial international network. With the establishment of the International Union for the Conservation of Nature (IUCN) in 1980, 'conservation' became the dominant modern approach to managing the non-urban and non-transformed natural environment.

Under the umbrella of the International Union for the Conservation of Nature (IUCN), large conservation NGOs such as Conservation International and WWF developed conservation methodologies and typologies of protected areas. They managed to gain influence in international policy circles, with landmark documents such as the Club of Rome's *The Limits to Growth* (Meadows et al. 1972) and the Brundtland Report (World Commission on

Environment and Development 1987), leading to the Rio Declaration (United Nations General Assembly 1992), and eventually to the Sustainable Development Goals (United Nations Sustainable Development knowledge platform 2015). Agreed a few months before the Paris Conference of Parties to the UN in November 2015, the Paris Agreement accepting these as international priorities came into force on 4 November 2016 (United Nations Treaty Collection 2016). This institutionalization of sustainability is dominated by a preoccupation with economic considerations and a tendency to address cultural, social and ecological concerns in ways compatible with economic growth.

SUSTAINABILITY TODAY

Several contributors (Hastrup, Homewood, Adams, Howell, Rival) trace 'sustainability' and its global connections by outlining institutionalized definitions of what constitutes sustainability with what happens locally when such ideas are applied. Universalizing discourses of development and progress tends to suppress political realities and local contingencies, a phenomenon that Ferguson (1990) named the 'anti-politics machine'. With the coupling of development to sustainability a similar process is produced. Development interventions are surprisingly rarely successful, especially when evaluated over time and according to the terms of their original aims. They often ignore or misunderstand social, political and cultural realities at the expense of ordinary people. As Katherine Homewood notes in Chap. 6, the Sustainable Development Goals aim at a convergence between economic development, social equity and environmental protection, and these goals are reformulated as a series of measurable and verifiable indicators, some of which are in contradiction with each other. For instance, the goal of 'eliminating poverty' (SDG 1) is in tension with the dominant approaches towards 'protecting terrestrial ecosystems' (SDG 15). This tension often produces contradictions between conservation and development aims. Debates about 'sustainable development' are, as Desmond McNeill has argued, characterized by conflicts of interpretation, notably between 'technicists' calling for technical solutions to environmental problems and 'humanists' promoting more political solutions (Maida 2007: 1, paraphrasing McNeill 2000). This separation between 'technicists' and 'humanists' is part of the legacy of the enlightenment conception of sustainability premised on a natural world separate from social and cultural life.

Such a perspective finds its logical conclusion in resolutions such as that proposed by the eminent biologist E.O. Wilson in his latest book

Half Earth (2016), which calls for half of the entire planet to be set aside for nature, arguing that this is the only way to avoid the disastrous effects of a sixth extinction. But the practical, political and economic implications of trying to enforce such a plan on the millions of people living outside mega cities and in a great diversity of relations with their environments are tyrannical. More so since most of the blame for the environmental ills facing the world lies with those societies dominated by massive urbanization dependent on industrial capitalism, not those living in close relations with the non-humans around them. Wilson's dystopian proposition to make all people into the type of people responsible for the grave situation we find ourselves in is no solution at all (Büscher et al. 2016).

The authors of this book converge on the urgency of drawing on anthropology to inform serious discussions on what desirable forms of future society must attend to. The intrinsic value of diversity—whether cultural or biological—emerges as the foundation stone of hope for a liveable future earth. In the Anthropocene, this now requires dominant societies be willing to learn from those most removed from industrial-capitalist modernity. Just as the Comaroffs (2012) emphasized the need for the 'North' (Europe and America) to learn about how to be flexible and diverse enough to cope with unpredictability from the global 'South', so Arturo Escobar stresses that currently the most inspiring alternative models come from indigenous groups, landless movements, black or feminist activists and other marginalized people, rather than from conservationists, academics or politicians (Chap. 14).

How easily these voices are marginalized in practice is described in Katherine Homewood's chapter. Here, a conservation model claimed to avoid undesirable consequences on local people of protected area conservation promises a 'triple win…that elusive convergence which sustainable development seeks between economic growth, social equity and environmental protection'. She explores how such globally hegemonic concepts of sustainability play out in East African Rangelands in one of the most celebrated 'successes' of sustainable development: 'Community Based Natural Resource Management' (CBNRM) in Tanzanian Wildlife Management Areas. She describes how, as international principles of sustainable development are applied, local customary common property resource tenure systems and practices are dismissed and local understandings of sustainability disregarded; local people end up enjoying fewer benefits from their natural resources, while the significant financial returns from their management are captured by state and foreign actors. Moreover, positive environmental conservation outcomes are not discernible.

The packaging of sustainable natural resource management into various forms of expert-led management regimes is not producing the environmentally and socially sustainable outcomes claimed. However, an institutionalized emphasis on technical tools and economic outcomes, and a reluctance among 'expert' teams to spend sufficient time getting to know local people, to understand local realities in local peoples' own terms, means that institutional actors ignore the human consequences of otherwise well-intentioned conservation programmes. It is because anthropologists do spend the necessary time to understand local realities that we can produce this kind of critical analysis.

When local populations are dispossessed of their customary lands, in return for scarce compensation, and forcibly kept out by armed patrols, such conservation has dubious claims to sustainability. If it excludes and further impoverishes populations, despite the 'triple win' claims of CBNRM—then how can it be sustainable? As Homewood mentions, it is primarily governments, rather than scientists or development practitioners, that routinely dismiss customary production and land use systems. The claim that customary activities such as pastoralism or swidden agriculture are archaic and unsustainable is not supported by sound science, but it persists among decision makers whose ideas of progress and modernity are part of the legacy of the social evolutionary ideology of colonialism. A major part of the problem, in other words, has to do with translating science into policy and finding ways to control the global resource grab by vested interests that is currently increasing rapidly as inequality continues to spiral (Hardoon et al. 2016; Hardoon 2017).

Globally, many kinds of activity have become unsustainable as a result of the growing human population and the scale of industrial capitalism, which requires and depends on the exploitation of resources in one part of the world to service demand in another. Yet legislation to protect forests or wildlife, which is intended to mitigate the degradation of landscapes and ecosystems due to these global movements of resources, tends to impose the greatest restraints on local populations rather than the consumers driving international trade. 'Top-down' conservation strategies rarely challenge the structural features of this situation. As William Adams describes, the reverse may be the case: while market-based 'conservation' instruments are sold as being able to 'unleash' energies 'from below', delivering outcomes without government control; in practice, they tend to move more power into the hands of those who 'design the mechanisms through which private investment and profits are made' (Chap. 7; Nelson and Agrawal 2008).

One of the few internationally agreed mechanisms has focussed on schemes for Reducing Emissions from Deforestation and Degradation (REDD+). REDD+ intends to provide an international architecture for compensating communities and governments for not deforesting, primarily in tropical countries with large areas of forest and significant rates of deforestation. Because of the vast amounts of expertise and bureaucratic oversight REDD+ projects require, few benefits trickle down to local communities. As REDD+ is gradually implemented in Suriname, top-down conservation's emphasis on 'evidence-based' conservation privileges experts and further centralizes power, simultaneously marginalizing traditional knowledge and customary practice (Brightman 2014, 2016).

Signe Howell (Chap. 8), describes an experience at one of the forums in which international guidelines for REDD+ were being elaborated and notes a paradox at the heart of many such deliberations: people are made central in the political discourse while being peripheral in practice. She points out how reluctant policy makers are to spend time understanding local perspectives, and how often this leads to the failure of intended outcomes. In a typical example, an indigenous woman trying to explain local forest peoples' concerns in a REDD+ workshop was repeatedly told to speak to the theme of the panel on 'incorporating women in REDD+', rather than appreciated for the local views she was sharing. Those concerned with sustainable development spend much of their time in local, national and international seminars rather than in the places where these policies will be applied. So guidelines are formulated for general application across large regions, yet tend to favour Euro-American priorities rather than local ones.

This state of affairs is often due to the divergence between local realities and global or regional institutions; it is a problem of translation across scales of action. For instance, the delegates involved in such negotiations are under pressure to produce universally applicable models, and when policy makers try to incorporate local realities they use generic concepts such as 'the community', 'conservation', 'local participation' or 'culture' that often turn out to be ambiguous and difficult to identify in practice at the local level. During project interventions, externally imposed time constraints often force external actors to hurry to complete their work and set up activities, causing them to ignore sometimes well-researched evaluation reports that describe the difficulties and mistakes of previous similar experiences. The temptation for implementers is to pay more attention to those funding their activities than those on whom the activities are imposed (Lewis 2008a). This is particularly the case for big international conservation organizations that are now dominated by corporate funding and business leaders in their decision-making and values, as William Adams' contribution describes (Chap. 7).

What Adams calls 'conservation from above' is strongly informed by the neoliberal enthusiasm for involving the private sector and the state in conservation, and an associated zeal for market-based approaches to addressing conservation issues. The outcome is an increasing commitment to conceiving of nature as 'natural capital', to be valued in financial terms and exchanged in global markets; and an increasingly direct role for conservation organizations in the valuation, control and marketing of nature through strategies such as payments for ecosystem services or eco-tourism. Another dimension of 'conservation from above' is its dependence on hierarchies of knowledge that devalue local perspectives and practices, instead privileging scientific practice and the development of corporate patterns of decision-making.

This approach, grounded in hierarchies of knowledge, follows the more general lines of global economic relations. Given the need for global measures, such as regulation, to address global sustainability, the question of how to resolve the problems arising from 'top-down' approaches seems to present an intractable challenge. Perhaps global solutions are better adapted to *global* phenomena such as the regulation of the activities of corporations, particularly oil and mining companies, but global regulation of this kind faces powerful resistance (Oreskes and Conway 2010).

As Homewood's case shows, strategies 'that do not reflect the interest, knowledge and values of the people they affect' entail 'real risks'. And arguably, they are 'not sustainable in the long run' because they cannot be maintained without coercion, displacement and dispossession. In contrast to this hegemonic approach, Adams introduces the idea of 'conservation from below', which includes 'things people do to establish or maintain good relations with nature' (Sandbrook 2014). This can include not only indigenous practices, but also many other things such as ethical attitudes to animal welfare, recycling, choosing local or organic food, reducing pollution, etc. In practice, Adams argues that conservation from below sometimes challenges conservation from above, and the question of which is accepted 'is central to the future of nature'.

Laura Rival (Chap. 11) offers us a perspective on how sustainability is advanced from below when not coercively imposed. Working in one of the world's mega cities, Rival introduces us to some urban agroecologists trying to live more sustainably through contributing to a socio-ecological project in a popular neighbourhood of São Paulo. She traces their determination to create positive change, describes the difficulties they face, and some of the controversies arising from their decisions and the actions they promote. She investigates the values, norms and principles referred to by the people seeking more sustainable lives. Rival's ethnographic exploration of the dynamic interface between natural environments and people trying to live more sustainably serves to illuminate the processes that produce sustainable actions. This puts in relief the importance of the value systems underpinning political processes and the frictions involved in sustainability mobilization, some of which involve disputes over the form in which human and non-human relations are to be conducted (or broken). Politics, Rival argues, 'needs to be rethought in terms wider than simple disagreements about modes of relationality or modes of emplacement'.

William Adams draws the similar conclusion that sustaining and protecting global biodiversity will require serious and committed engagements with the messy processes of politics, and the more fundamental issues of political economy: justice, wealth, poverty and powerlessness. As Adams reminds us 'conservation also bubbles up from below, a diversity of claims for a livable diverse world. The future of conservation demands nothing less than a re-imagining of conservation itself'. How does this apply to sustainability?

SUSTAINABILITY TOMORROW

Despite the popularity amongst governments and global elites of market-based mechanisms to achieve 'sustainability', so far these efforts are ineffective and do not understand sustainability in a rational sense, nor in an ethical sense. They incorporate a fuzzy and misleading definition of sustainability based on maintaining what already exists, as resilience thinking implies. Here we explore an anthropological understanding of what sustainability means by basing our analysis on ethnographic evidence exploring and documenting contexts of human adaptation to environmental challenge and examining what can be learnt from them.

An important case study that challenges facile assumptions about sustainability is offered by James Fairhead and Dominique Millimouno in Chap. 10 examining the 'Ground Zero' of the recent Ebola outbreak in

West Africa. A Ground Zero is a place where epochal events occur that break dramatically with the past and recalibrate the possibilities for the future. The term 'Ground Zero' emerged during the Manhattan Project to describe the place where an atom bomb would be detonated and came to describe Hiroshima's Shima Hospital. These are similar to what Nassim Taled labels 'Black Swans': a surprise event that transforms the reality that was hitherto felt to be normal and predictable. Fairhead and Millimouno consider the Ebola epidemic that first broke out in the small village of Meliandou in Guinea as Ground Zero, and as a Black Swan event. As such, it illustrates the antithesis of dominant understandings of sustainability because it transforms the possibilities for sustaining what went before.

Fairhead and Millimouno carefully examine the different explanations, and often conflicting rationalizations, made by some of those concerned to explain events, contrasting local narratives with those of international 'experts'. Fairhead and Millimouno describe these narratives as 'sustainability narratives'—attempts to tame such events by casting them into more familiar and predictable scripts for action and responses.

> These events present challenges to the language of sustainability. They are sometimes described as 'outliers.' But can one simply set them aside as exceptions? How foolish it would be to set aside such events if they play vastly larger roles than more regular, predictable and orderly occurrences more amenable to social analysis.

As the effects of anthropogenic climate change intensify, so too do the unpredictability of their consequences. How can sustainability simply mean sustaining what went before? Our reflections on sustainability must crucially take the unpredictability of such outliers into account.

Kirsten Hastrup (Chap. 9) offers further ethnographic insight on unpredictability from her research looking at the precarious existence of the Inughuit in Northern Greenland.

> Their land was defined by its unpredictable affordances, including the living and moving resources. These comprised the animals that were their main game, of course, but also new people, some of whom came from the south across the Melville Bay on large wooden ships bringing rifles and timber, while others came in the form of a small group of Baffin-landers crossing Smith Sound on dog-sledges, extending the gene-pool and reminding the Inughuit about forgotten technologies. The Inughuit could only sustain themselves

through new *social* relations, rescaling their community and counterbalancing
their deadly fewness in the frozen region. From within their horizon, sustainability was a simple matter of viability.

This challenges common assumptions that sustainability is in any obvious
way about remaining in ecological balance with 'nature', or based on
ensuring future predictability. For the meaning of sustainability to become
clear, it must embrace the uncertain and the unusual. As Hastrup points out,
this rescales the discussion of sustainability to incorporate absent and
unknown resources into possible futures.

Such a view is difficult to reconcile with sustainability strategies that aim
to perpetuate bounded or predictable systems over time. This is an important caveat to the Bruntland Report's formulation of sustainability as '*development that meets the needs of the present without compromising the ability of
future generations to meet their own needs*' (1987). Apart from basic needs
for fresh water, enough food, adequate shelter and the company of others,
only future generations will know their own needs. But the current popularity of 'throw-away' consumerism, the popular idolization of lavish lifestyles and extravagant living, and the runaway transformation of diverse
ecosystems into mono-cultures represent dominant cultural tendencies that
already are deciding for future generations. How a meaningful definition of
sustainability will address these dilemmas is illuminated by taking a closer
look at the label given to our current era: the Anthropocene.

THE ANTHROPOCENE

Humanity has again returned to the centre, in what Aït-Touati and Latour
provocatively call a 'surprising reversal' of the Copernican revolution
(Chap. 13). The idea that we have entered a new geological era, the
'Anthropocene', in which humankind is a major cause of physical change
on a geological scale, was first proposed by Crutzen and Stoermer in 2000
and has gained traction in disciplines across the sciences and humanities
(Crutzen and Stoermer 2000). In August 2016, an official expert group at
the International Geological Conference recommended issuing a formal
declaration that the earth has entered the Anthropocene once a consensus
is reached over the start date (Carrington 2016). Hamilton's insistence that
the Earth System supersedes ecology and environmental science (2015) is a
welcome move from the point of view of anthropologists who have long
been critical of the treatment of ecology or of the environment as something

outside, separate from or surrounding human culture and society (Bateson 1972; Descola 2005; Ingold 2001).

Interactions and changing relationships between human and nonhumans, ecological processes and all other aspects of the world around us contribute towards the functioning and changing of the Earth System. For this reason, it is important to tell these stories, or 'geo-stories' as Bruno Latour calls them, in order to contribute to understanding this system—let us call it Gaia, following James Lovelock (1972). Understanding the role of human action in the Anthropocene demands studying how people change ecosystems, for good or ill, intentionally and unintentionally. This can be done through fine-grained ethnographic studies that explore human–nonhuman relations without prioritizing human agency, such as Nicholas Kawa's recent book (2016). Kawa shows that people's influence on the Earth System is multifarious. Indeed, the 'anthropos' responsible for climate change is capitalist, industrial and modern, and to reflect this, some authors have offered alternative names for our era: the 'Econocene' (Norgaard 2013 in Hornborg 2016: 34), the 'Capitalocene' (Malm and Hornborg 2014) or, as Hornborg has suggested (2016: 34), the 'Technocene'. Donna Haraway offers another name that is more ambivalent in the potentialities it evokes: the 'Chthulucene' (2015). Nevertheless, 'Anthropocene' is the term that has taken hold, and we are left to interpret it and ponder its implications.

Bruno Latour opens this volume by doing this (Chap. 2). The Anthropocene is a gift for anthropology, he argues, because it recognizes that human activity is having a geological impact on the earth. Stratigraphers now find such clear signs of human agency in the sediments that they study that geologists are confident that any stratigrapher of the future will have no more difficulty detecting the distinctive layer of our epoch than they would that of the Cambrian or the Holocene. Natural scientists must now take human agency into account. As anthropologists are aware, combining these different casual agents into a coherent understanding is a challenging undertaking. The traditional division between the natural and the social sciences has long tested anthropology. By giving such pride of place to human agency, geologists have unwittingly opened an anthropological breach into mainstream natural science. The notion that social sciences are not really scientific because researchers are too involved in their subject matter has become applicable to most sciences, as it becomes clear to everyone that nature (the scientific object) is not really separate from culture after all. This adds weight to calls for cross-disciplinary alliances

(Palsson et al. 2012; Strang 2017), because of the moral as well as the material entanglements of our species with the Earth.

> The "anthropos" that is pushed centre stage by geologists is not the same passive entity that used to populate the older narrative full of "natural" causal agents. It is a being that is inevitably endowed with a moral and political history. To the great surprise of those who had tried to paint the human agent as a bag of proteins, computerized neurons and selfish calculations, it is as a *moral* character that human agency is entering the geostory of the Anthropocene. Bruno Latour (Chap. 2)

If modernism attributes value to nature in terms of its utility to people, Veronica Strang identifies the roots of this in the moral tradition of the Abrahamic religions, which proclaimed the moral dominion of humans over other species and the material world (Chap. 12; cf. White 1967; Taylor et al. 2016). Such values underlie concepts such as 'payment for ecosystem services' or 'carbon trading', which remain grounded in the very ontology that caused the crisis they claim to address.

Whether or not it is possible to identify one major religious tradition with the moral geostory of the Anthropocene, it makes no sense to tar all humans living on earth with the same brush. Amazonian Indians or Congolese hunter-gatherers, for example, have very different ecological impacts from the wealthiest 25% of humanity, and do not carry the same responsibility for the serious problems generated by this newly defined geological force.[1] The anthropos of the Anthropocene lives in modern growth-based market economies that have intensified resource extraction and consumption around the world, mostly externalizing the costs to nonhuman species and environments. Servicing the unrestricted demands of massive modern urban populations has replaced so much biodiverse biomass with human biomass and plantation monocultures that it has resulted in anthropogenic mass extinction at a rate only recorded after massive global catastrophes in the past. There is strong evidence that the world is on track for a 'sixth extinction', that is to say, a spike in the rate of species loss on a scale that has only occurred five times before in the history of the earth (Kolbert 2014).

Anthropos is a force causing so much disturbance to natural cycles such as climate, to environments such as oceans and forests and to diverse microbiomes on which life depends that it is rapidly reducing biological and cultural diversity. Along with many others in this volume, Latour sees this as an ontological struggle: 'Modernization is a war cry that has to be resisted everywhere'. Anna Tsing illustrates why in Chap. 3 by describing the impact of what she calls 'Anthropocene proliferation' on the diverse ecological systems that life and humanity depend upon.

At the heart of these modern projects are a combination of plantation ecologies, industrial technologies, state and imperial governance projects, and capitalist modes of accumulation. Together, these have moved more soil than the glaciers did and changed the earth's climate. They have done this by allowing investors to engineer large-scale projects across long distances for converting places to plantations. Meanwhile, extinction rates have rocketed. Anthropocene, then, is an epoch in which multispecies livability has become endangered.

To understand the Anthropocene we need to appreciate the Holocene. The Holocene began around 12,000 years ago at the end of the last Ice Age as the glaciers melted. This melting exposed new areas for colonization by those species that survived in refugia beyond the ice. In effect, as they colonized new places with what Tsing calls 'species agilities', their diversity increased in interaction with the new environments and each other, creating a resurgence of life in many forms on previously barren ice. Tsing refers to this phenomenon of remaking liveable landscapes such as forest, wetlands or meadows as *Holocene* resurgence. Such resurgence is the result of many organisms negotiating their differences over time to establish multispecies assemblages to support their combined lives. All ecosystems are so composed. Without such resurgence, human livelihoods cannot continue.

By contrast to Holocene resurgence, Anthropocene proliferation is an ecological phenomenon caused by the extraordinary force of plantation ecologies that engender new forms of biological movement that block resurgence. Justified by the ever-growing demands of urban populations, plantations are rationalized and simplified ecologies established to create assets for future profit through supplying urban demand. They kill off beings that are not recognized as assets and often favour the proliferation of many identical bodies. This novel ecological form has consequences for both the asset organisms—the oil palm, spruce tree or chicken—and for their pathogens. Plantations both cultivate and spread pathogens. The proximity of so many identical meals to a pathogen can augment its pathogenic abilities and sometimes change them. Over time, in non-plantation ecologies, pathogens are forced to adapt their virulence to the population dynamics of their prey species. In plantation ecologies, the supply of victims is constant so pathogens are not under selection pressure to be less virulent. As Tsing wryly observes: 'Welcome to the Anthropocene, in which alienated and disengaged organisms, including humans, multiply and spread without regard to multispecies living arrangements'.

To deepen this understanding, Henrietta Moore reminds us in Chap. 4 that the scientific conceptualization of what the environment is has undergone major change. Contemporary science understands the human body as an open system composed of a set of ecologies of microbial and human cells and microbial and human genes. Indeed, a healthy adult has ten times more bacterial cells than they have human cells derived from those of their parents. Since dietary and political–economic factors such as class, fashion or income shape the development of human microbiomes, so our bodies reflect our daily activities and cultural traditions, and are key to our health. The scientific revelation is that the human body is not a singular organism, but can only exist in symbiosis with complex bacterial and other communities. Our bodies are a series of nested environments composed of several multispecies living arrangements that are themselves embedded in larger systems. There is much variation in these arrangements between individuals and groups but it is a common feature of all living forms. So Moore argues,

> The bodies we have, and will have in the future, are the materialization of social relations, where forms of sociality cut across species... [and] the notion of environment has massively expanded to create new problems of scale and new problems of time. The environment now means everything from the level of the molecular to that of the biome. Environments are multiple and nested. There is no single environment.

Kirsten Hastrup's fascinating historical and ethnographic study of the remote Inughuit in Northwest Greenland demonstrates the complexity of understanding sustainability as a relationship with a bounded environment. However isolated the Inughuit may seem, or how circumscribed their local conditions are, their continued existence depended on chance encounters with an outside world. These unsolicited encounters provided them with unimagined innovations—from guns, timber and wood working technology, to new genes—that crucially helped to sustain them over historical time in their harsh environment. In the Anthropocene the environment is expansive not bounded. As Hastrup summarizes, 'Wherever we start from, and however 'isolated' our object of study, it is steeped in global connections'.

Taking these insights into consideration clearly challenges any definitions of sustainability that presuppose a predictable future in a bounded space where economic and political relations remain roughly constant over time. Rather, the evidence suggests a working definition of sustainability which emphasises that it is a principle based on the active cultivation of cultural, economic, political and ecological plurality, in order to be more likely to address unpredictability in future. At its core, sustainability demands practices that will foster, prize, support, defend and generate diversity at every level.

WHAT SORT OF WORLD FAVOURS 'SUSTAINABILITY'?

In practice, what sort of world will favour sustainability? To think more precisely about the prerequisites of a liveable future Mauro Almeida and Manuela Carneiro da Cunha remind us in Chaps. 15 and 16 of the important work of Nicholas Georgescu-Roegen. Georgescu explained that life needs three basic elements: matter (such as natural resources), energy and diversity (or more formally 'low entropy'). Living organisms obtain energy by taking advantage of the differences between states of matter that exist in a low entropy (diverse) environment by degrading the differences (consuming them) to produce energy and high entropy waste. In other words, life depends on the conversion of highly diverse matter into energy through processes that irrevocably degrade the diversity into waste—a uniform mix no longer able to produce energy for the organism that produced it.

Given that energy consumption has often been used as a measure of progress, Mauro Almeida proposes a 'thermodynamic critique of progress' (Chap. 16). Quoting the German physicist Ludwig Boltzman who considered the Second Law of Thermodynamics to be as important to understanding life as Darwin's principle of evolution '...the general law of struggle for existence of living beings is not a struggle for raw matter ... it is struggle for [low] entropy' (Boltzmann 1919[1906]: 40). Life depends on diversity. Almeida, like many authors in this volume, thus argues that the best way to support a future liveable world is to support a diversity of knowledge and practice. He, Moore and Escobar refer to this as 'ontological diversity' in its widest possible sense, encompassing nature and culture.

Manuela Carneiro da Cunha reminds us that 'a sustainable future hinges on diversity in every domain, and that people's diversity is a formidable contribution to that end' (Chap. 15). Her chapter provides vivid ethnographic testimony of how traditional people contribute to ensuring diversity

with an examination of agricultural biodiversity. Of 350,000 globally identified plant species[2] there are 7,000 species that have been used by humans
as food. In the Anthropocene today, 75% of the food eaten by human
beings is composed of just 12 crops and 5 animal species. Counter to this
trend, the indigenous Amazonian societies she discusses select for diversity
by cross-fertilizing different varieties of manioc to produce new diversity,
and using cuttings to clone new varieties. The result is that great diversity is
both maintained and produced. This celebration of diversity springs from
cultural pride in crop diversity and a cultural aesthetic that celebrates the
social networks that allow the exchanges of varieties that are needed to
produce beautifully diverse gardens. This agricultural system depends on
the much maligned 'slash and burn' method to create and rotate fields:
dormant sexually reproduced manioc seeds (i.e. new hybrids) only germinate and grow once a plot is burned.

Carneiro da Cunha shows that there is no immediate practical reason for
maintaining and producing such a wide diversity of manioc varieties. Yet,
unlike other farmers who simply select favoured varieties, indigenous Amazonians favour collection over selection since they do not discard varieties.
They both conserve and produce biodiversity for its own sake. Carneiro da
Cunha hypothesizes that 'this is but a particular case...of a much more
general law, one that demands diversity in every domain, societies included,
for life to go on'. Traditional forms of agriculture, especially shifting cultivation, have proven to be associated with high biological diversity, and more
than the diversity within gardens, it may also help preserve and even
enhance the diversity of forests themselves (Balée 1993; Posey 1985).
Many non-indigenous traditional societies—such as the rubber tappers of
the south-western Brazilian Amazon—as well as many small-scale peasant
societies, celebrate species diversity, and its defence is advocated in more
utilitarian terms by the global coalition of peasant movements, Via
Campesina, which calls for peasant rights along the lines of the indigenous
rights that are now enshrined in the Declaration of the Rights of Indigenous
Peoples (Desmarais 2008; Martínez Alier and Guha 1997).

This is just one example of a widespread tendency for cultural diversity
and biological diversity to co-exist and to be mutually reinforcing. There are
many others, and it is for this reason that some scholars now study
'biocultural diversity'. It is now clear that many landscapes beloved of
conservationists are very often not simply the product of wild nature but
have been shaped by a wide variety of human activities (Cronon 1995).

Almeida's chapter (Chap. 16) describes such a system of mutually reinforcing biological and cultural diversity among Amazonian rubber tappers, called Caipora. This ontology sometimes requires people to 'leave a part of the forest alone'. As he notes, such ontologies that produce diversity 'can in some cases converge in [their] pragmatic consequences with scientific ontologies'. A 1990s conservation approach called 'sink/source' prioritized the zoning of territory so that game animals would have places of refuge. This differs from the preservationist land sparing approaches dominating most conservation practice because it shifts in space according to need. Lewis (2008b) describes a similar system called *ekila* practised by Congo Basin hunter-gatherers.

Anthropogenic ecologies can be sustainable, but this requires a recognition that sustainability is not just a matter of human action and human decision-making. As Anna Tsing cogently argues, 'meaningful sustainability requires multispecies resurgence, that is, the remaking of livable landscapes through the actions of many organisms'. Why, she wonders, do so many scholars examining sustainability focus on human plans and actions? Blocking out the nonhuman makes 'sustainability a mean and parochial concept; we lose track of the common work that it takes to live on earth for both humans and non-humans'. When human societies sustain themselves over many generations, it is because they are aligned with the dynamics of multispecies resurgence. Rather than productivity, it is an ethic of encouraging, cherishing, celebrating, protecting and producing diversity that is at the heart of sustainability.

Currently, most initiatives to address the challenges of sustainability in the Anthropocene focus on 'harnessing the power of markets'. Paradigmatic among these are systems of 'payment for ecosystem services' (PES). There are arguably reasons to fear attempts to financialize life processes that are progressively turning all other beings, including key climate processes such as the rain cycle, into assets for trade and investment (Sullivan 2013). Investors' attempts to reduce all kinds of resources and life processes to the status of tradable assets is what engenders the 'terrifying ecologies' Tsing calls 'Anthropocene proliferations'. Handing a liveable world to our descendants requires moderating the processes of commodification in order to preserve, or even enhance the cross-species socialities on which we depend, and actively fighting for spaces that will ensure resurgence. Tsing reminds us that 'If human ways of life are sustained across generations, it is because they have aligned themselves with the dynamics of multispecies resurgence'.

If the financial instruments so dear to current global sustainability initiatives are produced by the modernist ideology of progress and development, then how can we identify ideologies more likely to promote sustainability? Arturo Escobar argues that these are most in evidence amongst groups fighting for resurgence on the frontline of ethno-territorial struggles against capitalist and statist expansion (Chap. 14). Escobar views these groups as engaged in 'pluriversal struggles', formulated by the Zapatistas as seeking to establish 'A world where many worlds fit'. Escobar views the territorial struggles by Afrodescendants, indigenous peoples, peasants and landless movements as ontological struggles because they 'interrupt the globalizing project of fitting many worlds into one'. These struggles are especially important because they produce and share knowledge that is most likely to inspire the search for post-capitalist, sustainable and plural models of life, since they emerge from outside modernity. Anthropology is the discipline best equipped to study these processes.

> From a theoretical and political position within anthropology – with all the limitations that this implies – the purpose of sustainability should surely not be to sustain just what already exists, but to sustain the capacity for further development and diversification of multiple ontologies and indigenous knowledge practices. Henrietta Moore (Chap. 4)

What Sustainability Does for Anthropology

The classic anthropological descriptions of cultures that were produced in the mid-twentieth century tended to be set in the 'ethnographic present'; the logic of cultural systems was presented as if it were timeless. The circular exchange of prestige objects among the Trobriand islanders, or the segmentary logic of Nuer social organization appeared to exist in timeless and bounded settings that were heuristic fictions. The ethnographic present was a rhetorical device that allowed anthropologists to document cultures as they observed them. It also resulted from the discipline's rejection of the ideas of social evolution that had been central to Victorian anthropology, and which modern practitioners realized were so flawed and biased that they were unsuitable as a framework for study. The solution was to study cultural systems on their own terms, challenging any attempt to place a specific social group at some point along a predetermined historical trajectory. This is in line with the epistemological and ethical position that we support. It allows us to take a critical stance towards assumptions about 'development' and 'progress' that underpin many areas of policy, and poses a challenge to them that is supported by decades of painstaking research. The implication of this for an anthropology of sustainability is not that all cultures should be preserved as they are, but rather that social and cultural variation in plans and aspirations for the future, and ideas about the good life, are key topics for study.

Global capitalism, the removal of trade barriers, the increasing mobility of populations, and improvements in communication technology, led anthropology to focus on situating the people they worked with in broader national and global processes. Many anthropologists today, whether or not they have an explicit interest in sustainability or the environment, study how global changes affect local systems, and many also think carefully about how local action can contribute to different kinds of global future. Our specialism in concrete and everyday realities and their relationship to wider phenomena and ideas leaves us well placed to offer insights into sustainability. After all, sustainability became a truly pressing problem when it began to be clear that it was a global problem, and yet the only way we can apprehend global changes is through abstract representations of numerical data, or through symbols such as the famous 'blue planet' photograph of 1968 that became an emblem of the environmental movement. Ordinary daily experience is limited to minute elements of these global changes—strange weather events or changes in the flora or fauna inhabiting our surroundings.

In order to try to make sense of the multifarious global phenomena that constitute today's world of 'accelerated change', Thomas Hylland Eriksen (2016) has developed a sophisticated framework, combining Batesonian concepts such as 'runaway processes', the 'double bind' and 'flexibility' with a strong emphasis on divergences between scales in social, physical, cognitive and temporal dimensions. This allows him to treat problems such as energy production and consumption, the mobility of goods and persons, urbanization, waste disposal and the information economy as elements in a complex global phenomenon that he calls 'overheating'. Eriksen brilliantly demonstrates the potential of anthropology for understanding globalization holistically, but he limits his task to the level of description, and he does not venture into normative terrain. We suggest that an anthropology of sustainability will be obliged to do more.

Anna Tsing reminds us that for too long most anthropologists 'have ignored the radical claim being made by environmental scientists: business as usual is killing us'. Nobody can continue to shut their ears, especially if they care about our collective future. At present, most frameworks and practices aimed at achieving sustainability at best reduce unsustainability, but take for granted the underlying world order and modernist vision that is at the root of our ecological crisis. Taking the question of sustainability, or future liveability, seriously requires rethinking the discipline and practice of anthropology within the academy, and has challenging political and ethical implications beyond it. This points to areas where anthropology will expand and develop in exciting new ways in terms of our research practice and the collaborations on which it depends. It implies identifying those areas we need to focus more carefully on, and on the types of policy and political debates our disciplinary knowledge should engage with more effectively. Ensuring a future for human cultural diversity requires more than simply studying it, but also supporting the struggles required to sustain it. Without territory or choice, many of the experiments in being human that our diversity represents, and on which our collective future may depend, may slip away before we have even realized they existed.

In this vein, Katherine Homewood reminds us that an anthropology of sustainability must foreground local voices, and this may demand a cultural and political analysis in conjunction with a willingness to challenge hegemonic ideology and practices, both locally and globally. Like Escobar, Homewood advocates a far stronger awareness of the political dimensions of sustainable development interventions. This may mean a willingness to resist and confront interventions in already sustainable local land use situations where human groups are embedded in functioning multi-species socialities. As Mauro Almeida stresses, an anthropology of sustainability offers the possibility of non-condescending anthropological activism. He suggests considering forging alliances with biological-human communities against aggressive projects of capitalist expansion seeking to alienate their natural resources through extraction, destruction or legislation. As Homewood affirms, 'Anthropology is now well placed to integrate qualitative and quantitative analysis, evidence and critique in ways that carry weight with policymakers, and to shape positive change'.

As Laura Rival observes in Chap. 11, 'Issues of knowledge and reasoning, as well as moral commitment and decision-making have clearly emerged as unavoidable theoretical cornerstones for this work'. In addition to challenging assumptions in other disciplines and translating between them, the anthropology of sustainability will need to engage more systematically with international institutions and the policy-making bodies they spawn, so we will have to find effective ways to describe bureaucratic contexts, decode the discourses of different interest groups, map ambiguities and contradictions, and assess claims. Rival continues:

> What makes 'development' (whether economic, social, human, or sustainable) anthropologically so interesting is the fact that descriptions *of* are always also (and unashamedly so) prescriptions *for*. This allows us anthropologists to trace over time and map over space the constant traffic of concepts, technical terms and metaphors within and between expert networks, academic circles and mobilised actors.

What this means for ethnographic research, as Rival emphasizes, is that we attend to what people do *in* as well as what they say *about* their environment, since the 'the dynamic interface between natural environments and human societies is necessarily mediated by actions as well as values, evaluations and judgments'.

MAKING ANTHROPOLOGY CONTEMPORARY AGAIN

Latour emphasizes that the Anthropocene has opened up new possibilities for anthropology: it is a gift! It has led scholars from disciplines such as geochemistry, economics, ecology, genetics and many others, to contemplate issues familiar to anthropologists: concerning human specificity and the diversity of human attachments, while situating human bodies in particular environments and cultural frameworks. They now join us in pondering what unites the human race while identifying the differences. Such reasoning resists the familiar reductionism of compartmentalized subjects seeking to maintain borders between themselves. Now we enter the disciplinary melting pot of the Anthropocene; as many of our authors point out, it is potentially a new era for anthropology. Latour predicts that anthropologists increasingly will populate 'critical zones' between the disciplines of the twentieth century, reconfiguring ourselves as specialists in facilitating dialogues of equals between different disciplinary and social ontological worlds. Thus, anthropology can make itself contemporary again. As Latour remarks, 'There is a huge difference between being "modern" and being "contemporary". Actually knowing how to become a contemporary, that is, of one's own time, is the most difficult thing there is'.

> We need to understand the human–nonhuman sympathies that make Anthropocene arrangements possible as well as the more-than-human historical trajectories that come together in both terrible hegemonies and patches of

hope or resistance. These are tasks that anthropologists have trained themselves to do. A new field is waiting for us—and it demands urgent attention. Anna Tsing (Chap. 3)

To attend to this new field of sustainability, as Henrietta Moore points out, requires anthropologists to be willing to integrate both biological and social relations in novel ways. For instance, the new models of humans and their environments emerging in contemporary science are surprisingly similar to what Escobar calls 'pluriversal'. Human bodies, like all life forms, turn out to be best understood as open systems, composed of multiple types of cells and organisms, all embedded and nested within each other in mutual co-existence. We are all multi-organisms. Moore remarks, 'The debates in modern science, with their complex relationalities that morph into socialities, look perplexingly like indigenous ontologies'. Anthropology is only beginning to explore the implications of such parallels (Kirksey 2014).

Escobar argues that an anthropology of sustainability needs a 'political ontology' approach that focuses on 'worlds and worlding'. He recommends examining both the powerful practices that bring a particular world or ontology into being, and the full range of interrelations within and among worlds. This should include the conflicts that follow when different ontologies strive to maintain their own existence in interactions with other worlds. Duration remains key, and as Signe Howell emphasises, research into local points of view takes more time than most research funders realize. Understanding sustainability requires the long view, as Kirsten Hastrup's and Anna Tsing's chapters beautifully illustrate, and this demands historical awareness to understand the multispecies relationships, chance meetings and sharings, that result in sustainable communities.

Veronica Strang argues that this suggests a new 'ethical theoretical model' to orientate anthropological research to firmly integrate human communities into the contexts of the living systems they inhabit and depend on. Environmental ethics has tended to be the preserve of philosophers, and from this perspective, the contributions to this volume imply advocating something closer to the emphasis on the relationality associated with the philosophy of Arne Naess and deep ecology, in contrast to the tradition of environmental ethics that emphasises the intrinsic value of individual organisms, places or landscapes: 'nothing exists separately, things only exist by virtue of the relations they sustain with the milieu in which they are immersed' (Afeissa 2015). Of course, this may exceed the knowledge and skill of many, and so, as Katherine Homewood also emphasizes, it will promote collaborations with those from other disciplines so that the theoretical insights and methodologies of each can serve to deepen and strengthen understanding. This is likely to be intellectually and strategically beneficial for anthropology.

Anna Tsing calls this 'A time for anthropology'! Emphasizing important new areas for research, she challenges anthropologists: While we have shown considerable ability in translating something of the many worlds successfully inhabited by humanity across the earth, we have been less attentive to document 'threats to livability'. In this volume, Tsing, Hastrup, Homewood, and Fairhead and Millimouno provide us with model examples of how to study encroaching 'unlivability'. They demonstrate the importance of an attention to history, to the wide-ranging connections between human and nonhuman actors, to an appreciation of international politics and institutions, and other disciplinary areas, as well as the people we traditionally work with. Latour, Homewood, Moore, Rival and Strang emphasize that seeking 'sustainability' has intensified collaborations, the sharing of concepts, technical terms, narrative devices and metaphors between scientific disciplines and the humanities, and also, as Rival points out, between activism and science.

WHAT IS AN ANTHROPOLOGY OF SUSTAINABILITY?

'Modernize' is a *mot d'ordre*. Not a concept. Not a thing. It destroys your ability to be the contemporary of what happens around you. 'It is a debilitating machine', asserts Latour.

'Modernize!' pushes those to whom it is uttered to put all their effort into progress towards an elusive future 'modern' state, rather than take stock of the present moment and respond appropriately. Can an anthropology of sustainability be contemporary? What is an adequate response? Anthropologists will need to 'stay with the trouble', to study the inner workings of unsustainable worlds to expose and change them (Haraway 2016). Escobar refers to the modernizing project as the One-World doctrine, and while acknowledging its aggressive expansion, he suggests that the ubiquity of the language of crisis when referring to planetary climatic, ecological, social, political and financial conditions is evidence that it is unravelling. This suggests urgent research questions for anthropology, challenges for social theory and, politically, an engagement in activism to support territorial struggles.

As many authors in the volume describe in powerfully different ways, the key struggle of our time is to support alternatives to neoliberal definitions of 'progress and development' among diverse societies and cultures. In different ways, many authors (Adams, Almeida, Carneiro da Cunha, Escobar, Homewood, Latour, Moore and Tsing) converge on the view that anthropologists continue to have a key role in supporting struggles to defend marginal spaces of ontological and biological diversity. Escobar asks, 'can [the One World World] be rearticulated in terms of a plurality of worlds?' Perhaps initiatives such as the Declaration of the Rights of Indigenous Peoples suggest ways in which this can be done, through engagement with and between traditional and indigenous communities, supporting their right to self-determination and their struggles to defend themselves against dispossession (Brightman 2008). Meanwhile, 'communities in the global north' may require constraints that might restrict their mobility, energy use and other excessive resource consumption, as Henrietta Moore notes in this volume. Critics of the 'green economy' paradigm support this view, arguing that the economics of green growth simply do not add up (Dale et al. 2016). According to these views, only when wealthy communities are so restricted will it be possible to slow the trajectory of climate change and resource depletion.

This implies, as Moore suggests, that 'anthropologists will have to engage not just with how communities are to be maintained, but with how they can be reworked, with what are the future desirable forms of society'. Mauro Almeida argues that logically for humans, this will eventually imply achieving 'anti-singularity': using technology to think, sense and imagine together with animals and plants (*this volume*). Escobar remarks that the most original contemporary thinking on 'realizable utopias' has emerged in the context of territorial struggles against capitalist expansion and the state. Such non-modernist communities committed to pluriversal ideals require the autonomy and liberty to design and (re)produce their worlds. This requires an autonomous space. So supporting territorial struggles is key to enabling the articulation of effective models for human societies to re-embed ourselves in the earth. This re-engagement with territoriality and materiality is worth emphasizing in our age of immaterial, digital communication.

CONCLUSION

Understanding sustainability meaningfully requires a shift—at very least a shift of emphasis—from 'sustainable production' to 'sustained ontologies' (Almeida, Chap. 16). If big NGOs and even governments began to recognize that local communities, whether they be East African pastoralists or Amazonian Indians or Paulistas, inhabit different worlds each of which is inherently valuable, then it may be possible that a diversity of worlds are supported as the surest way of ensuring a liveable earth. Thus, sustainability is something with lasting value for humanity and our relationship with other species on earth. Understood in this way, sustainability begins to converge in meaning with humanistic values such as peace and dignity. It need not require the elaboration of complex field methodologies by experts, but instead could be enacted as a sort of human principle of respectful engagement with others—with other cultures and societies, and other species.

Perhaps the biggest challenge to the modernization theory that drove international development in its heyday in the 1950s (Rist 1997) has been the realization that ordinary people's hopes for future prosperity can take many different forms. This message is powerfully conveyed by several chapters in this book, particularly by Arturo Escobar, who argues that the pluriverse of multiple worlds must be defended against the 'one world world' of pedlars of top-down development and outdated, ill-considered visions of 'progress', and by Henrietta Moore, who argues that sustainability depends on the freedom of different cultures, different ontologies, to continue to change following the paths they choose.

The tension between the unity and diversity of humankind has always been a feature of anthropology. Today we think it has a special relevance. From the late 1960s, when the images of our blue planet from space marked the beginning of the era of earth politics, to today, when concepts such as Gaia and the Anthropocene are becoming increasingly familiar, we tend more and more to discuss not only the common predicament of humankind, but that of all life on earth. As the titles of two recent conferences in Rio de Janeiro and in Santa Cruz put it, Gaia has 'a thousand names',[3] and there are many 'arts of living on [this] damaged planet'.[4] To evoke the Brundtland Report, there is not just one 'common future', but there are many common futures—those of different social groups, different nations, different species; different cosmologies. In Bruno Latour's language, sustainable futures belong to the 'earthbound', who face Gaia and engage with her, and we would do well to listen to their 'geo-stories'.

Given that our collective actions have become a planetary force that is destabilizing the very life systems on which our future depends, all humans must urgently formulate a more explicit project of transformation and transition. Anthropology's ability to respond to the current crises requires more of anthropologists than to describe and communicate the injustices being done by modernizing interests in the global south. If climate change and resource depletion are to be humanely addressed, anthropologists have a lot to offer.

> In conceiving of a sustainable human future, we need to do more than think about who we have been and who we are. We need rather urgently to focus on the question of 'who are we hoping to become' and how are we going to get there. (Henrietta Moore, Chap. 4)

We end the volume with Alf Hornborg's effort to do exactly this. Perhaps more than any other discipline, anthropology provides an appropriate and sophisticated tool for attempting such an ambitious goal and has unrivalled potential for leading interdisciplinary ventures (Strang, Chap. 12). We must carefully use our ethnographic and historically informed research to make propositions for change that address the key cultural creations that threaten future liveability. Hornborg tackles something at the root of Anthropocene proliferations and the Capitalocene—money, and the endless search for profit. Money, Hornborg reminds us in Chap. 17, is

> foundational to the sociological condition of modernity, frequently characterized in terms of inclinations toward abstraction, interchangeability, individualism, and alienation. The very concept of money is thus a pivotal cultural phenomenon that ought to be at the centre of anthropological deliberations on modernity, development, and sustainability.

Hornborg provides an example of Anthropocene anthropology. His chapter demonstrates the tremendous insight an anthropological point of view brings to envisaging a future that will open up new and plural opportunities, that encourages and supports diversity without compromising its range and possibility. Only once we have formulated clear ideas of what needs to be done can we begin to work towards achieving them.

As Hornborg remarks, 'History is not reversible, but we can take stock of millennia of historical experience in order to envisage our future'. In many surprising and ordinary ways, this volume provides profound insight into what sustainable living means for humanity to have a future on this one planet—it means more than supporting diversity in all its forms—but actively enhancing it through our engagement with all that surrounds us. Ignorance is no longer an excuse, and inaction no longer an option. As Kirsten Hastrup reminds us in Chap. 9:

The question of orientation in relation to climate change is therefore not a simple matter of making choices about remaining or moving away in some future, it is a constant and pressing need to assess the opportunities of the present, and to reason consistently about them on the basis of all available knowledge – because it is now that the future is shaped.

In a recent interview, James Lovelock, whose 'Gaia' anticipated the study of the earth as a total system, claims that climate change is of little importance because by the next century humans will have been superseded by our own creations: by artificial intelligence. Because electrons can travel a million times faster than neurons, computers can think, and evolve, at a vastly greater rate than humans; they are already able to design and improve themselves, and can adapt more easily to a changing climate. By the end of the twenty-first century, he believes, artificial intelligence will be as superior to human intelligence as human intelligence is to that of trees today. His remarks about machine learning seem to be supported by work on artificial intelligence (Bostrom 2014). These predictions, about which Lovelock himself is strangely sanguine, shed an alternative light on the challenges made by some authors in this volume to the anthropocentrism of much mainstream sustainability thinking.

If as Strang argues, humanity's current predicament calls for a new, interspecies morality, then what place does artificial intelligence or biotechnology have in this new ethics? In the Anthropocene will intelligent machines or technologically enhanced organisms exist on the same moral plane as humans and nonhuman animals and plants? If the Holocene provided optimum conditions for humans to thrive, does the Anthropocene ironically introduce the conditions for the prosperity of cyborgs and robots—humanity's own creations—at the expense of what we understand today as people? If, as Hornborg has argued (2016), technological innovation increases global inequalities by displacing energy, what will be the consequences of this blurring of the organic and the fabricated—will they lead to the kind of technological apartheid portrayed in dystopian visions of the future such as Margaret Atwood's *Oryx and Crake* (2003) or Paulo Bacigalupi's *The Windup Girl* (2009)? Or will the collapse of the nature-culture divide be addressed in a different way, by the generation of a 'biosingularity' that connects human, plant and animal intelligence as Almeida predicts (2017)?

Such questions carry implications for the 'earthbound' and confound assumptions about the relationship between life and 'nonlife' (Povinelli 2016), human and nonhuman. Predicting the future, even using the most sophisticated modelling, is a perilous business because unexpected changes can radically alter the parameters that one started with. But by placing both human and nonhuman diversity at the centre of one's system of values, and promoting, supporting and cultivating this diversity, we have the best chance of ensuring a liveable earth for future generations. This is what a sustainable future requires.

NOTES

1. It is for this reason that the Anthropocene is generally deemed to have begun with the industrial revolution and not, as a few authors have suggested, with the wave of large mammal (megafauna) extinctions that took place between 13,000 and 9,000 years ago (Doughty et al. 2010).
2. Collaboration between the Royal Botanic Gardens, Kew and Missouri Botanical Garden enabled the creation of The Plant List which has accepted 350,699 species names (www.theplantlist.org).
3. 'The Thousand Names of Gaia: From the Anthropocene to the Age of the Earth'. International colloquium, PUC/PPGAS do Museu Nacional, Federal University of Rio de Janeiro, 15–19 September 2014.
4. 'Anthropocene: Arts of Living on a Damaged Planet.' Institute for Humanities Research, University of California Santa Cruz, 8–10 May 2014.

REFERENCES

Afeissa, H-S. 2015. L'écosophie, qu'est-ce que c'est? *The Conversation.* https://theconversation.com/lecosophie-quest-ce-que-cest-49824

Atwood, M. 2003. *Oryx and Crake.* London: Bloomsbury.

Bacigalupi, P. 2009. *The Windup Girl.* London: Orbit.

Balée, W. 1993. Indigenous Transformation of Amazonian Forests: An Example from Maranhão, Brazil. In *La Remontée de l'Amazone,* ed. A-C. Taylor and P. Descola. *L'Homme* 126–128 XXXIII(2–4): 235–258.

Bateson, G. 1972. *Steps to an Ecology of Mind: Collected Essays in Anthropology, Psychiatry, Evolution, and Epistemology.* Chicago: University of Chicago Press.

Boltzmann, L. 1919[1906]. *Populäre Schriften.* 2nd ed. Leipzig: Johann Ambrosius Barth.

Bostrom, N. 2014. *Superintelligence: Paths, Dangers, Strategies*. Oxford: Oxford University Press.

Brightman, M. 2008. Strategic Ethnicity on the Global Stage: Perspectives on the Indigenous Peoples Movement from the Central Guianas to the United Nations. *Bulletin de la Société Suisse des Américanistes* 70: 21–29.

———. 2014. Audit sauvage: régimes de valeur de la terre et de la biodiversité en Amazonie. *Ethnographiques 27: Biodiversités*. www.ethnographiques.org/audit-sauvage-regimes-de-valeur-de. Accessed 17 Oct 2016.

———. 2016. Esperança e Compatibilidade Equívoca na Governança da Floresta: REDD+ e os Direitos Sobre a Terra Indígenas e Tribais no Suriname. *RURIS*.

Büscher, B., R. Fletcher, D. Brockington, C. Sandbrook, W. Adams, L. Campbell, C. Corson, W. Dressler, R. Duffy, N. Gray, G. Holmes, A. Kelly, E. Lunstrum, M. Ramutsindela, and K. Shanker. 2016. Half-Earth or Whole Earth? Radical Ideas for Conservation, and Their Implications. *Oryx* 1–4. doi:10.1017/S0030605316001228

Carrington, D. 2016. The Anthropocene Epoch: Scientists Declare Dawn of Human-Influenced Age. *The Guardian*. https://www.theguardian.com/environment/2016/aug/29/declare-anthropocene-epoch-experts-urge-geological-congress-humanimpact-earth. Accessed 29 Aug 2016.

Comaroff, J., and J.L. Comaroff. 2012. Theory from the South: Or, How Euro-America is Evolving Toward Africa. *Anthropological Forum: A Journal of Social Anthropology and Comparative Sociology* 22 (2): 113–131. doi:10.1080/00664677.2012.694169

Cronon, William, ed. 1995. *Uncommon Ground: Toward Reinventing Nature*. New York: Norton.

Crutzen, P.J., and E.P. Stoermer. 2000. The "Anthropocene". *Global Change. IGBP NewsLetter* 41: 17–18.

Dale, G., M. Matthai, and J. Puppim de Oliveira. 2016. *Green Growth: Political Ideology, Political Economy and Policy Alternatives*. Chicago: University of Chicago Press.

Descola, P. 2005. *Par-delà nature et culture*. Paris: Gallimard.

Desmarais, A. 2008. Peasant Resistance to Neoliberalism: La Vía Campesina and Food Sovereignty. *Human Geography* 1 (1): 74–80.

Doughty, C.E., A. Wolf, and C.B. Field. 2010. Biophysical Feedbacks Between the Pleistocene Megafauna Extinction and Climate: The First Human-Induced Global Warming? *Geophysical Research Letters* 37: L15703. doi:10.1029/2010GL043985

Eriksen, T. Hylland. 2016. *Overheating: An Anthropology of Accelerated Change*. London: Pluto Press.

Ferguson, J. 1990. *The Anti-Politics Machine: "Development," Depoliticization and Bureaucratic Power in Lesotho*. Cambridge: Cambridge University Press.

Foucault, M. 2009. *Security, Territory, Population: Lectures at the Collège de France 1977–1978.* New York: Palgrave.

Grober, U. 2012. *Sustainability: A Cultural History.* Totnes: Green Books.

Hamilton, C. 2015. Getting the Anthropocene So Wrong. *The Anthropocene Review* 2 (2): 102–107.

Haraway, D. 2015. Anthropocene, Capitalocene, Plantationocene, Chthulucene: Making Kin. *Environmental Humanities* 6: 159–165.

———. 2016. *Staying with the Trouble: Making Kin in the Chthulucene.* Durham: Duke.

Hardoon, D. 2017. *An Economy for the 99%: It's Time to Build a Human Economy that Benefits Everyone, Not Just the Privileged Few.* Oxfam Briefing Papers. Oxfam. doi:10.21201/2017.8616

Hardoon, D., R. Fuentes-Nieva, and S. Ayele. 2016. *An Economy for the 1%: How Privilege and Power in the Economy Drive Extreme Inequality and How This can be Stopped.* Oxfam Briefing Papers. Oxfam International. doi:10.21201/2016.592643

Hornborg, A. 2016. *Global Magic: Technologies of Appropriation from Ancient Rome to Wall Street.* New York: Palgrave.

Ingold, T. 2001. *The Perception of the Environment: Essays in Livelihood, Dwelling and Skill.* London: Routledge.

Kawa, N. 2016. *Amazonia in the Anthropocene: People, Soils, Plants, Forests.* Austin: University of Texas Press.

Kirksey, E., ed. 2014. *The Multispecies Salon.* Durham: Duke.

Kolbert, E. 2014. *The Sixth Extinction: An Unnatural History.* London: Bloomsbury.

Latouche, S. 1995. *La mégamachine: Raison scientifique, raison économique et mythe du progrès.* Paris: La Découverte.

Lewis, J. 2008a. Managing Abundance, Not Chasing Scarcity: The Big Challenge for the Twenty-First Century. *Radical Anthropology Journal* 2: 7–18.

———. 2008b. Ekila: Blood, Bodies and Egalitarian Societies. *Journal of the Royal Anthropological Institute* 14 (2): 297–315.

Lovelock, J.E. 1972. Gaia as Seen Through the Atmosphere. *Atmospheric Environment.* 6 (8): 579–580.

Lowe, Philip D. 1983. Values and Institutions in the History of British Nature Conservation. In *Conservation in Perspective*, ed. A. Warren and F.B. Goldsmith, 329–352. Chichester: John Wiley.

Maida, C., ed. 2007. *Sustainability and Communities of Place.* Oxford: Berghahn.

Malm, A., and A. Hornborg. 2014. The Geology of Mankind? A Critique of the Anthropocene Narrative. *The Anthropocene Review* 1: 62–69.

Martínez Alier, J., and R. Guha. 1997. *Varieties of Environmentalism. Essays North and South.* London: Earthscan.

McNeill, D. 2000. The Concept of Sustainable Development. In *Global Sustainable Development in the Twenty-First Century*, ed. K. Lee, A.J. Holland, and D. McNeill. Edinburgh: Edinburgh University Press.

Meadows, D., G. Meadows, J. Randers, and W. Behrens III. 1972. *The Limits to Growth*. New York: Universe Books.

Naess, A. 1989. *Ecology, Community and Lifestyle: Outline of an Ecosophy*. Cambridge: Cambridge University Press.

Nelson, F., and A. Agrawal. 2008. Patronage or Participation? Community-Based Natural Resource Management Reform in Sub-Saharan Africa. *Development and Change* 39: 557–585. doi:10.1111/j.1467-7660.2008.00496.x

Neocleous, Marc. 2013. Resisting Resilience. *Radical Philosophy* 178: 2–7. https://www.radicalphilosophy.com/wp-content/files_mf/rp178_commentary_neocleous_resisting_resilience.pdf. Accessed 12 Dec 16.

Norgaard, R. 2013. The Econocene and the California Delta. *San Francisco Estuary and Watershed Science* 11: 1–5.

Oreskes, N., and E. Conway. 2010. *Merchants of Doubt: How a Handful of Scientists Obscured the Truth on Issues from Tobacco Smoke to Global Warming*. London: Bloomsbury.

Palsson, G., B. Szerszynski, S. Sörlin, J. Marks, B. Avril, C. Crumley, H. Hackmann, P. Holm, J. Ingram, A. Kirman, M. Pardo Buendí, and R. Weehuizen. 2012. Reconceptualizing the "Anthropos" in the Anthropocene: Integrating the Social Sciences and Humanities in Global Environmental Change Research. *Environmental Science and Policy* 28: 3–13.

Posey, Darrell A. 1985. Indigenous Management of Tropical Forest Ecosystems: The Case of the Kayapó Indians of the Brazilian Amazon. *Agroforestry Systems* 3: 139–158.

Povinelli, E. 2016. *Geontologies: A Requiem to Late Liberalism*. Durham: Duke.

Rist, G. 1997. *The History of Development, from Western Origins to Global Faith*. London: Zed.

Sandbrook, C. 2014. What Is Conservation? www.thinkinglikeahuman.com; https://thinkinglikeahuman.com/2014/03/05/what-is-conservation/

Strang, V. 2017. The Gaia Complex: Ethical Challenges to an Anthropocentric 'Common Future'. In *The Anthropology of Sustainability: Beyond Development and Progress*, ed. M. Brightman and J. Lewis. New York: Palgrave.

Sullivan, S. 2013. Banking Nature? The Spectacular Financialisation of Environmental Conservation. *Antipode* 45 (1): 198–217.

Taylor, B., G. Van Wieren, and B. Daley Zaleha. 2016. Lynn White Jr. and the Greening-of-Religion Hypothesis. *Conservation Biology* 30 (5): 1000–1009.

United Nations – Sustainable Development knowledge platform. 2015. Transforming Our World: The 2030 Agenda for Sustainable Development. https://sustainabledevelopment.un.org/post2015/transformingourworld. Accessed 14 Oct 2016.

United Nations General Assembly. 1992. Rio Declaration on Environment and Development. http://www.un.org/documents/ga/conf151/aconf15126-1annex1.htm. Accessed 14 Oct 2016.

United Nations Treaty Collection. 2016. *Paris Agreement.* https://treaties.un.org/pages/ViewDetails.aspx?src=TREATY&mtdsg_no=XXVII-7-d&chapter=27&clang=_en. Accessed 14 Oct 2016.

White, L.T. Jr. 1967. The Historical Roots of Our Ecologic Crisis. *Science* 155: 1203–1207.

Wilson, E.O. 2016. *Half-Earth: Our Planet's Fight for Life.* New York: Liveright Publishing Corporation.

World Commission on Environment and Development. 1987. *Our Common Future.* Oxford: Oxford University Press.

CHAPTER 2

Anthropology at the Time of the Anthropocene: A Personal View of What Is to Be Studied

Bruno Latour

What does it take to 'produce anthropology'? Many things that you are much better able to envision than me. But maybe you need some help and you could do well with a gift and a little nudge forward. The gift is not mine, only the nudge is. What an amazing gift! Sure, it might be poisonous. But how silly it would be not to try to peek through the wrapping to take a glimpse of what is in store. Consider the situation: here is a battered scholarly discipline, always uncertain of its scientific status, constantly plagued by successive and violent 'turns' (the 'ontological turn' being only the more recent), a field which always finds itself dragged into harsh political conflicts, a discipline that runs the constant risk of being absorbed by neighbouring specialties and voted out of existence by deans and

This chapter was first presented as the Distinguished Lecture at the American Association of Anthropologists annual meeting held in Washington in December 2014.

B. Latour (✉)
Sciences Po Paris, Paris, France

© The Author(s) 2017
M. Brightman, J. Lewis (eds.), *The Anthropology of Sustainability*,
Palgrave Studies in Anthropology of Sustainability,
DOI 10.1057/978-1-137-56636-2_2

administrators impatient of its methods and ideologies, a discipline that accepts being crushed under the weight of all the violence and domination suffered by the many populations it has decided to champion—a lost cause among all the lost causes. It is to this same discipline, which a few years ago, an amazing present was offered: pushed from behind by the vast extent of ecological mutations and dragged ahead by philosophers, historians, artists and activists, a sizeable group of natural scientists are describing the quandary of our time in terms that exactly match the standards, vices and virtues of that very discipline. Yes, what a gift! It is really embarrassing, especially if it is not deserved!

I am of course referring here to the strange undertaking of the 'subcommittee of Quaternary stratigraphy' headed by my new friend, Jan Zalasiewicz, to name the geological period that might terminate the 13,000-year-old Holocene, with the amazing label of 'Anthropocene'. I know the label is still disputed. I am well aware that it is highly contentious (the dates vary wildly from 1945 to 3000 BCE; the proof from sediments are still unsettled; the politics of it are utterly fuzzy). And yet I really think Dipesh Chakrabarty (2008) was right to seize upon this tiny terminological innovation as something that could trigger an entirely different conversation among historians. What is true of post-colonial or Marxist historians should even be truer of anthropologists. In an earlier time, any anthropologists who would have claimed that even geology was made out of human activity would have been considered, and rightly so, as megalomaniacal. Or else what they might have meant was that such a connection between human and non-human, mountains and spirits, had been painted upon the frail fabric of myths because only myths were supposed to link sediments and sentiments. But here we are talking about a connection that is literal. Not symbolic. What a surprise.

I want to share with you some of the reasons why I am so interested (some would say infatuated) by the effects of the geologist's Anthropocene label upon this discipline for which I am an outsider, but towards which I feel the most loyalty.

If the idea of naming the period—or epoch, some say even era—'Anthropocene' resonates so deeply for the better, and maybe for worse (you will have to decide at the end of my chapter), with the name of your discipline, it is because it builds upon several of the same fault lines as those upon which anthropology had established its fragile tenements over many decades.

First, the very idea of the Anthropocene places 'human agency' (still undifferentiated, taken *en bloc* and generically) at the centre of attention. For you to be 'anthropocentric' does not come as a great surprise, but it is certainly a complete shock to stratigraphers used to studying million-year-old pebbles and to digging up sediments deposited long before humans ever appeared as a distinct species.

Second, this new concept defines the agency of humans by drawing on a bewildering range of entities, some clearly related to the 'natural' sciences—biochemistry, DNA, evolutionary trends, rock formation, ecosystem—while others clearly relate to what ethnographers have learned to register throughout their field work—patterns of land use, migrations of plants, animal and people, city life, the trajectory of epidemics, demography, inequalities, classes and state policies. In other words, to designate the present period as that of the Anthropocene is to tell all the other disciplines that the task of joining 'physical' and 'cultural' anthropology (I purposely use labels pertaining to the past of your discipline) is no longer your exclusive undertaking. Suddenly, without you having even asked for help, hundreds of subfields are also busy doing it. Everybody, it seems, is now converging on the same problem, ready to make the same mistakes and to live through the same traumatic experience that the discipline of anthropology as a whole had lived through since the beginning of the nineteenth century, namely, how to get bones and divinities to fit together.

Suddenly many hard science colleagues sit uneasily on the same fault line that has been the bane and the glory of your discipline, namely, surviving through an uneasy relation with evolutionary biologists, palaeontologists, archaeologists, as well as cultural and social ethnographers. Anthropologists everywhere, I am fairly certain, have stories to tell about how difficult it has been to connect the two sides of anthropology—the scars are visible even in the ways museums and departments and collections have been carved out. The French, being well known for their love of politicking, having even gone to the point of pitting two museums against one another: one for the Human bones—the Musée de l'homme—on the *Right* Bank and another one for art, gods and cultures—the Quai Branly—on the *Left* Bank. But the big novelty today is that those fights, those connections, those victories and defeats, now occupy many other people with new instruments, new agendas and coming from many different countries and disciplines.

At this point you could object that there is no reason to be excited by a replay of the boring old game of the 'physical' versus the 'social' in the definition of human evolution and habitation. To alternate once again between the twin dangers of 'naturalization', on the one hand, and 'social construction', on the other, seems rather depressing. I agree. But the concept of Anthropocene introduces us to a *third feature* that has the potential to subvert the whole game: to claim that human agency has become the main geological force shaping the face of the earth is to immediately raise the question of 'responsibility', or as Donna Haraway is fond of saying, 'response ability' (2008: 71).

The 'anthropos' that is pushed centre stage by geologists is not the same passive entity that used to populate the older narrative full of 'natural' causal agents. It is a being that is inevitably endowed with a moral and political history. To the great surprise of those who had tried to paint the human agent as a bag of proteins, computerized neurons and selfish calculations, it is as a *moral* character that human agency is entering the geostory of the Anthropocene. Its entry on the scene set by geologists is also its exit from the scene of 'natural history'.

Try to tell my neighbours, the farmers of Auvergne, as if it was just a straight 'scientific fact', that their soil is now sterile because of their imprudent land use and that the mouth of their river is now a 'dead zone' because of the way they use nitrates. Or try to utter without making it sound as an alarm, as an accusation, the sentence: 'Anthropic origin of climate transformation'. Try. And be prepared for tar and feathers! To state the fact and to ring the bell is one and the same thing. No amount of naturalization will clean this little statement from being read as an attribution of responsibility that requires action, and probably a fight. Such is the great paradox of the Anthropocene. There is nothing natural in the telltale signs left by this human agent in the sediments recorded by stratigraphers. Actually, this is exactly the reason why members of the subcommittee in charge of nomenclature assemble to compare their 'unnatural' findings in the sedimentary sections they have unearthed. It is because those sediments are so different that today geologists can say that any stratigrapher, a million years from now, will have no more difficulty detecting the neat mark of that geological period in the strata than the transition that marks the demise of dinosaurs. The topic of Zalasiewicz book's whose title is fairly typical *The Earth After Us: What legacy Will Humans Leave in the Rocks?* (2008). In the rocks! This is Elizabeth Povinelli's terrain (Povinelli 2016).

The human agent has grown to the dimension of a *natural* phenomenon (comparable, if you count in terawatts, to plate tectonics), but it has not become more *natural* for all of that. It has a history—a very short one compared to geological periods; it is burdened by responsibility, it depends on some moral economy; it is made to play an active role in this geohistory. A funny thing about this subcommittee of the Geological association is that it is so badly funded that they had to rely on the '*Haus der Kultur der Welt*' in Berlin to pay for their meeting. .... Artists financing geologists to decide upon the name of the *Zeitgeist*! The Anthropocene is a strange animal!

But there is something even more interesting in this concept: as soon as you give this pride of place to human agency, the exact nature of the assemblage is immediately thrown into doubt. This is the feature I find so fascinating in the short period during which scholars absorbed the geologists' innovation. As soon as historians, philosophers, anthropologists and activists stumbled on the name 'Anthropocene', they immediately realized that there was no sense whatsoever in lumping into one undifferentiated 'anthropos' all the human agents responsible for shaping the planet. Amazonian Indians, Alaskan seal hunters, Shanghai tycoons, Enron executives and slum dwellers of Valparaiso could not be ascribed the same responsibility in this newly defined 'geological force'. You just have to pronounce the sentence 'Anthropic origin of climate transformation' to get the immediate retort: 'But *who* is at the origin of that mutation? Certainly not *me*. Not *them*. Maybe *you* are!' So, as soon as the 'anthropos' became the centre of the collective attention of geochemists, economists, political scientists and many others, the idea of One Human in charge of that geostory exploded into pieces.

I hope you now recognize how familiar the question is. Anthropologists had been there all along! This is the defining question of our discipline, but not raised, this time, by ethnographers keen on solving the problem of the universality of human cultures, but by hundreds of new disciplines keen on attributing, eschewing or accepting responsibilities for thousands of different human situations. The old conundrum of what unites the human race is raised all over again from new quarters about issues such as deforestation, CO_2 credit swaps, urban dwelling, soot belching kitchen fires, steel mills, coal mines, fisheries, intestinal flora and soil degradation. It is in this sense that the very idea of defining our present period as that of the Anthropocene fits so readily within the older pattern of anthropology, as if all the older fights had to be fought all over again, but at a much bigger scale and with lots of new recruits. What is common to all humans and what is specific, that most essential of questions, is opened once again but on new terrain, even literally, on new soil.

Except that this old question takes another unexpected twist. Let me explain. In September 2014, I was lucky enough to participate in the

Climate March in downtown Manhattan with Timothy Mitchell, the historian of the Middle East, of economization and the author of a most important book, *Carbon Democracy* (2011). This Climate March had been cleverly sectioned into various slogans. So that, depending through which streets of New York you decided to join the march, you were enrolled behind a different banner. A great idea to transform the long snake of the demonstration into a sort of telegram easily decipherable by the media. At first, Tim and I had chosen the slogan prepared for scientists and (I am not inventing this) 'interfaith' followers. Their banner read, not surprisingly: 'The debate is over'. Which is true enough. But after a while, realizing that there weren't that many white coats walking behind that one, we decided to move ahead and give our support to another argument. We found ourselves chanting behind what I took to be the best banner of all: 'We know who is responsible'.

The 'anthropos' of the Anthropocene is not exactly any body, it is made of highly localized networks of some individual bodies whose responsibility is staggering. As Eduardo Viveiros de Castro and Deborah Danowski write: 'We have your names and your telephone number' (this is from a remarkable book, edited by Emilie Hache, on what the Anthropocene does to anthropology) (Danowski and de Castro 2016). Such an attribution of responsibility and this dispersion of the 'anthropos' into specific historical and local networks, actually gives a lot of weight to the other candidate for naming the same period of geohistory, that of '*capitalocene*'; a swift way to ascribe responsibility to those to whom it belongs.

So, as you may see, choosing the name Anthropocene brings together three features fairly familiar to anthropologists: the concentration on human agency; the necessity to tackle again the connection between what used to be called 'physical' and 'cultural' anthropology; and the reopening of the key question of what is common and what is specific in the various ways humans inhabit the earth. Is this enough of a gift? Or are you still worried that it might be poison in disguise?

Well, there is a *fourth* element brought in with the idea of the Anthropocene, and this one is not so familiar. Quite the contrary, it runs against what anthropology has most lamented about. Suddenly, with the question of the Anthropocene anthropologists are confronted head on with the question of urgency and political relevance. Of course, this has always been the case, but the political relevance of the ethnographer's field work has never been easily reconciled with the epistemological goal of establishing a science of the human. Relevance was an after effect, not a central goal. Most often it had to be resisted so as to save the sanctity of the quest. But to the bewilderment of many, all disciplines are now seized by the same feeling of urgency and the necessity of 'doing something', of influencing policy on hundreds of issues to which academics are suddenly pushed to the forefront. No need to be an '*anthropologue engagé*': the engagement comes to you as soon as you open your mouth.

If you doubt that this plight has become common, ask the climate scientists who are part of the Intergovernmental Panel on Climate Change (IPCC) to tell you how it feels to be messengers of alerts that are not being heard by those who are most directly impacted. And then compare this politicization of 'natural' science with the problems encountered by ethnographers forced to 'politicize' their own involvement with their 'people' (as the saying went) while keeping within the standards of objectivity. You will realize that the question of political relevance and urgency has spread from scholarly fields to hard sciences. All disciplines are now fighting with the urgent mission of assembling humans on newly defined territories— exactly the problems raised by anthropologists long ago.

In this sense, the concept of the Anthropocene pushes anthropology to centre stage and requests from it to be worthy of its original mission—a mission that anthropologists probably never really wanted to have! Or that many thought the discipline had definitely abandoned in favour of a glorified version of storytelling to which were added some radical pronouncements against power, injustice and domination. Remember the old concept of 'posthuman'? Posthuman! Just at the time when the Anthropocene brings the human back with a vengeance! You might be unprepared for a situation where too many people take your discipline too seriously.. ... It is in that sense that you might consider the gift of the Anthropocene handed to you by geologists as too much of a good thing.

Your decision, it seems to me, depends on whether or not I am right in thinking that both sides of the former division between physical and cultural anthropology are being reconfigured by the unexpected entry of the Anthropocene as the name defining our period. If I am wrong then we will simply be back where we were in the twentieth century. Natural scientists (aided by economists and cognitivists) will happily drown the results of ethnography with a few sets of 'natural forces' in the service of an even harsher round of 'modernization'. It *was* reductionism. It *will be* reductionism. Against this trend there will be no other game to play than the usual one we are so good at: we will be left insisting on the specificity, openness, rich situated and historical dimension of human agents. In this case, the very agency granted to the 'anthropos' by geologists will come split in two, just as before. And just as in an earlier time, what we take as the hallmark of our field—attention to the fragility, specificity and multiplicity of human attachments—will be considered as simply irrelevant. In other words, the fad of the Anthropocene will have been just another name for the attempts of neoliberalism to define the globe. The global will have gobbled up everything else.

Can the conversation really change? Imagine the cocktail conversation:

> What is your field?
> I am an anthropologist.
> Meaning?
> Meaning I am studying people who live in the Anthropocene.
> Do you mean *me*?
> Yes, you, in addition to many others. . . See?

This is a very different definition from the idea that anthropologists study *specific* people or specific *aspects* of being human.

To clarify this change in definition, I am afraid I have nothing more to offer than a few scraps of my recent experience. I called this chapter 'a personal view of what is to be studied' because there is no other way but for everyone to decide how he or she might accept, or not, the gift of living during a period of history named after the main topic of one's own discipline.

Let me start with the 'physical' side of things (even though I know the adjective 'physical' has become largely obsolete). The key thing here is the question of agency, or more precisely, of *animation*. All the scientific disciplines that are converging around the Anthropocene (in Paris, I lead a consortium of 22 laboratories of geochemistry, geology, geography, political sciences, law and media studies) have a specific style: they define the many entities that are proliferating in their models or field stations as being 'animated'. No, I exaggerate, they would not say 'animated' but they would say 'not dead' or 'surprising' or 'being dependent on other entities just as surprising'. For instance, I was struck when a renowned chemist from our consortium complained that there were so many types of carbon dioxides, that he needed a geopolitical map of CO_2s in the plural. . . 'Geopolitics' is his adjective. Too many different CO_2s? Even for an ethnographer of science like me who is used to the surprises of field work, this came as a shock. We immediately started a collaboration to bring metrics to try to map out this odd type of geopolitics.

This is what I mean by 'animated': surprising agencies where we expected no surprise, because we were supposed to deal with 'material entities'. For instance, Ian Zalasiewicz's book *The Planet in a Pebble* (is entirely animated, in the sense that it is freed from the 'cause reduces consequences to nothing' narrative that is paralysing so much scientific writing, and which is at the origin of what is called, strangely enough, the 'scientific world view'. His whole book is the history of one Welsh pebble, from the Big Bang to now. In his account, everything moves. Consequences *add* to their causes, a pragmatist tenet which is pretty hard to keep up with. It is not 'How forests think' (Kohn 2013), but rather 'how rocks register the transformations of history'. I take it as a very important sign that Zalasiewicz, the head of the now famous sub-committee on Quaternary nomenclature, is also able to write such an amazing book about a non-human, a mere pebble, a stone freed from the silly role given to 'mere objects' by scientific writers and their enemies (in epistemology, rocks and stones are usually used only for stoning relativists to silence). Is it not a good omen when totally unusual scientists meet totally unusual anthropologists to share some narrative strategies?

The great philosophical contribution of the Anthropocene is that *narrativity*, what I call *geostory*, is not a layer added to the brutal 'physical reality' but what the world itself is made of. Something on which novelists such as Richard Powers, anthropologists like Eduardo Kohn or Anna Tsing feed on. And it is also, as I have shown elsewhere, the great contribution of James Lovelock and Lynn Margulis (1974). When they say the planet is alive it does not mean there is one big organism that is to be called Earth, but that its many ingredients are all building their own world. 'Connected' does not mean 'holistic', any more than 'animated' means 'having a soul'. The range of animation entertained by scientists is much wider than what philosophers and even bio-semioticians are prepared to register. Why is it that, in our field, we take infinite precautions when Bororo 'say they are Arara' (Lévi-Strauss 1961) and that we jump to the conclusion that scientists are 'naturalists' when they say that 'Coal is made from sedimented life forms'? No, scientists are just as innovative; they too try to get out from under all sorts of metaphysical assumptions handed to them by philosophers that would result in them speaking of a dead planet. And not the one they live on with the rest of us.

My impression is that those scientists I meet around the 'Politics of the Earth at the time of the Anthropocene' (it's the modest name of our consortium!) are not so ready to present their objects of study as *de*-animated. They are so conscious of the multiplicity of factors they have to take into account and of the specificity of their field sites (many of those I follow are boots-in-the-mud types) that they don't buy the reductionist style of their colleagues. Especially when many of the cycles or loops they study include human actions distributed throughout.

This is where the Möbius strip quality of the Anthropocene has such an educating effect on all disciplines. Adding geochemistry on top of land tenure or agricultural subsidies on top of methane emissions (I say 'on top' on purpose to break down the notion of levels) has a sobering effect on every one of the partners. Especially when every paper and study they write is drawn into this other Möbius strip of restitution, reflexivity, media publicity and then back to science policy. And all the more so when you work under the urgent pressure of having to take a decision. Not respecting the sacrosanct distinction of fact and value has, in the end, a civilizing effect: be more careful of what you say about what others do, and be prepared to react quickly to the consequences of what has been agreed upon.

Remember this idea that social sciences could never be really scientific because the researchers were too involved with their subject matter? Well, the great thing about living in the Anthropocene is that this is common to pretty much everybody. No 'View from Nowhere' to be obtained here; nor any Great Unification to be expected. The consortium I had proposed to assemble is simply based on the project of learning to navigate in common a landscape of controversial data. Nothing to feed the rash impulse of reductionist predictions. But a great way to have data sets converge on, for instance, the questions of environmental inequalities if you can get soil scientists, chemists, lawyers, public health officials, to share their uncertainties.

The people with whom I study name their network '*critical zones*'. They define them as so many fully instrumented water catchments where they study everything from the top of the canopy to the mother rocks deep down. 'Critical zones'? Is this not an excellent name for collaboration with those who are so fond of critique—and so worried of its deferral? And is this not a term as excellent as those other concepts natural scientists keep inventing? Such as 'tipping points', 'planetary boundaries', 'great acceleration'—a zoo of concepts to absorb what it means to run inside such a roundabout. I am not even talking of the institutional innovations proliferating all around the world to handle those new anthropo*scenes* (a term used by artists where 'scenes' is now used as in scenography) the most famous of those innovations being the very protocol of the IPCC.

We always forget how recent the scientific enterprise is and how much leeway there is—there should be—for those many disciplines to evolve and change their tone and standing because of the change in the conflicts surrounding them. Having to deal with 'animated' agencies is just as difficult for soil scientists of Paris as for the Runa of Ecuador (Kohn 2013). And both are trying to invent how to resist the crisis destroying their own land. I have been studying scientists for 40 years and I really think that the pressure of the Anthropocene is making them willing to engage with our sorts of disciplines in a way that is really novel. The good news is that it has nothing to do with 'inter-disciplinarity'.

It might be worth betting that when former 'cultural' or 'social' anthropologists meet all those fields and sites, they will be surprised to see how little they resemble the 'natural sciences' they had learned to eschew in the name of the fight against 'naturalization' and biopower. How could you 'naturalize' anything anyway when the very ingredients of what used to play the role of 'natural forces' have been so transmogrified that they includes humans in pieces and morsels at every junction? I insist, once again: such intricate links between humans and non-humans in complex cosmograms have been described in every single ethnographic monograph but always with the risk of being seen as only 'symbolic'. Now it is literal. And that transforms everything, because it means that all field studies are studying devastated sites in crisis. To be on planet Earth at the time of the Anthropocene is not the same thing as being 'in nature' at the time of its modernization. *Cosmopolitics* is now the common situation for all collectives. There is no common world, and yet it has to be composed, nonetheless.

How does the situation sound when we turn to the other side—even though the whole point of my argument is that there are no longer two sides? Do we register the same amount of innovation, the same excitement, the same urge to collaborate, the same surprise at meeting at every juncture former non-human entities suddenly present with full blown agency? Is my beloved principle of symmetry applicable here, so that in the Anthropocene 'cultural' anthropologists are just as ready to shed their habit of using society and culture, as 'physical' anthropologists are to redistribute what count as 'natural forces'? No, I don't feel so; at least if I follow recent disputes around the 'ontological turn'. Nothing wrong, by the way, with taking many turns even if it makes you dizzy; it is possible that turning in ever-enlarging circles might be a necessity at the time of the Anthropocene to absorb the various loops that define the situation.

It seems to me that many anthropologists wish to keep the human in the centre, without always realizing that the centre has shifted, and that the human agent has been put in the centre also by geologists, climatologists, soil scientists and epidemiologists—before being redistributed again.

There is a tricky problem of design here: concentrating around the human could mean either maintaining this character apart from other entities—the former beings of 'nature' defining by contrast what could be called the 'humanistic' position—or it could mean accepting that, as soon as you take the human into consideration, it is suddenly redistributed (not *disintegrated*, that's the whole point, but *redistributed*) in many other roles and connections that make its earlier figurations unrecognisable. And with the great danger of losing its humanity in the process. This is the great risk of the Anthropocene, I agree. And that's what humanistic anthropologists warn against and rightly so.

Except if it is the case that 'producing anthropology' remains what it has always been, namely, producing the effect that every monograph always has had on its reader: first I don't recognize the usual face of humanity, and yet, on second thought, I do recognize it.

Such is the drama into which Chakrabarty has plunged all of us: What does it mean to redistribute human agency without being humanist, or post-human or anti-humanist? Where is the politics of assembling a character which is pushed to the centre but which simultaneously loses its boundary, consistence and definition because it is tied—morally tied—to all of what in earlier times would have been, to use a now famous subtitle, 'beyond the human'? That's what I mean by the tasks of *composition* (very much linked to that of *composting* as Donna Haraway emphasizes [2015]).

Those questions are at once central to anthropology—the human figure is a Western conceit, a naturalistic conception, everyone seems to agree—but they are also the questions that most anthropologists wish *not* to tackle head on since it would mean searching for alternative metaphysics. I use 'metaphysics' here just to avoid the O word. In reality, this is where, sorry to mention it, *ontological* questions are back. Attached to the Western conception of nature you also find the various conceptions of what sort of stuff society is, what role politics is supposed to play, how religion is to be located, what it is to have a mind, how law is bound to act, what can you expect from fiction, what is the standing of technical artefacts and so on. Modernism comes within a package. How strange it is to want to get rid of the Western definition of nature but to take as totally intangible, in the name of humanism, all the other notions, especially those of power, social order, critique and political struggle. It is as if you claimed to meet otherness but only on the condition that it fits exactly inside the same eternal and universal patterns of 'social life'.

I cannot help feeling that 'producing anthropology' also means re-describing what those who have never been modern have been up to. The reason has nothing to do with maintaining the modern/non-modern distinction. It is just the opposite: since 'we' have never been modern, there is no recognizable 'we' and 'they'.

Modernization is a war cry that has to be resisted everywhere. Anthropocene could offer another occasion to find an alternative to modernization. Another occasion to renegotiate the shape, boundary, limit and extent of the 'we' whose humanity is once again in question and that the Anthropocene is pressing upon everybody to answer, and fast.

To conclude: there is a huge difference between being 'modern' and being 'contemporary'. Actually knowing how to become a contemporary, that is, of one's own time, is the most difficult thing there is. This is probably the reason for my conversion to anthropology, 42 years ago, while I was supposed to be teaching philosophy in Ivory Coast, right on the frontier of a ruthless form of neo-colonialism. I converted not because I wanted to study the 'human'. Not because I was interested in some types of people by distinction to others. But because I realized at once that using 'modernization' as a shibboleth to understand the colonial situation would lead me nowhere—especially if I wanted also to study California scientists.

I felt that to stick to the concept of 'modernity' would have distracted me from the time and from the space I inhabited, that it would have forced me to encounter the wrong type of agency. I realized at once, that 'Modernity' could be a *topic* to study—I have done nothing else ever since—but never a *resource* to describe any situation whatsoever. 'Modernize' is a *mot d'ordre*. Not a concept. Not a thing. It destroys your ability to be the contemporary of what happens around you. It is a debilitating machine. It's made for that. While philosophy as a field was totally dependent on the concept of modernity, it appeared to me that anthropology could be an entry into the contemporary: precisely because it took ontology seriously at last. Not as symbolic representation. Not as those beliefs left on the wrong side of the modernizing frontier. But as life and death struggle to have the right to stand in one's own time and place.

In the same way as there is a shift from the modernizing frontier to the contemporary, there is a shift from the utopia of modernity to the relocalization of all the places and sites. By this I mean that everywhere the notion of territory is back, and even, that of the soil. And in the same way as becoming a contemporary is not a return to the past of modernity, this relocalization has nothing to do with attachment to the 'terroir'. What is to be reoccupied is not the post Renaissance idea of a territory, that is, a bounded piece of land viewed and ruled from a centre, but very much a new definition of an unbounded network of attachments and connections. It means that the search for *where* we are in space is just as complicated as to find *when* we are in time. This is why I think it is fair to say that in the same way as the idea of 'otherness' came in the sixteenth century from the 'great discovery' (in effect a land grab) of a new 'empty' continent, allowing the modern world to live for a few centuries in its utopia of an infinite frontier, a completely new definition of 'otherness' will come from this other 'great discovery' not, to be sure, of a new continent to be grabbed, but of another way for every piece of land to reside under the feet of those who have, at last, never been modern.

And yet, until recently, I had not met any alternative concept that would redefine spatial and time coordinates as well as the right type of agency, to root me back in my time and space (I toyed with 'ecology' but it didn't work too well). This is what the definition of the Anthropocene could do: it gives another definition of time, it redescribes what it is to stand in space, and it reshuffles what it means to be entangled within animated agencies. At the time of the Anthropocene, anthropology is not a specialized discipline; it is the name of what it is to reoccupy the time and space taken out of all of us by the modernising frontier. See why it is a gift? But I agree an embarrassing one and, in spite of what I said, you might be wise not to accept it! As I said: too much of a good thing. . .

References

Chakrabarty, D. 2008. The Climate of History: Four Theses. *Critical Inquiry* 35: 197–222.

Danowski, D., and E. Viveiros de Castro. 2016. *The Ends of the World*. Trans. Rodrigo Nunes. London: Polity Press.

Haraway, D. 2008. *When Species Meet*. Minnesota: University of Minnesota Press.

———. 2015. Anthropocene, Capitalocene, Plantationocene, Chthulucene: Making Kin. *Environmental Humanities* 6: 159–165.

Kohn, E. 2013. *How Forest Think. Towards an Anthropology Beyond the Human.* Berkeley: University of California Press.

Lévi-Strauss, Claude. 1961[1955]. *Tristes Tropiques.* Trans. John Russell. New York: Criterion.

Lovelock, J., and L. Margulis. 1974. Atmospheric Homeostasis by and for the Biosphere: The Gaia Hypothesis. *Tellus* 26 (1–2): 2–10.

Mitchell, T. 2011. *Carbon Democracy: Political Power in the Age of Oil.* London: Verso.

Povinelli, E. 2016. *Geontologies: A Requiem to Late Liberalism.* Durham: Duke.

Zalasiewicz, I. 2008. *The Earth After Us. What Legacy will Humans Leave in the Rocks?* Oxford: Oxford University Press.

CHAPTER 3

A Threat to Holocene Resurgence Is a Threat to Livability

Anna Lowenhaupt Tsing

"Sustainability" is the dream of passing a livable earth to future generations, human and nonhuman. The term is also used to cover up destructive practices, and this use has become so prevalent that the word most often makes me laugh and cry. Still, there is reason to dream—and to object—and to fight for alternatives, and that is the purpose of this volume. Rather than criticize the word, then, I'll take it seriously, repurposed as a radical argument in the face of hegemonic practice. This chapter argues that meaningful sustainability requires multispecies resurgence, that is, the remaking of livable landscapes through the actions of many organisms. Most scholars of sustainability focus only on human plans and programs. In contrast, I argue that where human ways of life are sustained across generations, it is because they have aligned themselves with the dynamics of multispecies resurgence. The converse is equally true—and an urgent message for our times. Where resurgence is blocked, more terrible ecologies take over, threatening livability. Using the term *plantation* in its largest sense, I point to simplified ecologies designed to create assets for future

A.L. Tsing (✉)
Department of Anthropology, University of California, Santa Cruz, CA, USA

Department of Anthropology, Aarhus University, Aarhus, Denmark

© The Author(s) 2017   51
M. Brightman, J. Lewis (eds.), *The Anthropology of Sustainability*,
Palgrave Studies in Anthropology of Sustainability,
DOI 10.1057/978-1-137-56636-2_3

investments—and to knock out resurgence. Plantations kill off beings that are not recognized as assets. They also sponsor new ecologies of *prolifera-tion*, the unmanageable spread of plantation-augmented life in the form of disease and pollution. In contrast to what I am calling resurgence, proliferation threatens life on earth. This should be a subject of concern not just for biology but also for anthropology, which is needed to track the cultural histories in which such more-than-human social relations come into being.

WHAT IS RESURGENCE?

Disturbances, human and otherwise, knock out multispecies assemblages—yet livable ecologies come back.[1] After a forest fire, seedlings sprout in the ashes, and, with time, another forest may grow up in the burn. The regrowing forest is an example of what I am calling *resurgence*.[2] The cross-species relations that make forests possible are renewed in the regrowing forest. Resurgence is the work of many organisms, negotiating across differences, to forge assemblages of multispecies livability in the midst of disturbance. Humans cannot continue their livelihoods without it. The dependence of human livelihoods on resurgence is particularly obvious in considering hunting and gathering: If animals and plants do not renew themselves, foragers lose their livelihoods. But, although both scholars and modern farmers are prone to forget this, such dependence is equally insistent for agriculturalists and keepers of animals—and thus, too, all those who live on their products. Farming is impossible without multispecies resurgence.

I first saw this dependence when studying shifting cultivation in the Meratus Mountains of South Kalimantan, Indonesia, in the 1980s and 1990s (Tsing 2004). Meratus Dayaks cut down trees to make small farms in the rainforest; after two years of growing grain, they allowed the forest to regrow amongst vegetable and tree crops. Within ten years, tree trunks as wide as a person's thigh filled former fields. Wild animals, herbs, and fungi joined this regrowing forest assemblage; after 50 years, old-growth species had arrived and begun to replace pioneers. The forest was a place for Meratus hunting and gathering as well as for the making of renewed new fields. Forest regrowth thus allowed Meratus to maintain the farming–foraging combination of their late twentieth-century livelihoods.

Meratus shifting cultivation embraces the forest; in contrast, fixed-field agriculture is often imagined as the antithesis of the wild. Perhaps it was this imaginary that led to my surprise to find that peasant farmers are equally dependent on forest regeneration.[3] In my more recent research on commercial mushroom collecting in northern temperate forests (Tsing 2015a), I found an equally intimate relationship between farmers and forests—at least in those areas where generations of peasants had created a longue-durée pattern of farming that might have any chance of being called sustainable. Peasant farmers need forests for many reasons. Their animals feed from forest plants; the forest fertilizes their fields; forest plants and animals meet farmers' everyday needs. The interplay of forest and field is essential to intergenerational livability for humans and their domesticates as well as other species. In what follows, I will call this interplay *Holocene resurgence* to point to its development over the last 10,000 years as well as its dependence on post-Ice Age species agilities. To see how this kind of resurgence contrasts with *Anthropocene proliferation*, let me turn to these ways of parsing ecology and time.

Holocene and Anthropocene: Indicators for the Human Condition

In the past few years, geologists have taken public thinking by storm by suggesting that a new geological epoch be named after the massive changes to climate and sedimentation caused by human activities. This proposed epoch is the Anthropocene. A lively debate has ensued about whether such an epoch should exist at all, and, were it to be established, when it should begin. Archaeologists have called for a "long Anthropocene" that charts the effects of human activities at least since domestication (e.g., Smith and Zeder 2013). But most other natural and human scientists have preferred to use the term to mark the overwhelming force of modern human projects (e.g., Lewis and Maslin 2015; Zalasiewicz et al. 2015).[4] At the heart of these modern projects are a combination of plantation ecologies, industrial technologies, state and imperial governance projects, and capitalist modes of accumulation. Together, these have moved more soil than the glaciers did and changed the earth's climate. They have done this by allowing investors to engineer large-scale projects across long distances for converting places to plantations. Meanwhile, extinction rates have rocketed. Anthropocene, then, is an epoch in which multispecies livability has become endangered.

Naming the modern as "Anthropocene" invites us to look back at the previous geological epoch, the Holocene, to see what it might contribute to knowing sustainability. About 12,000 years ago, at the end of the Ice Age, the earth's climate warmed and stabilized.[5] Humans spread, and they increasingly began to use new modes of living involving crops and domestic animals. Many species were disadvantaged by the spread of humans, most dramatically those large animals whose extinction followed the late Pleistocene and Holocene expansion of humans. In comparison to modern environmental destruction, however, it is possible to think of the Holocene as an epoch in which human farming managed to co-exist with a wide variety of other living beings. If there is any meaning to the term sustainability, we must look for it in Holocene ecologies—including those that have managed to hang on in the contemporary world.

How did farming maintain its longue-durée viability during the Holocene? Holocene farming privileged the same resurgence processes and forest species assemblages as the multispecies expansion that followed the Ice Age, including both local succession and the long-distance travel of plants.[6] Plants had to travel to survive: The cold and drought of Ice Age glaciation pushed out many species. Spaces where those species wiped out elsewhere continued to thrive became *refugia*. When the glaciers retreated and the world became warmer and wetter, living things spread out from refugia, remaking forests, wetlands, and meadows. In temperate lands, after the first wave of ruderal (or weedy) plants, forest-forming trees came to occupy once frozen places. Trees are mobile—and thus they can respond to farming. In their spread from refugia, plants showed the lively initiative that has helped them survive human disturbances. Holocene farmers cut back forests, but every time farms were abandoned, forests took back the land. Mimicking their post-Ice Age spread, forests kept returning. Meanwhile, both crops and domestic animals depended on nutrients gained from forests. Farming not only cut but also impoverished forests, and yet forests bounced back.

Holocene farming might be said to have encouraged the continual enactment of post-Ice Age successions. In their advance, both glaciers and farms push back earlier ecologies; in their retreat, both tap multispecies agility in ecological renewal. Luckily, such agility is not gone. Holocene modes of existence, in this sense, are still part of the contemporary world, although pressed by powerful modern alternatives. To recognize this continuing importance, I need a specialized usage: In this chapter, Holocene and Anthropocene will not offer a singular chronology but instead point to diverging ecological modes that entangle and co-exist across historical time, even as they make histories. To preserve livability, we will need to conserve Holocene ecologies—and to do so, we need to pay attention to them.

Plants don't just automatically occupy places; their assemblies are formed in cross-species negotiations. In the rest of this chapter, I use the relations between fungi and plants to stand in for the many kinds of multispecies relations through which Holocene resurgence, on the one hand, and Anthropocene proliferation, on the other, emerge. Fungi are important actors in landscape making; they are also little noticed by most of us—and thus a good ambassador for the many hidden worlds that make the sustainability of human livelihoods possible. In what follows, I consider two distinctive fungal ways of life, which we might consider "hunting" and "farming."[7] My fungal hunters are decomposers. They locate vegetable prey and settle in to feast upon it. They make forest succession possible by culling stressed trees, and by providing nutrients for newcomers. My fungal farmers form symbiotic connections called *mycorrhiza* with the roots of trees. Like human farmers, they care for their plants, providing them with water and nutrients. In turn, plants provide them with a carbohydrate meal. Both modes of life are important to Holocene resurgence, but I focus on mycorrhiza. I turn then to decomposers to show how the plantation blocks resurgence and generates unmanageable proliferation.

Matsutake Enables Holocene Resurgence

My recent research has followed ecological and commercial connections involving that cluster of related mycorrhizal mushrooms called matsutake (Tsing 2015a).[8] Matsutake have a powerful and distinctive smell, and that smell has made them a gourmet treat in Japan. Prices rose spectacularly in the 1970s and 1980s as the domestic supply of matsutake from Japan's forests sharply declined. Matsutake have never been successfully cultivated. But it turned out that forests around the northern hemisphere support matsutake, and since the 1980s a lively trade has brought mushrooms to Japan from forests in North America, China, North Africa, Nordic Europe, and other regions.

Matsutake grow in nutritionally challenged forests; where rich soils are available, other fungi displace them. In East Asia, they are associated with peasant forests—and they depend on farmers' disturbances, which open the forest in ways that advantage them over other contenders. Here I stick with matsutake in Japan, where admiration for the mushrooms has encouraged a great deal of research and reflection. How do matsutake make Holocene resurgence possible?

Most of Japan's central island, Honshu, was not covered by ice in the last glaciation; still, the climate was cold and dry, and conifer forests covered most of the land (Tsukada 1983). As the region warmed at the end of the Ice Age, broadleaf trees moved in, and conifers retreated to the high central mountains. The only conifers in the hills and valleys (that is, outside of the central mountains) were those that could grow interspersed with broadleafs, such as *sugi* (*Cryptomeria*) and *hinoki* (Japanese cypress). In the first part of the Holocene, humans seem to have managed trees but not to have made extensive clearings in the regrowing broadleaf forest (Crawford 2011). Then, several thousand years ago, farmers started cutting down trees for intensive agriculture. Suddenly, pines, which had disappeared from hills and valleys since the end of the Ice Age, were back (Kremenetski et al. 2000: 102). Pines' partners in this return were matsutake. Together, they answered the need for ongoing resurgence.

Japanese peasants on Honshu have long cultivated a distinctive village landscape, enshrined as traditional practice (Takeuchi et al. 2003). Flat valleys are spots for rice paddies, vegetable fields, and houses. Irrigation channels slow down scouring mountain streams as they also water the rice. Since the nineteenth century, timber plantations of sugi and hinoki have become increasingly common. Yet the heart of the village landscape is the anthropogenic woodland on surrounding steep hills, the *satoyama* forest. Satoyama forest is intensively used. It may be cleared for timber and shifting cultivation; trees are also regularly cut for firewood and charcoal. Forest products such as wild vegetables, fruits, and mushrooms are gathered. And fallen leaves and humus are raked for green manure for the fields. The satoyama forest is an essential part of village life, supplying everyday needs and fertilizing the fields.

Farming depends upon forests—and forests require the resilience of resurgence. Matsutake shows us repeated beginnings of this process. Pines colonize bare mineral soil, laid bare by peasant practices, through their partnership with matsutake. Matsutake make nutrients available for pine from the mineral soils; pine give matsutake their carbohydrate fix. As pines and matsutake rehabilitate bare land for forests, broadleafs follow. If farmers did not continue disturbing the area, pines would eventually die out. But farmers' continuing use of the forest repeats the need for pioneering succession again and again. Pine and matsutake oblige. This is the opening act of Holocene resurgence. If Japanese peasant landscapes might be said to be "sustainable"—and indeed they have had a long viability—it is because of their relationship with pine, matsutake, and forest resurgence, which enables farming as a way of life.

In recent years, satoyama forests have declined. Some have been replaced—by suburban development, on the one hand, and by timber plantations, on the other. Others have transformed through multispecies responses to farmers' abandonment. During Japan's late twentieth-century economic boom, many farming families moved to the city, leaving their farms in the hands of the elderly. Meanwhile, those who stayed on the farm replaced green manure with chemical fertilizers and replaced firewood and charcoal with fossil fuels. Without human disturbance, a different successional process overtook the satoyama forest: Evergreen broadleaf trees moved in from the south, smothering pines and even deciduous broadleafs. Another forest emerged, one that no longer supported farming. Matsutake were missing from this new forest, and along with them a suite of flowers, birds, amphibians, and insects.[9]

Such transformations bring us to modern farming's efforts to disengage with forest resurgence. Let me move directly to the plantation and the new forms of biological movement it engenders, which I call proliferation. My example is another fungus, this one a decomposer: a hunter that is killing ash trees across Europe.

Ash Dieback and Anthropocene Ecologies of Extinction

In the early 1990s, a strange dying was reported among ash trees in Poland. A rapidly spreading fungus—something new that had not been reported—was shown responsible, *Hymenoscyphus pseudoalbidus*. Since then, the fungus has spread across almost all of Europe. In many places, more than 90% of the trees are infected by the fungus, which causes leaf spots, cankers, wilting, and tree death. In Denmark, one field study of 39 trees found only one with less than 10% damage (McKinney et al. 2011). At first, mycologists thought the fungus might be a new and virulent mutant of *Hymenoscyphus albidus*, an inoffensive saprobe of ash leaves on the Eastern European forest floor. But subsequent detective work has suggested that the fungus is a recent Asian import (Gross et al. 2014). Its Asian cousins are the same species, yet they do little harm to Asian ashes, remaining in the foliage rather than infecting the tree (FAO 2014: pt. 53). In Europe, a new fungal life cycle has been initiated in which the fungus grows from the leaves into the stem of the tree, eventually causing death. Annual obligate sexual reproduction, requiring a new host, has spread the fungus rapidly and kept it flexible in dealing with the responses of the genetically heterogeneous population of European ashes (Gross et al. 2014). This disease is spectacular and seemingly unstoppable. It is possible that Europe will lose most or all of its ash trees. Like matsutake in Japan, ash is culturally significant: In Nordic mythology, it is Yggdrasil, the tree at the center of the world, and its death means chaos. Ecologists point out too that ashes are keystone species, supporting much more life than just themselves. There are insects, lichens, fungi, mollusks, and birds that are entirely dependent on ash trees. As one group of researchers puts it, "The loss of a high proportion of ash trees is likely to have a cascade of ecological effects on ecosystem services and biodiversity" (Pautasso et al. 2013: 41).

How did ash dieback develop? It is hard to separate its rapid spread from the industrialization of the nursery trade in Europe. Ash is a common tree throughout Europe, and it thrives as a companion to human settlement. There has been no need to import it. Yet hundreds of thousands of young trees were shipped for replanting programs, both public and private, in the very places that ash is common. Here is how the situation in Europe is described in an FAO report (2014: II, 7–10):

> Until 40–50 years ago, horticulture trading was done mostly at local level. Nurseries raised plants close to where they would be planted.... From the 1970s onwards, however, the industry changed rapidly.... From that time, seedlings or cuttings were produced by specialized nurseries, transported to other nurseries as "liners" for potting into two or three litre containers, then taken from that stage into larger pots.... The development of international trade in plants largely followed from the widespread uptake of containerized transport: the availability of space in container ships, some capable of carrying over 18,000 standard-sized containers means that tens of thousands of plants can be shipped by sea, reaching their intended distribution points within days to a few weeks.... Inevitably, plant production condensed.... Young plants were often supplied by nurseries in regions where employment costs were lower, initially Central and Eastern Europe, then beyond Europe, as far as Asia, Africa, and North and South America.

Managers see industrial tree production and long-distance shipping as economical and efficient, but this view takes for granted the very hegemonies anthropologists might want to open up. The industrial nursery trade is an instance of the reorganization of the living world into assets, that is, resources for further investment. This is the principle behind what I am calling the plantation. Plantations discipline organisms as resources by removing them from their life worlds. Investors simplify ecologies to standardize their products and to maximize the speed and efficiency of replication. Organisms are removed from their native ecologies to keep them from interacting with companion species; they are made to coordinate only with replicas—and with the time of the market.

Plantation simplification intentionally deprives organisms of their ordinary ecological partners, since the latter are imagined as hindrances to asset production. On the one hand, then, almost identical organisms are packed together; on the other hand, they are alienated from all others. This is a strange ecological form—and it has consequences not just for the asset organisms but also for their predators. Imagine the feast for "hunter" fungi: an endless meal of helpless and identical prey.

Plantations are incubators, then, for pests and diseases, including fungal pathogens. Plantation ecologies both create and spread virulent microorganisms. Plantations are long-distance investments, and markets spread their products globally and with unprecedented speed. Through the industrial nursery trade, for example, soil, with its microorganisms, is gathered from around the world to transfer everywhere. Nor is the spread of pathogens limited to other plantations. The borders of plantation and forest have blurred: Because ash trees grown in nurseries are mixed into self-seeded landscapes, ash dieback spreads into the forest. Ironically, this spread seems an instance of the very movement of fungi and plants I celebrated in discussing Holocene resurgence—but speeded up unrecognizably. Speed matters. Plant pathogens have always attacked plants; but when this process happens slowly, landscapes recover. The speed of multiple attacks is something new, and a product of the dominance of the plantation form. That the attacks come even at those trees that have stood up to human disturbance is particularly frightening: The death of those trees threatens the resurgence on which we depend.

Plantations do more than spread pathogens; they also cultivate them. The proximity of so many purified and identical asset bodies—meals to pathogens—both augments pathogenetic abilities and also sometimes changes them entirely. In the rub of many bodies, fungal reproduction may take off with a new vigor, making use of otherwise minor abilities, such as alternative forms of reproduction. Furthermore, the plantation economy offers opportunities for fungal pathogens to meet close relations from other regions and to discover new prey. In this feast and family reunion, new virulent forms that leap from one prey species to another are formed. It seems likely that this was the situation for ash dieback. And the feast goes on and on, never lacking for new dishes. In more ordinary ecologies, pathogens become less virulent over time, as they adjust to the population dynamics of their prey. In the plantation, however, the supply of bodies is constantly refreshed. There is no reason for pathogens to reduce their virulence.

Welcome to the Anthropocene, in which alienated and disengaged organisms, including humans, multiply and spread without regard to multispecies living arrangements. Such proliferation makes no adjustments for previous residents and shows no signs of limits. Ash dieback is one of many products of the plantation economy, set loose into the world. These feral biologies block Holocene resurgence—and threaten the livability of multispecies landscapes.

Consider ash dieback, then, through its spread through containerized shipping, a floating plantation. This has not been a casual introduction, an ordinary result of travel. The thoroughfares for the fungus are the nodes of industrial plantation exchange: from really low-cost nurseries in Asia to still low-cost nurseries in Eastern Europe; from Eastern Europe to the Netherlands, the center of industrial nursery shipping; from the Netherlands to the rest of Europe. This has been the route for a reason: the organization of the industrial nursery trade. The FAO report I quoted continues: "Once in the EU, the plants are considered 'clean,' having passed the border inspections, even if not inspected. Further trade within the EU ensues, with huge numbers of plants shipped to countries other than the initial importing state" (FAO 2104: 21). In 2012, UK journalists reported that local nurseries relabeled their imported ashes as "British," hoping to please customers (Gray 2012). Ash dieback has spread by bringing the plantation into the forest.

In his celebration of ash trees, British botanist Oliver Rackham put the problem as follows (2014: 8–10):

> The greatest threat to the world's trees and forests is globalisation of plant diseases: the casual way in which plants and soil are shipped and flown around the globe in commercial quantities, inevitably bringing with them diseases to which the plants at their destination have no resistance. This has been subtracting tree after tree from the world's ecosystems: if it goes on for another hundred years how much will be left?

A TIME FOR ANTHROPOLOGY

Anthropologists, on the whole, have not taken threats to livability very seriously. In part this is because our ethnographic methods predispose us to notice success in livability, even where people are struggling with environmental challenges. To study encroaching unlivability, we need longer histories than fieldwork usually allows as well as attention to far-flung and difficult-to-trace connections. In part, too, anthropologists distrust the arrogance of experts, and we want to show them that local people know more about the situation than scientists allow. We reject generalizations about environmental destruction, especially where they involve accusations against poor and marginalized groups. We think of ourselves as radical critics of the authorities. But in the process, we have ignored the radical claim being made by environmental scientists: Business as usual is killing us. This chapter argues that we cannot continue to shut our ears—and certainly not if we care about sustainability.

The encroaching unlivability of Anthropocene arrangements could be an exciting challenge for anthropological research. Anthropocene natural scientists have been the first to admit that, given their training and methods, they cannot tackle these problems alone. We need to understand the semiotic *and* material nature of Anthropocene ecologies. We need to track back and forth between ethnographic observations rooted in particular communities, on the one hand, and broad histories and connections, on the other. We need to understand the human–nonhuman sympathies that make Anthropocene arrangements possible as well as the more-than-human historical trajectories that come together in both terrible hegemonies and patches of hope or resistance. These are tasks that anthropologists have trained themselves to do. A new field is waiting for us—and it demands urgent attention.

To appreciate Anthropocene challenges, however, we need to pay more attention to the cross-species socialities on which we all depend. As long as we block out everything that is not human, we make sustainability a mean and parochial concept; we lose track of the common work that it takes to live on earth for both humans and nonhumans. Besides, it does not work: Investors' attempts to reduce all other beings to assets have engendered the terrifying ecologies I have called Anthropocene proliferations. While my example showed the death of ash trees, I could have focused on those human pathogens similarly born in plantation-like ecologies of simplification.

To get to know other organisms, however, is a new challenge for anthropology. Yet we have what it takes: We know how to learn about social processes and about places and those who live in them (Tsing 2013). We merely need to expand our repertoire of the "people" we might meet to include other living beings. We can learn about them using all our skills: There is no reason not to combine what we learn from observation, indigenous cosmology, scientific reports and experiments, political mobilizations, and written and unwritten histories. Each of our sources must be assessed, of course, in relation to its methods for knowing and "doing" the world. But there is no reason, I argue, to throw any of these out on first principles, even if they do not fit together neatly.

This lack of unified sources might be exactly what we need to understand a patchy and fragmented ecological scene, part Holocene resurgence and part Anthropocene proliferation. The distinctive ecological modalities I signal with the terms Holocene and Anthropocene co-mingle in our times; they do not add up to a single whole. We need tools particularly to follow this patchiness. When pieces do not fit together seamlessly, a variety of ways of knowing can be of use. Indeed, this refusal to add up is an argument for anthropology's usefulness. Anthropology is one of the few disciplines that can identify patchiness and show its importance. Identifying those patches where Holocene resurgence still runs strong may be critical to our survival at every level.

This chapter has argued that sustainability is a multispecies affair. If we have any dreams of handing a livable world to our descendants, we will need to fight for the possibilities of resurgence. The biggest threat to resurgence is the simplification of the living world as a set of assets for future investments. As the world becomes a plantation, virulent pathogens proliferate, killing even common plants and animals. I can only repeat botanist Rackham's warning: "if [this] goes on for another hundred years how much will be left?"

NOTES

1. *Disturbance* is a comparatively quick change in ecosystems conditions; it is not necessarily bad—and not necessarily human. Unfortunately, humanists often misunderstand the term as a way of criticizing humans; without this (mistaken) implication, it could be a useful term for an anthropology of a world always in motion. See Tsing (2015a, Chapter 11). Meanwhile, there is no implication here that post-disturbance ecologies are the *same* as those they replace.

However, they are also not randomly different. Post-disturbance resurgence dynamics are studied as *succession*.

2. Resurgence thus forms part of a cluster of words concerning ecological health that includes *resilience* and *remediation*. I chose resurgence because it is not narrowly defined for quantitative exactness and thus retains its polysemy, with poetic overtones. The term forms part of my effort to expand the terrain in which natural scientists, humanists, and social scientists might engage in open-ended discussions without allowing demands for philosophical correctness, on the one hand, or quantitative models, on the other, to block creative work together. See Tsing (2015a, b).

3. I use the term "forest" in the American sense to mean a landscape with trees. My usage is synonymous with English "woodland."

4. Each of the citations in this paragraph offers quite different start dates for the Anthropocene, from 12,000 BP to 1945. The open-endedness of current debate is my excuse for an alternative use of the terms in this chapter: Holocene and Anthropocene here are used to refer to ecological modalities that can co-exist in particular times.

5. In official geological discourse, the Holocene epoch begins 11,700 years ago, following the Pleistocene.

6. Vegetation change in the Holocene followed different patterns in different regions. The spread of vegetation after the retreat of the glaciers in the northern hemisphere is particularly clear. In contrast, in other regions climate change followed more locally particular patterns. For example, the increased humidity of the Holocene allowed forest vegetation to recolonize Ice Age deserts. However, it seems to me that the label Holocene (and worse yet Quaternary) privileges the global north, and some serious rethinking about earth processes needs to be done from the perspective of the south.

7. These are not essences; as with human "hunters" and "farmers," their descendants may change. In explaining these ways of life, I make acquaintance but do not imprison them in fixed identities.

8. My research formed part of the work of the Matsutake Worlds Research Group. See Matsutake Worlds Research Group (2009). "Matsutake" here refers to a cluster of related species, with special attention to *Tricholoma matsutake* and *T. magnivelare*.

9. A Japanese citizens' movement, concerned that this landscape no longer makes the connection between multispecies resurgence and human livability, has emerged to bring back satoyama forests. See Tsing (2015a, Chapter 18).

REFERENCES

Crawford, Gary. 2011. Advances in Understanding Early Agriculture in Japan. *Current Anthropology* 52 (S4): S331–S345.

FAO (Food and Agriculture Organization of the United Nations), Regional Conference for Europe. 2014. The Impact of Global Trade and Mobility on Forest Health in Europe. www.fao.org/docrep/meeting/030/mj554e.pdf

Gray, Louise. 2012. Gardeners Sold 'Native' Ash Trees Grown Abroad. *The Telegraph*. http://www.telegraph.co.uk/news/earth/earthnews/9649565/Gardeners-sold-native-ash-trees-grown-abroad.html

Gross, Andrin, Tsuyoshi Hosoya, and Valentin Queloz. 2014. Population Structure of the Invasive Forest Pathogen *Hymenoscyphus pseudoalbidus*. *Molecular Ecology* 23: 2943–2960.

Kremenetski, Constantin V., Kam-biu Liu, and Glen M. MacDonald. 2000. The Late Quaternary Dynamics of Pines in Northern Asia. In *The Ecology and Biogeography of Pinus*, ed. David Richardson, 95–106. Cambridge: Cambridge University Press.

Lewis, Simon, and Mark Maslin. 2015. Defining the Anthropocene. *Nature* 519: 171–180.

Matsutake Worlds Research Group (Timothy Choy, Lieba Faier, Michael Hathaway, Miyako Inoue, Shiho Satsuka, and Anna Tsing). 2009. Strong Collaboration as a Method for Multi-sited Ethnography: On Mycorrhizal Relations. In *Multi-sited Ethnography*, ed. Mark-Anthony Falzon, 197–214. London: Ashgate.

McKinney, L.V., L.R. Nielsen, J.K. Hansen, and E.D. Kjær. 2011. Presence of Natural Genetic Resistance in *Fraxinus excelsior* (Oleraceae) to *Chalara fraxinea* (Ascomycota): An Emerging Infectious Disease. *Heredity* 106 (5): 788–797.

Pautasso, Marco, Gregor Aas, Valentin Queloz, and Ottmar Holdenrieder. 2013. European Ash (*Fraxinus excelsior*) Dieback—A Conservation Biology Challenge. *Biological Conservation* 158: 37–49.

Rackham, Oliver. 2014. *The Ash Tree*. Dorset: Little Toller Books.

Smith, Bruce, and Melinda Zeder. 2013. The Onset of the Anthropocene. *Anthropocene* 4: 8–13.

Takeuchi, Kazuhiko, R.D. Brown, I. Washitani, A. Tsunekawa, and M. Yokohari, eds. 2003. *Satoyama: The Traditional Rural Landscape of Japan*. Tokyo: Springer-Verlag.

Tsing, Anna. 2004. *Friction: An Ethnography of Global Connection*. Princeton: Princeton University Press.

———. 2013. More than Human Sociality: A Call for Critical Description. In *Anthropology and Nature*, ed. Kirsten Hastrup, 27–42. New York: Routledge.

———. 2015a. *The Mushroom at the End of the World: On the Possibility of Life in Capitalist Ruins*. Princeton: Princeton University Press.

————. 2015b. Aura's Openings. *More than Human: AURA Working Papers.* Vol 1. http://anthropocene.au.dk/more-than-human-aura-working-papers/

Tsukada, Matsuo. 1983. Vegetation and Climate During the Last Glacial Maximum in Japan. *Quaternary Research* 19: 212–235.

Zalasiewicz, Jan, Colin N. Waters, Mark Williams, Anthony D. Barnosky, Alejandro Cearreta, Paul Crutzen, Erle Ellis, Michael A. Ellis, Ian J. Fairchild, Jacques Grinevald, Peter K. Haff, Irka Hajdas, Reinhold Leinfelder, John McNeill, Eric O. Odada, Clément Poirier, Daniel Richter, Will Steffen, Colin Summerhayes, James P.M. Syvitski, Davor Vidas, Michael Wagreich, Scott L. Wing, Alexander P. Wolfe, Zhisheng An, and Naomi Oreskes. 2015. When Did the Anthropocene Begin? A Mid-twentieth Century Boundary Level Is Stratigraphically Optimal. *Quaternary International.* doi:10.1016/j.quaint.2014.11.045

CHAPTER 4

What Can Sustainability Do for Anthropology?

Henrietta L. Moore

Human/environment relations have been a topic of enquiry since the earliest days of anthropology as a discipline. Anthropology's commitment to localised differences, both cultural and geographical, initiated early debates on the intersection between livelihoods and ways of living that have had long-run salience in the discipline. Over the decades, intellectual and activist frameworks have shifted, moving through adaptive ecology to environmentalism, biodiversity and sustainability. No genealogy can be exact, since there have been many detours via development, resilience, conservation, postcolonialism, postcapitalism, bioethics and the pluriverse. However, what has remained constant is anthropology's political commitment to the autodetermination of the world's peoples, and the interdependence of cultural diversity and biodiversity. The focal point of critique has altered over time from the state to capitalism and onwards to the non-human, but the discipline has cleaved steadfastly to the importance of ethnography for demonstrating the viability of alternative life-ways and values.

H.L. Moore (✉)
Institute for Global Prosperity, University College London, London, UK

© The Author(s) 2017
M. Brightman, J. Lewis (eds.), *The Anthropology of Sustainability*,
Palgrave Studies in Anthropology of Sustainability,
DOI 10.1057/978-1-137-56636-2_4

Thus, anthropology's theories of sustainability as they have emerged have been tied up with a certain politics, even for those practitioners not directly involved with policy impacts, NGOs, activism and government. At root, as several chapters in this volume suggest, this is because of the presumption that conservation or sustainability is necessarily opposed to development, with an implicit working assumption that change for communities is rarely a positive process as they become drawn into forms of resource management and power relations they can do little to influence. Anthropology has contributed to the critique of models of development (e.g. Escobar 2012; Mosse and Lewis 2005) and has maintained a critical stance even as anthropologists have engaged with, worked in, and conducted ethnographic studies of development projects and processes (Bornstein 2003; Li 2007; Mosse 2013). However, anthropology as a discipline has yet to fully embrace the potentially larger auto-critique that is emerging as a consequence of a more rigorous engagement with the larger politics of sustainability and social transformation (Escobar 2015). In this chapter, I begin therefore not with what anthropology can do for sustainability, which is well-represented by excellent literature (e.g. West 2005)—including this volume—but with what sustainability might do for anthropology.

WHY THINKING ABOUT SUSTAINABILITY IS GOOD FOR ANTHROPOLOGY

Sustainability is the organizing principle of many areas of contemporary life: sustainable food consumption, sustainable waste management, sustainable development and so on. The word is in everyday use around the globe. In academic texts, policy documents, presidential speeches and television documentaries, its meaning seems obvious, but there is no universally agreed definition. What is apparent is very widespread agreement that the current planetary situation is unsustainable because we are consuming and/or degrading the resources which sustain us, an alarming form of destructive self-consumption. Consequently, one of the most common understandings of sustainability is as the inverse of unsustainability, particularly at the planetary level. But, what might actually be involved in achieving planetary sustainability, how we would move back within planetary boundaries to occupy safe operating spaces is much less clear (Rockström et al. 2009; Dearing et al. 2014), especially with a growing world population, many of whom are already suffering immiseration through poverty, ill-health and injustice.

WHAT IS IT THAT WE SHOULD SUSTAIN?

It is not just that there are complex tradeoffs and hard choices to be made, but that while we understand many of the technical issues surrounding such issues as CO_2 emissions and temperature rises, and the appalling pollution of the oceans, when it comes to social and economic questions, it is much less clear what changes would be needed, and how they would be implemented, to achieve sustainability. A number of writers have pointed out that despite societal awareness that the established structures, values and practices of advanced consumer societies are unsustainable and require fundamental change, little has been done in the global north to address the fact that the world is living beyond its means.

'Sustainability is interpreted by national governments as well as transnational bodies such as the EU first and foremost as sustained economic growth and competitiveness', something that is intended to 'secure the continuation of established lifestyles and patterns of societal development' (Blühdorn 2009: 2, 2013; Blühdorn and Welsh 2008). The rhetoric of commitment to sustainability is underpinned by ideas of environmental security and safeguarding which in turn support the aspiration for continued economic growth. Sustainability thus marks not a commitment to change, but a desire for continuity in ways of being and doing. Where this becomes problematic is when discussion turns—which it rarely does—to a consideration of constraints, to the fact that established rights and freedoms, including general principles of choice, autonomy etc., will likely have to be reconsidered if problems of climate change, energy resources, biodiversity loss and other challenges are to be seriously addressed (Kallis et al. 2015).

Sustainability is not just a matter of fixing the current technical problems of climate change, water, food security and so on, but a larger project of changing values which themselves will require novel social and economic institutions, possibly even innovative ideas about some of the fundamental prerequisites of communities and societies as they have been conventionally understood in anthropology, such as sociality, trust, companionship. So the problem of sustainability is a problem of change in the most general sense, but one which potentially places new ethical requirements on anthropology. For example, the global south is bearing the brunt of much of the impact of climate change, with the result that many indigenous and island communities are at serious risk. The need for action is extremely pressing, but it is understandably much easier for anthropology to concentrate on the injustice being done to those communities, rather than to ask how and in what way should constraints be placed on communities in the global north that would potentially restrict their mobility, use of energy, life opportunities and capacity for individualization. Such restrictions have the force of natural justice behind them, but if the trajectory of climate change and resource depletion is to be altered, anthropologists will have to engage not just with how communities are to be maintained, but with how they can be reworked, with what are the future desirable forms of society.

But how well is anthropology as a discipline equipped to cope with change, and with time? As a modernist project, anthropology's roots lie in very specific practices of change, in engagements with colonial policies, development projects, policy initiatives and so on. But, what do theories of change now look like in anthropology, and most particularly theories of change related to future sustainability? As anthropologists we work with the diversity of sustainability—culturally-specific definitions of what sustainability is and performative accounts of practices that fall within the rubric of sustainability. We know that there are many different ways of being sustainable, and this is a view shared by many other disciplines. The joint UNESCO/UNEP report on cultural and biological diversity made the link explicitly, arguing that the interconnection of the two is essential for long-term sustainability for the planet. 'Sustainable development requires that the moral vision of human beings be harnessed in as much harmony with local cultural aspirations as possible. Cultural diversity guarantees sustainability because it binds universal developmental goals to plausible and specific moral visions. Biological diversity provides an enabling environment for it' (UNESCO/UNEP 2002: 7). The vision is a compelling one and it emphasizes an ethic of conservation and stewardship. The anthropologist Arjun Appadurai played a key role in developing this vision, and the case it makes for moral justice cannot be gainsaid. However, it still leaves unexplored a larger issue about time and change.

The interconnectedness of cultural and biological diversity is key to long-term sustainability, but it cannot be so from an implied adherence to the status quo. In the broadest sense, the human condition is one of change, both for individual organisms and for societies and communities—to live is to change. Living in this sense encompasses the many different terms anthropology has used to understand this engagement: dwelling, existing, being, performing. Humans are embedded in living systems that are themselves open, self-organizing and interactive with their environments. These very notions and values are frequently made explicit through ethnography, and most especially through ethnographies based on the life-worlds of indigenous peoples (e.g. Descola 2005; Viveiros de Castro 1998, 2004), but they are found in more silent forms in the theories, values and cosmologies of a wide range of societies across the globe. We live in living systems, and while we do much to manage these systems, they are neither separate from nor subsumed by human agency. The human–environment interface is a dynamic one. So what does sustainability mean in this context and especially in relation to time?

Sustainability is one of those terms whose productive potential arises precisely because of its resistance to purification. However, one of the challenges such litheness provides is that we have great difficulty in specifying or even recognizing what it is that is to be sustained. (I will come on to the question of who does the sustaining and for whom later on.) More demanding still is how this question of what is it that is to be sustained relates to future sustainability, that is sustainability in the long term. For the most part, it is assumed that what needs to be sustained is made up of three parts or elements: the planet or the environment itself, including biodiversity; the relationship between humans and the environment; and the life-ways, cosmologies and ontologies of the humans concerned. However, logically speaking, we cannot really speak of sustaining any of these three things. They will all change—not necessarily at the same rate—so what we are sustaining is the ability for all three elements—the ecosystem, the ontology and the relation between the two—to have some future state, some future form of existence, a future life, a future. Human-ecological systems are never bounded or closed systems. This is true of even the most isolated and remote communities and is a point made most elegantly by Kirsten Hastrup in her contribution to this volume. However, while many scholars recognise the perils of treating sustainability as if it were without temporal performativity, anthropology within the larger disciplinary frame most often stays close to its modernist project, to the idea that local communities and systems are part of larger wholes that may—and most likely will—have deleterious effects on them. Here sustainability sometimes slips dangerously close to maintenance, the desire to maintain life-ways or ensure their auto-determination from larger processes. This is in itself not a sustainable position. Reflecting on the challenge of sustainability should turn anthropological thinking more directly towards the proposition that in living systems it's not simply about preserving existing diversity, but about enhancing it for the future.

The Challenges of Space and Time

The theorization of time in relation to sustainability is actually rather weak, and this is true of many other disciplines, as well as anthropology. This is partly because the scale and pace of change, and indeed of forms of reproduction, exchange and coalescence, across life-forms and systems are not singular. Cellular replication, for example, does not move to the dance of the history of human time. However, the weakness of theories of change in anthropology seems to be connected to pre-theoretical assumptions inherent in theorizations of the spatial. It is probably fair to say that in many, if not most, instances within the discipline of anthropology, the notion of sustainability is premised on ideas of embeddedness, location and context. People live in a place—they have an environment—and ideally they are at one with that environment. The environment may have suffered degradation, people may be suffering immiseration, exploitation, ill-health, there there may be conflict over resources, but the anthropological presumption is that if all things are well with the world—if none of these ravages hold true—then people would ideally be at one with their environment/ecological systems or at least living in productive symbiosis with them. Hence, the links between cultural and biological diversity and moral visions. However, there is a risk in many anthropological accounts, and especially those that emphasize the incommensurability of indigenous ontologies and western mononaturalism, that the singularity of cultural alterity is over-emphasized and reinstated inside a set of spatial coordinates within which its specific content has a unique function.

The result is the erasure of heterogeneous topographies and spatialities—even as these may be documented within the detail of the ethnography. They get overridden by the assumption of oneness of people and environment. In fact, as geographers argue eloquently, social/spatial relations must always be spatiotemporal, but more than that they are also formed in multiplicity. In effect, all worlds are 'a kaleidoscopic mix of space-times, constantly being built up and torn down. These space-times normally co-exist, folding into one another, existing in the interstices between each other, creating all manner of bizarre and unexpected combinations [...] Some space-times are more durable. Their reach is able to be extended by intermediaries, metrics and associational knowledges [...]

Other space-times flicker out of existence' (Thrift 2004: 91). Strictly speaking, there can be no oneness or singularity between a culture and its environment because together they make up a living system which is subject to non-linear change.

We have to pick our way carefully here because in the recent ontological debate in anthropology, what its practitioners emphasize is the potentiality of alterity, and the importance of processes of becoming where complex relationalities that are not premised on the subject/object, nature/culture divide—radically different ontologies—hold sway (e.g. Descola 2005; Escobar 2011, 2015; Latour 2004; Viveiros de Castro 1998, 2004). Such different ontologies seem to be premised on the multiplicity of space-times, both within and across contexts. In many Amazonian settings, for example, all natural beings are considered subjects and agents, but subjectivities can mutate and shift across corporeal forms. However, shared perspectives between humans and other natural beings presuppose a uniculturalism which persists across their corporeal differences: 'one single culture, multiple natures one epistemology, multiple ontologies' (Viveiros de Castro 1998: 478). This is a set of body-views, a kind of embodied standpoint theory, but it is not an unchanging one. Multiple realities emerge and are acknowledged, but they are the product of engagements, of historically and dynamically situated encounters between being and becoming (McCallum 2014: 506). These are not, therefore, versions of the world, in the sense of differing representations, but historically and experientially located forms of engagement. However, within this world of becoming, and taken on its own terms, it makes little sense to argue for a pre-given or static notion of ontology, as McCallum suggests (see above), and even less to assume that it implies a oneness with location, a single spatial–temporal framing encompassed by a relational natural world. Ontologies, like much else, are emergent, and have multiple space-times.

Within one specific view of the pluriverse, it is often argued that the ontologies that comprise it are so radically different that they are incommensurable with any others. This seems a strange position to adopt given the processual temporalities of perspectivism and its entailments. The ontologies involved are themselves living forms and are engaged in dynamic interrelations, including with other ontologies. The dynamic, processual nature of ontologies implies that they have histories and that they will change over time as part of living systems. In many instances, they have clearly endured—over long periods in many cases—but we cannot assume that they are unchanging. Such a view finds resonances in environmental and ecological philosophy, where relational, embodied spatiotemporal engagements are always necessarily multiperspectival, multispecies projects (Rose 2012: 131; Tsing 2012) because metabolic processes flow across species and systems. If this is so, we might need to think much harder about what it is that is to be sustained.

Clearly, it cannot be a singular relation between cultural ontology and an ecosystem, since this would imply stasis. Nor can it be the sustainability of the ontology per se since that is dynamically (perspectivally) produced in context, a living spatiotemporal form of embodied engagement with the world. One possibility would be to argue that what should be sustained is the ability to produce ontologies, and that such forms of becoming require enabling conditions, such as specific ecosystems. Yet, we need a further step because surely it could not be just to argue that an ontology or specific set of ontologies could only be sustained under a particular ecosystem state, for this would imply that there be acknowledged limits to the kinds, forms and numbers of system-states within which such ontologies might pertain. However, when making these arguments it is important to keep in mind that power differentials and forms of exclusion and extraction set clear limit conditions. Since it matters not one whit what future possible states of being or systems might be if the actions of others have already deprived indigenous communities of their lives, lands, traditions and life-ways.

If by autodetermination of indigenous communities, we mean the ability to withstand or to be protected from extermination, dispossession and immiseration, then we need look no further, but if by autodetermination we mean the assumption that stasis, disengagement or isolation is necessarily desirable and/or feasible, then the situation might be more complex, and especially with regard to sustainability. From a theoretical and political position within anthropology—with all the limitations that this implies— the purpose of sustainability should surely not be to sustain just what already exists, but to sustain the capacity for further development and diversification of multiple ontologies and indigenous knowledge practices. New knowledge practices come most often from trafficking across borders, and so it must surely be a matter for communities themselves as to what they traffic, and on what terms, how much use they wish to make of other systems, knowledges and practices. Writing of the incommensurability of knowledges does not make much sense in the face of the involvement of indigenous communities in a wide range of knowledge practices: using digital technologies for community monitoring and mapping, engagement with international biopiracy laws, selling carbon offsets, access to both traditional and modern medicine, using the internet to fight for community rights, and so on (see Ramos 2012).

MISCONCEIVED ALTERITIES

Perhaps more interesting though than this kind of argument would be to explore commonalities across knowledge systems, and work to enhance collaborations that would potentially bear fruit for the whole planet. A very wide spectrum of philosophies around the world are not premised on subject-object divides, maintain in different ways that causal relationships are not unified into a single whole, focus on the performativity of relationality, and insist on the continuities between living, non-human and organic entities. These include Shintoism, African cosmologies, North and MesoAmerican philosophies and societies in the Andes, Mongolia, Melanesia and the Amazon. Such ideas existed, of course, historically in Europe. In eighteenth-century France, Bishops were called upon to try and persuade encroaching glaciers to retreat. In present-day Europe, a whole suite of ideas about agency from actants and actor network theory to new materialism, and the strange space-time materialities of quantum physics, raise questions about forms of distributed agency, and the complex relationalities of humans to the systems that sustain them, as well as their vain efforts to control them.

The ontologies of indigenous communities and their vision of a world of relationalities is often portrayed, both inside and outside anthropology, as the opposite of something called western thought, and in particular western science. At one level, there might be something to recommend this position, but on another it totally misrepresents the emerging forms of explanation and enquiry in contemporary philosophy and science, as well as portraying both these activities as western instead of complicating the accounts of where and how both are performed, financed and institutionalized. For example, both microbial research and epigenetics are changing the very notion of human bodies through attention to the histories of those bodies in their environments. Modern science sees the human body not as a closed system, but as a set of ecologies composed of microbial and human cells, and microbial and human genes. A healthy adult has about 100 trillion bacteria in their gut alone, 10 times as many bacterial cells as those inherited from our human parents. Specific dietary and political–economic factors shape the development of human microbiomes, and so they reflect our daily habits, diets and cultural traditions, and they are also key to our health.

The revelation is that the human body is not a singular organism, but contains, in mutual symbiosis, complex bacterial communities. It is not entirely clear how these communities relate to human communities—variation occurs among individuals within communities—but it does suggest that in terms of any argument about sustainability, and the future of the planet and its biotic diversity, anthropologists may need to think again about how the communities they study relate to and are entangled with other living communities. For the human body itself is a series of nested environments inhabited by several 'more-than-human socialities' (Tsing 2013) which are themselves affected by their own embeddedness in larger systems. Content and context become enmeshed (Landecker and Panofsky 2013: 351).

Such questions reappear in other guises in contemporary science. The human body may be multiply constituted as a series of ecologies rather than a single organism, but it is also a fundamentally open system. Epigenetics—heritable changes in gene expression that do not involve changes to the underlying DNA sequence—shows that environmental factors play a significant role in the development and expression of life-forms. There are many contexts of relevance, but a key area is connected to foetal development and toxins. In the case of methylmercury contamination of fish in the USA, for example, fish consumption advice is issued to women of child-bearing age. Racial disparities in exposure to contaminated food means that such fish are eaten primarily by women of colour and it is their children who are most exposed to changes in foetal neurodevelopment. In this instance, the non-bounded relation of body and environment means that differences in diet can lead to biological differences in people, in this case between people of different races (Mansfield 2012). The social and cultural factors influencing diet literally become inscribed within the body, and 'race becomes the material effect of this epigenetic biopolitics of fetal neurodevelopment' (Mansfield 2012: 353). Suddenly, race is a newly emergent feature and rethought as a feature of altered neurodevelopment. Previously important boundaries between organism and environment—skin, mucous, membranes etc.—are not particularly significant to the organization of causal networks at the molecular level, since these networks are self-organizing. However, such biological networks are embedded within larger systems of social and cultural environments, and systematically affected by their own embeddedness within these larger systems, where the interpretations and representations of environments by the humans who inhabit them play a critical role (Landecker 2011; Niewöhner 2011).

Epigenetic change is heritable and forms part of human history, and there are two key points here. The first is that the social—as it has historically been conceived in the social sciences—is a causative factor in the biology of humans. The bodies we have, and will have in the future, are the materialization of social relations, where forms of sociality cut across species. Second, the notion of environment has massively expanded to create new problems of scale and new problems of time. The environment now means everything from the level of the molecular to that of the biome. Environments are multiple and nested. There is no single environment. New understandings of what it means for humans to be biologically cultural are emerging because environment includes social interactions and representations that can be transduced into molecular form and self-perpetuated epigenetically (Landecker and Panofsky 2013: 341), and because organisms we assumed to be bounded by membranes, such as the skin, turn out to be made up of multiple communities. 'Insofar as organisms constitute each other's environments through sociality, these biologically modulated social environments become the socially modulated biologies of further generations of organisms. The causal arrows go both ways, and the ontology of the gene as content and the environment as context cease to make sense' (Landecker and Panofsky 2013: 351). Social and biological anthropology have come back together again in ways that we might not have anticipated, but what is clear is that the new models of humans and their environments arising in contemporary science cannot profitably be dismissed as a manifestation of western ratiocination that is the incommensurable opposite of indigenous ontologies. The debates in modern science, with their complex relationalities that morph into socialities, look perplexingly like indigenous ontologies.

However, the character of bodies and their environments are being materially rewritten not just by epigenetics, but by new materials that are the product of science and technology. Contemporary humans are using living systems to build things that did not previously exist in nature. These new natural forms—synthetic biologies—are forms of life, and as these new materialities emerge, they are changing forms of consciousness. Human beings are involved, as they always have been, in redesigning life-forms. The involvement of engineering, computer science and nanotechnology in these processes of design produces some startling results, many of which are routinely dismissed by academics and publics alike as Frankenstein monsters. Playing God, failure to manage ethical conflicts, the further reinforcement of social inequalities, and many other worrying developments, are all significant issues in these areas. However, on a planet challenged by scarce water, rising temperatures and increasing pollution, engineered microorganisms can make many of the things our production processes rely on, but do so using less energy, producing less waste and without relying on fossil fuels. Synthetic biology is developing organisms to remove pollutants by consuming toxic chemicals in water and soil, and rerouting the crisis of antibiotic failure by developing probiotics that will remove antibiotic-resistant genes from the body. The hyperbole of the high-tech is always with us, and the political and moral challenges are acute and will no doubt increase. However, it would be quite wrong for anthropologists to dismiss these developments as the unlikely products of a western science that will never be of relevance to most of the communities anthropologists study. The issue is not about technological fixes, which as history has amply demonstrated often result in failure and always have unintended consequences, but about the future relation of humans to their environments.

CONCLUSION

All the environments humans live in are the result of human envisioning, and this is as true of contemporary science as it is of indigenous cosmologies. Anthropology's view of the environment has always been characterized by ethnographic diversity, but it has most usually been conceived of as context, the spatial location within which human agency takes place. It is precisely this conceptualization—and its space/time constitution—that a review of sustainability and of what it is that is to be sustained brings into focus. The current situation of planetary challenge and ongoing economic crisis finds us perhaps in an altered relation both to space and to time, and one that anthropology is just beginning to grapple with. In conceiving of a sustainable human future, we need to do more than think about who we have been and who we are. We need rather urgently to focus on the question of 'who are we hoping to become' and how are we going to get there.

REFERENCES

Blühdorn, I. 2009. Locked Into the Politics of Unsustainability. *Eurozine*, October 30. http://www.eurozine.com/articles/2009-10-23-bluehdorn-en.html
———. 2013. The Governance of Unsustainability: Ecology and Democracy After the Post-democratic Turn. *Environmental Politics* 22 (1): 16–36.

Bluhdorn, I., and I. Welsh. 2008. *The Politics of Unsustainability: Eco-politics in the Post-ecologist Era*. London: Routledge.

Bornstein, E. 2003. *The Spirit of Development: Protestant NGOs, Morality, and Economics in Zimbabwe*. New York: Routledge.

Dearing, J., et al. 2014. Safe and Just Operating Spaces for Regional Socio-ecological Systems. *Global Environmental Change* 28: 227–238.

Descola, P. 2005. *Par-delà Nature et Culture*. Paris: Gallimard.

Escobar, A. 2011. Sustainability: Design for the Pluriverse. *Development* 54 (2): 137–140.

———. 2012. *Encountering Development: The Making and Unmaking of the Third World*. 2nd ed. Princeton: Princeton University Press.

———. 2015. Degrowth, Postdevelopment, and Transitions: A Preliminary Conversation. *Sustainable Science* 10 (3): 451–462.

Kallis, G., F. Demaria, and G. D'Alisa. 2015. Introduction: Degrowth. In *Degrowth: A Vocabulary for a New Era*, ed. G. D'Alisa, F. Demaria, and G. Kallis. London: Routledge.

Landecker, H. 2011. Food as Exposure: Nutritional Epigenetics and the New Metabolism. *BioSocieties* 6: 167–194.

Landecker, H., and A. Panofsky. 2013. From Social Structure to Gene Regulation, and Back: A Critical Introduction to Environmental Epigenetics for Sociology. *Annual Review of Sociology* 39: 333–357.

Latour, B. 2004. *Politics of Nature*. London: Harvard University Press.

Li, T. Murray. 2007. *The Will to Improve: Governmentality, Development, and the Practice of Politics*. Durham: Duke University Press.

Mansfield, B. 2012. Race and the New Epigenetic Biopolitics of Environmental Health. *BioSocieties* 7: 352–372.

McCallum, C. 2014. Cashinahua Perspectives on Functional Anatomy: Ontology, Ontogenesis, and Biomedical Education in Amazonia. *American Ethnologist* 41 (3): 504–517.

Mosse, D. 2013. The Anthropology of International Development. *Annual Review of Anthropology* 42: 227–246.

Mosse, D., and D. Lewis, eds. 2005. *The Aid Effect: Giving and Governing in International Development*. London: Pluto Press.

Niewöhner, J. 2011. Epigenetics: Embedded Bodies and the Molecularisation of Biography and Milieu. *BioSocieties* 6 (3): 279–298.

Ramos, A. 2012. The Politics of Perspectivism. *Annual Review of Anthropology* 41: 481–494.

Rockström, J., et al. 2009. A Safe Operating Space for Humanity. *Nature* 461: 472–475.

Rose, D. 2012. Multispecies Knots of Ethical Time. *Environmental Philosophy* 9 (1): 127–140.

Thrift, N. 2004. Summoning Life. In *Envisioning Human Geographies*, ed. P. Cloke, P. Crang, and M. Goodwin, 81–103. London: Arnold.

Tsing, A. 2012. On Nonscalability: The Living World Is Not Amenable to Precision-Nested Scales. *Common Knowledge* 18 (3): 505–524.

———. 2013. More-Than-Human Sociality: A Call for Critical Description. In *Anthropology and Nature*, ed. K. Hastrup. London: Routledge.

UNESCO/UNEP. 2002. *Cultural Diversity and Biodiversity for Sustainable Development*. Nairobi: UNEP.

Viveiros de Castro, E. 1998. Cosmological Deixis and Amerindian Perspectivism. *Journal of the Royal Anthropological Institute* 4 (3): 469–488.

———. 2004. Perspectival Anthropology and the Method of Controlled Equivocation. *Tipití* 2 (1): 3–22.

West, P. 2005. Translation, Value and Space: Theorizing an Ethnographic and Engaged Environmental Anthropology. *American Anthropologist* 107 (4): 632–642.

CHAPTER 5

Interlude: Perceiving Human Nature Through Imagined Non-human Situations

Marcus Coates

M. Coates (✉)
London, UK

© The Author(s) 2017
M. Brightman, J. Lewis (eds.), *The Anthropology of Sustainability*,
Palgrave Studies in Anthropology of Sustainability,
DOI 10.1057/978-1-137-56636-2_5

Fig. 5.1 Goshawk (Self-portrait), 1999
Silver gelatin print, dimensions variable
Photography by Jet

Fig. 5.2 Human Report, 2008
Digital video, 7:16 min.
Broadcast at 8.26 pm on 23 May 2008,
Channel 9 TV, Galapagos, Ecuador
While artist-in-residence on the Galapagos Islands, Coates approached the family-run local television station Channel 9 TV Galapagos. He offered to make a short news report for them as an outsider. His report was broadcast as a news item, appearing between coverage of a beauty contest and the football results. Dressed in his hand-made cardboard costume, Coates reports on the human society (population approx. 30,000) from the perspective of a blue-footed booby, an iconic bird of the Galapagos. Coates had asked research scientists working on the island what they would report about the human situation if they were a visiting bird. Much of the report is informed by their responses.
Photography by Elke Hartmann

Fig. 5.3 The Great Auk (Pinguinus impennis) and Egg, 2010
MDF, emulsion paint
Bird: 85 × 27.5 × 27.5 cm
Egg: 12.4 × 7.6 × 7.6 cm
'The last pair (great auks), found incubating an egg, were killed there
   (Eldey Island, Iceland) on 3 July 1844, with Jón Brandsson and
   Sigurður Ísleiffsson strangling the adults and Ketill Ketilsson smash-
   ing the egg with his boot.'
Ellis, Richard, No Turning Back: The Life and Death of Animal Species,
   New York: Harper Perennial, 2004
Photography by Andy Keate

Fig. 5.4 Platonic Spirit: Running Grey Wolf, 2012
MDF, emulsion paint (colour: Mid Grey), 204 × 98 × 33 cm
A running grey wolf at full gallop measures 204 cm from nose to tip of
tail, 98 cm from ear to floor and 33 cm from shoulder to shoulder.
Photography by Andy Keate

Fig. 5.5 Journey to the Lower World, 2004
Performance, digital video, 28:13 min.
Single or dual channel video installation
Client:
Residents of Sheil Park
Location:
Liverpool, UK
Question:
Do we have a protector for this site and what is it?
Coates stayed in a 24-storey housing block in Liverpool, which was
    scheduled for demolition. After getting to know the residents, he
    invited them to participate in a ritual, where he would enter into a
    trance and communicate with animal spirits. Dressed in a stag pelt, he
    dances and makes animal and bird calls in front of the residents, before
    recounting how his encounter with these animals might relate to the
    residents' question.
Photography by Nick David

Fig. 5.6 (a, b) The Plover's Wing: a Meeting with the Mayor of Holon, Israel, 2009
Performance, digital video, 22:41 min.

Client:
Moti Sasson, The Mayor of Holon
Location:
The Mayor's Office, Holon, Israel
Question:
Will the Israeli-Palestinian conflict be solved through investing in better
    education and reducing the violence among young people?
[Marcus Coates performs a ritual for the Mayor in his office. He under-
    takes this ritual in an effort to seek an answer to a problem described
    by the Mayor.]

INTERPRETER [GALIT EILAT]	I would like to introduce you, Marcus Coates and Moti Sasson, Mayor of Holon.
MAYOR	Shalom.
MARCUS COATES	Shalom.
	Thank you very much for inviting me to Holon, Israel. I'm here to offer my services to you and your city. And I want you to ask me a question, a question that is important to you. I want to take that question to a spirit world, to talk to animal and bird spirits, to see if I can use their guidance to help you answer the question.
MAYOR/ INTERPRETER	There is a problem among the young people, the youth in the city, which is related to violence and he needs help to solve this problem.
MC	OK, and does this relate to a wider issue about the Israeli and Palestinian problems?
MAYOR/ INTERPRETER	OK, I think it's about investment in the future, so to try to reduce the violence among the young people is our investment for the future, because they will be the leaders of the future, and they will know better how to deal with different kinds of issues, argument and conflict. So in this sense, will the Israeli-Palestinian conflict be solved through investing in better education and reducing the violence among young people?
MC	OK, thank you, I'll try my best.
	[Marcus Coates performs his ritual. He makes the calls of a jackdaw, bittern, moorhen, coot, red

grouse, heron, raven, sparrowhawk, badger cubs, cuckoo. MC finishes and sits down.]

INTERPRETER How are you?

MC OK, that was interesting. There were many interesting animals and birds there. Most of them I am seeing, talking to and I'm listening to them. But there was one particular bird that wouldn't respond to me. I am not good at its call, I don't know its language very well. This particular bird is called a plover. It's a small bird, it nests on the ground on fields.

MAYOR/ What is the colour of the bird?
INTERPRETER

MC It's a white bird with beautiful green and black wings and has a small crest – tuft – on top of its head and it has very rounded ends to its wings, it's a beautiful flyer, and it nests on the ground. I saw this bird, I didn't see a nest, I just saw this bird on the ground and it was looking at me from the side and walking away with its wing dragging on the floor and I knew that's what this bird does, it's pretending to have a broken wing and it's trying to take me away from the nest, to distract my attention. And I followed the bird for a while and then it flew off, that's what happened, that's what I saw. In a way there was nothing unusual about that behaviour, it's what I'd expect from that bird. Which leads me to think that this question is a universal question, it's not necessarily a specific problem to you, but it's something that's affecting you a great deal at the moment. It's difficult to understand the meaning of this, but my immediate interpretation is that I knew I wasn't a threat to that bird. But the bird assumed anyone going up to its nest or into it, was a threat. It's automatically defensive. And in that way it feels like the bird or what the bird represents here is the idea of identifying with a certain position, identifying with a victim position. Whereas the bird wasn't a victim at all, it was just assuming whenever there was a circumstance like that, it was a victim. It was almost a default situation for that bird, it was an automatic response.

I think in conflict situations especially – and this happens with young people, with old people, I think it happens with everybody, I think it happens with nations – it's easier sometimes to take on what is seemingly a victim position, because you are defending yourself. And from this position you can do very extreme things and feel you are in the right.

I think that young people, especially here, need to learn that in a conflict situation they need to be able to identify with the person who they are in conflict with. They need to identify with other people's situations and with other sides of arguments. And that is a very difficult skill to learn. That's really it, I'm not sure how you teach young people, I'm not sure how you teach nations to identify with other people's positions. But I'm sure it starts with young people and it starts with education.

MAYOR/ INTERPRETER	They have an openness to be changed.
MC	Indeed. Do you have any questions for me?
MAYOR	No.
MC	Thank you very much.
	Cheers.
	[MC and the Mayor raise their coffee cup and glass and take a drink.]
INTERPRETER	It was strange – bizarre?
MAYOR/ INTERPRETER	He says that you are feeling things from the inside and it is important for you. It is real, not a play.

(Transcript excerpt)

CHAPTER 6

"They Call It Shangri-La": Sustainable Conservation, or African Enclosures?

Katherine M. Homewood

This chapter looks at the way global, hegemonic concepts of sustainability play out at the local level. It starts by setting out the global vision as encompassed in the current Sustainable Development Goals (SDGs). It goes on to use a case study of Maasai villages in East African rangelands to explore the experience that results for local people, and the very different concepts of sustainability they express. What emerges looks more like accumulation by dispossession, than the improved social and environmental sustainability that policymakers and practitioners claim to bring about.

SUSTAINABILITY: THE GLOBAL VIEW

Global visions of sustainability are perhaps epitomised by official UN literature. Over the last decades, and particularly in the last few years as international agencies have increasingly focused on following up the Millennium Development Goals, these documents have come to express the hegemonic concept of sustainability as a convergence between the three key dimensions of economic development, social equity and environmental protection

K.M. Homewood (✉)
Department of Anthropology, University College London, London, UK

© The Author(s) 2017
M. Brightman, J. Lewis (eds.), *The Anthropology of Sustainability*,
Palgrave Studies in Anthropology of Sustainability,
DOI 10.1057/978-1-137-56636-2_6

(e.g. UN 2012). That vision is now becoming crystallised in the UN SDGs (SDGs: UN 2015:6).

SDG 1 is to "End poverty in all its forms everywhere"—an aspirational goal, not least considering the 2030 deadline. Further down the list, goals 13, 14 and 15 deal with climate change, marine environments and resources, and terrestrial ecosystems, respectively. Goal 15 is thus to "protect, restore and promote sustainable use of terrestrial ecosystems, sustainably manage forests, combat desertification, and halt and reverse land degradation and halt biodiversity loss". SDGs 16 and 17 deal with social justice, institutions and sustainable development.

It is important to understand that these sweepingly broad goals are then reformulated as a whole series of potentially measurable and verifiable indicators, effectively intended as yardsticks against which governments are held to account. The data required to populate those indicators, and to allow such evaluation, are drawn from sources that range from standard government population statistics and surveys through to ad hoc reports from civil society and other organisations of events such as earthquakes, floods or forced evictions. So there is active encouragement by international bodies for member states to institute the processes these statistics seek to measure, and to perform well on the "measurable and verifiable" indicators that result.

Juxtaposing SDG 1 (eliminating poverty) and SDG 15 (protecting terrestrial ecosystems) underlines the inherent challenge enshrined within the idea of sustainable development. There is a deep-rooted contradiction between conservation and development. As the human population approaches nine billion, global demand for food, fuel and fibres is rising, alongside the demand for the land and water to grow them. Biodiversity is demonstrably collapsing through the habitat loss and direct exploitation driven by those demands (Lambin and Meyfroidt 2011; Rockström et al. 2009). Convergence between the three core dimensions of economic growth, social equity and environmental protection can appear not only a challenge but also a virtual impossibility. But a new orthodoxy has emerged over the last few decades, just at the point where rural livelihoods, biodiversity conservation and expanding large-scale cultivation collide. International agencies, and the big international nongovernmental organisations (NGOs) that both shape and facilitate their policies, increasingly view these tradeoffs as open to being resolved at the local level through community-based natural resources management: CBNRM. The present chapter explores how this chain—from global visions of sustainability achieving a convergence of economic growth, social equity and environmental protection, through to local, supposedly community-based management of the tradeoffs involved—plays out in the context of East African rangelands. The paper looks first at key dimensions of the economic, social equity and environmental issues in this region. It then goes on to consider the particular case of Tanzania's programme of Wildlife Management Areas (WMAs). They are analysed here as a case study of the local implementation of hegemonic sustainable development concepts through national CBNRM policies, and of the ways these are experienced by local people.

East African Rangelands: From Global to Local Understandings of Sustainability

Three main factors shape the interplay of conservation and development in East African rangelands. First, these rangelands are home to unique and spectacular large mammal savanna wildlife populations, which are known to be in drastic decline (Ottichilo et al. 2001; Ogutu et al. 2011). Second, the rangelands are also home to iconic pastoralist groups—peoples such as the Maasai, Samburu, Turkana, Mursi. The environmental implications of these and other pastoralists' land use practices are hotly contested (e.g. Vetter 2005; Homewood 2008, Homewood et al. 2001), as also is the productivity of pastoralism (e.g. Behnke and Muthami 2011). Without going into the detail of those debates here, they are relevant to this chapter's argument. Most immediately relevant though is the wide, deep and persistent poverty which characterises most sub-Saharan African pastoralists, including most of those living in the East African rangelands. That poverty is variously attributed to a perceived low efficiency and productivity of customary pastoralism (e.g. see current Ministry of Livestock policy documents for both Kenya and Tanzania: GoK 2006b, 2007; URT 1997), or conversely to the common social and political marginalisation of pastoralist peoples (Galaty and Bonte 1992). The third factor is the value of the tourism business, which earns East African countries like Kenya and Tanzania well over US$1 billion per year each, constituting one of the top contributors to gross domestic product (GDP) in these countries (GoK 2006a, 2010; Homewood et al. 2012). Not surprisingly, many observers see this conjunction of biodiversity, poverty and tourism as a strong case for CBNRM, and more specifically community-based conservation (CBC). Briefly, the idea is that if local people set aside land, wildlife populations will proliferate there, and attract increased tourist numbers. The tourism will bring in revenues and that money acts to lift people out of poverty. Given that the whole process operates on environmentally sustainable conservation, it holds out the promise of a triple win, that elusive convergence which sustainable development seeks between economic growth, social equity and environmental protection. This theory of change and desired objective is repeated across innumerable conservation and development initiatives:

> The central idea of CBNRM is that when local communities have ownership of natural resources and they derive significant benefits from the use of those resources, then those resources will be sustainably managed...This involves shifting control of natural resources from the state to the community and the development of opportunities for local residents to earn income from the resources newly under their control. (WWF 2014: 2)

Tanzania's Wildlife Management Areas

Tanzania's WMA programme exemplifies one specific case of such a CBNRM intervention. At Independence, the Tanzanian state owned and controlled all land as a strongly socialist government under Julius Nyerere. Though Tanzania underwent economic liberalisation from the mid-1980s onward, there is still strong state control over land. In the late 1990s, governments around the global South were encouraged to produce Poverty Reduction Strategy Papers. Tanzania produced *Mkukuta I* which focused on rural development through CBNRM. More recently, *Mkukuta II* focuses more strongly on economic development (URT 2005) but CBNRM remains a key mechanism, and Tanzania has instituted major programmes of participatory management for forests (PFM: Lund and Treue 2008), coastal resources (e.g. Verheih et al. 2004) and terrestrial wildlife (WMAs: WWF 2014).

Over 40% of Tanzania's land surface already comprises protected areas where local people have neither access to nor use of natural resources (Fig. 6.1). In addition to established protected areas (National Parks, Game reserves, Ngorongoro Conservation Area), a new category of WMAs is now being implemented. These WMAs represent "community-based" conservation areas which are effectively state designed, state driven and international NGO facilitated. Currently, there are 22 operational WMAs, and 38 are planned in total. This will add up to another 13% of Tanzania's land area set aside for conservation, directly impacting some two million people and indirectly affecting many more. It is important to

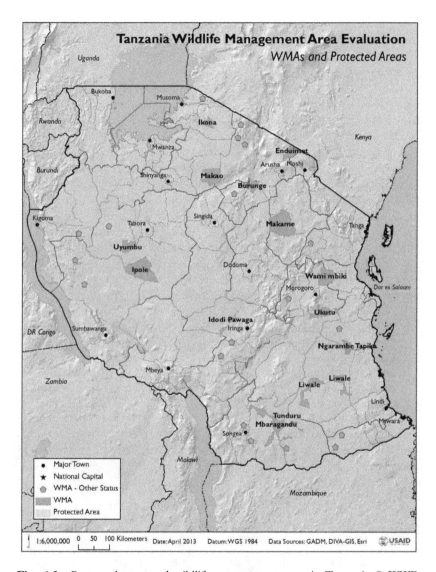

Fig. 6.1 Protected areas and wildlife management areas in Tanzania © WWF-Tanzania 2014 (The material and the geographical designations on the map do not imply the expression of any opinion whatsoever on the part of WWF concerning the legal status of any country, territory or area, or concerning the delimitation of its frontiers or boundaries)

understand how the WMA programme, conceived as an expression of a global vision of sustainable development and affecting very significant numbers, is playing out across this still very poor country (ranked no.159 in the World Bank's Human Development Index 2013[1]).

The case study outlined here was documented as part of a mixed methods research project on the social and ecological outcomes of Tanzanian WMAs, focusing, in particular, detail on three Northern (savanna) and three Southern (woodland) WMAs (Fig. 6.1). The present chapter focuses on qualitative findings for two Northern savanna WMAs, Enduimet and Makame, in Longido and Simanjiro Districts, respectively. This chapter does not go into the quantitative and statistical research design or results, but the quantitative findings of the wider study support the qualitative ones discussed here.[2] In particular, quantitative data and analyses show how representative of the wider national situation the qualitative findings are, while supporting the more nuanced differences between North and South, and between individual WMAs implemented at different times, and in somewhat different ways, across the varied contexts of pre-existing differences between villages and communities.

The central objectives of the WMA programme are to

- increase the **participation** of local communities in the management of wildlife resources;
- enable local communities to derive **benefits** from wildlife resources; and
- enhance the **conservation** of wildlife resources (WWF-USAID WMA status report 2014: 13) (emphasis added)

In evaluating the impacts of the WMA programme, this chapter therefore focuses on these three key dimensions: participation, benefits and wildlife conservation.

Enduimet Wildlife Management Area

Enduimet WMA was established in 2007 on the western slopes of Mt. Kilimanjaro. Prior to its inception, in 2004, we carried out livelihoods surveys of several hundred households in this area (Homewood et al. 2009). Household incomes were very low, with per capita income averaging US $0.16/day. Whatever the limitations of income measures and international poverty datum lines, these people are in economic terms very poor (increasingly so, as they become connected directly to global markets). The same survey established that on average around two-thirds of household income in cash and in kind came from crops and livestock. Households received on average negligible returns from wildlife tourism activities (around 1% of mean annual household income).

In 2007, the gazetting of Enduimet WMA set aside 110,000 ha, leaving 11,000 ha for farming and settlement. The gazettement effectively set aside 90% of the land held by nine villages, leaving 10% for households to farm, herds to graze and families to build homesteads. There are differences between the nine villages incorporated into Enduimet WMA. The WMA distributes equal shares of revenue to participating villages. However, some villages lost larger areas of their productive resources (including pre-existing wildlife enterprises). Others may have profited from gaining access to equal shares of wildlife-related income, which formerly they did not have, while retaining productive land outside the WMA.

PARTICIPATION

With the proliferation of schemes claiming community participation in NRM governance, there have been numerous analyses of quite what "participation" means. There is now widespread awareness that "participation" is a complex and compromised concept. So-called "participatory" systems often amount to little more than further ways to co-opt local people into externally devised and controlled projects that ultimately benefit outsiders more than those they supposedly engage (Cooke and Kothari 2001). The "participatory" processes deployed in development interventions may obscure relations of power, rather than factor them into ways of managing social equity and justice (Comandulli 2015). While fully accepting the complexity and ambiguities that the concept encompasses, the present paper deliberately chooses to evaluate participation on the terms on which it is understood by the international and national agencies promoting CBNRM. In this light, the extent to which participation is meaningful and successful relies on key dimensions such as the extent to which local people have themselves debated, prioritised and set the agenda; the extent to which they have made the rules, enforce the rules, evaluate the outcomes, and to which their assessment shapes the ongoing evolution of the system. Downward accountability of leaders is a key dimension of meaningful participation, though rarely observed. Analysing participatory forest management in Tanzania, Lund and Treue (2008) document instances where local committee members are able to censure or remove peers who fall short of expected standards (horizontal accountability, with leaders keeping one another in check) within a more general pattern of coercion, harassment and extraction of payments from poorer members of the community.

We spoke with members of the NGO-funded team who carried out the "participatory mapping" of village lands in Longido District in the runup to formalising WMA boundaries. They followed a participatory land use planning (PLUP) protocol based on a comprehensive and detailed manual available online and in hard copy (FAO 2009). Briefly, the NGO team arranges to meet with village government (VG) members for each registered village targeted for incorporation into a WMA. The VG is invited to identify seven individuals who will represent the village in an ensuing three-day process of participatory mapping intended to identify areas for set aside. Those seven individuals are given a brief training. The participatory mapping then involves creating an initial map of current land use, and current key resources (areas of settlement, water points, livestock dips, schools, health facilities)—a snapshot of how things are at the time of the planning process. This is followed by an exercise in imagining possible futures, and the creation of a second map, this time to show how land use will be in the future under new zoning which includes set aside. As implemented in Longido District, the facilitators stipulate that any features documented on the first map should not be displayed on the second map (creating some potential for confusion and conflict when key resources not highlighted on the second map are inadvertently lost to set aside). The process culminates in a village or participatory land use plan, to be signed off by the VG. However, it multiplies different "final" versions of the plan that may emerge and remain in circulation. The VG person signing off the (English-language) version considered official by the visiting planners may not be equipped to understand the contents nor how these may differ from the understanding of the villagers, leading in some cases to ongoing misunderstanding and conflict (Corey Wright, pers com.).

Throughout the period during which participatory mapping and land use planning was being facilitated by the NGO African Wildlife Foundation (AWF), a separate and parallel process of participatory mapping was being led in the same districts by the International Institute for Environment and Development (IIED), an NGO interested inter-alia in resource rights and governance in arid and semi-arid lands. This team used Google Earth visualisation in village meetings in an attempt to capture a more representative view of people's land use wants and needs and ensure their local environmental knowledge could be mainstreamed into participatory land use planning (Hesse 2013). This process has produced a separate and different set of outputs, begging questions as to what extent the participatory process may be empowering and conversely to what extent it coopts local people and situates them within the outsiders' own maps (Wood 2010).

Thus, a few teams each of seven local individuals, chosen ad hoc and without prior warning by VG members present on the day of the NGO team visit, and given the briefest of explanation and training, are assumed to be appropriate representatives for a population of some 50,000 people. They participate in a process unfamiliar to local people but all too familiar to the NGO team, which culminates after a couple of days in the planned set aside of very significant proportions of the land of the group of villages designated for a WMA. This chapter does not go into the detail of the lengthy bureaucratic process of establishing an 'authorised association' and the stages of finalising the WMA. Bluwstein and Lund (2016) go in detail into the implications of the multiple divergent understandings of the boundaries of the set aside in Burunge WMA (Simanjiro District); similar confusion and misinformation as to set aside boundaries applies in Southern WMAs (Noe and Kangalawe 2015).

Local people's own comments on their experience give a grounded view of the extent to which the WMA is meeting the stated objectives of people's participation, benefits and environmental conservation.

LOCAL VOICES: PARTICIPATION

In the case of the Northern WMAs, including Enduimet, people are clear that it is not the community but the state and the big conservation NGOs facilitating CBNRM who jointly drive the WMA process:

> For the community, devolution of power is not real to them. The government owns and the partners prepare the WMAs. The community...is not much involved. (G.W., Executive Secretary, AAC,[3] Arusha, February 2014)

A key dimension of participation is recognised as the extent to which local people make and enforce the rules. In Enduimet and other WMAs, local people have no authority to decide or change a WMA tourism operator, however, unsatisfactory that operator may prove to be

> the village can make a formal complaint, but has no right to remove a problematic [tourism] company. (D.A.N., District Legal Officer, Longido, February 2014)

This weak participation in managing the key dimension of rule enforcement is further highlighted by community spokesmen, who see enforcement as directed against, not by, the community:

Conservation has police, the community does not: there is no conversation... [the] WMA has many police: brothers and sisters but with guns. (A.M., spokesman for pastoralist communities, Arusha inception workshop, February 2014)

The Enduimet WMA authority confirmed that much supposedly community-oriented activity (and associated WMA funding) is in fact focused around enforcement against the local community. Anti-poaching operations attract significant wildlife NGO support. Though there are few functional health, education or other facilities, Enduimet WMA maintains patrol vehicles, a SWAT team of armed, masked enforcement officers and sniffer dogs, and the capacity to pursue suspects well beyond the boundaries of the WMA, including joint cross-border operations with Kenya. By his own account, the role of Enduimet WMA Authority's community officer focuses largely on anti-poaching, including operating an informer system monitoring households.

A further dimension of meaningful participation should reside in local people's ability to evaluate an intervention and to act upon that evaluation to either shape or terminate the intervention. However, as an international land rights organisation interviewee told us in December 2014, "there is no exit mechanism".

BENEFITS

As with participation, the concept of benefits (and of disbenefits or costs) is complex and contested. There is an increasing emphasis on multidimensional well-being, on both objective and subjective dimensions, as opposed to purely economic measures (Woodhouse et al. 2015). Beyond economic assets, security of food and livelihoods, common dimensions considered to contribute to well-being include subjectively perceived and objective measures of health, good collective social relations, autonomy, and personal and physical security (Woodhouse et al. 2015).

In economic terms, people's perception is that the livelihoods costs of Enduimet WMA overwhelmingly outstrip economic benefits. Typical comments from local informants on WMA benefits were "Revenues are small.

Outgoings are large" and "The community education video shows 50% WMA benefits going to the village. People ask where that has gone—they don't see it."

This impression of costs outweighing benefits is strongly backed up by our quantitative data. Where people have been told 50% of benefits should come to the villages, they have been given a half-truth. The state topslices at source roughly one-third of what the WMA earns. According to the state regulations, the remaining two thirds are meant to be split 50:50 between WMA, covering its administrative costs, and the governments of the villages participating in the WMA. At least in principle, each VG get its equal share of the remaining third of total WMA earnings. However, this does not go to households—it is used by the VG for community-level projects (building a school classroom, or funding school fees for a couple of students per village). These are real benefits, if at the community not the household or individual level. They may even attract further state co-funding (such as salaries for health or education personnel staffing facilities built on shared conservation revenues). However, in order to qualify to receive them, Enduimet WMA villages have given up 90% of their productive land, representing significant opportunity costs in terms of crops not grown, of livestock potentially excluded from dry season grazing and failing to survive droughts, and restrictions on access to non-timber forest products. A quick analysis of published figures (WWF 2014) shows that while WMA finances are complex, with multiple distinct income streams each of which is designated for a differential proportional share between state, WMA authority, district and VG, overall revenues to Enduimet WMA work out at around US$0.50/person/year, a derisory sum by contrast to the crop and livestock revenues foregone; it does not come directly to people; the services it buys overlap with those which—elsewhere—the state may provide as a matter of course.

There are significant disbenefits. People feel disempowered and disadvantaged:

> These wildlife management areas are...not a local concept....Do these resources belong to investors or to local people?...The people feel cheated. WMAs are seen as an avenue to take their land, their resources and their homes. (AM., Maasai spokesman. Arusha, February 2014)

Local people resent the restrictions placed on their gathering non-timber forest products. "You have to get permits to cut poles or thatching grass.

People feel taking poles is their right: they do not want to get permits." People now bear the additional costs of living in close proximity to wildlife, with the attendant risks of disease, loss of property and of lives, human as well as livestock. They resent the asymmetry which they see favouring wildlife over people "Hyaenas kill our livestock: but if you kill even one hyaena you will go to jail. People are really angry" (NS, Chairman, Namba 1 village; February 2014). This sense of people being valued less than wild animals is brought home most acutely with cases of injury or death caused by elephants and large predators, including the 2014 death of one of a group of young children out herding. In theory, there is a form of 'consolation payment' for such loss. In practice, no consolation payments have been made by WMA or by the state.

There is an obvious resonance between global visions of sustainability and the myth of Shangri-La's magical valley, where people live in harmony with nature and no one grows old; between the perfect cone of snow in the Shangri-La myth, and Mount Kilimanjaro on whose western flank Enduimet WMA lies. It is ironic then that the Enduimet tourist camp named Shangri-La illustrates so poignantly the disjunct between global vision/myth, and the practical realities on the ground, and challenges so strongly the widespread claims of participation and social equity, of benefits/and economic development:

> The tourist camp is called Shangri-La. The company refused to pay the villagers, as they say they pay the state. The villagers blocked passage of the tourists' vehicles....they were going to burn his camp...local people want him out but up till now he is still operating.
>
> He has no WMA contract, pays no fees and has many visitors. He is unwelcome. He is not allowed into the village. He cannot take pictures of people. He just shuttles visitors in and out as usual...
>
> The operator is always dodging....At the WMA meeting the villagers expressed the wish he should leave. He has no contract with the WMA. He paid the Division of Wildlife direct. He has political backing....No one can get rid of him.
>
> They dislike him....The MP knows the problem. This has gone to parliament: where does the strength come from to evict him? (Villagers meeting in Sinya government offices, February 2014)

Makame WMA

A second Northern WMA is also of interest. In Makame, proposals for a WMA were initially rejected. However, registered village members were eventually persuaded to join, on the basis of two significant inducements. This is an area which has received many in migrants: some being well-heeled outsiders looking for additional land to farm; the majority being people displaced by conservation or development interventions elsewhere. Evicted from their homes, and having not been given any alternative place to go, they have settled as squatters on outlying village lands. The state representatives whose role it was to persuade local residents to sign up for a WMA promised registered villagers they would evict non-registered in-migrant farmers from village lands set aside for the WMA. They also promised dry season grazing access. Makame WMA is thus seen as a way of securing both tenure and grazing access for local people. However, government colleagues collaborating on our joint research told us the villagers 'will be disappointed when they see how it turns out'. Again, villagers have been given false expectations.

Emboreet village has consistently resisted incorporation into the WMA:

> Wildlife? *"Faidha ndogo sana kwetu"*.[4] We try to keep livestock but there are wildlife problems—disease, losses—We try to farm but there are wildlife problems. The antelopes used to eat our maize. Now hyaenas eat our maize too. There are human casualties from predator attacks. (*Diwani* (Councillor) of Emboreet, February 2013)

Ecological Outcomes of WMA

Maasai are renowned for their environmental knowledge, but this resource has largely been disregarded by policymakers and practitioners (Goldman 2003). Their environmental knowledge has been ignored and eclipsed in official discourse by powerful narratives around environmental degradation (Homewood 2008:69 et sequ). Similarly, customary production and land use systems are consistently dismissed by East African governments (Homewood et al. 2012), though rarely by scientists or development practitioners (Behnke and Muthami 2011, Catley et al. 2012).

By contrast, policymakers and practitioners pay close attention to technical data, and our current work uses those data to bring home the extent to which ecological objectives of CBNRM interventions are achieved (or not). We use remotely sensed and aerial census data to analyse changes in vegetation state and wildlife population numbers, respectively. We also use a "before/after, control/impact" research design that allows causal attribution, making it possible to exclude confounding factors so as to tease out changes due to WMAs. Briefly, both vegetation state and wildlife numbers show large fluctuations, as expected for notoriously variable and unpredictable arid and semi-arid lands, but the changes observed are minimally attributable to the implementation and presence of WMAs.

LOCAL VISIONS OF SUSTAINABILITY

There is no word in Maa, the lingua franca of the northern rangelands, that maps to the term 'sustainability' in current international use. Swahili words commonly used in official documents (*endelevu; hifadhi*) tend to convey quite other, often negative connotations among local people. However, people commonly express local visions of modestly aspirational futures centred on security of tenure, of food and of livelihoods. These are generally phrased in terms of social, political and economic rather than environmental characteristics. Tenure security focuses on personal or communal ownership, control, access, use, and the right to exclude outsiders from land and key pastoral resources of grazing, water, mineral licks and migration corridors. Food security hinges on people's control of livestock and crop production (de Luca 2004). Livelihoods security encompasses access to and involvement in farming and herding; ability to manage drought strategies through grazing access to set aside; and engagement with education for the future of Maasai youth. This focus on dimensions of security is not some manifestation of a conservative culture resisting change—Maasai livelihoods are already very diversified, with people getting on average around one-third or more of their income from business or other off-farm activities (Homewood et al. 2009).

This is also not to say that there is a single shared local vision of a sustainable future. Attitudes to education provide a good example of the diversity of such visions. There is a widely expressed enthusiasm for young people to get the education that would allow them to compete for local jobs that currently go to outsiders; or to go for jobs outside the region. But the enthusiasm masks some strongly divergent attitudes. Maasai women are customarily treated as juridical minors. People now see that with education, women not only can earn their own income but can also support their children's education. Some parents support this actively, but others are unwilling to pay girls' secondary school fees. These parents see girls' education as a wasted investment, because girls will marry and relocate to the husband's homestead or that of his natal family, and her labour is lost to them. It is common for fathers to say girls have dropped out of school, or moved away or even died, and collude with teachers to remove their names from the school lists. There is a rush of marriages after exams, so that many girls who complete primary school and sit the final exams are married away before they find out whether they have done well enough to win a secondary school place.

DISCUSSION

In pursuit of social and environmental sustainability, local customary common property resource tenure systems and practices have been dismissed, local visions of sustainability disregarded, local participation in natural resources management and in benefits reduced, natural resource management returns captured by state and foreign actors, and environmental conservation outcomes until now not discernible. How is it that claims to secure local tenure and control play out as dispossession? How is it that interventions that purport to be community based, to enhance participation, benefits, local control and environmental conservation either have no measurable effect or may commonly play out as making things worse?

Tanzanian WMAs offer a classic example of the political ecology workings of sustainability interventions. In this case, as elsewhere (Robbins 2012) the intervention is driving commodification of commons, with WMAs converting grazing land commons into rents for elites.

Beyond WMAs, the Tanzanian state is engaged in land grab on a grand scale. Examples include the repeated attempts to evict 40,000 Maasai to establish a Qatari hunting concession in Loliondo[5] (most recently in December 2014), and Tanzania's implementation of SAGCOT,[6] whereby the state identifies and leases 'unused' village land to investors. More generally, Nelson and Agrawal (2008) have shown that across eight nations of East and Southeast Africa, "decentralisation" of natural resource management has in reality led to greater centralisation and state control, moves driven by these states' rent seeking behaviour, and facilitated by official narratives of degradation and poor productivity attributed to customary land use practices. These represent only a few of the many examples proliferating around the global south. They represent classic cases of accumulation by dispossession, through encroaching upon and dismantling traditional commons, culminating in elite appropriation. The African commons may be particularly vulnerable to resource grab (Berry 1993, 2009; Peters 2009). These outcomes map directly to political ecology predictions.

The process of dispossession may start out with the best of intentions on many levels and from multiple perspectives. Donor governments seeking to support poverty reduction ally with big international conservation NGOs concerned with environmental protection and with South states focusing on economic growth to address that convergence of economic growth, social equity and environmental protection held up by global hegemonic visions of sustainability. Are these willing partners naïvely co-opted by national and local politics, a process exacerbated by insufficient downward accountability? Either way, neoliberalisation of natural resource management is not producing the environmentally and socially sustainable outcomes claimed in global hegemonic visions and national policy discourse. Anthropology's view of sustainability foregrounds local voices; demands a cultural and political analysis; and challenges the hegemonic discourse globally and locally. It argues for a far stronger awareness of the political and political ecology dimensions of sustainable development interventions, for resistance to interventions in already sustainable local land use situations, for more attention to large scale processes of resource grab, conversion and extraction. Anthropology is now well placed to integrate qualitative and quantitative analysis, evidence and critique in ways that carry weight with policymakers, and to shape positive change.

Acknowledgments This work was carried out in the context of the PIMA research project (Poverty and Ecosystems Impacts of Wildlife Management Areas http://www.ucl.ac.uk/pima/sNE/L00139X/1) funded with support from the ESPA programme. The ESPA programme is funded by the DFID, the ESRC and the NERC. I am grateful to the United Republic of Tanzania for their permission to undertake the research and to the local communities with whom the work was carried out for their willingness to discuss the issues presented here.

NOTES

1. http://countryeconomy.com/hdi/tanzania
2. This work forms part of the collaborative research projects Biodiversity, Ecosystem services, Sustainability and Tipping points (BEST) NERC-NE/I003673/1, and Poverty and ecosystem Impacts of payment for wildlife conservation initiatives in Africa: Tanzania's Wildlife Management Areas (PIMA) NERC-NE/L00139X/1, both funded by the Ecosystem Services for Poverty Alleviation (ESPA) programme. The ESPA programme is funded by the Department for International Development (DFID), the Economic

and Social Research Council (ESRC) and the Natural Environment Research Council (NERC).
3. Before a WMA is established, the participating villages are required to form an Authorised Association. The Consortium of Authorised Associations (AAC) is thus the official body representing the WMAs in national political life.
4. "wildlife? They are of absolutely minimal benefit to us."
5. http://www.bbc.co.uk/news/world-africa-22155538
6. Southern Agricultural Growth Corridor of Tanzania: http://www.sagcot. com

REFERENCES

Behnke, R., and D. Muthami. 2011. *The Contribution of Livestock to the Kenyan Economy.* IGAD LPI Working Paper No. 03–11. Intergovernmental Authority for Development in Eastern Africa. Ababa: IGAD LPI Communications Office.

Berry, S. 1993. *No Condition is Permanent: The Social Dynamics of Agrarian Change in Sub-Saharan Africa.* Madison: University of Wisconsin Press.

———. 2009. Property, Authority and Citizenship: Land Claims, Politics and the Dynamics of Social Division in West Africa. *Development and Change* 40 (1): 23–45.

Bluwstein, J., and J.F. Lund. 2016. Territoriality by Conservation in the Selous-Niassa Corridor in Tanzania. *World Development.* doi:10.1016/j.worlddev. 2016.09.010

Catley, A., J. Lind, and I. Scoones, eds. 2012. *Pastoralism and Development in Africa: Dynamic Change at the Margins,* Pathways to Sustainability Series. London: Routledge.

Comandulli, C. 2015. *Beyond Development: Designing Alternative Worlds with the Ashaninka from Apiwtxa.* MPhil/PhD upgrading report, Anthropology, UCL.

Cooke, B., and U. Kothari, eds. 2001. *Participation: The New Tyranny?* New York: Zed Books.

DeLuca, L. 2004. *Tourism, Conservation, and Development Among the Maasai of Ngorongoro District, Tanzania: Implications for Political Ecology and Sustainable Livelihoods.* Unpublished PhD thesis, Ann Arbor.

FAO (Food and Agriculture Organisation of the United Nations). 2009. *Sustaining Communities, Livestock and Wildlife: A Guide to Participatory Land Use Planning.* Rome: FAO with AWF, ILRI, URT, GEF, and the World Bank.

Galaty, J.G., and P. Bonte. 1992. *Herders, Warriors, and Traders: Pastoralism in Africa.* Boulder: Westview Press.

GoK (Government of Kenya). 2006a. Ministry of Tourism and Wildlife, Republic of Kenya. Statistical Analysis of Tourism Trends. Central Planning Unit. http://www.tourism.go.ke/ministry.nsf/doc/Tourism_Trends_OCT2006_Revised.pdf. Accessed Nov 2008.

————. 2006b. *Draft National Livestock Policy.* Nairobi: Ministry of Livestock and Fisheries Development.

————. 2007. *Draft Wildlife Bill Nairobi: Ministry of Tourism and Wildlife.*

————. 2010. *Facts and Figures.* Ministry of Tourism. http://www.tourism.go.ke/ministry.nsf/pages/facts_figures. Accessed 14 Mar 2012.

Goldman, M. 2003. Partitioned Nature, Privileged Knowledge: Community-Based Conservation in Tanzania. *Development and Change* 34 (5): 833–862.

Hesse, C. 2013. *Maps that Build Bridges.* http://pubs.iied.org/pdfs/17193IIED.pdf

Homewood, K. 2008. *Ecology of African Pastoralist Societies.* Oxford: James Currey and Ohio UP.

Homewood, K., E. Lambin, E. Coast, A. Kariuki, I. Kikula, J. Kivelia, M. Said, S. Serneels, and M. Thompson. 2001. Long-Term Changes in Serengeti-Mara Wildebeest and Land Cover: Pastoralism, Population or Policies? *Proceedings of the National Academy of Sciences* 98 (22): 12544–12549.

Homewood, K., P. Kristjanson, and P. Trench, eds. 2009. *Staying Maasai? Livelihoods, Conservation and Development in East African Rangelands.* New York: Springer.

Homewood, K., P. Chenevix Trench, and D. Brockington. 2012. Pastoralist Livelihoods and Wildlife Revenues in East Africa. *Pastoralism: Research, Policy and Practice* 2: 19. (Online, open access).

Lambin, E.F., and P. Meyfroidt. 2011. Global Land Use Change, Economic Globalization, and the Looming Land Scarcity. *Proceedings of the National Academy of Sciences (PNAS) early edition* 108: 3465–3472. doi:10.1073/pnas.1100480108

Lund, J.F., and T. Treue. 2008. Are We Getting There? Evidence of Decentralized Forest Management from the Tanzanian Miombo Woodlands. *World Development* 36 (12): 2780–2800.

Nelson, F., and A. Agrawal. 2008. Patronage or Participation? Community-Based Natural Resource Management Reform in Sub-Saharan Africa. *Development and Change* 39 (4): 557–585.

Noe, C., and R.Y.M. Kangalawe. 2015. Wildlife Protection, Community Participation in Conservation and (Dis)empowerment in Southern Tanzania. *Conservation and Society* 13 (3): 244–253.

Ogutu, J.O., N. Owen-Smith, H.-P. Piepho, and M. Said. 2011. Continuing Wildlife Population Declines and Range Contraction in the Mara Region of Kenya During 1977–2009. *Journal of Zoology* 285: 99–109.

Ottichilo, W., J. de Leeuw, A. Skidmore, H. Prins, and M. Said. 2001. Population Trends of Large Non-migratory Wild Herbivores and Livestock in the Masai Mara Ecosystem, Kenya, Between 1977 and 1997. *African Journal of Ecology* 38: 202–216.

Peters, P. 2009. Challenges in Land Tenure and Land Reform in Africa: Anthropological Contributions. *World Development* 37 (8): 1317–1325.

Robbins, P. 2012. *Political Ecology: A Critical Introduction*. Second ed. Chichester: Wiley-Blackwell.

Rockström, J., W. Steffen, K. Noone, Å. Persson, F. Stuart Chapin, E. Lambin, T. Lenton, M. Scheffer, C. Folke, H. Schellnhuber, B. Nykvist, C. de Wit, T. Hughes, S. van der Leeuw, H. Rodhe, S. Sörlin, P. Snyder, R. Costanza, U. Svedin, M. Falkenmark, L. Karlberg, R. Corell, V. Fabry, J. Hansen, B. Walker, D. Liverman, K. Richardson, P. Crutzen, and J. Foley. 2009. A Safe Operating Space for Humanity. *Nature* 461 (7263): 472–475.

UN. 2012. *Sustainable Development: From Brundtland to Rio 2012*. UN High Level Panel on Global Sustainability 2010. http://www.surdurulebilirkalkinma.gov.tr/wpcontent/uploads/2016/06/Background_on_Sustainable_Development.pdf

———. 2015. *Open Working Group Proposal for the Sustainable Development Goals*. https://sustainabledevelopment.un.org/content/documents/1579SDGs%20Proposal.pdf. Accessed 3 Mar 2015.

URT (United Republic of Tanzania). 1997. *Livestock and Agriculture Policy*. Section 4: Range Management pp. 127–131. Dar es Salaam: Policy statements, United Republic of Tanzania.

URT. 2005. *Mkukuta: Tanzania's National Strategy for Growth and Reduction of Poverty*. United Republic of Tanzania: Vice-President's Office.

Verheih, E., S. Makoloweka, and H. Kalombo. 2004. Collaborative Coastal Management Improves Coral Reefs and Fisheries in Tanga. *Tanzania' Ocean & Coastal Management* 47 (7–8): 309–320.

Vetter, S. 2005. Rangelands at Equilibrium and Non-Equilibrium: Recent Developments in the Debate. *Journal of Arid Environments* 62: 321–341.

Wood, D. 2010. *Rethinking the Power of Maps*. New York/London: The Guildford Press.

Woodhouse, E., K. Homewood, E. Beauchamp, T. Clements, J. McCabe, D. Wilkie, and E. Milner-Gulland. 2015. Guiding Principles for Evaluating the Impacts of Conservation Interventions on Human Wellbeing. *Philosophical Transactions of the Royal Society (B)* 370: 20150103. http://dx.doi.org/10.1098/rstb.2015.0103

WWF (World Wide Fund for Wildlife). 2014. *Tanzania's Wildlife Management Areas: A 2012 Status Report*. Dar es Salaam: WWF, 72pp.

CHAPTER 7

Conservation from Above: Globalising Care for Nature

William M. Adams

We work closely with communities, governments, businesses and many others because we make a bigger impact when we work together.
Website, Conservation International, http://www.conservation.org/Pages/
default.aspx, 4 May 2015

INTRODUCTION

In 1999, the US-based international conservation organisation Conservation International (CI) published a coffee-table book describing critical
'hotspots' for international conservation (Mittermeier et al. 1999). In
2008, a *Hotspots* movie was released, describing 'efforts worldwide to rescue
habitat and species from extinction' (http://www.imdb.com/title/
tt1295907/).

The idea of 'hotspots' as a way of prioritising conservation action was
originally suggested by Norman Myers (1988) in the context of the loss and

W.M. Adams (✉)
Department of Geography, University of Cambridge, Cambridge, UK

© The Author(s) 2017   111
M. Brightman, J. Lewis (eds.), *The Anthropology of Sustainability*,
Palgrave Studies in Anthropology of Sustainability,
DOI 10.1057/978-1-137-56636-2_7

conservation of tropical forest. Soon after the foundation of CI in 1987, the organisation adopted his concept as the guiding principle for their programme of conservation investment. The book's stunning photographs supported a description of 25 zones, covering 2.1 m Km^2, containing 44% of the earth's plant and 35% of vertebrate species. In describing this new approach to conservation planning in the journal *Nature*, Myers et al. (2000, p. 853) argued that 'by concentrating on areas where there is greatest need and where payoff from safeguard measures would also be greatest, conservationists can engage in a systematic response to the challenge of large-scale extinctions ahead.'

Those concerned about the protection of nature or wildlife were key players in the growth of western environmentalism through the twentieth century. Environmentalism has been dominated by anthropocentric concern for the use-values of nature and the idea of sustainable development, yet the idea of the protection of nature from human use (and abuse) has been a powerful and central theme within wider environmental thinking. It was important for the development of mainstream sustainable development in the 1980s and 1990s (Adams 2009): the World Conservation Strategy, produced in 1980 by the World Wildlife Fund, International Union for the Conservation of Nature (IUCN) and United Nations Environment Programme (UNEP), was one of the first formulations of the idea of sustainable development.

CI's idea of hotspots reveals an aspiration on the part of international conservation organisations for a scale of operation and a global reach that was new. It represented what Peter Brosius and Diane Russell (2003) call 'conservation from above': the planning and delivery of the protection of nature by experts within powerful conservation organisations.

CONSERVATION FROM ABOVE OR BELOW?

In a sense, much conservation's history is one of top-down imposition of protection for nature. The default mode of capitalism was the capture and conversion of natural resources and natural areas. In industrialised countries, the conservation movement arose in opposition to the resulting destruction (Sheail 1998; Adams 2004). However, for much of the twentieth century, conservation organisations were small, poor and relatively powerless. Some (like the Wildlife Conservation Society in New York) built their work around successful zoos, others (like the Society for the Preservation of the Wild Fauna of the Empire in London) were effectively small elite lobbying groups. Their successes mostly came by persuading governments to take action, chiefly by passing legislation to protect nature, to set aside land in protected areas of various kinds and to conclude international agreements. They had spectacular success in colonised territories such as the USA, where the cleared lands and dramatic landscapes of the West allowed the development of the first national parks, and in the vast European colonial territories, particularly those of the British Empire (Neumann 2004). Colonial conservation, like other areas of government, was classically top-down: arbitrary, at best paternalistic and at worst coercive (Neumann 1998; Adams 2003).

The legacy of colonial ideas about nature and society persisted into conservation thinking beyond the end of Empire (Neumann 2002; Garland 2008). Non-governmental organisations grew in number and influence following the end of the Second World War (Adams 2004; Brockington et al. 2008), with the umbrella organisation of the IUCN (established in 1948, and combining both governments and non-governmental members), but the role of conservation organisations as advisers and lobbyists remained. The outcome was an unprecedented growth in land dedicated to conservation (18.4 million km^2, 12.5% of the terrestrial earth by 2014).

Conservation has continued to struggle with the coercive tendencies associated with the top-down imposition of protection (Peluso 1993). In particular, there has been extensive debate about the displacement of indigenous and other rural people associated with the creation of protected areas (Dowie 2009; Brockington et al. 2008), and the wider phenomenon of 'green grabbing' (Fairhead et al. 2012).

In parallel with a global conservation whose default mode was imposition 'from above', there has also been a concern to promote 'conservation from below' (c.f. Abrams et al. 2009). The language reflects an analogy with the shift in the dominant discourses of development that took place in the 1970s, in which 'top-down', 'technocratic', 'blueprint' approaches to development were criticised for failing to deliver promised economic growth and social benefits (Turner and Hulme 1997). An alternative agenda proposed to deliver 'development from below' through participation, 'putting the last first' (Chambers 1983).

In the 1980s, this approach was copied in conservation, and the language of conservation began to undergo a radical change, to emphasise social inclusion rather than exclusion (Adams and Hulme 2001). The IUCN General Assembly passed a 'Resolution on the Protection of Traditional Ways of Life' at its meeting in Kinshasa in 1975, calling on governments to take specific account of the needs of indigenous populations (Colchester 2004). Relations between protected areas and local people were discussed at the decennial World Congresses on National Parks and Protected Areas in 1982 and 1992, and the park managers were urged to consider the needs of local communities for education and healthcare, to allow them to participate in park management and to allow activities such as hunting, gathering, grazing and religious practices (Western et al. 1994). The 'Durban Accord', agreed at the World Parks Congress in Durban in 2003, spoke of a new paradigm for protected areas, 'equitably integrating them with the interests of all affected people', such that they provide benefits 'beyond their boundaries on a map, beyond the boundaries of nation states, across societies, genders and generations' (World Conservation Union 2005, p. 220). The Durban Action Plan called for 'free and informed prior consent' before the creation of protected areas and recognised a range of forms of governance, including those managed by communities as 'indigenous or community conserved areas'.

In the 1980s, 'community conservation' therefore became a central motif of conservation, important throughout the developing world (Western et al. 1994; Adams and Hulme 2001; Hulme and Murphree 2001). In theory, this placed the needs of local people were placed at the core of the conservation planning agenda. This seemed at the time a triumph for the idea of 'conservation from below', although as Brosius and Russell (2003) noted, 'bottom-up conservation' was more widely talked about than delivered.

Arguably, 'conservation from below' never fully took root (Hutton et al. 2005). The case for the strict protection of biodiversity was strongly restated in the 1990s (Oates 1999; Terborgh 1999; Kramer et al. 1997), in what has been described a 'resurgence' of the 'protectionist paradigm' (Wilshusen et al. 2002). In fact, ideas in conservation do not tend to change as fully as talk of paradigms suggest. Conservation is, and has always been, diverse in both ideology and practice. It is true that 'community conservation' was widely proposed as a new approach, principle or paradigm for conservation in the 1980s and 1990s, but it was proposed as an argument about what conservation should seek to be, not a finished and agreed organisational principle.

Belief in the need for strict protection to secure a future for biodiversity persisted and was an important motivator for the work of the new and ambitious organisation, CI, in the 1990s. Their work epitomised a renewed formulation of 'conservation from above'.

THE NEW CONSERVATION FROM ABOVE

So what are the features of the new 'conservation from above'? CI's adoption of the idea of 'hotspots' represented a new departure for global conservation organisations in several important respects. Here, I tease out five: (i) its global frame; (ii) its deployment of and dependence on science; (iii) its corporate shape; (iv) its neoliberalism; (v) its dependence on hierarchical systems of knowledge.

First, the need for conservation action is expressed within an explicitly global frame—not simply as an undifferentiated 'global problem' (such as 'rainforest loss'), but as a set of spatially explicit targeted priorities, each of which was argued to be of 'global' importance. CI's hotspots were just the first of a series of scientifically based attempts to define global priorities in conservation, each associated with a different conservation organisation. Thus WWF launched a global biogeographic classification (Olson and Dinerstein 1998), the Nature Conservancy outlined a programme based on 'Ecoregions' (The Nature Conservancy 2000) and BirdLife International defined 'Important Bird Area' (IBAs) programme (Stattersfield and Thirgood 1992).

Second, the new conservation from above draws on the power of science. There is nothing new about the centrality of science in conservation (Adams 2009), but the nature of that science has undergone change. The success of CI's hotspots reflected their deployment of science to define them, and (more importantly) to justify the choice, thereby legitimising them as priorities. These initiatives comprised one element in a new 'conservation biogeography' (Whittaker et al. 2005), a revolution in applied scientific research perfectly timed to contribute to the rise of the 'mission-driven' discipline of Conservation Biology, founded in 1986 (Meine et al. 2006). They were enabled by advances in digital technologies, particularly in the relatively cheap global coverage of satellite remote sensing (culminating in the ubiquitous surveillance of Google Earth), and the rising power and falling cost of computing. Facilities of analysis and modelling, once the preserve only of elite organisations like the International Institute for Applied Systems Analysis (IIASA, http://www.iiasa.ac.at/), became available to any organisation with a bright computer geek and a suitable laptop. New data were assembled within new algorithms that served as tools for planning (Brosius 2004), notably in the science of 'conservation planning' (Margules and Pressey 2000). This planning was global and scientific. It was by its very nature elitist and top-down.

Third, the new 'conservation from above' was highly corporate in style and organisation. A number of NGOs based in the developed world (particularly the USA) had grown relatively wealthy and powerful, and had developed global programmes (Brockington and Schofield 2010). In a seminal article in *Worldwatch Magazine*, Mark Chapin (2004) took the three largest (CI, The Nature Conservancy and the Worldwide Fund for Nature, dubbed 'Conservation BINGOs', or 'Big International NGOs') to task for their close relations with corporations and their disregard for local and indigenous peoples. In promoting their hotspots, CI used the techniques of commercial advertising, at the same time, highlighting the idea of hotspots, the fact that CI as a corporate entity had uniquely and cleverly identified them and the specific attributes of the places themselves. The characteristics of specific hotspots (e.g. the primate diversity of Madagascar or the floral diversity of the South African *fynbos*) demonstrated the value of the whole set, the idea of the whole set, and the importance of the organisation identifying them.

By the end of the twentieth century, conservation organisations had built significant alliances with corporations. Commercial sponsorship had become essential to conservation programme funding, and the network of interactions was dense (Hoffman 2009). The attraction of such arrangements for conservationists included not only the money to undertake their programmes, but also the possibility that they might influence corporate decision-making, and help 'save' biodiversity by 'greening' corporate boardrooms. In pursuit of both aims, closer personal ties were established, with current or former executives (including wealthy 'dot com' millionaire philanthropists) invited to serve as members of many corporate boards. The benefits of such engagements have been questioned both from a theoretical and pragmatic perspectives (Buscher et al. 2012; Robinson 2011; Holmes 2012), but the interpenetration of corporate and conservation boardrooms is everywhere commonplace.

Fourth, the new 'conservation from above' is strongly informed by neoliberal ideas about the role of private sector and state in conservation, and an associated enthusiasm for market-based approaches to conservation (Brockington et al. 2008; Büscher et al. 2012). Such a move for conservation is perhaps unsurprising, given the influence of corporations and corporate leaders in conservation decision-making. However, it is hard to separate cause and effect, since neoliberalism has washed throughout government and global institutions, transforming ideas about governance of the environment as so much else (Castree 2008; Peck 2010). The outcome is not in dispute: first, an intensifying commitment to the idea of nature as 'natural capital', that may be valued in financial terms and exchanged; second, a direct role for conservation organisations in the valuation, control and marketing of nature through strategies such as payments for ecosystem services (Igoe et al. 2010; Corson et al. 2013; Castree and Henderson 2014).

In terms of 'conservation from above', the use of market-based instruments might be seen as an unleashing of energies 'from below', with the market's 'hidden hand' delivering conservation outcomes without direct government control. In practice, the emancipatory promises of liberalism are not features of neoliberal governance. In fact, neoliberal conservation involves opportunities for government to extend its ability to protect nature (Hodge and Adams 2012); furthermore, it provides opportunities for corporations to expand control (Apostolopoulou and Adams 2014). Far from empowering people to achieve the conservation they wish, neoliberal strategies move power into the hands of corporations that have the capital to invest in order to profit from the marketisation of nature, and the governmental and non-governmental organisations that design the market mechanisms through which private investment and profits are made.

The fifth dimension of the new 'conservation from above' is its dependence on hierarchies of knowledge. This grows naturally from the intensification of scientific practice and the development of corporate patterns of decision-making. Brosius and Russell (2003) highlight the importance of legibility in modern biodiversity governance and the power of conservationists' maps and spatial data. Bryant (2002) describes how a process of strategic conservation planning in the Philippines was based on the mapping of biophysical data alone: data on people were not mapped, and local people were not involved in the planning process. Plans for the protection of nature were drawn up by the scientific planners, later to be imposed on local communities, who would be schooled in their correct response in a process of negotiation with outsiders. This case study is far from unique: Fairhead and Leach (2003) describe essentially the same process half a world away, in Guinea, West Africa: a planning process that seeks to bring in 'experts' with knowledge of the nature of concern to draw up a plan.

The nature of expertise is fundamental to the new 'conservation from above'. While Smith et al. (2009) include 'local groups' as actors (with government agencies) who must be allowed by researchers to set research agendas and decide how to implement results, even their agenda places researchers in a controlling position. Such an agenda is central to calls for 'evidence-based' conservation, an approach to science-based policy-making which copies the approach used in medicine (e.g. Pullin and Knight 2001; Fazey et al. 2004). Advocates point to increased cost-effectiveness if policy is based on peer-reviewed science, and statistically robust meta-analysis of case studies rather than rules-of thumb or accumulated field experience. However, as Adams and Sandbrook (2013) argue, Evidence-Based Conservation's framing of conservation in the language of medicine reveals a simplistic understanding of policy, involving a linear pathway from evidence to decisions and an associated narrow understanding of conservation action as a series of discrete 'interventions'. It privileges formal scientific evidence over other forms of knowledge, such as that of local people, who are not scientifically trained, and whose experience is not captured in formal literature. An 'evidence-based' approach strengthens the centralisation of power to make (and hence implement) plans in the hands of experts and those people working in formal conservation organisations. Even where the value of indigenous and local knowledge to inform conservation decisions is recognised (e.g. to extend short runs of formal scientific data), the emphasis is on testing and translation into a form that can be incorporated into scientific planning processes (Sutherland et al. 2014).

A NEW CONSERVATION FROM BELOW?

What are the implications of the new 'conservation from above'? The first, and perhaps most fundamental, is its narrow framing of conservation itself. In its contemporary guise, conservation is dominated by the ideas of established conservation organisations, and the burgeoning success story of growth in number, size and budgets of conservation organisations, the expansion of landholdings by state and non-state actors (Adams 2004).

However, while this history of this dominant, indeed world-bestriding, Anglo-American model is powerful, it is not complete. If one stands back from what could be called 'actually existing conservation', and asks what conservation is, the answer is less monolithic. Conservation can be defined as the outcome of choices about human relations with the non-human. Conservation needs to be understood as a socio-technical practice, combining social and technical dimensions into organisational structures and processes. This approach focuses attention on the relations between ideas and action in conservation. Both are highly diverse. Conservation ideas have manifold sources (ethics, self-interest, opportunity, cultural norms), and are highly complex (Sandbrook et al. 2010). All involve deliberate choices about how people (and human society in aggregate) should interact with non-human nature—how, in the common parlance of conservation, nature should be managed (and, more often, how human engagements with nature should be managed and nature utilised or protected). It is this 'management' that comprises the technology of conservation, be it hoe, fire, bulldozer or DNA sequencer.

Not all conservation can be lumped within the formal bounds of the work of conservation organisations. Sandbrook (2014) nicely defines conservation as 'things people do to establish or maintain good relations with nature'. This definition manages to capture the idea of conservation action and excludes those actions that are irrelevant or damaging to nature; it recognises that in some cases, good relations already exist and it leaves open debate about how exactly 'good relations' and 'nature' are defined. The formal practices of conservation are embedded in and arise from a much wider, informal individual responses to nature. Following Brosius and Russell, one can call these practices 'conservation from below'. What does it include?

Most obviously, 'conservation from below' includes practices of indigenous people (whatever their motivation, which might include shamanistic rejection of nature/human dualism, or simply long practical experience of interacting with non-human nature in place). Evidence, from anthropologists and others, on the profound depth and breadth of indigenous cultural engagements with nature and landscape are legion (e.g. Croll and Parkin 1992; Berkes 1999; Pretty et al. 2009; Pilgrim and Pretty 2010).

However, not all 'conservation from below' is confined to the ideas and practices that arise from shared cultures that are non-indigenous. Such ideas might include ethical attitudes to animal welfare, recycling, local or organic food, or shared practical ideas about the effects of nitrogen runoff from fields, or the problem of waste management. Many of these ideas reflect the work of conservation organisations, whose values are contested or normalised, shared and embedded in wider cultural norms in various kinds of 'environmentalities' (Agrawal 2005; Fletcher 2010). Thus, 'conservation from below' would include modern choices of diet or lifestyle (whether to eat meat, drive a car or fly on holiday) as well as the decisions of rural people about land or resource management (whether to clear or plant trees, to refuse to feed antibiotics to livestock, to use pesticides, to reduce net mesh size in fishing). Such choices are also 'conservation', just as much as the formal practices of 'conservation from above' (Bearzi 2009). Sometimes 'conservation from below' takes the form of local opposition to resource claims of government (e.g. for dams) or corporations (e.g. mines). Sometimes it can mean opposition to conventional 'conservation from above', for example, in attitudes to crop or stock raiding, or attempts to prevent small scale and traditional resource use, in protected areas.

The question of whose version of conservation comes to dominate is central to the future of nature. In a letter to the journal *Nature*, Reed Noss (2010, 424) rejects the call of Smith et al. (2009) to 'let the locals lead' in conservation; instead, he places his confidence in academic researchers, conservation non-governmental organisations 'and other "foreign" interests', because they are 'better informed, less subject to local political influence and more experienced in conservation planning than local agencies'. He precisely believes that conservation must come down from above, from those who know: 'Local agencies' capabilities are likely to be even more of a problem in developing countries. Letting them set the conservation agenda by themselves could therefore be a mistake' (p. 424). This is 'conservation from above' at its clearest and most pragmatic: only 'conservation from above' works, ordinary people are not to be trusted, and politics and self-interest corrupts every decision.

There are real risks in this strategy, and they lie in the political vulnerability of conservation strategies that do not reflect the interest, knowledge and values of the people they affect. Where such 'conservation from above' is unpopular, it leads to more of the same: a call for bigger and better-funded conservation organisations with more strongly defined and scientifically based strategies, and more resources to persuade other parties to adopt them. Conservation organisations seek support from central governments, international donors and corporations, and knowledge from scientists based in research institutions, most often overseas. Conservation renews its values and its programmes from such sources, and repeats its search for 'solutions' from above with renewed vigour.

Arguably, imposed models of conservation are not sustainable in the long run (Brosius and Russell 2003); certainly, they cannot be maintained without coercion, population displacement and dispossession (Brockington 2003). Sachedina (2010) describes the pathology of 'conservation from above' in one leading conservation NGO, the African Wildlife Foundation. As it grew through the 1980s, its managers (of whom he was one) became 'locked into certain ways of behaving and being from which it was difficult to escape' (p. 619). He comments that 'the people who end up mattering most to international conservation NGOs are donors in the west and African government elites, not the poor communities marketed in glossy communications materials' (p. 619). Sachedina's description would be true of many international NGOs, and it explains why conservation, presented from above, is so widely rejected by local communities; however, assiduously they are courted as 'partners' or 'participants'. To echo the title of the famous book by Robert Chambers (1983), this is 'conservation as if people did not matter'.

It is not, of course, a simple dichotomy between 'up' and 'down'. The writers of papers might love the rhetorical pizazz of black and white, but the world is everywhere grey. The challenge is therefore, as Abrams et al. (2009) puts it, 'to bring the top-down strategy to a point where it meets bottom-up conservation' (p. 803), to bring about 'a new kind of relationship between grassroots groups and international organizations' (Brosius and Russell 2003, p. 55). That requires an engagement with the messy processes of politics, and the more fundamental issues of political economy: justice, wealth, poverty, and powerlessness. This much is widely recognised (e.g. Brockington et al. 2008; Büscher et al. 2012).

At present, the dominant idea of conservation is something that comes from above, from those who are trained to understand the problem of biodiversity loss. It is an ideology forged in the industrialised world and offered as a global blueprint for future relations between humanity and other forms of life. But conservation also bubbles up from below, a diversity of claims for a liveable diverse world. The future of conservation depends on the balance struck between these conservation visions. The future of non-human biodiversity depends on the possibility of re-imagining conservation itself.

REFERENCES

Abrams, R.W., E. Anwana, A. Ormsby, D. Dovie, A. Ajagbe, and A. Abrams. 2009. Integrating Top-Down with Bottom-Up Conservation Policy in Africa. *Conservation Biology* 23: 799–804.

Adams, W.M. 2003. Nature and the Colonial Mind. In *Decolonizing Nature: Strategies for Conservation in a Post-Colonial era*, ed. W.M. Adams and M. Mulligan, 16–50. London: Earthscan.

———. 2004. *Against Extinction: The Story of Conservation*. London: Earthscan.

———. 2009. *Green Development: Environment and Sustainability in a Developing World*. London: Routledge.

Adams, W.M., and D. Hulme. 2001. If Community Conservation Is the Answer, What Is the Question? *Oryx* 35: 193–200.

Adams, W.M., and C. Sandbrook. 2013. Evidence and Conservation: The Need for a New Approach. *Oryx* 47: 327–335.

Agrawal, A. 2005. *Environmentality: Technologies of Government and the Making of Subjects*. Durham: Duke University Press.

Apostolopoulou, E., and W.M. Adams. 2014. Neoliberal Capitalism and Conservation in the Post-Crisis Era: The Dialectics of "Green" and "Ungreen" Grabbing. *Antipode* 47: 15–35.

Bearzi, G. 2009. When Swordfish Conservation Biologists Eat Swordfish. *Conservation Biology* 23: 1–2.

Berkes, F. 1999. *Sacred Ecology: Traditional Ecological Knowledge and Resource Management*. London: Taylor and Francis.

Brockington, D. 2003. Injustice and Conservation – Is "Local Support" Necessary for Sustainable Protected Areas? *Policy Matters* 12: 22–30.

Brockington, D., and K. Scholfield. 2010. Expenditure by Conservation Nongovernmental Organisations in Sub-Saharan Africa. *Conservation Letters* 3: 106–113.

Brockington, D., R. Duffy, and J. Igoe. 2008. *Nature Unbound. Conservation, Capitalism and the Future of Protected Areas*. London: Earthscan.

Brosius, P. 2004. *Seeing Natural and Cultural Communities: Technologies of Visualization in Conservation*. EP Colloquium, University of California Berkeley. globetrotter.berkeley.edu/EnvirPol/ColloqPapers/Brosius2004.pdf

Brosius, J.P., and D. Russell. 2003. Conservation from Above: An Anthropological Perspective on Transboundary Protected Areas and Ecoregional Planning. *Journal of Sustainable Forestry* 17: 39–66.

Bryant, R.L. 2002. Non-governmental Organizations and Governmentality: 'Consuming' Biodiversity and Indigenous People in the Philippines. *Political Studies* 50: 268–292.

Büscher, B., S. Sullivan, K. Neves, J. Igoe, and D. Brockington. 2012. Towards a Synthesized Critique of Neoliberal Biodiversity Conservation. *Capitalism, Nature Socialism* 23: 4–30.

Castree, N. 2008. Neoliberalising Nature: Processes, Effects, and Evaluations. *Environment and Planning A* 40: 153–173.

Castree, N., and G. Henderson. 2014. The Capitalism Mode of Conservation, Neoliberalism and the Ecology of Value. *New Proposals: Journal of Marxism and Interdisciplinary Enquiry* 7 (1): 16–37.

Chambers, R. 1983. *Rural Development: Putting the Last First*. London: Longman.

Chapin, M. 2004. A Challenge to Conservationists. *World Watch* 17 (6): 17–31.

Colchester, M. 2004. Conservation Policy and Indigenous Peoples. *Cultural Survival Quarterly* 281: 17–22.

Corson, C., K. MacDonald, and B. Neimark. 2013. Grabbing Green: Markets, Environmental Governance and the Materialization of Natural Capital. *Human Geography* 6 (1): 1–15.

Croll, E., and D. Parkin. 1992. Cultural Understandings of the Environment. In *Bush Base: Forest Farm: Culture, Environment and Development*, ed. E. Croll and D. Parkin, 11–36. London: Routledge.

Dowie, M. 2009. *Conservation Refugees: The Hundred-Year Conflict Between Global Conservation and Native Peoples*. Cambridge: MIT Press.

Fairhead, J., and M. Leach. 2003. *Science, Society and Power: Environmental Knowledge and Policy in West Africa and the Caribbean*. Cambridge: Cambridge University Press.

Fairhead, J., M. Leach, and I. Scoones. 2012. Green Grabbing: A New Appropriation of Nature? *The Journal of Peasant Studies* 39 (2): 237–261.

Fazey, I., J. Salisbury, D. Lindenmayer, J. Maindonald, and R. Douglas. 2004. Can Methods Applied in Medicine be Used to Summarize and Disseminate Conservation Research? *Environmental Conservation* 31 (3): 190–198.

Fletcher, R. 2010. Neoliberal Environmentality: Towards a Poststructuralist Political Ecology of the Conservation Debate. *Conservation and Society* 8 (3): 171.

Garland, E. 2008. The Elephant in the Room: Confronting the Colonial Character of Wildlife Conservation in Africa. *African Studies Review* 51: 51–74.

Hodge, I., and W.M. Adams. 2012. Neoliberalization, Rural Land Trusts and Institutional Blending. *Geoforum* 43: 472–482.

Hoffman, A.J. 2009. Shades of Green. *Stanford Innovation Review* 7 (2): 40–49.

Holmes, G. 2012. Biodiversity for Billionaires: Capitalism, Conservation and the Role of Philanthropy in Saving/Selling Nature. *Development and Change* 43: 185–203.

Hulme, D., and M. Murphree, eds. 2001. *African Wildlife and Livelihoods: The Promise and Performance of Community Conservation*. Oxford: James Currey.

Hutton, J., W.M. Adams, and J. Murombedzi. 2005. Back to the Barriers? Changing Narratives in Biodiversity Conservation. *Forum for Development Studies* 32 (2): 341–370.

Igoe, J., K. Neves, and D. Brockington. 2010. A Spectacular Eco-tour Around the Historic Bloc: Theorising the Convergence of Biodiversity Conservation and Capitalist Expansion. *Antipode* 42: 486–512.

Kramer, R.A., C.P. van Schaik, and J. Johnson, eds. 1997. *The Last Stand: Protected Areas and the Defense of Tropical Biodiversity*. New York: Oxford University Press.

Margules, C.R., and R. Pressey. 2000. Systematic Conservation Planning. *Nature* 405: 243–253.

Meine, C., M. Soulé, and R.F. Noss. 2006. "A Mission-Driven Discipline": The Growth of Conservation Biology. *Conservation Biology* 20: 631–651.

Mittermeier, R.A., N. Myers, P.R. Gil, and C.G. Mittermeier. 1999. *Hotspots: Earth's Biologically Richest and Most Endangered Terrestrial Ecoregions*. Mexico City: CEMEX and Conservation International.

Myers, N. 1988. Threatened Biotas: 'Hotspots' in Tropical Forests. *Environmentalist* 8: 187–208.

Myers, N., R. Mittermeier, C. Mittermeier, G. de Fonseca, and J. Kent. 2000. Biodiversity Hotspots for Conservation Priorities. *Nature* 403: 853–858.

Neumann, R.P. 1998. *Imposing Wilderness: Struggles Over Livelihood and Nature Preservation in Africa.* Berkeley: University of California Press.

———. 2002. The Postwar Conservation Boom in British Colonial Africa. *Environmental History* 7: 22–47.

———. 2004. Nature-State-Territory: Towards a Critical Theorization of Conservation Enclosures. In *Liberation Ecologies: Environment, Development, Social Movements*, ed. R. Peet and M. Watts, 195–217. London: Routledge.

Noss, R. 2010. Local Priorities Can be Too Parochial for Biodiversity. *Nature* 463: 424.

Oates, J. 1999. *Myth and Reality in the Rain Forest: How Conservation Strategies are Failing in West Africa.* Berkeley: University of California Press.

Olson, D.M., and E. Dinerstein. 1998. The Global 200: A Representation Approach to Conserving the Earth's Most Biologically Valuable Ecoregions. *Conservation Biology* 12 (3): 502–515.

Peck, J. 2010. *Constructions of Neoliberal Reason.* Oxford: Oxford University Press.

Peluso, N. 1993. Coercing Conservation: The Politics of State Resource Control. *Global Environmental Change* 3: 199–217.

Pilgrim, S., and J. Pretty, eds. 2010. *Nature and Culture: Rebuilding Lost Connections.* London: Earthscan.

Pretty, J., W. Adams, F. Berkes, S. de Athayde, N. Dudley, E. Hunn, L. Maffi, K. Milton, D. Rapport, P. Robbins, E. Sterling, S. Stolton, A. Tsing, E. Vintinner, and S. Pilgrim. 2009. The Intersections of Biological Diversity and Cultural Diversity: Towards Integration. *Conservation and Society* 7 (2): 100–112.

Pullin, A.S., and T.M. Knight. 2001. Effectiveness in Conservation Practice: Pointers from Medicine and Public Health. *Conservation Biology* 15 (1): 50–54.

Robinson, J.G. 2011. Corporate Greening: Is It Significant for Biodiversity Conservation? *Oryx* 45 (3): 309–310.

Sachedina, H.T. 2010. Disconnected Nature: The Scaling Up of African Wildlife Foundation and its Impacts on Biodiversity Conservation and Local Livelihoods. *Antipode* 42: 603–623.

Sandbrook, C. 2014. What Is Conservation? *Thinking Like a Human.* http://thinkinglikeahuman.com/2014/03/05/what-is-conservation/

Sandbrook, C., I. Scales, B. Vira, and W.M. Adams. 2010. Mission Impossible? Diversity in the Values Held by Conservation Scientists. *Conservation Biology* 25 (2): 285–294.

Sheail, J. 1998. *Nature Conservation in Britain: The Formative Years.* London: The Stationery Office.

Smith, R.J., D. Verissimo, N. Leader-Williams, R. Cowling, and A. Knight. 2009. Let the Locals Lead. *Nature* 462: 280–281.

Stattersfield, A.J., and S. Thirgood. 1992. *Putting Biodiversity on the Map.* Cambridge: BirdLife international.

Sutherland, W.J., T.A. Gardner, L.J. Haider, and L.V. Dicks. 2014. How Can Local and Traditional Knowledge be Effectively Incorporated into International Assessments? *Oryx* 48: 1–2.

Terborgh, J. 1999. *Requiem for Nature.* Washington, DC: Island Press.

Turner, M., and D. Hulme. 1997. *Governance, Administration and Development: Making the State Work.* London: Macmillan.

Western, D., M. Wright, and S. Strumm, eds. 1994. *Natural Connections: Perspectives in Community-Based Conservation.* Washington, DC: Island Press.

Whittaker, R.J., M. Araújo, P. Jepson, R. Ladle, J. Watson, and K. Willis. 2005. Conservation Biogeography: Assessment and Prospect. *Diversity and Distributions* 11: 3–23.

Wilshusen, P.R., S.R. Brechin, C.L. Fortwangler, and P.C. West. 2002. Reinventing a Square Wheel: Critique of a Resurgent "Protection Paradigm" in International Biodiversity Conservation. *Society and Natural Resources* 15: 17–40.

World Conservation Union – IUCN. 2005. *Benefits Beyond Boundaries.* Proceedings of the Vth World Parks Congress. Cambridge, UK: World Conservation Union.

CHAPTER 8

Different Knowledge Regimes and Some Consequences for 'Sustainability'

Signe Howell

Coming from Norway where 'sustainability' was effectively put on the map by the Brundtland Commission on Environment and Development in their report *Our Common Future* published in 1987, I feel a special responsibility to consider if and how anthropologists may contribute to policies for alleviating the current ecological crisis we are facing in the so-called Anthropocene Age. According to the report, 'sustainable development' is development that 'meets the needs of the present without compromising the ability of future generations to meet their own needs' (1987: 8, 43). The report further insists that development is not just about how poor countries can ameliorate *their* situation, but what the entire world, including developed countries, can do to ameliorate *our common* situation.[1]

Some basic premises of the Brundtland Report would appear to be compatible with an anthropological approach. For example, it promoted the idea that while the 'environment' was previously perceived as 'a sphere separate from human emotion or action', and while 'development' was a term habitually used to describe political goals regarding economic progress, it is more appropriate to understand the two terms in relation to each other (ibid.: Chap. 1). Moreover, the Report insisted upon the environment

S. Howell (✉)
Department of Social Anthropology, University of Oslo, Oslo, Norway

© The Author(s) 2017
M. Brightman, J. Lewis (eds.), *The Anthropology of Sustainability*,
Palgrave Studies in Anthropology of Sustainability,
DOI 10.1057/978-1-137-56636-2_8

being 'something beyond physicality, going beyond that traditional school of thought to include social and political atmospheres and circumstances'. Few anthropologists interested in environmental anthropology would disagree with these statements. Indeed, most of us who have undertaken studies of small-scale societies whose livelihood and quality of life are dependent upon interaction with the natural environment within which they live, argue that nature and society are mutually implicated in the ontological schema in question (Hastrup 2013). The challenge, however, is how—if at all—we can make our knowledge of other people's life-worlds relevant to our current ecological situation. Disappointingly, the Brundtland Report did not offer much guidance on how they imagined that policy makers could build on the insight that the environment is entangled with economics, politics, religion or indeed, in contemporary jargon, ontology. This lack of guidance notwithstanding, the Report immediately caught the imagination of politicians and ordinary citizens alike. However, the optimism of the Brundtland Commission has not been vindicated by subsequent events. Despite the wide attention paid to the report and the many subsequent number of summit meetings, little has been achieved. Arguably, the situation has gone from bad to worse (Lee et al. 2000). A major reason for this may be attributed to a subsequent tendency to focus upon economic growth at the expense of the wider understanding of environment. Universal models for sustainability and development are still being sought within the fields of economics and technology while lipservice continues to be paid to "the importance of culture". Studies of alternative values and practices continue to be ignored. However, solutions to a sustainable future (however defined) are today as dependent on political will as on finding new models to be implemented.

In this chapter, I shall not discuss the ontological turn in Anthropology. I am well aware of trends in Anthropology that argue for a dissolution of the division between humanity and nature and for radical alterity. I have commented on this elsewhere and shall not do so here (Howell 2013a). Having worked with one group of people (Chewong on the Malaysian Peninsula) whose ontological understanding is both animistic and perspectivist (Howell 1984), I nevertheless argue for human exceptionalism on the simple grounds that to do otherwise is to deny human commensurability. Comparison is difficult enough as it is without introducing posited non-human conscious beings into the discourse. Moreover, a post-human position limits the scope for anthropological contribution to the challenges of the Anthropocene Age; a scope that already is rather limited. Rather, I shall try to respond to what I interpret to be the intention of the conference to inaugurate the new Centre for Anthropology of Sustainability, namely a critique of the current situation and the search for an anthropological contribution to an understanding of the issues involved with a view to provide insight to policy makers.

The term 'sustainable development' has a certain immediate appeal. It sounds so obviously sensible and has been characterized as an example of 'an idea that makes a difference' (McNeill 2000: 10). However, the definition of the term has been subjected to serious critiques (e.g. Lee et al. 2000). What is meant by it, according to McNeill, depends on whether one is seeking a definition or a description of actual circumstances; whether it falls within the realm of academia or practice—or, indeed, the interface between the two; and whether the emphasis is on sustainability or on development. (ibid.: 12). Whichever one's approach, there are epistemological as well as policy consequences that need to be taken account of— but which usually are not, largely because of the failure to question one's premises and purpose. To combine two aims, such as sustainability and development is particularly challenging. Based on her study of a conservation-as-development project in Papua New Guinea (PNG), West (2006) argues that such dual purpose projects cannot easily be achieved, not least because the aims of development and conservation are generally in conflict. Another reason for the failure in PNG is, according to West, the radically different understanding of the premises for and aims of the project between the local population and the American employees of the environmental Non-Government Organizations (NGO) that initiated the project—a difference that was never resolved because neither party was able to take on board the implications of each other's cultural assumptions. I will discuss this kind of resulting cross-purposes communication below. I further shall question if knowledge of apparently sustainable small-scale societies are in fact helpful in the quest for a sustainable global future. Indeed, it is likely that small-scale societies may be sustainable precisely because they are small-scale. I wish to emphasize three simple points: the enormous variability of human solutions to existential and environmental challenges; practices in these regards are ontologically constituted; and 'culture' is not superficial.

REDD

Twenty years after the Brundtland report, a new global initiative to counteract global warming and ensure a sustainable future, entitled *Reducing Emissions from Deforestation and Forest Degradation* (REDD)[2] was inaugurated at the Bali COP in 2007 when, once again, Norway was a leading actor. Since that time, REDD has emerged as one of the more highly profiled initiatives to combat climate change (Angelsen 2012). REDD springs out a recognition that the loss of the world's rainforest has for decades been a serious, global environmental problem. Still 13 million hectares of tropical forest disappear every year (Rainforest Foundation Norway 2012). When REDD was established as a mitigating measure in 2007, it was initially linked to the carbon market. As an important carbon sink, forests play a major role in reducing CO_2 emissions and REDD was initiated as a cheap, quick and 'win–win–win' way to reduce greenhouse gas emissions (Stern 2006). The core idea is to make performance-based payment to forest owners who protect their forests. After its initial launching through bilateral and multilateral funds, the idea was that it would pay for itself through the international carbon market. This 'commodification of nature' approach is in line with contemporary neoliberal thinking and policy in the North and, as such, has provoked criticism from many international and national environmental and human-rights organizations. In effect, REDD is yet another attempt to achieve the twin goals of conservation and development. Expected co-benefits from REDD included enhancing both biodiversity and adaptations to climate change through sustainable forest management (SFM). One obstacle that immediately presented itself was that there is no universally agreed-upon definition for sustainability with regard to forest management. The most widely accepted is the one expressed in the non-legally binding instrument (NLBI) on all types of forests of the United Nations Forum on Forests which states: 'Sustainable forest management as a dynamic and evolving concept aims to maintain and enhance the economic, social and environmental value of all types of forests, for the benefit of present and future generations' (2007: 3). SFM was linked to the REDD initiative, but no attempts were made to concretize these vague aims. From an anthropological point of view it has been interesting to note that in the process of formulating REDD, the focus has shifted from a rather simple-minded preoccupation with saving trees and forests employing a range of technical methods, to a project that, on paper at any rate, seeks to take full account of the people who live in and of forests. This shift can be attributed to the many vocal national and international activists who argue that only a rights-based approach developed in co-operation with the people themselves will succeed in saving forests sustainably (Howell 2013b, 2014).

In much REDD rhetoric, we find shades of the Brundtland Commission's insistence on the environment being more than the physical world to include social and political circumstances. This is turning out to be far from easy to either define or implement. The politics of the Anthropocene is fraught with both practical and ideological complications. While many policy makers today state that the nature–human distinction may be flawed and must be subjected to critical examination, and that one must learn from local understandings and practices, how to incorporate that insight into actual plans is proving very difficult. My own and my students' studies of actual attempts to implement REDD—or in most cases REDD Readiness projects—in several countries have demonstrated that statements of intent are made regarding the significance of 'local cultural beliefs and practices' in policy documents, but that little or no concrete suggestion are forthcoming on how to learn what these are, or how to accommodate them into practice. Based on my research on REDD,[3] I shall reflect on the failure to usefully transfer anthropological knowledge about other life-worlds to those professions who are directly engaged in creating a sustainable future (Howell 2013b, 2015). I shall question if such knowledge is indeed transferable— let alone implementable. To know that many small-scale societies in the South are organized in such ways that their relationship with the natural environment may be characterized as 'sustainable' in the sense that no permanent damage is resulting is interesting and indeed encouraging, but is it in any practical sense useful to the situation in the rest of the world today? There are really two separate, albeit related, issues involved. One is whether and how anthropological knowledge about one particular society or locality can be made useful to externally initiated conservation or development projects in that society. The second is how/if knowledge about indigenous knowledge regimes and practices are capable of being generalized and integrated into initiatives at a global level.

In order to illustrate my argument, I shall draw on examples from Southeast Asia. In many parts of Southeast Asia we can observe how massive environmental degradation has resulted from a range of externally initiated activities such as mining, legal and illegal logging and oil-palm plantations. Despite the introduction of a 'green rhetoric' of some of the companies involved, little effect of this can be observed. Apart from devastating local and global effects of these activities, environmental degradation often leads to the marginalization and loss of livelihood of poor subsistence communities; communities that previously had lived in a kind of symbiosis with their natural environment. According to the political ecologist Paul Robbins, it might be logical to assume that externally initiated projects that deal with conservation and preservation of environmental systems will result in community sustainability and the protection of livelihoods (2012: 166). However, as he points out, this is far from the case in most instances. West's study from PNG confirms this. So far, the fate of the global REDD initiative further proves his point when we examine actual local REDD projects. While the overall purpose of REDD was to save and protect tropical forests, the stated co-benefits for affected forest populations should result in alternative and sustainable livelihoods that would be environmentally friendly, sustainable and preserve biodiversity. So far, this has rarely proved to be the case. Much of what is happening on the ground in actual REDD projects are disappointingly similar to what has been reported from a number of the community forestry projects throughout the South that were initiated in the wake of the Brundtland Report (viz. CIFOR conference 2010).[4]

In the rest of this chapter, I will try, first, to suggest some reason why policy makers and implementing agents fail to learn from well-documented evaluation reports that deal with analogous experiences, and continue to make the same mistakes. Then, drawing on research from small-scale societies in Southeast Asia, I will ask if any use can be made of the ontologically constituted practices of such small-scale societies more generally in planning a global sustainable future.

FROM TREES TO PEOPLE

Activists and others involved in REDD argue for 'people-based' projects on the basis of human rights as specified in the UN Declaration of the Rights of Indigenous Peoples (UNDRIP). Demands are made for Free Prior and Informed Consent (FPIC), transparency and participation in decision-making processes. An underlying argument is that sustainability can be achieved only on such basis. What is done less frequently is to try to ensure that REDD projects are planned and implemented in line with local understandings and practices. In other words, despite claims to the contrary, REDD tends to be a top-down project based on contemporary understanding, values and priorities from the North. Ironically, the value of human rights is also a top-down one, but that is not subjected to critique. I suggest a paradox is discernable in REDD discursive practices in which people are made central to the political discourse at the same time as they are rendered peripheral in practice. Our research has revealed again and again how idealistic outsiders are reluctant to spend time in selected REDD communities. Rather, much time is spent in seminars locally, nationally and internationally in which general guidelines are formulated that, it is assumed, can be applied everywhere. Ultimately, the priorities of policy makers and NGOs spring out of Euro-American concerns, not local ones. One consequence is that local knowledge becomes irrelevant. This is nothing new. Anthropologists have argued along these lines for several decades. However, given the amount of effort that is put into promoting the rights of affected communities and the argument that sustainable forestry can only be achieved with the full participation of communities, it is perplexing to note a disinclination on the part of external agents to undertake in-depth studies of local conditions that can help to ensure projects that are relevant. The Centre for International Forestry Research (CIFOR), the UN agency that has undertaken most studies on REDD, including a recent workshop on 'Sustainable landscapes in southeast Asia', initiated at the outset a huge project in order to obtain a comparative understanding of affected communities' situation and priorities. This was done as a questionnaire survey that tried to elicit information about everything—from peoples' income from different sources, to land ownership, to the role of women. Masses of data resulted, most of which is, at best, very 'thin', at worst, incorrect.

DEFENCE MECHANISM AND REPRESSION OF KNOWLEDGE

I have suggested elsewhere that the persistent failure of external agents to act upon the insight that local practice and ideology provide may be characterized as a repression of knowledge (Howell unpublished manuscript). By this I mean defense mechanisms in the mind that protect against feelings and thoughts that are too difficult for the mind to cope with; mechanisms that keep inappropriate or unwanted thoughts from entering the conscious mind (Cherry 2010) in order to "avoid the dreaded assignment" http://psychology.about.com/bio/Kendra-Van-Wagner-17268.htm.[5] I do not doubt that policy makers, representatives of bi- and multilateral organizations, and NGOs all wish to do what is best for the people as well as the environment in their conservation projects. Environmental NGOs, in particular, are established as the result of idealistic motivations. Most state that the success of community forest projects of all kinds is dependent upon plans being made in conformity with local ideas and priorities. They write this in their documents. They reiterate it at conferences and meetings. Yet, away from the meetings, faced with getting a project off the ground, they too often fail to take the consequences of this knowledge. There are several reasons for this repression of knowledge, some of which are externally imposed, such as the time constraint imposed by donors—always in a hurry; the desire for universally applicable models; while others arise out of a sense of uncertainty regarding what to do.

Anthropologists do not help. On the rare occasions when ethnographic studies have been commissioned, the ethnographer often fails to offer simple and applicable advice as to what should be done. This leads to a sense of frustration and uncertainty on the part of the implementing agents. Unable to figure out how to implement ethnographic findings, they revert to methods which they know to be unsatisfactory. This course of action may spring out of a 'repression of uncomfortable knowledge'. Another and more disturbing reason, I suspect, is that many do not actually fully appreciate the significance of 'culture'. It seems to be hard to accept that local perceptions and values are embodied knowledge, constitutive of the way that people act in the world and that it can be elicited only through an examination of ontology and epistemology in each specific case. The idea formulated in the Brundtland Report that the environment should not be perceived as a sphere separate from human emotion or action ought reasonably, I suggest, to proceed to an acknowledgement that society and nature are mutually implicated, never more so than in small-scale forest communities. That to separate them without proper consideration will usually lead to failure of an externally introduced project is not part of most outsiders' imaginaries. This devaluing of local knowledge may lead to feelings of humiliation on the part of the local people, thus further contribute to the failure of projects. This was one of the stated criticisms by local NGOs of the Australian REDD project in Indonesia—the *Kalimantan Forest and Climate Partnerships* (Howell 2014). As a result of the criticism, the Australian government decided to close the project before its completion. Despite their avowals to listen and learn, the Australians were unable to do just that. What they were told by the local people did not correspond to their own expectations and goals and, whether they suppressed any knowledge of local understanding or not, the result was a massive failure of communication.

I will now briefly exemplify my argument by reference to observations made at a recent global gathering to discuss progress of REDD+.

NORWAY, REDD+, AND UNINTENDED CONSEQUENCES

As mentioned, Norway is one of the main initiative takers to REDD and a major donor, and my ethnographic starting point will be a recent gathering in Oslo entitled *The Oslo REDD+ Exchange 2013* that was organized by the *Norwegian and International Climate and Forest Initiative*. More than 400 participants from the countries and organizations that Norway supports, including representatives from governments and multilateral organizations, the private sector, NGOs and academia, attended this high-profile event. The aim was 'to review the forests and climate change agenda in light of experience to date, and respond to rapidly changing physical, financial, and political landscapes' (http://www.norad.no/en/oslo-redd-exchange-2013). The presentations and the discussions confirmed my earlier claim, (see Howell 2013b, 2014, 2015) that the focus in REDD has changed from a concern with forest preservation, sustainability and biodiversity, to so-called co-benefits: alleviating poverty, improving local livelihoods, improving forest governance and protecting rights (Angelsen 2012: 312). Indeed, the co-benefits dominated the discussions. The overall purpose of REDD which is climate mitigation, together with enhanced biodiversity and enhanced adaptations to climate change, were hardly mentioned at all during the two-day conference.

At the end of the Oslo REDD Exchange, a voting exercise was organized in plenary in order to assess current priorities. These showed a, to many, surprising emphasis on socio-economic issues, such as poverty alleviation, securing tenure rights and gender equality, while issues of forest conservation, sustainability and securing biodiversity were less emphasized. To the question 'what is the most urgent domestic and international constraint' (to successful implementation REDD+), 'political will' received the highest score while issues of tenure came second. To the question of what is the highest priority, 'land tenure and rights' received 51%, 'poverty' 26% and 'biodiversity' 8%. Referring to these and similar votes, the chair in her summing up, noted that the conference had demonstrated a shift in the priorities of REDD+. She then asked 'how can REDD+ be offered as an instrument to achieve those objectives?' The conference offered few concrete answers.

REDD AND SITUATIONAL REPRESSION OF KNOWLEDGE

This shift in priorities might be interpreted as a move toward incorporating human values in planning. Given this emphasis on local communities, it was interesting to observe the cool reception given to the only speaker who seriously tried to articulate indigenous people's concerns. In a session entitled 'How can REDD+ policies, programs, and projects support transformative change for gender and poverty', an activist from the Philippines presented an account of a group of indigenous Philippines' understanding of themselves and their forest environment. In order to alert the audience to the necessity for taking serious account of local perceptions when planning REDD projects, she gave a detailed account of how the ontology of the people she represented is predicated upon a profound relationship between humans and other species (plants, animals, natural features such as rivers and mountains) in their environment. Theirs is a true symbiotic relationship, she argued, and insisted that chances for achieving sustainable forest conservation and poverty alleviation are remote if local understanding is ignored. In a session where others spoke of nature and gender inequality from a Western perspective, she argued that it was not meaningful in this case to make a clear separation between nature and culture, or between men and women in these societies as both carried elements of its opposite. A continued respectful relationship between the human and spirit world is, she argued, essential for the maintenance of a sustainable life in the forest. Outsiders who had arrived to establish a REDD Readiness project failed to appreciate this and, as a result of their activities in the forest, a number of unfortunate events had started to occur. Her talk fell on barren ground. She was interrupted several times by the convener and asked to speak to the theme of the workshop ('thank you, can we move on to discuss policies for incorporating women in REDD'). No questions or comments were directed to her.

In her comment on the session as whole, one member of the audience expressed the opinion that the main future challenge was to 'mainstream women into REDD'. She had worked on mainstreaming women into development projects for more than 20 years, she added, and her main question remained 'why is it so difficult to integrate women?' Had she perhaps listened more carefully to the Philippine activist, she might understand that local ontologies and practices must be properly taken account of and that no generally applicable solution can be found.

What the Philippine activist tried to communicate was that ontology, epistemology and morality are not superficial add-ons (add-on to what, one may ask), but integral to people's sense of identity and how they orient themselves in their daily lives in their 'natural environment'. It is this that seems to be so hard to understand. So, as policy makers preach the need for a 'broader and better integrated approach, with a broader focus on the domestic agenda' (plenary speaker) they still hope for a 'simple model to integrate all' (ibid.). I suggest that the incident illustrates what West (2006) has called 'rendering technical', that is, conceiving and rearranging social relations and inherently political processes in alignment with expert design (Mosse 2013: 229).

WHAT CAN BE LEARNT FROM INDIGENOUS KNOWLEDGE?

One challenge is how to integrate local knowledge into specific individual conservation projects, and another is how to draw upon indigenous knowledge systems more generally in developing models for sustainable environmental practices in the North as well as the South. Can they in any way contribute to the achievement of a sustainable global future? If groups such as the one described by the Philippine activist lead a sustainable life style, this is due to a number of factors: their metaphysical schema, the fact that they are small-scale and there is no pressure on land. It has little to do with people's conscious decisions to act ecologically. Ellen has argued that until the 1960s, from a 'combination of ignorance and arrogance'—"top-down" development paradigms and educational agendas were routinely bereft of local expertise and relevance (2000: 163). However, from the 1960s, a new green politics enthused about the environmental wisdom of traditional 'eco-cosmologies'. This was taken up by a number of indigenous movements, especially in North and South America. Ellen is critical of this romanticism regarding 'indigenous knowledge' and the 'noble ecological savage'. Piecemeal and decontextualized extraction of knowledge fails to lead to sustainable new environmental projects, he argues. He suggests one might be better served by examining practices rather than decontextualized ideas (ibid.).

What we notice in the REDD discourse on affected populations today in contrast with that of the 1980s and 1990s is less focus on indigenous cosmology and knowledge. Arguments phrased in terms of eco-cosmology, mother nature, Gaia and human-nature entanglement are replaced by rights (Doolittle 2012)—rights to ownership of natural resources, rights to tenure or cultivation and extraction of land, forests, rivers and lakes. This is a noticeable shift in activist rhetoric and is promoted by a range of indigenous, national and international human rights and environmental NGOs. Being phrased in familiar legalistic language, Western stakeholders appear to be more open to these arguments than they have been to the Gaia type rhetoric.

CHEWONG AND LIO LAND RIGHTS

I will end by briefly considering the possible relevance of indigenous knowledge and environmental practices based on my experience with two very different societies I have studied in Southeast Asia: the hunting, gathering, shifting cultivating Chewong of Peninsular Malaysia and the agricultural Lio of the highlands of eastern Indonesia.[6] My argument will be that the detailed study of both contributes to an enhanced understanding of human potential and the range of solutions to existential and environmental challenges. However, the ontologically constituted practices of either can contribute little to initiatives toward a sustainable global future. As with the example from the Philippines, fragments of their knowledge regimes cannot be taken out of context and refitted into the dominant Euro-American ones. I will illustrate with a brief consideration of their respective attitude to land. In both cases, land is not a neutral part of a separate nature to be exploited by humans according to their practical needs. Rather, in the words of Daniel de Coppet, people belong to the land (1995) and as such, human personhood is not separate from the land upon which they live and work. Albeit in very different ways, both Chewong and Lio relationship with the land and with everything non-human that also lives on it, is predicated upon an understanding of profound mutuality. A number of prescriptions and proscriptions that I call cosmo-rules because they integrate the cosmos in their daily lives, guide daily action in both cases. However, the social and cultural differences between them are major. Chewong ontology and metaphysis are profoundly egalitarian. An egalitarian ideology permeates all relations between human and between humans and the part of their environment that is perceived as animated, rendering Chewong society co-existent with their environment. No meaningful boundary exists between society and cosmos. Chewong ontology is typical animistic and may broadly be characterized as perspectivist (for details see Descola 2006, Howell 1984, Viveiro de Castro 1998). The forest and everything in it belongs to everyone and may be exploited by everyone. People's daily behavior is guided by cosmo-rules all of which specify their interaction with each other as well as with the non-human conscious and non-conscious beings and objects. Failure to adhere to these leads to mishap of some kind, but never to retribution by fellow humans. Chewong sociality incorporates the animated forest; adherence to the cosmo-rules ensures a continued life of fecundity—and sustainability as viewed from outside. It is possible to argue that by default, not by design, Chewong lead a life in the forest that is sustainable. Swidden cultivation does not destroy the forest, their hunting and fishing do not deplete the game or fish in the rivers. However, this is due to three main factors: their population is small, the land capacity is not strained and their technology is simple.

As the outside world has started to impinge, a noticeable change in Chewong practice may be observed. Outside logging has depleted much of Chewong forest. Encouraged by the authorities, many Chewong families are settling at the edge of the forest, engaging in more settled agriculture and in a cash economy. Forest land is still free for all, but notions of ownership of cultivated areas are appearing. People are moving from harvesting forest produce for own consumption to harvesting non-timber products for sale to outsiders. Three such items have been in much demand in recent years: *gaharu* wood, *damar* resin and live frogs. Pursuit of these has been so extensive that they are all virtually extinct. While Chewong are aware of this, the fact does not lead to more wide-ranging reflections upon the long-term consequences of such action. Accompanying these and other shifts in practice I have noted a move away from the permeating significance of cosmological knowledge that constituted all behavior during my first field work. Due to larger settlements and to decrease in hunting and gathering, the constitutive cosmo-rule that all forest produce must be shared is less observed. Moreover, the injunction to share is not extended to money and that which is bought by money, including food stuff. The pursuit of cash and cash-bought food and consumer durables shows signs of leading to inequality (Howell and Lillegraven 2013). Cultural sustainability is on the wane in parallel with ecological sustainability.

Lio, by contrast, is a thoroughly hierarchical society—both as regards social organization and metaphysical constitution (e.g. Howell 1996). Theirs is a highly complex order and I can only touch on some central elements. Social, political and religious life is orchestrated by a council of priest-leaders who hold their office by virtue of decent and marriage. Their authority is legitimized through an ontology that is predicated upon an elaborate mythology about origins. The original ancestors descended from a sacred mountain and spread out into the surrounding landscape settling in various places; taking possession of the land and cultivating it. In the process, they developed patri-clans that are reproduced through prescriptive matrilateral cross cousin marriage. Each patri-clan is under the authority of a priest-leader and his wife. To be able to narrate one's descent from these original ancestors gives the priest-leaders mystical as well as political control over the clan land and the people who live on it. By virtue of their kin position, they maintain good relations not only with ancestors but also with the numerous spirits that inhabit the land. This is a prerequisite for fertility—agricultural and human. As clan leaders, they hand out land for cultivation to commoners. All who ask are given land, but they must acknowledge their dependency upon the priest-leader through an annual ceremony when they present him with a range of prescribed items.

Lio have been less willing to exploit their natural environment for commercial purposes than have the Chewong, but they have a long tradition of selling and bartering rice. As with the Chewong, Lio land is not scarce, but unlike the Chewong, it is not free for all to exploit at will. So far, Lio are resisting all offers to sell land and the priest-leaders banned the use of chain saws—not for environmental reasons but because the spirits objected. While Indonesian authorities are being pushed (by NGOs) to pass laws that give rights over land to indigenous populations, they have no interest in the vast variety of socio-political attitudes and practices that involve land.

In Conclusion

Both Lio and Chewong ontology are empirical examples of the Brundtland Report proposition that 'environment is something beyond physicality, going beyond that traditional school of thought to include social and political atmospheres and circumstances'. They both also—at least until now—have led a sustainable way of life. But to return to my two questions regarding a possible application of local ontology and practices by outsiders in developing plans for sustainable development elsewhere, this is far from unproblematic. As regards applying local ideology and practices in establishing particular environmental projects locally, I would argue that such knowledge could and should be used. That this has hardly been successfully achieved does not mean that it is impossible. Despite the recent claims of some, we do not live in radically incommensurable worlds. But it requires genuine interest and sensitivity on part of the outsiders, as well as willingness to render complexity comprehensible on part of the anthropologists. Policy makers and implementers need to take on board the fact that 'culture' is not superficial. It is questionable if knowledge of Chewong values and practices would be useful in the establishment of an environmental project with the Lio—and vice versa. Interestingly, in light of recent changes, it is questionable if either social group is ensuring the conditions for their own future generations that was a major aim of the Brundtland Commission.

As regards the second question, I am doubtful whether knowledge of Chewong and Lio ontology and epistemology (or that of small-scale forest communities generally) in which agency is distributed across a range of domains, beings and materiality can be used by outsiders in search of new global models for implementing a sustainable future. Animistic and totemic modes of thought (Descola 2006) are grounded in their own realities. Despite the recent fashion for various post-humanist theoretical positions, to generalize from ontologies such as those of the Lio and Chewong is full of epistemological, not to mention methodological, challenges. As anthropologists, we can try to elicit the premises for alien metaphysics and render them probable. That is what we are good at. In itself, that is a political act as it questions our own assumptions (see Escobar in this volume). I fear that post-humanist approaches are not going to help, in the current ecological crisis. It remains an undisputed fact that human behavior is the major cause of global warming; not practices by trees, mushrooms, rivers or whatever. In light of this, it does not seem in any way useful to drop human exceptionalism, or insist on incommensurability of human worlds in the search for remedial practices for the survival of the globe.

NOTES

1. It further insists that "...the 'environment' is where we live; and 'development' is what we all do in attempting to improve our lot within that abode. The two are inseparable".
2. Although REDD has received a number of + since the original acronym to indicate a number of co-benefits, I do not include these in this chapter.
3. I initiated in 2010 an anthropological comparative study of the implementation of REDD in a number of countries in Latin America as well as Tanzania and Indonesia. Master students undertook six months fieldwork according to a research plan developed by myself. Since 2011, the project in Indonesia has been undertaken in collaboration with the Anthropology Department at Universitas Gadjah Mada, Jogyakarta, and supported by the Norwegian Foreign Office.

4. CIFOR organized an international workshop "Taking stock of smallholder and community forestry. Where do we go from here?" in 2010. I attended in order to familiarize myself with the issues before started the project on REDD.
5. When I presented a version of this paper at the Institute for Science, Innovation and Society, University of Oxford, Professor Steve Rayner drew my attention to Mary Douglas' work on institutional memory, and her notion of "uncomfortable knowledge" (see also Rayner 2012). The idea that the "achievement of non-knowledge can serve as a tool of political and social authority" (Rayner ibid: 108) is evocative of my own problematic.
6. Fieldwork with Chewong began in 1977–79 supported by the UK Economic and Research Council. Subsequent shorter visits have made between 1982 and 2010. Fieldwork with the Lio started in 1984 and return visits were made in 1986, 1989, 1994 and 2001.

REFERENCES

Angelsen, A., ed. 2012. *Analysing REDD+: Challenges and Choices.* Bogor: CIFOR.

Cherry, K. 2010. *The Everything Psychology Book: Explore the Human Psyche and Understand Why We do the Things We Do.* Everything Books. New York: Simon & Schuster.

de Coppet, D. 1995. Land Owns People. In *Cosmos and Society in Oceania*, ed. Daniel de Copet and A. Itéanu. Oxford: Berg.

Descola, P. 2006. Beyond Nature and Culture. *Proceedings of the British Academy* 139: 137–155.

Doolittle, A.A. 2012. The Politics of Indigeneity: Indigenous Strategies for Inclusion in Climate Change Negotiations. *Conservation and Society* 8 (4): 256–261.

Ellen, R. 2000. Local Knowledge and Environmental Sustainable Development in Developing Countries. In *Global Sustainable Development in the 21st Century*, ed. K. Lee, E. Holland, and D. McNeill, 163–186. Edinburgh: Edinburgh University Press.

Howell, S. 1984. *Society and Cosmos: Chewong of Peninsular Malaysia.* Singapore: Oxford University Press. Reprinted 1989 in paperback by Chicago University Press.

———. 1996. Many Contexts, Many Meanings? Gendered Values Among the Lio of Indonesia. *Journal of the Royal Anthropological Institute (MAN n.s.)* 2 (2): 253–269.

———. 2013a. Metamorphosis and Identity: Chewong Animistic Ontology. In *The Handbook of Contemporary Animism*, ed. G. Harvey. Durham: Acumen.

———. 2013b. Divide and Rule: Nature and Society in a Global Forest Programme. In *Anthropology and Nature*, ed. Kirsten Hastrup. London: Routldge.

———. 2014. 'No Rights-No REDD': Some Implications of a Turn Towards Co-benefits. *Forum for Development Studies* 41: 253–272.

————. 2015. The Politics of Appearances: Some Reasons Why the UN-REDD Project in Central Sulawesi Failed to Unite the Various Stakeholders. *Asia Pacific Viewpoint* 55 (1): 37–47. (Special issue: *From Global Policy to Local Politics: The Social Dynamics of REDD+ in Asia Pacific*).

Howell, S., and A. Lillegraven. 2013. Cash, Culture and Social Change: Why Don't Chewong Become Entrepreneurs? In *Embedded Entrepreneurs: Market, Culture and Economic Action in Southeast Asia*, ed. E. Bråten. Leiden: Brill.

Lee, K., A. Holland, and D. McNeill, eds. 2000. *Global Sustainable Development in the 21st Century*. Edinburgh: Edinburgh University Press.

McNeill, D. 2000. The Concept of Sustainable Development. In *Global Sustainable Development in the 21st Century*, ed. A. Holland, K. Lee, and D. McNeill, 10–30. Edinburgh: Edinburgh University Press.

Mosse, D. 2013. The Anthropology of International Development. *Annual Review of Anthropology* 42: 227–246.

Rainforest Foundation Norway. 2012. *Rights-Based Rainforest Protection*. Oslo: RFN.

Rayner, S. 2012. "Uncomfortable knowledge: the social construction of ignorance in science and environmental policy discourse" *Economy and Society*, 41 (1): 107–125.

Robbins, P. 2012. *Political Ecology: A Critical Introduction*. 2nd ed. London: Wiley-Blackwell.

Stern, N. 2006. *The Stern Review on Climate Change*. London: HM Treasury: The Cabinet Office.

Viveiro de Castro, E. 1998. Cosmological Deixis and Amerindian Perspectivism. *Journal of the Royal Anthropological Association* 4: 469–488.

West, P. 2006. *Conservation is Our Government Now: the Politics of Ecology in Papua New Guinea*. Durham: Duke University Press.

World Commission on Environment and Development. 1987. *Our Common Future. (The Brundtland Report)*. Oxford: Oxford University Press.

CHAPTER 9

The Viability of a High Arctic Hunting Community: A Historical Perspective

Kirsten Hastrup

Over the past nine years, I have worked with people of Avanersuaq ('The big North'), also known as the Thule Region, in North West Greenland. If they have a name, it is Inughuit (or Polar Eskimo in the older literature), but the inhabitants are mixed and often see themselves simply as North West Greenlanders, living in the northernmost part of Greenland. The total population today is around 700, and they are distributed between one town and three smaller settlements, all of them quite isolated from the rest of the country, not to mention the rest of the world. They are still primarily hunters of marine mammals and polar bears, with seabirds, reindeer, and muskox and some fishing as subsidiary game. With some interruptions, they and their predecessors have inhabited the high Arctic coastal fringe of the ice-covered mainland for the better part of 4500 years, when the first wave of immigration from North America crossed the narrow strait between Ellesmere Island and Greenland on the ice and left their traces in the landscape.

The world has changed dramatically since then, but in the far North, the radically changing seasons of light and darkness and the omnipresence of the ice have been constants in the shaping of a social life based on hunting. Through my investigations into the history of this community and my

K. Hastrup (✉)
Department of Anthropology, University of Copenhagen, København, Denmark

© The Author(s) 2017
M. Brightman, J. Lewis (eds.), *The Anthropology of Sustainability*,
Palgrave Studies in Anthropology of Sustainability,
DOI 10.1057/978-1-137-56636-2_9

conversations with the present inhabitants over the past years, it has become abundantly clear to me that however isolated these people may seem, and however circumscribed the local living conditions have been, they are part of an unbounded and shifty world, and have always been. This poses an immediate challenge to the concept of sustainability, presupposing a bounded space and a clear sight of the future that may not be warranted. These features seem to be implied by the oft-cited Brundtland Report of 1987, where sustainability is defined as *development that meets the needs of the present without compromising the ability of future generations to meet their own needs.* In the high Arctic, where people have based their lives on living resources for consumption, it is impossible to speak of needs, present or future, as negotiable.

As observed by Fricker, the noble definition of sustainability in the Brundtland Report defies both objective interpretation and operational implementation (Fricker 2006, 192). Who knows about the needs of future generations, except very basic needs for fresh water and enough food to simply survive? This is rarely enough for humans endowed with reflexivity and agency. The anthropological contribution to a refashioning of the concept lies with its ability to ground it in social life in all its particularity. By exploring the notion of sustainability from *within* social life, we can make a case for the co-constitution of needs and knowledge and the different concerns that scale the environment (Hastrup 2013a).

In this chapter, I shall make my argument in three moves, each relating to a particular phase in the historical course of social life in Avanersuaq, and implicitly challenging any fixed concept of sustainability.

DISCOVERY: MEETING A NEW PEOPLE

Let us move North towards the Inughuit in Avanersuaq, also known as the Thule Region. They became known to the outer world, including the rest of Greenland, only in the nineteenth century, and have remained on the edge of vision until far more recently. The first to report on their existence was Captain John Ross, who had been sent out by the British admiralty to find the North West Passage in 1818. In this, he did not succeed, finding or rather assuming the Baffin Bay to be hermetically sealed at the top by ice. He made other important discoveries, however, notably of a small group of unknown people. The account is fascinating. Captain Ross, a Scotsman, was quite taken by these fur-clad savages, whom he affectionately referred to as

Arctic Highlanders, an interesting analogy between the foreign and the familiar. He wrote:

> The origin of the Arctic Highlanders, or inhabitants of Prince Regent's Bay, is a question as yet involved in peculiar obscurity. They exist in a corner of the world by far the most secluded which has yet been discovered, and have no knowledge of anything but what originates, or is found, in their own country; nor have they any tradition how they came to this spot, or from whence they came; having, until the moment of our arrival, believed themselves to be the only inhabitants of the universe, and that all the rest was a mass of ice. (Ross 1819, 123–124)

In this case, the discovery goes both ways; Ross and his crew discovered an unknown tribe, and the Arctic Highlanders did the same. For both parties, the people from beyond caused wonder and excitement. How far the Arctic Highlanders believed themselves to be alone in the universe is debatable. All of Greenland had actually become populated from the North Western corner, where Inuit from North America had crossed the narrow strait in several waves of immigration and moved south. There had been no communication between the far North and the rest of Greenland for a couple of centuries, but it seems that there were at least rumours or tales about 'the others' in both north and south, and not very flattering ones.

In the wake of Ross' daring voyage across the Melville Bay, whalers and explorers soon followed; it became such a regular recurrence that each summer the Arctic Highlanders—or at least a number of them—would congregate at Cape York, a promontory in the southern part of the region, hoping for opportunities for barter. The sailors were ready to comply and provided timber, guns and utensils in exchange for furs. Elisha K. Kane, who visited the region from 1853 to 1855 and stayed long enough to count the entire population, suggested that there were about 140 souls. At this point in time, the people were suffering from famine and saw themselves as doomed. Still, their sense of community was remarkable, as was their keeping track of each other. Kane writes:

> The narrow belt subjected to their nomadic range cannot be less than six hundred miles long; and throughout this extent of country every man knows every man. There is not a marriage or a birth or a death that is not talked over and mentally registered by all. I have a census, exactly confirmed by three separate informants, which enables me to count by name about one hundred

and forty souls, scattered along from Kosoak, the Great River at the base of a glacier near Cape Melville, to the wind-loved hut of Anoatok.

Destitute as they are, they exist both in love and community of resources as a single family. The sites of their huts—for they are so few in number as to not bear the name of villages—are arranged with reference to the length of a dog-march and the seat of the hunt; and thus, when winter has built her highway and cemented into one the sea, the islands, and the main, they interchange with each other the sympathies and social communion of man, and diffuse through the darkness a knowledge of the resources and condition of all. (Kane 1856 vol. II, 211)

At this time, the distinct sense of community across the region went along with a growing sense of an outer world offering new possibilities for an insufficient subsistence economy. However, ten years after Kane's report, the population was allegedly close to barely 100 people according to Isaac I. Hayes, the next in line to report his encounter (Hayes 1866, 386). Part of the price paid by the Inughuit, eagerly awaiting the arrival of foreigners and goods, was to be exposed to epidemics that tolled considerably in a non-resistant population (Gilberg 1976). This may account for the rapid decline noted by Hayes, even if it cannot be verified. Also, the harshness of their environment, where the Little Ice Age held its grip longer than elsewhere in the North Atlantic region, gave people hard times hunting, not only because of a decline in the living resources but also for want of wood. Previously, a trickle of driftwood had reached their shores by the tail-end of a sea-current going up along the west coast of Greenland, but this had failed for a long time, and left their hunting gear remarkably reduced.

Ross, Kane and Hayes all of them commented on dog-sledges made entirely out of walrus and narwhal bone, meticulously pieced together by sealskin string. But the full extent of the technological loss due to the absent wood, only occurred to a group of American Inuit, who migrated across the narrow strait between Ellesmere Island in Canada and North West Greenland in the late 1860s. They amounted to a total of 15 people, and they knew what to expect of a proper hunting community. A few of them lived to tell their story to Knud Rasmussen in 1903 (Rasmussen 1908).

Not only did the small contingent of Baffin Landers contribute vitally to a boosting of the population, they also taught people to use the (now) available wood for bows and arrows, fishing spears and not least kayaks. An old man said 'we taught them to build kayaks, and to hunt from kayaks. Before that they had only hunted on the ice, and had been obliged during the spring to catch as many seals, walruses, and narwhals as they would want for the summer, when the ice had gone' (Rasmussen 1908, 32). With time, their old technological skills had been forgotten.

With or without kayaks, the people depended on the open-water polynya, the North Water, being the breathing and feeding place of marine mammals and seabirds. This Arctic oasis also attracted the whalers, who had all but depleted the stock of big whales further south in the Baffin Bay. The local hunt had taken place from the ice-edge, and once it was broken and the sea-ice had become unstable, their access to the prey was circumscribed. Thus, the reinvented kayaks vastly extended their hunting grounds in spring and summer when the sea and the fjords gradually opened up. The pulse of the ice, short term or long term, opening or closing, always heavily affected the game in the region, and by implication the social community (Vibe 1967).

When Robert Peary came in 1891, staying and coming back over a period of 18 years, the population had increased to about 250 persons; clearly things had improved with access to new materials. Peary's ambition was to reach the North Pole, and he could only do so by the help of the locals. His more or less continuous presence meant that rifles and ammunition were now accessible on a more regular basis, and hunger could be kept at bay. Still, Peary described the tribe as living in complete independence and isolation, under the utmost stress of the savage environment, without government and religion, and with only two objects in life, something to eat and something with which to clothe themselves, and therefore apparently near the bottom of the scale of civilization. However, 'closer acquaintance shows them to be quick, intelligent, ingenious, and thoroughly human' (Peary 1898 vol. I, 481). A significant element in their ingenuity was (and still is) to catch the moment; no opportunity should ever be wasted—the future depended upon it.

Peary gives a detailed description of their life, and their almost inconceivable destitution due to the restriction on the available materials. 'Is it to be wondered at that under these circumstances a man offered me his dogs and sledge and all its furs for a bit of board as long as himself; that another offered me his wife and two children for a shining knife; and that a woman offered me everything she had for a needle?' (ibid., 483). Having listed their hardships, Peary admits to being very impressed by their knowledge and capability to make the most of their barren country, and he ends his narrative by wishing for them that they shall never be converted or civilized;

at such prospect of ending up like the half-bred Greenlanders further south, Peary exclaims:

> 'No; God grant no civilisation to curse them.' What I have done in the past, and shall continue to do in the future, is to put them in a little better position to carry on their struggle for existence; give them better weapons and implements, lumber to make their dwellings drier, instructions in a few fundamental sanitary principles, and one or two items of civilised food, as coffee and biscuit—allies to rout the demons, starvation and cold. (Peary 1898 vol I, 508)

Peary obviously speaks in two tongues here; he wants to keep these people at some distance of civilization, while also acknowledging their needs for certain things from outside. The people saw themselves as lingering on the brink of extinction, and they more than welcomed sailors and explorers from elsewhere, supplying them with modern goods. They were even willing to go to the North Pole, in spite of the fact that there were neither games nor other people. They laughed at the idea, but went along.

What would sustainability mean in this case? Clearly, the community was not viable on its own account under the prevailing climatic conditions. They knew that as well as Peary did, but while he feared for their being corrupted by civilization, they could hardly get enough of it. The knowledge of foreign technologies deeply affected local needs. This challenges an implicit idea in some interpretations of sustainability 'that it is possible to live in harmony with nature' (Kalland 2003, 161); this has been attributed to traditional or indigenous peoples in particular. But nature opens and closes, and harmony makes no sense when seen from the point of view of the inhabitants, struggling to survive and importing whatever is available from elsewhere. The guns and the gear that the Inughuit wanted so badly, of course did more than simply affect their 'material sustainability' (cf. Minnegal and Dwyer 2011, 198). It also vastly extended their environment. This rescales the discussion of sustainability and incorporates absent resources into the idea of the future.

This is particularly important to note in this case, because the notion of sustainability has 'contributed to uphold the notion of the ecologically noble savage' (Kalland 2003, 161)—as if he or she was ever beyond worldly concerns of improving local life conditions. The Inughuit meeting the sailors at Cape York had no qualms about importing guns and selling their labour to wild men like Peary, aiming for the completely insignificant Pole.

In this environment, self-sufficiency was a luxury that could not be sustained, which again was expressed in a local practice of sharing the hunt, as the luck was likely to shift over time and between families.

Given their own acute sense of doom in the nineteenth century, the Inughuit took the opportunity of extending their social relations to new-comers to once again become self-sustained, if in a new sense. Their land was defined by its unpredictable affordances, including the living and moving resources. These comprised the animals that were their main game, of course, but also new people, some of whom came from the south across the Melville Bay on large wooden ships bringing rifles and timber, while others came in the form of a small group of Baffin-landers crossing Smith Sound on dog-sledges, extending the gene-pool and reminding the Inughuit about forgotten technologies. The Inughuit could only sustain themselves through new *social* relations, rescaling their community and counterbalancing their deadly fewness in the frozen region. From within their horizon, sustainability was a simple matter of *viability*.

DISPERSAL: CUTTING THE NOMADIC LANDSCAPE

The community was more permanently extended in 1909–10, when a mission and a trade station was established in the region on a private Danish initiative; this was the Thule Station, founded by Knud Rasmussen. The entire region was deemed outside of state interest because it was beyond regular reach—and without any real commercial value. The latter turned out to be wrong. In fact, already in 1819, Ross had suggested that there was an untapped economic asset, which could benefit both locals and merchants. Ross wrote:

... it is more than probable, that a valuable fur trade might be established; numbers of black foxes were actually seen by the officers and men, who were on shore at Crimson Cliffs, and also the traps used by the natives in catching them; and we were informed that the country abounded in them. There can be no doubt that people who are of so harmless a disposition as the Arctic Highlanders, might be easily instructed to collect these skins, which they do not seem to value, or make so much use of as those of the seal and the bear. The ivory of the sea-unicorn, the sea-horse's teeth, and the bear's teeth, may also be considered articles of trade. All these could be procured for European commodities, such as knives, nails, small harpoon-heads, pieces of iron, wood of any description, crockery ware, and various cheap and useful utensils and tools; both to the great benefit of the merchant, and to that of this secluded race of human beings. (Ross 1819, 119–20)

This was eventually to become organized by the Thule Station. For many years, the trade of fur, mainly from polar fox, was quite profitable and allowed the people to get guns and ammunition, utensils and cooking pots, new food items and not least a steady supply of timber. The social situation had changed again. As Johannes Fabian has suggested, when the expedition turns into a station, the relations between the newcomers and the local community change (Fabian 2000, 47–48). In many ways, the Thule Station also turned into a scientific field station—at the instigation of Knud Rasmussen, the owner of Thule. The surplus from the trade contributed to the funding of his many Thule-Expeditions, whence their name (Hastrup 2016).

At Thule, the widely distributed nomadic population began to congregate more regularly around the trading station; small stone and turf houses were built along the wooden houses of trade and mission, and the small settlement grew into a village, Uummannaq, named after the heart-shaped mountain. It was not simply the relations between insiders and newcomers that changed; it was the constitution of the entire community. People still moved all over the region, hunting for polar bear north and south, walrus in particular fjords and narwhal in others, seal all over the place and seabirds in extensive colonies in between, where foxes were likewise abundant. The nomadic landscape—in the sense of Deleuze and Guattari—as such was unaffected, even if there now was a dominant nodal point (Deleuze and Guattari 2004; Hastrup 2009a). In early twentieth century, the Thule people, as they were now often called, had become used to people from elsewhere and relied very much on their presence and the regular arrival of all kinds of provisions.

The Thule Station was geographically situated in mid-district, and it gradually evolved into a social and political centre in an otherwise anarchic society. It was a trading post, where the hunters could exchange their goods, mainly fox fur and eider down, for foreign commodities. A specific Thule-law was made in 1929, again on private initiative. The region was still outside of the colonial interest of the Danish state, but Knud Rasmussen made sure that the Ministry for Greenland approved of the law, and thus acknowledged the special status of Thule. With this law, a hunters' council was established with three representatives from among the hunters, from the North, the South and the Middle district, in addition to the residing doctor, the station manager and the priest. One of the main objectives, apart from signalling 'civilization' by emulating international trends, was to regulate the hunt. It became increasingly clear that the process of centralization that had followed in the wake of the establishment of the Thule Station was beginning to toll too heavily on the living resources in the Wolstenholme Fjord, notably walrus and eider duck, even if the semipermanent population at Thule only counted some 100 people. The council urged able-bodied people to regularly disperse, as they had before, and ruled that it was inadmissible to stay for more than three years in one row at Thule, unless they were sick or too old to move; then they would be taken care of by the Station.

This was a sign of acute concerns about sustainability and of the need for hunting regulation. The preamble to this part of the Thule-law is significant:

Any free hunter may provide food and hides for himself and his family through hunting. But the game is no longer available in unlimited numbers. All over the world, independent people have therefore decided that the game animals must be protected at those times of the year, when they are breeding, because there shall otherwise be less and less game for every year. In our land, it is particularly important to protect eider ducks, foxes and walruses against extinction, and any free hunter should be pleased to go along with such protective measure, because these animals otherwise would be extinct, when those people, who are children now, become adult. (*Thule-law* 1929, 16; author's translation)

The law further stresses that if the hunters do not comply with these measures of protection, they will hurt not only the present generation but also the following generations. This is the Brundtland Report live, so to speak, from 90 years ago. To encourage people to disperse and thus to redistribute the hunt in the entire nomadic landscape, two auxiliary shops in the northern and the southern regions were established, in 1929 and 1934, respectively, creating new if minor centres in the region that again served as points of commodity exchange. This gradually came to function reasonably well and a sense of social stability took root, allowing the populations of both people and animals to remain stable and eventually to grow. Some of the elderly inhabitants of Thule still refer back to their childhood in the 1930s and 1940s as wonderful, although there are also reminiscences of years of starvation and epidemics—the latter partly curbed by the permanent presence of a doctor since 1929.

This sense of stability was not to last. The Cold War came to Thule in the shape of an American Airbase that was built in the early 1950s—at the very heart of Thule. It is still there, bearing the name of the Thule Airbase. This was the outcome of secret negotiations and surreptitious claims that the land really did not belong to anybody. The Danish state had been recognized as the supreme ruler over the entire Greenland by a verdict at the international court in Hague in 1933, but the Thule region was still outside of the normal jurisdiction of the state—in spite of the fact that it had been acknowledged as part of the Danish realm in 1936, when the state bought the Station from Knud Rasmussen's widow after his death. The Thule-law remained in force until 1963, however, as the only legal framework of Thule. The region remained too vast and too thinly populated to seem to matter, or even to be seen as somebody's lived space of multiple affordances. It looked empty on any map; if ever the distinction between dwelling and building made sense, this is it (Ingold 2000).

The heavy transport vessels, the aeroplanes and the thousands of military personnel that descended on Thule disturbed the animals and destroyed some of the most important hunting grounds around the station. This became the pretext for a forced relocation of the entire population of the Thule settlement, including the trading station, the hospital, the church and the rest of the village in 1953. People could move wherever they wanted, but Qaanaaq was chosen as the new centre for the 'official' buildings and installations; until then it had only been a site of temporary hunting camps. The main issue was not the place, however, it was the abruptness of the decision and the secrecy of the entire plan that was (and still is) troubling. The Danish state authorities (or at least some of them) and the American military powers succeeded in keeping the larger plan secret, not only to the Inughuit but also to the managers of the trading post, and to the Greenlandic authorities. Clearly, they saw it as a no-man's land; it was *used* but not really claimed, as in appropriated by the state.

With very short notice—four days, to be precise—people had to abandon the middle part of their region; the break-up not only regrouped people, it also destroyed the integrity of their tiny and vastly dispersed community. In the first few years after relocation, people would occasionally stop over at their old houses on their way towards either the northern or the southern hunting grounds. After all, it was mid-way, and one could still hope for a walrus in the fjord for the dogs when passing by. The military management in the backyard would not allow it, and—adding insult to injury—it was decided to burn down the settlement so as not to tempt people back, if only for a short stay (Harlang et al. 1999, 126ff). This happened in 1956–57, reinforcing the sense of being severed from the past, which still lingers today (Walsøe 2003). Erik Holtved, an archaeologist who had worked extensively in the region up until and during the early days of American presence, describes the establishment of the airbase as possibly the most severe turning point in the eventful existence of the Polar Eskimos, and he notes that their 'minds had lost their former equilibrium due to a feeling of uncertainty regarding the future' (Holtved 1967, 11).

Quite apart from destroying the community by cutting it up, it also introduced a new fear of radiation; first because of experiments under the ice with nuclear power (Martin-Nielsen 2012), later because of a crash of a B52 plane carrying plutonium bombs and contaminating the fjord at the old Thule in 1968. Even today, the relocation and the plane crash linger in a deep sense of ill health and fear of radiation, according to a recent health assessment in the region (Bjerregaard and Dahl-Petersen 2010). 'The last kings of Thule,' as Jean Malaurie (1956) had called them, were definitively dethroned by military power. People had become outcasts in their own country.

There is a thought-provoking historical development embedded in this discussion that challenges any notion of sustainability as a bounded or systemic issue. Just a generation earlier, the Hunters' Council at Thule had ruled that people should disperse and that the game congregating in the vicinity of the Thule Station should be protected. This was deemed a legitimate measure of sustainability, if not in those words. Yet, in the 1950s, it was foreign power that not only destroyed the habitat of animals and people by their technologies and pollution, but also entirely denigrated the local sense of land and living resources. In more ways than one, it hit their heart, and people still suffer.

As anthropologists, we cannot overlook the weight of past experience on present actions—by which the future is gradually shaped. This again questions the concept of sustainability from within so to speak. As Richard Wilk has it, while the 'rich countries want to focus on the present and the future, the legacy of past injustice and inequality will not go away in debates over sustainability' (Wilk 2009, 266). Perhaps the larger challenge to the concept of sustainability here is, as Kalland has suggested, that 'the notion that everything is connected with everything else denies any role to coincidence' (Kalland 2003, 164). In this case, the coincidence of Thule lying on the direct line between New York and Moscow at this particular moment in time made their world explode.

While the dispersal of the people by the rulings of the hunters' council left their landscape intact, and still accessible, the relocation that was later forced upon them destroyed that very landscape. The network of the nomadic landscape was cut up, and both the social and the individual *vitality* were at stake.

DISLOCATION: ASSESSING CLIMATE CHANGE

The defining feature of high Arctic Greenland is the ice: the sea-ice, the ice-cap, the permafrost and the way in which the settlements are connected to each other and to the hunting grounds by sledge routes on the sea, on the ice-foot or across glaciers. In such environment, the ice 'has a profound *social* ontology, an existence as a social object by virtue of the deep-seated meanings and relations that connect to Inuit life' (Bravo 2010, 446). In recent years, the ice has melted off rapidly, which deeply affects the community and its means of subsistence, and people have become dislocated in a new sense.

In general, the people in Avanersuaq live in a world of intensifying movement; there is the changing environment, but also a changing political system in Greenland, and new international measures of wildlife protection (Nuttall 2009). This greatly affects the diagrammatic reasoning that people have used to master the challenges of the region because places, sledge-roads and authority structures are destabilized (Hastrup 2013b). Living in the Arctic has always meant living in an animate world, partly because of the massive seasonal changes, partly because of the mobile resources, but in recent years, it has become truly elusive, pointing to a constellation of processes rather that a thing (cf. Massey 2005, 141).

Hunting means orientation in relation to a destination that is the epitome of an elusive place, such as the shifty ice-edge where one might get a narwhal for instance. The narwhals would normally migrate along relatively predictable routes in different seasons, but 'normalcy' has been suspended. The whales often choose to remain for very long in the outer part of the Whale Sound (undermining the semantics of the place name), where winds and currents are much more unpredictable and hunting from kayak impossible. The entire community, including people who are not active hunters, is engaged in a permuting conversation about the relative merits of different hunting grounds for narwhal and their increasing unpredictability. The yardstick is that of the condition of the ice, not the number of animals; it is accessibility rather than species depletion that worries them. And as narwhal plays a major role both in the subsistence and in the cash economy (the *mattak*, the skin, is sold as a delicacy to south Greenlanders), now an indispensable supplement to the subsistence economy, the theme concerns everybody.

Eventually, the decision of when and where to go is made on the basis of individual and collective reasoning, as well as a general feeling of the time being 'right' (cf. Brody 2002, 37). While the anthropologist may find the waiting time empty (i.e. of action), the hunters are continuously engaged in an act of assessing the affordances of places that are as elusive as their 'companion species' (Haraway 2008). While the hunters' knowledge may look different from scientific knowledge in its being less governed by established laws, it is neither less systematic nor less theoretical, even if more unruly. Speaking of the Incan knowledge system, David Turnbull says that 'being grounded in the specificities of local conditions and practice, it is the combination of diversity, complexity, vagueness and imprecision which gives it its essentially flexible, dynamic and strategic character' (Turnbull 2003, 32). This could be said also for the way of knowing in the highly elusive Arctic landscape.

The point I want to make is that there is no such thing as local knowledge as opposed to scientific knowledge; they are equally *located*, if clad in different spatial vernaculars, possibly upsetting the geometric habits of conventional cartography, by being 'fluid, not flat, unsettling coordinates of distance and proximity; local and global; inside and outside' (Whatmore 2002, 6). The spatial vernacular in Avanersuaq is based upon an age-old engagement with non-human agents, including the ice, as well as present concerns raised by the Intergovernmental Panel on Climate Change (IPCC) for instance—of which they are recurrently reminded by passing scientists measuring the changes in ice-cover, assessing the relative salinity of the seawater given the influx of freshwater from the rapidly calving glaciers, and counting the stocks of the big marine mammals. The question of orientation in relation to climate change is therefore not a simple matter of making choices about remaining or moving away in some future, it is a constant and pressing need to assess the opportunities of the present, and to reason consistently about them on the basis of all available knowledge—because it is now that the future is shaped. Given the co-constitution of peoples and places (Hastrup 2014b), the intensifying elusiveness of place hits the Inughuit hard.

When the hunters send their sons and daughters south for an education beyond the schooling offered in the region, they implicitly acknowledge that the future does not lie with hunting. And they will be proved right, because of their present choice on behalf of the next generation. For those who stick it out, the hunt is becoming increasingly circumscribed; antici- pating the whereabouts of the game has become more difficult (Nuttall 2010; Hastrup 2013b). There is the melting ice, making it more difficult to access the game by the sea-ice; there is the seismic noise from ships explor- ing the sea bottom hundreds of kilometres away and disturbing the migra- tion routes of the narwhals (Heide-Jørgensen et al. 2013); and there are the increasingly strict quotas on the hunt of polar bear, narwhal and walrus. People have no objection to quotas, but they do have an issue with the unjust (in their view) distribution of these, given the more cavalier attitude to the hunt outside of Avanersuaq.

People in Avanersuaq are staunch adherents to species protection, and they still only allow themselves to hunt narwhal by kayak and harpoon in the spirit of the old Thule-law, of which they are very proud. This protects the whales from random shooting and loss, they explain, and by their use of sealskin floaters and long harpoon lines they make sure that the captured narwhal does not sink or disappear. Elsewhere, motorboats and shooting upset entire schools of whale, and result in major losses that are never counted—I am told. Thus, the general wish for a sustainable hunt is fraught with ambiguity, as subsistence and more commercial hunting economies have to share the general quotas, even within Greenland. As Kalland has it about whale hunting elsewhere, 'commercial native hunters distort the picture' (Kalland 2003, 170). For whom is it to make a just decision about who is the more deserving part?

Another unknown factor in the present versatility of the regional affordances is the geopolitical race for the Polar Sea. It echoes Peary's quest for the North Pole, added to which is a new Cold War that may eventually explode in the face of the Inughuit, having—potentially at least, so far it is non-existent—the last port of call in Greenland, both for the North West Passage and for the Polar Sea. Climate change certainly holds some economic promises for the population, if again at the cost of a sustainable relationship to the companion species.

It seems to me that whatever notion of sustainability we entertain when approaching Thule today, it does not sit easily with the actuality of the place as inhabited and lived. The place itself is elusive and people are implicated in global connections, and this calls for a situational rather than a systemic notion of sustainability. We need, perhaps, to re-invoke the planetary consciousness that emerged with the enlightenment quest for discovery (Pratt 1992). This time, however, the enlightenment must be far more pragmatic, and less classificatory. Sustainability itself must be acknowledged as historical as implied by Sverker Sörlin and Paul Warde in their book, *Nature's End:*

> When we talk of sustainability as one of the most crucial environmental concepts of our time, codified by the United Nations Commission on Environment and Development in 1987, headed by Gro Harlem Brundtland, it is clear that we mean the environment. Nature cannot be unsustainable—can it? It is when we in societies transform it and create an environment that we create the possibility of unsustainability. This quest for survival and sustainability is historical, the (eternal) sustainability of (pure) nature is not. (Sörlin and Warde 2009, 4)

This is an important clarification, but it leaves us with a new burden of delineation related to the question of how far the environment stretches. In the Anthropocene, there are no limits to the environment. Wherever we start from, and however 'isolated' our object of study, it is steeped in global connections—troubling or promising as the case might be. Nature has not become, indeed cannot be, unsustainable, but when the rest of the planet has become environment to communities of multiple designs and vastly unequal numbers, ranging from the small community in the Thule to megacities, the question is whether the notion of sustainability is of any use. Certainly, with the current climate change processes all over the world, the sense of dislocation feeds into a disquieting question of the future *liveability* of homely places.

DISPOSITIONS: SUSTAINABILITY IN UNBOUNDED ENVIRONMENTS

The history of the discovery, dispersal and dislocation of the Inughuit has shown how the question of sustainability cannot easily be answered in systemic terms. Even the most isolated people reach out to and connect with others given half a chance. Social resilience is not the ability to bounce back and remake the old form, but to actively respond to new challenges through new connections, for instance (Hastrup 2009b). To be human is to be flexible and to anticipate new openings and possibilities when old ways no longer hold. Social relations are part of this, and meeting other people, exchanging goods and ideas may be vital for survival, as we have seen. Sustainability is historical, and horizons of expectation are always in the making, yet this is very often downplayed in sustainability science. As suggested by Libby Robin, who has worked in Australia:

The imperatives of sustainability have influenced biology and other disciplines such as economics (in particular, ecological economics), but they have yet to engage seriously with some branches of knowledge. Take history, for example. Despite the fact that sustainability is a concern in management over time—'for the long haul'—and that the time scales offered by history might inform the state of an ecological community, there has been only limited historical interest in such questions. (Robin 2009, 204–5)

Robin suggests that a partial explanation for the lack of historical engagement is to be found in 'wilderness' thinking, where a place is valued mainly for the lack of human interference. Yet, neither the Australian outback nor the Arctic highlands can be seen as a terra nullius; the landscapes are historicized because they are *lived*. This is what makes an anthropological perspective on sustainability invaluable.

If sustainability is historical, it cannot at the same time be abstract—if applied to actual social life. By assembling the lessons from three historical phases in the social life of the Inughuit, I have wanted to show how sustainability cannot be an objective measure of the relationship to the environment; it is already embedded in the relationship. This implies that sustainability is a feature of how people see themselves in the world and identify their opportunities. In the Anthropocene, the truth of this has not diminished; on the contrary, it has been sharpened. I would like to cite Werner Krauss, who says:

There is more at stake in the Anthropocene than a simple addition of natural sciences and those concerned with *anthropos*. It is also not sufficient to identify planetary boundaries, tipping points and limits of growth from a scientific perspective in order to successfully implement sustainable development or effective climate politics. We have to take into account the double challenge of global change, which affects our environment *as well as our intellectual dispositions*. The Anthropocene challenges the familiar distinction between nature and culture, which structured the order of knowledge and disciplines for such a long time. (Krauss 2015, 74; emphasis added)

The call for new thinking on sustainability is related to current ambitions to integrate the social and human sciences with the natural sciences more fully into our understanding of the natural environment (Palsson et al.

2013, 6). Anthropology itself works on the edge of worlds; our intellectual dispositions now afford an unprecedented view of the integration of nature and society (Hastrup 2014a). The price, of course, is to give up on the notion of the idea of a *natural* environment. The environment is shaped by particular, historical horizons, scaling the anthropological object in multiple possible ways.

This intellectual challenge to anthropology is of great potential, also with respect to the notion of sustainability. We need to develop new ways of thinking, given the momentous present, where we—like the hunters in Avanersuaq—inadvertently meet the future halfway.

Acknowledgements The author wants to acknowledge the European Research Council (ERC AdG no. 229459) and the Carlsberg and Velux Foundations for making recurrent fieldwork in North West Greenland possible. Thanks also to Jerome Lewis and Marc Brightman for organizing the conference of which this volume is a result and for their generous comments on this chapter.

REFERENCES

Bjerregaard, P., and I.K. Dahl-Petersen. 2010. *Sundhedsundersøgelsen i Avanersuaq 2010.* København/Odense: Statens Institut for Folkesundhed.

Bravo, M. 2010. Epilogue: The humanism of sea-ice. In *SIKU: Knowing Our Ice. Documenting Inuit Sea-Ice Knowlecge and Use,* ed. I. Krupnik, C. Aporta, S. Gearhead, and L.K. Holm, 445–453. New York: Springer Press.

Brody, H. 2002. *Maps and Dreams. Indians and the British Columbia Frontier.* London: Faber & Faber.

Deleuze, G., and F. Guattari. 2004. *A Thousand Plateaus. Capitalism and Schizophrenia.* Trans. Brian Massumi. London/New York: Continuum.

Fabian, J. 2000. *Out of Our Minds. Reason and Madness in the Exploration of Central Africa.* Berkeley: University of California Press.

Fricker, A. 2006. Measuring Up to Sustainability. In *The Environment in Anthropology. A Reader in Ecology, Culture, and Sustainable Living,* ed. N. Haenn and R. Wilk, 191–202. New York: New York University Press.

Gilberg, R. 1976. *The Polar Eskimo Population, Thule District, North Greenland,* Meddelelser om Grønland. Vol. 203, no. 3. Copenhagen: Nyt Nordisk Forlag Arnold Busck.

Harlang, C., A. Lynge, and H.K. Nielsen. 1999. *Retten til Thulelandet.* København/Nuuk: Dike/Atuagkat.

Hastrup, K. 2009a. The Nomadic Landscape. People in a Changing Arctic Environment. *Danish Journal of Geography* 109 (2): 181–189.

————. 2009b. Arctic Hunters, Climate Variability and Social Flexibility. In *The Question of Resilience. Social Responses to Climate Change*, ed. K. Hastrup, 245–270. Copenhagen: The Royal Danish Academy of Letters and Sciences.

————. 2013a. Scales of Attention in Fieldwork. Global Connections and Local Concerns in the Arctic. *Ethnography* 14 (2): 145–164.

————. 2013b. Anticipation on Thin Ice. Diagrammatic Reasoning in the High Arctic. In *The Social Life of Climate Change Models. Anticipating Nature*, ed. K. Hastrup and M. Skrydstrup, 77–99. London/New York: Routledge.

————., ed. 2014a. *Anthropology and Nature*. London/New York: Routledge.

————. 2014b. Of Maps and Men. Making Places and Peoples in the Arctic. In *Anthropology and Nature*, ed. Kirsten Hastrup, 211–232. London/New York: Routledge.

————. 2016. Knud Rasmussen: Explorer, Ethnographer, and Narrator. In *Early Inuit Studies. Themes and Transitions, 1850s–1980s*, ed. Igor Krupnik, 111–136. Washington, DC: Smithsonian Institution Scholarly Press.

Haraway, D. 2008. *When Species Meet*. Minneapolis/London: University of Minnesota Press.

Hayes, I. 1866. *The Open Polar Sea. A Narrative of a Voyage of Discovery Towards the North Pole, in the Schooner United States*. London: Sampson Low, Son and Marston.

Heide-Jørgensen, M.P., R.G. Hansen, K. Westdal, R.R. Reeves, and A. Mosbech. 2013. Narwhals and Seismic Exploration: Is Seismic Noise Increasing the Risk of Ice Entrapments? *Biological Conservation* 158: 50–54.

Holtved, E. 1967. *Contributions to Polar Eskimo Ethnography*, Meddelelser om Grønland. Vol. 182, no. 2. Copenhagen: C.A. Reitzels Forlag.

Ingold, T. 2000. *The Perception of the Environment*. London: Routledge.

Kalland, A. 2003. Anthropology and the Concept of 'Sustainability': Some Reflections. In *Imagining Nature. Practices of Cosmology and Identity*, ed. A. Roepstorff, N. Bubandt, and K. Kull, 161–177. Aarhus: Aarhus University Press.

Kane, E.K. 1856. *Arctic Explorations. The Second Grinnell Expedition in Search of Sir John Franklin, 1853–55*. Vol. I & II. Philadelphia/London: Childs & Peterson/Trübner & Co.

Krauss, W. 2015. Anthropology in the Anthropocene: Sustainable Development, Climate Change and Interdisciplinary Research. In *Grounding Global Climate Change*, ed. H. Greschke and J. Tischler, 59–76. Dordrecht/New York: Springer.

Malaurie, J. 1956. *Les derniers rois de Thulé*. Paris: Plon.

Martin-Nielsen, J. 2012. The Other Cold War: The United States and Greenland's Ice Sheet Environment, 1948–1966. *Journal of Historical Geography* 38: 69–80.

Massey, D. 2005. *For Space*. London: Sage.

Minnegal, M., and P.D. Dwyer. 2011. Appropriating Fish, Appropriating Fishermen. Tradable Permits; Natural Resources and Uncertainty. In *Ownership and Appropriation*, ASA Monographs 47, ed. V. Strang and M. Busse, 197–215. London: Berg.

Nuttall, M. 2009. Living in a World of Movement: Human Resilience to Environmental Instability in Greenland. In *Anthropology and Climate Change: From Encounters to Actions*, ed. S.A. Crate and M. Nuttall, 292–310. Walnut Creek: Left Coast Press.

———. 2010. Anticipation, Climate Change, and Movement in Greenland. *Études/Inuit/Studies* 34 (1): 21–37.

Palsson, G., et al. 2013. Reconceptualizing the 'Anthropos' in the Anthropocene: Integrating the Social Sciences and Humanities in Global Environmental Change Research. *Environmental Science & Policy* 28: 3–13.

Peary, R.E. 1898. Northward over the "great ice". In *A Narrative of Life and Work Along the Shores and Upon the Interior Ice-Cap of Northern Greenland in the Years 1886 and 1891–1897*, vol. I & II. London: Methuen & Co.

Pratt, M.L. 1992. *Imperial Eyes. Travel Writing and Transculturation*. London: Routledge.

Rasmussen, K. 1908. In *The People of the Polar North. A Record*, ed. G. Herring. London: Kegan Paul, Trench, Trübner & Co. Ltd.

Robin, L. 2009. A New Science for Sustainability in Ancient Land. In *Nature's End. History and the Environment*, ed. S. Sörlin and P. Warde, 188–211. London/New York: Palgrave Macmillan.

Ross, J. 1819. *Voyage of Discovery, Made Under the Orders of Admiralty, in His Majesty's Ships Isabelle and Alexander, for the Purpose of Exploring Baffin's Bay, and Inquiring into the Probability of a North-West Passage*. London: John Murray.

Sörlin, S., and P. Warde. 2009. Making the Environment Historical: An Introduction. In *Nature's End. History and the Environment*, ed. S. Sörlin and P. Warde, 1–20. London/New York: Palgrave Macmillan.

Turnbull, D. 2003. *Masons, Tricksters and Cartographers. Comparative Studies in the Sociology of Scientific and Indigenous Knowledge*. London/New York: Routledge.

Vibe, C. 1967. *Arctic Animals in Relation to Climatic Fluctuations*, Meddelelser om Grønland, bd. 170, no. 5. Copenhagen: C.A. Reitzels Forlag.

Walsøe, P. 2003. *Goodbye Thule. The Compulsory Relocation in 1953*. Copenhagen: Tiderne Skifter.

Whatmore, S. 2002. *Hybrid Geographies. Natures, Cultures, Spaces*. London: Sage.

Wilk, R. 2009. Consuming Ourselves to Death: The Anthropology of Consumer Culture and Climate Change. In *Anthropology and Climate Change. From Encounters to Actions*, ed. S.A. Crate and M. Nuttal, 265–276. Walnut Creek: Left Coast Press.

CHAPTER 10

Ebola in Meliandou: Tropes of 'Sustainability' at Ground Zero

James Fairhead and Dominique Millimouno

This chapter begins at 'Ground Zero'. Two locations have recently acquired the epithet of 'Ground Zero'; the Twin-Towers of the World Trade Centre in New York and the small Guinean village of Meliandou. 'Ground zero', however, was coined by members of the Manhattan project during their development of nuclear weapons as the point on the Earth's surface closest to a nuclear detonation. It entered public consciousness to describe the location of Hiroshima's Shima Hospital.

The concept has other connotations. Ground Zero captures an epochal event that recalibrates time itself. Its use could be back-dated to describe the fall of the Bastille at the inception of the French Revolution or that graveyard in Kyrgyzstan that marks the spillover location for the Black Death that claimed some 200 million of our ancestors and transformed global society (Herlihy and Cohn 1997).

If anything can evoke the antithesis of 'sustainability', it is 'Ground Zero'. A ground zero event is also a quintessential 'Black Swan' event, in

J. Fairhead (✉)
Department of Social Anthropology, University of Sussex, Brighton, UK

D. Millimouno
Centre for Development Research, Kissidougou, Guinea

© The Author(s) 2017
M. Brightman, J. Lewis (eds.), *The Anthropology of Sustainability*,
Palgrave Studies in Anthropology of Sustainability,
DOI 10.1057/978-1-137-56636-2_10

the language of Nassim Taleb; a massive event that comes as a surprise, but has major consequences and a dominant role in history (Taleb 2007). These events present challenges to the language of sustainability. They are sometimes described as 'outliers'. But can one simply set them aside as exceptions? How foolish it would be to set aside such events if they play vastly larger roles than more regular, predictable and orderly occurrences that are more amenable to social analysis. I am reminded of all those anthropologists who participated in the Second World War—Edmund Leach, Edward Evans-Pritchard—but who in their subsequent years suppressed this experience in their books that still helped anthropologists to focus on the orderliness of things (Price 2008).

Taleb encourages us to embrace the disproportionate role of high-profile, hard-to-predict, and rare events that are beyond the realm of normal expectations whether in history, science, finance or technology. He chides all social sciences either for ignoring them, or when we do not, of inappropriately rationalising them after the fact with the benefit of hindsight. In this chapter, I am going to look at the ex-post rationalisations and explanations that have been made for the Ebola outbreak. I will examine the narrative framings—tropes or clichés—that have been used to tame it, to make it orderly after all and to link it to the language of sustainability.

Anthropologists have not been as silent on Black Swan events as Taleb suggests. The arrival over the horizon of Captain James Cook in Hawaii is a quintessential 'Black Swan' moment. In the 1990s, Marshal Sahlins (1985, 1995) and Gananath Obeyesekere (1992) thrashed out contradictory readings. Sahlins quite reasonably encouraged us to interpret the unfolding interplay of these radically different worlds in terms of the structure of such conjunctures. How did their radically contrasting interpretive grids shape their encounter—and how did that encounter, in some ways, reshape those grids? Or why did it not? Much modern anthropology now turns on 'events', tracking the social, economic and emotional fallout of 'global encounters' in localities.

Spillover at Meliandou is most definitely 'an event'. Since December 2013, radically different worlds have come into conjuncture in the village, so how has the dialectical interplay between them been unfolding? The events at Meliandou throw into sharp relief (and relativise) the interpretive grids and the social worlds of the agonists involved. In particular, I am interested in the contrasting ways that those involved have rationalised the spillover event, and what each then makes of the other. This, I think, helps us to an 'anthropology of sustainability'—at least an aspect of it, which is to discern how orderliness and the sources of disorder are envisaged and acted upon and how competing readings of orderliness are shaped in the global encounters that they shape. As I shall argue, it makes methodological sense in anthropologies of 'sustainability' to examine how the antithesis—Black Swan events—are 'rationalised'—'explained' or rendered orderly.

To begin, I look at explanations of spillover at Meliandou in the scientific and journalistic publications that examine it, with which we will be more familiar and comfortable. These trace a broadly ecological (albeit political ecological) explanation for spillover associated with unsustainable resource use. After probing the validity of such explanations, I want then to examine contrasting explanations as they have unfolded in Meliandou. A caveat is in order: the focus here is on the spillover of Ebola from the natural world. I am not engaging with narratives on why Ebola then spread so dramatically in West Africa.

We can begin with the UN World Health Organization (WHO 2015) which published a quasi-official document that explained the causes of spillover in the following terms:

> The remote and sparsely populated village of Meliandou . . . is located in Guékedou District in what is known as the Forest Region. Much of the surrounding forest area has, however, been destroyed by foreign mining and timber operations. Some evidence suggests that the resulting forest loss, estimated at more than 80%, brought potentially infected wild animals, and the bat species thought to be the virus' natural reservoir, into closer contact with human settlements. Prior to symptom onset, the child was seen playing in his backyard near a hollow tree heavily infested with bats. During the country's long years of civil unrest, natural resources were exploited by mining and timber companies. The ecology in the densely-forested area changed. Fruit bats, which are thought by most scientists to be the natural reservoir of the virus, moved closer to human settlements. Hunters, who depend on bushmeat for their food security and survival, almost certainly slaughtered infected wild animals—most likely monkeys, forest antelope, or squirrels.

Many journalistic reports echo this environmental reading. After visiting Meliandou, Coen and Henk write that:

> In recent years thousands of people have migrated to the area around Meliandou, among them many refugees from the civil wars in Sierra Leone and Liberia. The villages grew, the distance between the houses shrank and the rainforest, which once seemed impenetrable, yielded to fields, farms and

mines. The humans forced Nature to obey their laws. They left only a perimeter of trees around Meliandou, trees that bear mangos and papayas . . . . The virus did not invade the habitat of humans. Quite the contrary: humans invaded the habitat of the virus. (Coen and Henk 2014)

The scientific literature dovetails with these views. Bausch and Schwarz (2014) were among the first,[1] writing that 'The effect of a stalled economy and government' creates 'poverty' that:

> drives people to expand their range of activities to stay alive, plunging deeper into the forest to expand the geographic as well as species range of hunted game and to find wood to make charcoal and deeper into mines to extract minerals, enhancing their risk of exposure to Ebola virus and other zoonotic pathogens in these remote corners.

These works narrate a 'history of Guinea, where decades of inefficient and corrupt government have left the country in a state of stalled or even retrograde development' (Bausch and Schwarz 2014), and one where: 'The Guinea forest region, traditionally comprised of small and isolated populations of diverse ethnic groups who hold little power and pose little threat to the larger groups closer to the capital, has been habitually neglected, receiving little attention or capital investment. Rather, the region was systematically plundered and the forest decimated by clear-cut logging, leaving the "Guinea Forest Region" largely deforested'. It is now 'home to tens of thousands of refugees fleeing . . . conflicts (ibid.)'.

In short, the scientific and journalistic communities 'know' (rationalise after this Black Swan event) that there has been spillover from an animal reservoir (probably bats) but this is associated with degrading natural resources (Laporta 2014), itself associated with foreign timber firms, mining, civil unrest and lawlessness, migrants, refugees from the terrible conflicts in Liberia and Sierra Leone, a stalled economy, and inefficient and corrupt government. If it derives from a need for charcoal, hunting or scavenging unclean foods, the agency behind this is attributed to poverty.

Explanations thus have the decency to project the "good local" by projecting culpability and evil-doing outwards into the regional and global political economy (e.g. also Obilade 2015). This gives a 'social analysis' to ecological causes; a 'political ecology' as it were, and it is a 'feel good' political ecology at that. The narrators and audience feel good: both feel an uncanny worry in coming to know their own culpability but find some

Fig. 10.1 Meliandou showing the village surrounded by a forest island (Google Earth 2015) nestled under the 'Four hills' (Kongonani)

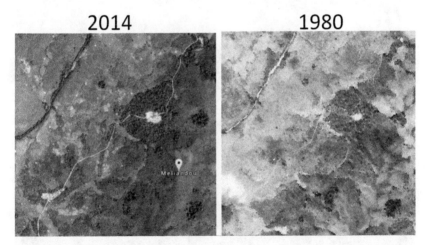

Fig. 10.2 Comparison of vegetation of village of Meliandou between 1979/80 (JICA) and 2014 (Google Earth, rendered black and white)

absolution in confessing their sins. And policy can do something positive. As we are half-way to understanding unsustainability, so we are half-way to intervening to address it. We can enjoin with other 'saviours' in this time of darkness and enact a more environmentally sustainable development.

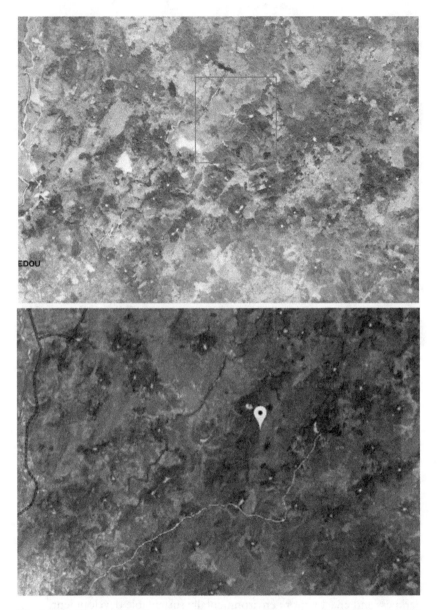

Fig. 10.3 Comparison of vegetation at smaller scale between 1980 (*top*) and 2014 (*bottom*) that shows broad continuity of vegetation cover. Blue box shows area in Fig. 10.2

There is a problem with this, however, and raised by earlier research in this region that focused on a village just 15 miles from Meliandou and reported in *Misreading the African Landscape* (Fairhead and Leach 1996). Comparing air photographs from 1979/1980 and modern satellite imagery reveals that there has been no deforestation, or at least none worthy of the name (Figs. 10.1, 10.2 and 10.3). This is a fragmented landscape, to be sure, but it has been so for more than a hundred years, perhaps many hundreds. One hundred years ago, colonial agricultural officer Nicholas described the same landscape that we see today (though he also interpreted it as recently deforested): 'From Kissidougou to Gueckedou all has been cut. . . . A region so fertile has become a complete desert. Now there remains no more than a little belt of trees around each village, and that is all' (Fairhead and Leach 1996: 17). Spillover has happened, but the narratives deployed to explain it, linked to recent environmental catastrophe, are wanting.

I could spin a political ecology narrative of causality and could have made it convincing to Western readers who are so well predisposed to believe it. And yet we can see, now, that these are 'rumours' of deforestation; rumours attributing Ebola to it. It would be incorrect, however, to understand the emergence and persistence of the deforestation analyses simply as the persistence of rumours. A lot more work would need to be done to examine what renders this analysis credible (scientific), looking at the history of ecological science and its relationship to administration in the colonial and 'development' eras, a project that I have earlier addressed in a trio of books (Fairhead and Leach 1996, 1998, 2003a). Here, however, I simply want to recognise these political ecological explanations as structuring the 'scientific' 'expert' side of the conjuncture in Meliandou, and to realise that these explanations are invoking a causal link (deforestation) between social processes and the disease, that has demonstrably not happened. Indeed, it is so obviously flawed as to be laughable to those living in Meliandou, just as their explanations have been ridiculed by scientists and journalists who 'know' that deforestation is the cause.

EVENTS IN MELIANDOU

Let us now turn to events in Meliandou, and unfolding explanations there. In February 2015, there were 16 international visits to the village in the space of 3 days, most of them made by journalists or scientists, but one of them by Dominique Millimouno. Key events can be traced from the profusion of writing about the village that has emerged. The chapter thus traces events that are now 'public knowledge', but we thicken the description with the 'corn flour' of our past ethnography.

The facts are these: Etienne Oumouno is a 30-something farmer and occasional hunter. In 2013, he had fallen out with his mother-in-law who also lived in the village, and this had either caused problems between Etienne and his wife, Sia, or was caused by such problems depending on perspective. By December 2013, Sia had moved back to her parent's house with their youngest son, one-year-old Emile. Sia was heavily pregnant. Her other children stayed with Etienne, who by now had married a second wife (Sia's co-wife) who now lived in Etienne's house.

The one-year-old, Emile, fell ill and his father Etienne joined in desperately seeking healthcare. When Emile died on December 28, 2013, becoming 'Patient Zero' (Saéz et al. 2015) it was at his fathers' house. Etienne's four-year-old daughter, Philomene, fell ill too, and died a week later. And then Sia died. She was eight months pregnant.

Western media report that a 'midwife' from another village was called to deliver her baby, stillborn. Whether this delivery was before or after her death is still a little confused. It seems that the person called on was not simply a 'midwife'. In this region, the death of a pregnant woman brings a particular kind of calamity to the 'order of things'. A woman must not be buried with a fetus inside her (Paulme 1954; Anoko 2014a; Fairhead 2016). This is because a fecund world is an orderly one in which human, animal and crop reproduction must occur in their separate places, and the reproductive cycle for each must be rigorously separated from the next. Death is part of this cycle, being envisaged as a rebirth into the ancestral world—into the 'village of the dead'—which those who die aspire to join. Birth is an arrival from that world. To mix the generations in death by burying a pregnant woman confuses this order, and disrupts the ancestral world too. The 'midwife' was, I infer (as these things are kept secret) a *sulukuno;* the leading figure of the women's initiation society in the vicinity that manages these aspects of reproductive life. The *sulukuno* presided over the necessary rituals that would put things back on track—the dead baby being delivered of the dead mother by caesarean prior to their separate burial. All men, and indeed all women of reproductive age, would have been excluded from these feared and revered ceremonies. Women manage all mortuary rites of women which include preparing the body.

The *sulukuno* was infected and she died too. Etienne's mother-in-law who he had fallen out with (i.e. patient zero's grandmother) died. Indeed, three senior women from the village died in February, and the disease was thus observed not only to be killing women but all the leading 'wise women'. The senior women themselves attracted large funerals. At this time, one interpretation afloat in the village was that women were to be the only victims. Not long after a man died, as did men who washed his body, so that idea was scotched. 'They were the ones called to care for people when they became ill', said Suzanne Leno. 'Who will care for us now?'(Chalvon 2014).

Etienne Ouamouno, however, remained unscathed. He had lost six family members in less than a month, though he had three surviving children. As he says, he believed these mysterious deaths were caused by witchcraft. Others did too. Suspicions, we can infer, fell on the fraught in-law relations as they often do. According to Etienne: 'I thought my village was against me. I thought my whole family will die. I lost all hope . . . ' (Palitza 2014). And: 'We all thought it was a curse . . . . Everyone who touched my child was doomed to die (Coen and Henk 2014).'

After the simultaneous loss of the three leaders of the women's society, the village authorities hired in a witch hunter—a 'Wulomo'—in the hope of identifying who or what had brought this calamity and to exorcise the village. As part of their practice, apparently, in one of the village alleys they planted a banana stem to which they attached specialist pouches. 'Should the banana grow, the village would be released . . . ', at least according to Cécé Kpoghounou, the school principal (Chalvon 2014).

We do not know (and do not seek to know) exactly who was found to have cursed who, and how the complex ricochets and rebounds of the curses were envisaged as they encountered modes of personal protection.[2] The deaths continued. Burials in the village left tombs marked by small stone circles everywhere (Chalvon 2014).

The medication and funeral ceremonies had been very expensive and the work of the specialists—the dead *Sulukuno* and the *Wulomo*—more so. Not only had Etienne and his family taken on debts in treating the ill and in their funerals, but they took on debts for these ceremonies too. Their debts emptied the village coffers and worse, many others who had also borrowed money to help fund these events also died. Those remaining had to take on the debts of each of those who died before the dead could be buried. With every death, the living became ever more indebted, and yet the village economy itself collapsed as it became isolated. Those from the neighbouring villages that were tainted by these events (by the curses) became angry. Mourners initially refused to eat food or drink the water— an insult. Then, they refused to attend funerals—a bigger insult. Then, they even cut the bridge that gave Meliandou access to the only working well and main road. In a world where celebrations concerning the clearing of a path is a sign of kinship and alliance, cutting a path signals a terminal insult. The villagers could not sell their crops, such as rice, corn, and banana, slashing the town's income. The clinic shut. The school shut. The paramedic left.

Hardly surprisingly, young men now left too 'in the belief that the Ouamouno family or the entire village was cursed' according to the village chief (Associated Press 2014). Some say 100 went, some say 200. Four hundred remain. Among those who fled was Etienne Ouamouno's own father Fassinet, 47, who 'grabbed his children and grandchildren and travelled more than 400 kilometres in crammed minibus taxis to the town of Siguiri, where he stayed for eight months (Palitza 2014)'. He has only recently returned to Meliandou. 'There is still so much stigma,' he says. 'As soon as people hear we are from Meliandou, they are scared or run away. They think we are contaminated (Palitza 2014).'

'Ebola'

For the first three months, the epidemic spread and ravaged the regional hospitals and health centres until eventually the unprecedented disease drew international attention that identified and declared 'Ebola' as the cause. Health workers soon visited Meliandou and informed the villagers how to prevent transmission. Residents burnt everything in the homes where each patient had died: mattresses, bedding, clothing, towels, sometimes even agricultural equipment. 'People were crazed by fear. They burned the few belongings they had,' says village chief Amadou Kamano, pointing to heaps of ashes at the back of the houses 'Now we are even poorer than we were before' (Palitza 2014). Within a couple of weeks, however, they managed to contain the outbreak, but 26 people had died.

Until 'Ebola' was declared the cause, the causes were being construed in part as social, related to curses and the maleficent dead or living. Healthcare was sought, but was ineffectual. Yet once 'Ebola' was confirmed, and a new name was given to the illness, villagers (and those in the region) began to speculate on what had brought this new disease. Just as 'scientists' were sense-making in attributions to the knock-on effects of 'deforestation' (a cursed nature biting back) so those in the village began to speculate in frames that made sense to them. Whilst 'instability' or 'non-sustainability' had been framed in relation to curses, we now encounter another set of very different unsustainability narratives.

The narratives in the village and region are not environmental. There is little in the vegetation and the environment that is experienced as precarious or unstable—and such instability as there is (occasional droughts, pests, etc.) might easily be attributed to social faults. Despite all that is thrown at it, the vegetation and fauna in the landscapes provide a bedrock of stability for people here. The environment has never been 'a problem'. It is certainly not a powerful enough trope or cliché in which to make sense of this Black Swan catastrophe. Those who wield such explanations could be dismissed at best as ignorant or perhaps as maleficent.

The environmental narratives that scientists and journalists rolled out to 'explain' Ebola spillover might be dated back to the Ancient Greeks, or perhaps to the *Bible*, to Descartes, to the enlightenment, to colonial encounters, to the psychological impact of the First World War, or perhaps to all of these and more. They certainly date back. The narrative is deeply sedimented in everything from European language and philosophy, to its imagery, institutions and emotions. There has been similar sedimentation in the explanatory frameworks within which people began to make sense of Ebola in Meliandou and neighbouring districts. They date back and are instituted, but they do not relate to the environment.

But in this region, history has sedimented the pertinence of very different frames of reference, and these concern, particularly, the capriciousness of outsiders. Perhaps, this dates to 'memories' of the 'Slave Trade' (Shaw 2002), perhaps to the maelstrom of conflict known locally as the 'tribal wars' but associated with that precarious period of mercantile capitalism between Atlantic slavery and Colonisation (Fairhead et al. 2003b). Perhaps it relates to the murderous and extractive colonisation itself in which Kissi leaders were hung sowing division among them that left the land cursed (e.g. Anoko 2014b; Iffono 2010). Perhaps too, the capriciousness of outsiders could be traced to post-colonial Marxist revolutionary 'modernizers' who were experienced as bringing alien iconoclasm and ethnic domination (McGovern 2013). And now it is the neoliberal Kleptocracy. In each there is a malicious, distant and often white driving force and an African connivance. There is enough and more in this history to shape powerful narratives on the external causes of instability.

The material paraphernalia of Ebola response, of the surveillance, of the 'kidnapping' of the ill to Ebola Treatment Units, and of deaths and disappearances associated with these places, not only was playing into these histories long sedimented into local practices, emotions and institutions, but also played into modern experiences of those from the region who experienced the apartheid of foreign-owned mining; the quashing of arti sanal Guinean youth in their mining; the apartheid and extreme inequality that is international development in practice; the horrors on the trans-Saharan migration trail, of migrant life in Morocco, of the illegal crossings to Spain, of border police and of racism in everyday Europe (Fairhead 2016).

Ebola, it was now thought, was disseminated by white people seeking the deaths of blacks; by a measles vaccination campaign; by the Lab testing of bats to create a vaccination against the virus; by ethnic rival politicians; by white miners looking to exploit a nearby mountain of iron ore (Faul 2014). As the grid of international intervention cranked up (not just Médecins Sans Frontières (MSF), but a tidal wave of astonishingly well-resourced outsiders), it was these narratives that rendered legible its symbolic load. In June 2014, even the president of Guinea accused Médecins Sans Frontières of 'seeking money on the backs of Guineans'.

Those in Meliandou and the vicinity did not need convincing of the existence of Ebola: by May and June, many villages throughout Guékedou were felling trees and pulling down road bridges to isolate themselves from MSF and health services that were at its origin (Fairhead 2016). Outside agencies and their African collaborators were suspect. This was not the stuff of speculation and of Scottian 'foot dragging', it was a matter of life and death. Villagers in Guékedou attacked international vehicles penetrating their territories. Many districts became 'off-limits' to Ebola surveillance. The region where local fear was the most palpable was next to the Simandou Iron Ore mountain—that has become iconic in Guinea and beyond, of global corruption and white greed. What might those capable of billions of dollars of fraud and their African political accomplices also be capable of? In the small town of Womey, when a delegation of doctors, politicians, journalists, and aid workers visited in September 2014, villagers murdered eight in an orchestrated act of resistance and then attempted to track down and kill those who had escaped (Guineenews 2014a, b; Ouendeno 2014).

These causal explanations are ridiculed by the knowing policy and development community that dismisses their content as 'rumour'. But what differs between this locally rooted explanatory frame and the external frame tracing cause to deforestation? One makes a deductive leap (invoking deforestation) in otherwise compelling arguments about political ecological processes, whereas the other makes a deductive leap (invoking biological warfare) in otherwise compelling arguments about political economic processes. In the terms of Taleb, this Black Swan event is being rationalised in hindsight—and in inappropriate ways. In identifying sources of instability, both can be seen to evoke framings of 'sustainability'.

ANXIETY IN THE LAND

Those in Meliandou and the vicinity do not turn to deforestation or to fruit bats as harbingers of evil in their aetiology of Ebola. They have not lived through deforestation and they and their ancestors have lived closely with bats since the depths of time. Those fruit bats that Etienne and villagers in Meliandou were initially told by outsiders might have brought the disease are said to migrate to the village in February or March, as Etienne pointed out, not in December, when Emile fell ill. Etienne himself has no confidence in that explanation.

Villagers also reject a more recent, better-researched narrative which is that 'patient zero' (Emile) was infected whilst playing next to a hollow tree where 'free-tailed' bats roosted (Saéz et al. 2015), a variant of the fruit bat hypotheses that is also usually also contextualised in the wider narrative of environmental decline (Firger 2014; Turk 2015). Those in Meliandou are not impressed: the child was simply too young to have played there.

A few months later, Meliandou villages seemed to have little confidence (or to have lost confidence) in capricious outsiders as being the cause as well. Events had moved on and international visits to the village had escalated in intensity. Every day Etienne was asked to go on expeditions into the bush to probe the landscape and trap bats. He was asked for radio interviews, and to answer researcher's questions, and those of humanitarians, politicians and others.

This intensity and external concern with the landscape has instilled new fears within the village. In late March 2014, Guinean authorities forbade the hunting of bats or any other animals, and those in Meliandou were prevented from raising domestic animals for fear that spillover from the as-yet-unknown reservoir might recur. Those in the village had grown fearful of the paths, fields, swamps, caves and woodlands that had once been their refuge in everyday routines. Farms were left untended. Paths went un-walked and have grown over. Every aspect of the landscape became tainted. When Dominique Millimouno probed the potential role of caves, he was met with anxious questions: should one continue to visit them or use the water that comes from them? Are the trees and lands around the caves dangerous to use? Every outside researcher's question asked in the hope of reaching resolution to Ebola's cryptic reservoir instilled a new fear.

BLACK SWANS AND THE ANTHROPOLOGY OF 'SUSTAINABILITY'

Explanatory frameworks in Meliandou have thus shifted from initial reflection on social causes within their community, to social causes linked to outsiders, and then to the landscape that sustains them. In the latter case, there is no successful resolution; no successful rationalisation. There is debilitating uncertainty.

In this shifting framing, the communities of knowledge ('epistemic communities' as conceived by Haas 1992) that shape ideas concerning the nature of order and the causes of 'unsustainable' disorder have altered—from those in the village(s), to those in the wider region in contradistinction to the 'outside world' of Ebola response, to those in the global community inclusive of the Ebola response. Only in the latter case are the causes left unknown and so there can be no local discourse of sustainability. This 'Black Swan' event has thus been rationalised within very different tropes, from intra-community curses to the capricious outsider, and then to an unspecified danger lurking in the landscape. The first two make the event more predictable and provide a script for action in response. Narratives taming such events—sustainability narratives—are intimately tied to such scripts and make sense within the lived worlds that produce them. Only in the latter case is this not possible.

Expert scientific explanations have not changed much. The deforestation narrative and its environmental script for action are surprisingly tenacious despite the counter-evidence and community critique. The external 'global' epistemic community espousing the political ecological explanation has not been open to the critique emergent within the community (who reject deforestation and the culpability of fruit bats). This global epistemic community remains quaintly amused in learning of the local fear of curses, and is shocked by the 'irrationality' credulity and ignorance of the 'rumours' that recast the 'white saviour' as bringing the very evil that they seek to overcome. The same community, however, cannot see the implausibility of their own explanation. In the unfolding 'structure of conjuncture', the expert narrative finding the ultimate origin of the disease in 'unsustainable resource use' has remained fixed, unchallenged by the encounter that has prompted several reframings in Meliandou.

By observing how Black Swan events are rationalised we not only reveal tropes of unsustainability—of disorder—but can also appreciate how social communities themselves are mutually constituted in relation to these visions, and thus how they become the locus of social othering.

NOTES

1. See also Alexander et al. (2015).
2. For an understanding of medicines affording such protection, see, for example, Paulme (1954), Højbjerg (2007).

REFERENCES

Alexander, K.A., et al. 2015. What Factors Might Have Led to the Emergence of Ebola in West Africa? *PLOS Neglected Tropical Diseases* 9 (6): e0003652.

Anoko, J. 2014a. La réparation de la malédiction générale suite à l'enterrement d'une femme enceinte avec le bébé dans le ventre. Une approche anthropologique pendant l'épidémie de la Maladie à Virus Ebola en Guinée.

———. 2014b. Communication with Rebellious Communities During an Outbreak of Ebola Virus Disease in Guinea: An Anthropological Approach. http://www.ebola-anthropology.net/case_studies/communication-with-rebellious-communities-during-an-outbreak-of-ebola-virus-disease-in-guinea-an-anthropological-approach/. Accessed 8 Apr 2015.

Associated Press. 2014. Life at Ebola's Ground Zero: Confused, Hungry and Angry, the Villages That Believes It is Cursed By Deadly Disease (December 10). http://www.dailymail.co.uk/news/article-2868284/Debt-hunger-birthplace-Ebola-Guinea.html. Accessed 11 Apr 2015.

Bausch, D., and L. Schwarz. 2014. Outbreak of Ebola Virus Disease in Guinea: Where Ecology Meets Economy. *PLOS Neglected Tropical Diseases*. doi:10.1371/journal.pntd.0003056

Chalvon, S. 2014. Meliandou, le "Ground Zero" d'Ebola tente de se reconstruire (15 December). http://afrique.lepoint.fr/actualites/melliandou-le-ground-zero-d-ebola-tente-de-se-reconstruire-10-12-2014-1888609_2365.php. Accessed 11 Apr 2015.

Coen, A. and M. Henk. 2014. How the Virus Came Into This World (November 24). http://www.zeit.de/feature/ebola-afrika-virus. Accessed 11 Apr 2015.

Fairhead, James. 2016. Understanding Social Resistance to Ebola Response in the Forest Region of the Republic of Guinea: An Anthropological Perspective. *African Studies Review* 59 (3): 7–31.

Fairhead, J., and M. Leach. 1996. *Misreading the African Landscape*. Cambridge: CUP.

———. 1998. *Reframing Deforestation*. London: Routledge.

———. 2003a. *Science, Society and Power*. Cambridge: CUP.

Fairhead, J., M. Leach, T. Geysbeek, and S. Holsoe. 2003b. *African American Exploration in West Africa*. Bloomington: Indiana University Press.

Faul, M. 2014. The Village of Meliandou: Guinea's Ground Zero for the Ebola Virus (December 10). http://en.radiovaticana.va/news/2014/12/10/the_

village_of_meliandou_guineas_ground_zero ebola_/1114310.   Accessed 11 Apr 2015.

Firger, J. 2014. Child's Encounter with a Bat May Have Sparked the Ebola Outbreak (December 30). http://www.cbsnews.com/news/ebola-childs-encounter-with-a-bat-may-have-started-outbreak/. Accessed 11 Apr 2015.

Guinéenews. 2014a. Ebola et la poudrière de la Guinée Forestière. Part 1. http://Guineenews.org/dossier-ebola-et-la-poudriere-de-la-Guinee-forestiere/. Accessed 8 Apr 2015.

————. 2014b. Poudrière Forestière : la part d'erreurs de sensibilisation dans le drame de Womey (2ᵉᵐᵉ Partie). http://Guineenews.org/dossier-poudriere-forestiere-la-part-d%e2%80%95erreurs-de-sensibilisation-dans-le-drame-de-womey-2eme-partie/. Accessed 8 Apr 2015.

Haas, P. 1992. Introduction: Epistemic Communities and International Policy Coordination. *International Organization* 46 (1): 1–35.

Herlihy, D., and S. Cohn. 1997. *The Black Death and the Transformation of the West*. Harvard: Harvard University Press.

Højbjerg, C. Kordt. 2007. *Resisting State Iconoclasm Among the Loma of Guinea*. Durham: Carolia Academic Press.

Iffono, A.G. 2010. *Le peuple Kissi (Guinée, Liberia, Sierra Leone) face aux colonisations*. Paris: l'Harmattan.

Laporta, G. 2014. Landscape Fragmentation and Ebola Outbreaks. *Mem Instituto Oswaldo Cruz, Rio de Janeiro* 109 (8): 1088–1088 (December 2014). http://www.scielo.br/pdf/mioc/v109n8/0074-0276-mioc-109-8-1088.pdf. Accessed 11 Apr 2015.

McGovern, M. 2013. *Unmasking the State : Making Guinea Modern*. Chicago: University of Chicago Press.

Obeyesekere, G. 1992. *The Apotheosis of Captain Cook: European Mythmaking In The Pacific*. Princeton: Princeton University Press.

Obilade, T. 2015. The Political Economy of Ebola Virus Disease (EVD) in West African Countries. http://hdl.handle.net/10919/51641. Accessed 11 Apr 2015

Ouendeno, M. 2014. Rapport de la mission dans la sous-préfecture de Womey, Préfecture de N'Zérékoré du 15 septembre 2014.

Paltiza, K. 2014. Despair in the Time of Ebola: In the Village of "Patient Zero" (October 25). http://www.dpa-international.com/news/international/despair-in-the-time-of-ebola-in-the-village-of-patient-zero-a-43061064-img-1.html. Accessed 11 Apr 2015.

Paulme, D. 1954. *Les Gens du riz*. Paris: librarie Plon.

Price, D. 2008. *Anthropological Intelligence: The Deployment and Neglect of American Anthropology in the Second World War*. Durham: Duke University Press.

Saéz, Almudena, et al. 2015. Investigating the Zoonotic Origin of the West African Ebola Epidemic. *EMBO Molecular Medicine* 7: 17–23.

Sahlins, M. 1985. *Islands of History*. Chicago: University of Chicago Press.

————. 1995. *How 'Natives' Think: About Captain Cook, For Example*. Chicago: University of Chicago Press.

Shaw, R. 2002. *Memories of the Slave Trade: Ritual and Historical Imagination in Sierra Leone*. Chicago: University of Chicago Press.

Taleb, N. 2007. *The Black Swan: The Impact of the Highly Improbable*. London: Allen Lane.

Turk, V. 2015. Tracing the Origin of the Ebola Outbreak Is Really Hard (January 5). or http://motherboard.vice.com/read/tracing-the-origin-of-the-ebola-outbreak-is-really-hard-2. Accessed 11 Apr 2015.

WHO. 2015. Origins of the 2014 Ebola Epidemic (January 2015). http://www.who.int/csr/disease/ebola/one-year-report/virus-origin/en/. Accessed 11 Apr 2015.

CHAPTER 11

Anthropology and the Nature-Society-Development Nexus

Laura Rival

INTRODUCTION

Now that the oxymoron (sustainable development) is decisively being let to blur into fuzziness (sustainability), anthropologists will have to pay attention, more than ever, to what has been elided (development). The economy that can continue forever is not developing in the same way or at the same rate or level as the economy that is asked to grow limitlessly; its nature has altered. Thinking anthropologically about human environmental relationships will thus remain incomplete, unless we provide an explanation of how people conceptualise nature and act in and in relation to it under current conditions of economic development and globalisation. Issues of knowledge and reasoning, as well as moral commitment and decision-making, have clearly emerged as unavoidable theoretical cornerstones for this work. It has also become clear that such an endeavour cannot be carried out from within the discipline of anthropology alone. With what other academic disciplines should anthropology carry out the project of documenting human environmental relationships from a nature, society and development perspective? This question raises the issue of knowledge co-creation,

L. Rival (✉)
Queen Elizabeth House, Oxford University, Oxford, UK

© The Author(s) 2017
M. Brightman, J. Lewis (eds.), *The Anthropology of Sustainability*,
Palgrave Studies in Anthropology of Sustainability,
DOI 10.1057/978-1-137-56636-2_11

familiar enough to those involved in 'action research.' What kinds of ethnographic collaboration will be recognised as ethically acceptable by those embarked on transition journeys towards 'sustainability'? Although neither of these two questions are novel, they take on new meanings (and have different implications) now that the very purpose of research seems to have shifted quite significantly. Not only are we to examine commitments to values that are deeply implicated in our common future, but we are also expected to work collectively at bridging different values and interests as we seek workable solutions to intractable and complex problems, not least because our research must demonstrate its 'impact.'

'Sustainability' has intensified the traffic of concepts, technical terms and metaphors between activism and science. Development keywords do not necessarily come from academia, but may end there, whether they have journeyed through policy cycles or not (Martinez-Alier et al. 2014). Whatever else it will do, the anthropology of sustainability will thus have to describe bureaucratic contexts, decode discourses, map ambiguities and contradictions, and assess claims. Jeffrey Sachs (2015), for instance, announces in his new book that: 'sustainable development (SD) is a central concept of our age. It is both a way of understanding the world and a method for solving global problems.'[1] Those among us who have followed the tribulations of SD over the last thirty years take note of the subtle changes in conceptualisation, meaning and intent, as well as the general evolution of aspirations, structures and process that Sachs' words imply. What makes 'development' (whether economic, social, human or sustainable) anthropologically so interesting is the fact that descriptions *of* are always also (and unashamedly so) prescriptions *for*. This allows us anthropologists to trace over time and map over space the constant traffic of concepts, technical terms and metaphors within and between expert networks, academic circles and mobilised actors. There is however something new in the discourse of sustainability underpinning the 'sustainable development goals.'[2] The call is no longer meant for governments and corporations alone; it mobilises every citizen. Each of us must stop behaving unsustainably; each of us must be the change we wish to see in the world.

Given that there are many collective ways of experiencing the world, the dynamic interface between natural environments and human societies is necessarily mediated by values, evaluations and judgements. Anthropological research is predicated on the dilemma of portraying the 'native point of view' without having necessarily to share it. This separation, however, becomes difficult to maintain when examining commitments to values that are deeply implicated in our common future. Difficult, but not impossible, as I shall try to demonstrate in this chapter. Anthropology can usefully contribute to the committed study of sustainable development if it renews its attention to the values, norms and principles marshalled by people as they act to make the world a better place. To research sustainability as a value, I start where an anthropological enquiry always starts, with an ethnography. I focus on a socio-ecological project in a popular neighbourhood of São Paulo, and follow a number of actors bent on living their lives sustainably. I discuss their determination to create positive change through professional actions and personal commitments, the difficulties they face, and some of the controversies arising from the decisions, choices, and course of actions they promote. These actors self-identify as agroecologists, and I show how sustainability comes to figure as a central value in this movement, which is widespread throughout Latin America. I conclude with a few general remarks aimed at guiding further research on and analysis of what I call, for lack of a better term, sustainability mobilisation.

A PROJECT TO COMBAT SOCIAL EXCLUSION ECOLOGICALLY

Projeto Arcadia[3] is an educational centre attended daily (after or before school) by 700 children age 5–15. Children take their meals at the centre, and can choose activities from a wide range of performing arts, computing courses and sports. The centre was created in the early 1990s by a group of artists and wealthy citizens in response to the plight of street children—so graphically depicted in films such as *Pixote* (1981). Projeto Arcadia is located in one of the newer and poorer neighbourhoods surrounding São Paulo on a site that was acquired in the early 1980s by a well-known architect with a view to develop it. Government regulations aimed at curtailing urban sprawl in the conservation areas that protect the city's water supplies were passed shortly after the acquisition. Faced with a stalled housing development, the architect accepted to make the thirty-hectare site available free of charge for the development of his friends' philanthropic project.

As an association dedicated to fighting social exclusion through a holistic vision of personal development, Projeto Arcadia is not dissimilar to other well-known Paulista alternative education programmes. The amount of land it controls is unique, though, and so is the abundance of aquifers and fragments of Mata Atlantica (native rainforest) it contains (see Fig. 11.1). In the thirty years or so Projeto Arcadia has been on the architect's land, it has

Fig. 11.1   Remnants of Mata Atlantica in Arcadia, by a creek

never used more than 10% of it, leaving the rest to informal (and often illegal) neighbourhood uses, such as the pursuit of recreational activities, cattle grazing or plant growing for medicinal and religious purposes. There have also been regular attempts to invade this land over the years. Each time, this privately held property has benefited from the intervention of government authorities. Shacks built overnight in haste have been systematically destroyed, and their occupants swiftly removed.

When I first visited the centre, about ten years ago, the calendar year was punctuated with popular events, especially the carnival parade in February. In addition, talent shows were organised periodically to bring the children attending Projeto Arcadia together with those attending privileged schools in richer neighbourhoods. The goals have broadly remained the same over the years, even if changes in personnel, board members, trustees, sources of funding and other factors have meant that education is increasingly being considered as a means to finding employment, rather than as a source of personal fulfilment. Offering a holistic education (regarded as the birth right of all children, regardless of their social or economic background) remains the primary goal of Projeto Arcadia's staff and volunteers. In recent years, however, a more 'business-like' view of cultural activities, with an emphasis on 'priority skills' has progressively replaced the ethos of beauty appreciation and the valorisation of artistic performance. Many literacy and numeracy classes today are offered by volunteers sourced through the social corporate responsibility programmes of large companies. Rugby and other sponsored sports events have gradually replaced the hubbub of *capoeira* classes, theatre performances, circus skills and carnival rehearsals. Whereas attempts at bringing an ecological outlook to the site gained prominence ten years ago, the issue of social housing has come back to the fore today.

To better understand the arguments of those involved at Projeto Arcadia who wish to combat social exclusion ecologically and those who tend to think that nature conservation is a matter for the rich, I present below the ethnographic portraits of two friends, Dill and Andrea, whose dream it has been to make the centre more 'ecological.' I then discuss a recent land invasion. The demands to build a social housing complex on the thirty-hectare site will leave little or no place for the agroecological activities initiated by Dill, Andrea and their supporters. I end with a visit I made with Dill to an ecopark some years ago to illustrate further the tensions between different versions of sustainability and ecology through which Saõ Paulo's urban fabric is being reconfigured today.

When I first met her, Andrea (an actress) was working full-time for Projeto Arcadia, while her friend Dill (a multi-media artist) only came to the centre occasionally. Dill's interest in ecology was at the time more developed than Andrea's. Dill, who liked running workshops and sharing her artistic skills, nourished the dream of opening an alternative environmental education centre in the western part of São Paulo state, which is still largely rural. She had herself taken tens of short training courses on a wide range of practical topics broadly relating to agroecology.[4] The knowledge and experience she had acquired by joining the agroecology movement percolated through her daily life and her artwork in many different ways. Practical and spiritual ecology had become a part and parcel of her personal identity and lifestyle. Agroecology to her was an *art de vivre*, which she liked sharing widely with those around her, from friends and neighbours to the children she taught.

Andrea's interest in ecology was partly triggered by the managing director of Projeto Arcadia, who decided one day to organise an agroecology course. The land had become a kind of commons criss-crossed with public paths, and the director was looking for new ways of using the 90% or more of the site's surface that were not supporting educational activities directly.

Several models of what to do with the land had been talked about over the years, including various forest conservation projects, as in one less frequented corner the forest had even grown back. Conversations with the director, members of the pedagogical team and trustees confirmed that alongside ecological awareness, a desire to explore a range of alternatives for the full use of the property (and by so doing lower its running costs while increasing its revenues) played a role in the decision to organise the course. Should the land be used for an eco-housing project that would provide accommodation for core staff and generate rent revenues? Should there be a kitchen garden to provide some of the food used in preparing the daily meals (at least 1200) served at Projeto Arcadia? Should the property be reforested as a plantation to produce valuable commercial timber in thirty years' time? Or should the regeneration of the Mata Atlantica be further encouraged and the site transformed in a botanical garden or an ecopark opened to the public?

When Andrea invited Dill to participate in the course, she was happy to go along, even if she knew most of what was to be taught. What appealed to her was the promise of new contacts (with their cohort of possibilities, encounters and chance opportunities) that a course always presents. Dill thus made use of the course very much as she had done in the past with other courses she had taken. It became an additional source of practical ideas to increase the presence and benefits of plants and animals in her immediate environment. She also looked at the course as a means to renew her artistic sensibilities. Some months after the completion of the course, she invited me to see the art projects that she had been inspired to design. In addition to beautiful objects made with clay and fabric, there were the plans of an interactive workshop built around the theme of rainwater storage. Dill had created this pedagogical exercise especially for a deprived primary school where educationalists from the University of São Paulo (USP) had initiated a community garden as part of their experiments in non-formal education. Having learnt rudimentary measurement techniques (quantities, volumes and ratios), as well as simple agroecological techniques, the school children researched climate reports and calculated average rainfall rates in their part of the city. With Dill's guidance, they started to think about roofs in terms of the total amount of rainwater that can be intercepted and stored. They focused their attention on the roof of a church adjacent to the school, as well as on various school buildings with large roofs. Paper models at various scales were created, as well as clay and wood models of rain catchment devices. When I last saw Dill during that year, she was hoping to create an art installation that would illustrate various agroecological techniques to irrigate the school garden.

Andrea's involvement with agroecology was more sudden, passionate and short-lived than Dill's. Unlike her friend, Andrea had grown and lived all her life in apartment blocks, with no garden. The agroecology course was designed to get a wide range of users to think about the site from different perspectives, all aimed at grasping the complementary needs and potentials of the many kinds of people, plants and animals living in and around it. For the first time in the eight years, she had worked at Projeto Arcadia, Andrea actually walked all over the site, both alone and with various groups of learners, each tasked with specific activities, such as looking for insects, finding wildlife, examining streams or tree species and more. I got the impression that the course gave coherence to what Andrea had picked up about agroecology from conversations with Dill and other friends. This may be the reason why it had such a deep impact on her. Through conversations, I came to realise that she was now thinking in terms of the site as a whole, while before she would refer mainly to what was taught in the classrooms that bordered the site's entrance. The course made another type of impression on Andrea; it taught her (the hard way as we shall see below) that wildlife had made itself at home on large stretches of the land. 'The wildlife has figured out that humans only use very specific parts of the site,' she told me one day, 'and well-trodden paths,' she added. One day, one of the agroecology instructors took Andrea's team downhill to a place where the site's complex topography could be apprehended readily, not very far behind the caretaker's house. By so doing, he had inadvertently disturbed a ground nest of feral Africanised honeybees.[5] The swarm viciously attacked the intruders, as well as the caretaker's dogs, who had followed the party. Andrea and three other learners had to be taken to hospital; two young dogs, stung to death, died during the night. A local beekeeper came in the morning to remove the nest, which he accommodated next to his beehives. When she came back to Projeto Arcadia a couple of days later, Andrea involved herself even more intensely with the course, asking many questions, reading avidly, and developing strong bonds with the instructors.

The course over, Andrea created a play with the children to whom she was teaching drama, as if moved to express through her trade—theatre—the stronger bond she had developed with the land. The play, which involved plants, healing and a number of agroecological themes, was performed and toured for several months, after which Andrea campaigned for the creation of a community garden at Projeto Arcadia. Having convinced at least some of the trustees and members of the management team of the propriety of her proposal, she obtained the right to spend 50% of her time on the development of this new line of activity. During the two years that followed, and with the full backing of the managing director and the active participation of a group of children and some parents, Andrea committed herself entirely to the budding community garden. She took courses in horticulture, seed savings, composting and rainwater harvesting, while building contacts with a number of conservation NGOs, with which she partnered to write funding applications. Thanks to donations and a small grant, tools, seeds and equipment (as well storage and drying facilities) soon filled the two classrooms earmarked for the garden project. Work parties were organised to build a rainwater tank and a nursery. One weekend, volunteers from a large Brazilian corporation joined project workers and parents to plant hundreds of fruit trees on the slope where Andrea had been stung by Africanised bees. With additional funding, a small lake was dug at the foot of the hill, below the orchard. Produce from the kitchen garden started to make their way into the daily meals served daily at Projeto Arcadia (Fig. 11.2).

Fig. 11.2   Meeting at Projeto Arcadia

Andrea's passion and success grew, but so did the opposition to the agroecology project. She had supporters (the children, staff, mothers, neighbours and board members involved in the gardening work), but not everyone was on her side. Tensions grew when it became clear that the agroecology project was not just an additional line of activity, but an entirely new way of looking at Projeto Arcadia's objectives, goals and overall purpose, as well as, and more critically, the future of the site as a whole. Conversations I have had with a range of protagonists highlight the divide between those who understood and embraced the concept of including nature conservation within the city's poor neighbourhoods, and those who saw this concept as antithetical to progress and social justice. The poor need affordable housing and education, I was told. Projeto Arcadia is a *projeto social* (a 'social project') people often added, implying that the land should be used to shelter people, not to conserve habitats or to grow food. As months passed, the dispute grew more personal; it now opposed Andrea directly to the architect who had once granted the land, and who was now slowly coming back on the scene. When the pro-agroecology managing director left for another job in the north of Brazil, and the architect was elected chair the Board of Trustees. Gradually, and through a process of organisational restructuration, he became increasingly involved in the day-to-day running of Projeto Arcadia. Clashes with Andrea multiplied, until she finally resigned. Resigning had been a very painful decision, she told me a few years later. Her emotional and professional investment in Projeto Arcadia's community garden had been such that she had found it difficult to work elsewhere. For months, she tried to involve herself in various social and/or conservation projects around São Paulo, but she could no longer muster the same level of commitment. Depressed and unemployed, she decided to resume her career as an actress instead. The last time I met Andrea, she was happily married with a baby. She works today for a leading national organisation that offers a wide range of cultural and educational activities based on strong ideals of social progress. She no longer has time for agroecology.

Dill does not see Andrea very often these days. She too has had a series of disappointments with her agroecological projects. The lay and clerical personnel in charge of the church and the primary school where she had hoped to create the art installation were not impressed with the children's models of rainwater catchment techniques. As for the idea of using the church roof to collect rainwater, it was, to them, simply preposterous; spending money on it was out of the question. Dill has since gone back to making art objects for individual clients. Their orders have a spiritual or a personal dimension that leave little place for her agroecological dreams and inspirations. Her life also has changed. Now a grandmother, she often travels long distances across São Paulo to help her son or her daughter with childcare. She has therefore less time to look after street cats or rescued dogs; even the worms in her wormery have suffered from erratic feeds. She has also decided to give up her garden allotment, which went to a close friend with more time on her hands. One day, she hopes, when her grandchildren are older, she will go with them to a piece of land she timeshares in the countryside. 'The state of São Paulo is extensive; many parts are still rural,' she tells me. 'Crossing the giant metropolis to reach the countryside takes so long, though, especially at the weekend.' Moreover, Dill loves the city, and cannot envisage moving to the countryside permanently; she'd feel too isolated. Agroecology has increasingly become for her a set of aspirations and spiritual values that nourish her inner life and orientate her aesthetic appreciation of both urban and rural landscapes. Circumstances, opportunities, and situations she feels she has little control over constrain Dill's agroecological applications and techniques. Given her current priorities (to make a living as an artist and to care for her family), she has had to put on hold practical and material realisations.

After Andrea's departure, the community garden lost much of its impulse. The two classrooms reverted to literacy and numeracy activities, and the remaining tools and equipment were shifted to the greenhouse. During my latest visit (Summer 2015), I saw no plant or seedling in the greenhouse, which had become a kind of storage space. The downsized garden area had been fenced off. Weeds had taken over, except for a bed or two that kitchen staff still cultivated. More dramatically, the orchard and the fragments of Mata Atlantica had entirely disappeared under a sea of undulating iron. Projeto Arcadia had been invaded two summers earlier by 1200 families 'without roofs.'[6]

This land invasion caused much commotion and disarray among staff, management, children, parents, neighbours and supporters of the project alike. People I spoke with described to me how well organised and politically determined the invaders were. They had arrived one night by car, setting the camp in less than a day, connecting the shacks hastily built to the electrical grid and to water supplies, drilling holes for toilets and opening roads. Two years on, I could observe many solar panels on the roofs, as well as hyperbolic TV antennas. There have been five other land invasions in the locality since, all in conservation areas 'protected' through government legislation. Legally speaking, the invasion of Projeto Arcadia is of a different order, given that the charity privately owns the land. However, in the minds of many,[7] Projeto Arcadia legitimately owns only the part used for educational activities; the rest of the property is considered to have been left idle and empty, including the orchard and the fragments of Mata Atlantica.[8] The board of trustees could have used the force of the law to expel the invaders (as it did many times previously), but given Projeto Arcadia's social aims and the size of the invasion (and the leaders' determination), the decision was taken to offer political support to the families demanding 'decent social homes for the poor.' Under the architect's leadership, therefore, the trustees have fostered peaceful dialogue between the invaders and the government, and facilitated a series of mediation, hoping for the speedy delivery of the 'Minha Casa Minha Vida' (My House, My Life) project. The plan agreed so far is to divide the property in various parts. Projeto Arcadia would only retain the land it already occupies for its educational and cultural activities, and sell back to the government the land needed to create a social housing park, a commercial centre and a primary school complex. The status of the remaining area (and whether it will be used for nature conservation) is still under discussion.

AGROECOLOGY PROJECTS AS WORLDS

How one goes about combatting social exclusion in a megalopolis like São Paulo? For Dill and Andrea, agroecology was part of the solution—at least for a while, until the obstacles they faced multiplied, thwarting their efforts and those of the children, parents and co-workers with whom they had started developing a community concretely rooted in its natural environment. As their story illustrates, the paths agroecological projects tread are full of difficulties and uncertainties; not many evolve into resilient worlds.

In continuation, I focus on three particular land practices (provisionally called cultivating, sheltering and rewilding) to shed light on Andrea's and Dill's ecological vision of world making and on the obstacles they have faced. I discuss these land practices in relation to three related stories: (1) a visit with Dill to an ecopark located at a walking distance from her home in the Pinheiros district of São Paulo; (2) the recommendations made for the social housing project to be developed on the Projeto Arcadia site by one of the instructors of the agroecological course mentioned earlier; and (3) an agroecological encampment at the Cúpula dos Povos during the Rio+20 summit.[9]

CULTIVATING THE LAND

All agroecologists see cultivation as the most basic (in the sense of the most fundamental) relationship humans may develop with the places they choose to occupy. Cultivating the land means working together to produce the nutrients that feed a community, as well as the surpluses that widen a community's exchanges, activities and partnerships. In the context of Projeto Arcadia, cultivating also meant reviving people's knowledge of the land with its complex webs of ecological interactions, while ensuring both the spread of this knowledge throughout the entire neighbourhood, and its transmission to the children attending the centre. To cultivate thus also meant strengthening already existing peasant and folk land uses, for instance, pasturing cows and growing medicinal herbs and magical plants.

The ecopark Dill brought me to visit and to photograph one afternoon 'is not about cultivation,' she remarked as we passed the gate. 'It is beautiful, but it has no soul,' she added (Fig. 11.3).

Fig. 11.3 The neat beds of Pinheiros' EcoPark

Fig. 11.3 (continued)

Look at the neat rows of salads, carrots and other vegetables. They are to be relished visually, not to be turned into food. I have asked employees about these vegetables. No one knows. It does not matter whether they are eaten or not; they are part of the design. They are grown for their colours, their patterns, and their appearance. Can you feel how deserted this place is? I get intimidated when I come here. Let's go to the art centre now. You can create your "trash art" with brand new products (i. e. not recycled). What about that?

Dill laughed at the absurdity of turning agroecology into an aesthetics for urbanites. Having walked straight to the ecopark from her house made me realise the extent to which the latter had become a cohesive world. Even if small, rented and surrounded by high-rises that threatened to march on and close in, Dill's house beat at the rhythm of her cultivating skills. Her minuscule garden was full of edible plants, as well as soil making and rainwater collection devices. Humans, cats, dogs, ants, plants, banana stalks, objects, seeds, seedlings, songs, worms, spirits and more all seemed to form part of a giant organism that opened and closed to the outside world in tune with the house's inner life. The art project she was working on at the time, entitled 'Life's Fabric,' captured the house's pulse perfectly.

Cultivation reskills, boosts resilience and self-reliance, and enhances the confidence of individuals and communities. Cultivation can happen at any scale, large or small, depending on the size of the community that cultivates. With the site now squatted by a social movement pressuring the government to build more social housing, new cultivation ideas are emerging. As the site is so densely settled at present, it is no longer practical to develop extensive food-growing areas within Projeto Arcadia. The vast orchard having been destroyed and the extensive community garden largely abandoned, there are talks of cropping on building roofs. One adviser to the project has suggested that 'Minha Casa Minha Vida' blocks of flat could be equipped with micro-scale structures that would support individual or collective gardening. A multitude of small businesses supported by financial incentives could be created for growing fresh food to be sold in the commercial centre, which could become a hub for new ideas and practices. This would help create new, diversified income streams in an area where unemployment is high. Roberto (one of the agroecological instructors) has even talked of partnering the new social housing complex with a not too distant agroecological farm. This would reconnect people with food supplies in many ways, as well as ensure the supply of fresh products that are essential for people's health. Various 'community supported agriculture' schemes could be developed, including arrangements allowing for social housing recipients and their children to escape from the city and spend some time on the farm in the countryside. Cultivation, in short, blurs the entrenched divides between rural and urban areas, and opens up new ways of thinking about the land and using it through living on it.

SHELTERING WITH NATURE

Dill invested more of her energy, time and agroecological creativity in her home than Andrea did. I have not discussed this with them, and do not know for sure whether this fact represents a difference in temperament, or circumstances.

An agroecological approach to sheltering reveals a primary concern with ecological functions. A roof, for instance, is seen first and foremost as an opportunity to collect rainwater to be used as a source of water for drinking and washing as much as to irrigate a garden. A window functions to let sunlight in, but also to modulate heat penetration and retention. Communal living arrangements are preferred over single habitation. Dill has always shared her house with housemates, even before she divorced and before her children left the nest. To recreate an ecologically functional and meaningful world, agroecologists also try to live where they work or to develop their projects where they live. One of the difficulties Andrea faced in Projeto Arcadia when she was developing the community garden is that her flat was two hours away from it, a fact partly reflecting the deep inequalities that structure São Paulo's urban fabric.[10] It is in the neighbourhoods around Projeto Arcadia though that Andrea found many of the architectural ideas that she hoped to introduce in the community garden. As already mentioned, agroecology is rooted in popular wisdom, peasant resourcefulness and folk ecological knowledge.

Neighbourhoods such as the ones that surround Projeto Arcadia are neither rural nor urban; self-made buildings cluster among fields, orchards or fragments of Mata Atlantica. The developing infrastructure seems to offer the promise that the government has now decided to treat these neighbourhoods as an acceptable extension of the city. If the concrete houses look built for permanence, their inhabitants continue to live transient lives, moving in and out according to work opportunities and the state of their relationships. Although less transient and impermanent than the agroecological camp at Rio+20,[11] the camp set up by the families who invaded Projeto Arcadia in the summer of 2013 shares more traits with it than with the social housing complex by which it will be replaced one day.[12] The planned housing park of cheap, minimal and unimaginative concrete blocks could not be further away from agroecological sheltering principles. Yet, activists have tried to lobby the architect and the construction firm to improve the design. To them, design challenges for housing, school buildings and commercial buildings are structurally similar. In all cases, the idea is to harmonise the lives of humans with plant life, solar cycles, and water cycles. Housing can be designed ecologically to enhance the quality of life of all. These activists have tried to convince the architect to attend to priority alterations that would accommodate, among others, rainwater catchment systems, grey water recycling and ecological waste management. There was also talk of creating biological niches and offer bio-remediation through multiple uses of plants. During my last visit, as the activists were getting nowhere with their recommendations, they tried to convince the construction company at least to ear-mark one building as a prototype to demonstrate the validity of agroecological principles for the social housing sector. Simple and cheap proposals for retrofitting were also made, as a means to influence the companies involved in delivering low-cost housing for the public sector.

I wish I could have listened to more conversations between invaders, local authorities, local dwellers, architects, building companies and activists. Projeto Arcadia had reached a critical point of its existence; land use and purpose were being fundamentally redefined in the midst of a national political crisis. Although much more ethnographic research is needed to fully grasp the meanings, values, and moral framings at work in the unfolding of this popular urban development, enough has been presented, I hope, to illustrate that sheltering with nature faces challenges and difficulties of a higher—one may wish to add structural, order. The realities that are being disturbed by agroecological activists (homelessness, encampment, transience, mobility, sedentariness, housing markets, planning regulations or speculation) clearly show that what is in the making in marginal zones of social exclusions such as the site occupied by Projeto Arcadia is a new vision of human habitation on earth.

INVITING WILDERNESS BACK

As readers will remember, Andrea's commitment to transforming Projeto Arcadia into an agroecological project grew in the aftermath of a traumatic encounter with stinging Africanised bees.[13] Like her, many of the staff, parents and children who took the course were astonished to find wildlife in the remnants of rain forest scattered in the lower part of the site, especially along the creek that runs at the bottom. To the conservation NGOs and the government authorities with which Andrea tried to partner, these rain forest patches were as many visible signs of the disappearing ecosystem, which the state and the prefecture of São Paulo are legally bound to protect. Ironically, the laws that restrict housing development allowed Projeto Arcadia to be created in the first place.[14] Ironically as well, it is the conservation of the last unspoilt (and miraculously surviving) areas of Mata Atlantica long considered to be a priority, which has framed protection efforts until today. Being located in the upper reaches of the watershed on which São Paulo's drinkable water depends, the conservation of such areas was also justified according to links established scientifically between forest cover and water supplies. Andrea and the agroecologists who were helping her did not contest this language of pristine rainforest conservation, but instead insisted on the need to supplement ecological restoration efforts with agroforestry activities, stressing, in other words, the positive complementarity between cultivation and forest protection. In so doing, they insisted on the compatibility between human access and the maintenance of biological diversity.

Having first come to Projeto Arcadia straight from the Amazon region, I was struck by the commonalities of arguments being used in favour of biodiversity enrichment and community conservation initiatives. The species that make the Mata Atlantica differ from those present in the Amazon rainforest, but the ecological structures share much in common, and I could readily see that the forest fragments in Projeto Arcadia were healthy and thriving, devoid from alien species, viral invasions or deadly pathogens. As in so many parts of the world, these fragmented ecosystems seemed to recover best when left alone. It was of course surprising that no one had disturbed these patches gone feral. I heard stories of murdered corpses being dumped in their depths. It could be that such haunting presence deterred people from entering. The whys and hows of people's apparent disinterest in Projeto Arcadia's forest remnants can be established only through further research. In the Amazon region, where the demographic collapse that took place in the sixteenth and seventeenth centuries significantly complexified a long and slow history of forest anthropogenisation, what westerners take for pristine wilderness is more often than not the result of abandonment.[15] In this part of the Mata Atlantica, it suddenly occurred to me, faunal and floral species have found refuge in forest fragments out of neglect rather than abandonment. Of course, it is possible that with the 2013 land invasion some of these fragments will have disappeared forever, but it is also possible that some of them, perhaps because of their impractical location, have continued to survive undisturbed.

So what processes of land recovery and disturbance have unfolded here? One may take a historical–ecological view of these forest fragments as the material bearers and physical retainers of human activity, and, in so doing, think about these fragments as the products of the irreversible passage of time. By reflecting upon the multiplicity of times they embody, one comes to see that the future of these forest patches does not entirely depend on an emerging consciousness about humanity's fundamental dependence on non-humans (see Tsing's chapter). Rather, their future is irremediably linked to the ways in which they are being conceptualised and fought over. The agroecologists who planted an orchard at the interface between the forest patches and the community garden aimed at promoting a new form of intervention. By implementing a number of agroforestry techniques, they sought to weave seamlessly the cultivated and the non-cultivated, while allowing parts of nature to exist beyond direct human control, with a view that no matter how small a piece of land, some parts must be 'left alone.' By treating the forest as a place in need of recovery, they thus encouraged a different form of neglect, while blurring distinctions between intervention and non-intervention.

These forest patches have remained a headache for the architect and the designers of the social housing complex. While they would like to use the 'without roof' invasion as an excuse to increase the overall surface dedicated to human occupation, the conservation laws that prevented the urban development are still in force, and still need to be abided by. Several conversations with the architect have made me realise that the tension between urban development and forest conservation is caused by unexamined ideas linking the poor, the rich, housing and space for the forest. Neither the architect nor anyone else working on the social housing complex seems to be able to approach forest conservation as non-intervention, or even better, *neglect.*

The parts that are not built over are thought of as requiring even more control and surveillance—hence costly resources, than the built ones. Whether a botanical garden, a green commons, an ecopark, or an educational reforestation project, the conservation area will need to be created, maintained, and guarded against encroachments. The government imposes conservation laws, I was told, but does not allocate credits to implement them. This is the bone of contention. Who owns, and who is responsible for 'green areas'? No one knows for certain. No public authority or private actor is willing to assume the cost or the responsibility of protecting the natural environment. 'This is why we have a headache on our hands' I was told. Pushing the discussion further, though, I quickly realised that the main difficulty lay in defining the location and the boundaries of the conservation area; the problem was not simply one of financing it. For many of the well-to-do decision makers involved, the poor were either undeserving of a conservation area, or unfit for it. Philanthropy concerned the facilitation of state-provided social housing. 'These people need homes, not green spaces' I was told, before being informed of all the risks of vandalism and the costs of security and maintenance.

I did not have the opportunity to discuss these issues with the families sending their children to Projeto Arcadia, or with the families that invaded the site, for that matter. It is quite probable that they share the view that the poor need housing, not green spaces, especially given their demand for 1500 housing units, and the fact that the local authorities are prepared to grant them no more than 350. It is quite possible that they would see the forest patches as unnecessary luxury. After all, one of the most striking differences in São Paulo between a poor and a well-to-do neighbourhood is the number of trees that line the latter, and the absence of greenery in the former.

There seems to be a shared view of nature as a burden or a liability, as something socially and economically unproductive, a luxury that only the rich can afford or appreciate. In such a perspective, the ecopark in Dill's neighbourhood is not in any way out of place. Its manicured grounds and its museum-like collections of plants perfectly illustrate for the city dweller what ecological functions have been, and, perhaps one day, were. Projeto Arcadia's agroecological vision, on the other hand, held the promise of an entirely different interaction between people and their natural surroundings, one inspired by the extractive reserve model found in parts of the Brazilian Amazon (e.g. Ruiz Murrieta and Pinzón Rueda 1995).[16] Whereas in the ecopark, trees and other plants are neatly aligned as in any colonial plantation (the resulting grid effect being an intrinsic feature of the aesthetic effect sought after), the Projeto Arcadia's short-lived agroforestry experiments offered the promise of a world inhabited according to close observation of ecological processes, a world where people eventually become indigenous to a place (Rival 2009). There is no space here to explore the reasons why agroecology is so closely related to social forestry and conservation programmes in Brazil. Agroecology's subversion of the idea that nature is best conserved as a collection of unproductive places made to be toured by visitors in search of leisure is in any case part of the explanation. If it is the presence or not of nature that materialises the separation of poor and rich neighbourhoods in São Paulo, it is the recognition or not of the value of human labour that differentiates extractive reserves and other conservation areas in the Amazon region (Rival 2012).

Conclusion

By following the tribulations of a socio-ecological project at the periphery of one of the world's megalopolises, São Paulo, I was able to investigate the circumstances under which actors involved in such projects mesh together the 'environmental' and the 'social' with the aspiration of creating meaningful worlds. In this chapter, I have explored ethnographically some of the ways in which people transform dynamic interactions with ecological opportunities and historical constraints into choices and values. As I have endeavoured to show, if such interactions are without a doubt embedded within sensory and investigatory experiences, they are also framed by enduring discourses on nature, society and development, which often thwart individual and collective attempts to break away from dominant forms of world inhabitation.

The nature/culture dualism has thrown contemporary anthropological theory in a crisis state (Rival 2014). While the material world in which we live is heading for an ecological crisis of global proportion, our leading conceptual frameworks deal with imagined worlds that have no reference to the land we walk on (see Gregory 2005).[17] The way out of this problem is not simply to reassert the merits of a materialist approach against radical virtualism, but, rather, to reconnect the imagined worlds of our subjects (including fellow anthropologists) to the material conditions that give rise to them. As the ethnography presented here illustrates, modes of adaptation are grounded in imagined worlds, which emerge through close observation of ecological processes and inevitably lead to processes of indigenisation. Such knowledge systems do not disappear overnight, nor do they remain unchanged; rather, they evolve historically, through frictions and clashes with the homogenising forces of capitalist trade. Moreover, the processes of indigenisation brought about by globalisation and commodification transform traditional environmental knowledge in unpredictable ways.

After fifteen years of existence as an 'art against social exclusion' project, Projeto Arcadia was re-planned to grant new values to its land base. Staff, parents and children learnt to see that the forest was growing back amidst the trash on parts of the site. Looked at by some as a whole, the site appeared to offer new socio-ecological possibilities. Gardens were cultivated, trees planted and a lake dug. The agroecological practices I have briefly evoked in this chapter illustrate the ways in which life and matter come to form an integral part of human social worlds that no longer set nature apart from technology. Agroecologists give shape to lived landscapes by inserting a multitude of ecological relations within social dynamics, thus redrawing the boundaries between living kinds and artefacts. Not everyone, however, chose to look at Projeto Arcadia through an agroecological lens. Instead of seeing the site as a whole-world-in-the-making, some members focused on the growing real-estate value of the property, and, when Brazil's social housing politics heated up, divisions grew more entrenched. Whereas some still defended that 'more ecology in the economy is what we need to create a sustainable world,' others firmly defended the view that Brazil's poor need 'more social progress,' not 'more ecology.'

The ethnographic portraits I have presented in this chapter reveal the extent to which agroecology draws on forms of indigenous intelligence that offer people practical ways of assembling worlds at different scales, and through which new ways of relating ecological and social possibilities may be learnt. I have stressed that world making through agroecology relates primarily to an ability to see and articulate 'the whole,' that is, a whole from which one's natural surroundings are not excluded. Sustainability is mobilised in this context as a core value to articulate the whole and to change the world for the better. This preliminary analysis can do no more than outline the contours of the value system underpinning the political nature of sustainability mobilisation. It has, nevertheless, shed some light on the dynamics of political friction. More specifically, we are now in a better position to understand why whole-world-making projects may trigger political disputes involving tensions over forms of 'disrelations' between humans and non-humans. Politics, therefore, needs to be rethought in terms wider than simple disagreements about modes of relationality or modes of emplacement.

NOTES

1. 'As an intellectual pursuit,' he continues, 'sustainable development (SD) tries to make sense of the interactions of three complex systems: the world economy, the global society, and earth's physical environment,' before adding that: 'SD is also a normative outlook on the world, meaning that it recommends a set of goals to which the world should aspire.' 'The sustainable development goals (SDGs) will guide the world's economic diplomacy in the coming generation' (Sachs 2015: 12).
2. The United Nations General Assembly decided in September 2014 that the report produced by the Open Working Group on Sustainable Development Goals (after two years of deliberation) would form the basis for integrating

the SDGs in the post-2015 development agenda. The SDG list can be found at https://sustainabledevelopment.un.org/ accessed on 29/12/2015.

3. All the names used in this chapter are pseudonyms.

4. Agroecology is at once a science, a set of practices and a movement (Wezel et al. 2009; Altieri and Toledo 2011). Agroecological studies began in the late 1920s as the study of how crops interact with their ecosystems, before expanding in scope in the 1980s in response to the limitations of the Green Revolution. While the fusion of these three dimensions of agroecology is especially prevalent in Latin America, agroecology as a grassroots movement is very active in the south of Brazil.

5. *Apis mellifera scutellata* Lepeletier. Africanized bees, which are common in Brazil, are more dangerous to humans than normal bees (see http://entnemdept.ufl.edu/creatures/misc/bees/ahb.htm).

6. See   http://juntos.org.br/2013/12/juntos-na-luta-com-a-ocupacao-Arcadia/, accessed on 12 July 2015. The Movimento dos Trabalhadores Sem Teto (MTST, in English, Movement of Workers Without a Roof) has been very active throughout the country, but especially in São Paulo and Rio de Janeiro under the presidency of Dilma Rousseff, who created a vast social housing programme called 'Minha Casa Minha Vida' (my house, my life). See the MTST website at www.mtst.org and Rousseff's housing programme at http://www.brasil.gov.br/governo/2015/08/voz-do-brasil-dilma-rousseff-entrega-residencias-do-minha-casa-minha-vida-no-ceara

7. Locals do not consider themselves to be different from invaders, given that this neighbourhood of the southern periphery of São Paulo was created through the same process of land invasion in the 1970s and the 1980s.

8. People in interviews referred to 'um terreno baldio' (an empty, idle land). More research is needed on popular and administrative representations of land use and land conservation.

9. Cúpula dos Povos refers to the parallel event entitled 'Peoples Summit for Social and Environmental Justice in Defence of the Commons' which took place during the United Nations Conference on Sustainable Development in Rio de Janeiro in June 2012. See http://rio20.net/en/, accessed on 2 October 2015.

10. The 'non-agroecological' nature of the ecopark I visited with Dill has a lot to do with the fact that it is a park; people do not live in it, or depend on this land for food or shelter. It is a place earmarked for urban strolling and visual appreciation. Moreover, it is located in a neighbourhood undergoing drastic renovation, where modest family houses with gardens are being replaced with expensive multi-storey office blocs. The ecopark is now the only bit of 'nature' present in a very dense urban patch.

11. It took me a while to notice the agroecologists' presence on a patch of grass behind the Bank of Brazil Foundation's exhibition booth. What caught my

eye at first is a recycled art sculpture in the shape of a tree that was being assembled day by day. Like this tree, grown bit by bit, the encampment was taking shape slowly. The installation would have grown more visible, had the agroecologists been allowed to stay overnight; but their display was diurnal. Each day upon arrival, they would open the bundles of blankets and sheets they had left on the ground. Children were playing as they helped unpack the bundles. There were sacks of seeds and produce from their farms, which were sold at low cost. The materials needed for the art installation were heaped in a corner. Simple tools and devices were set up for passers-by to try out. On a large blanket in the middle, a group sat cooking and eating while conversing. Later on in the day, two young men came to the edge of the sidewalk, barefoot, their hands full of *Physalis peruviana* seeds, urging passers-by to get some. The weed's nutritional and medicinal properties were vaunted. More, there was no need to plant *Physalis peruviana*; it was enough to throw the seeds gently in the air above a patch of soil. I bought a bottle of perfume from a young man, and a video telling the story of the farm on which he lived; he had made both.

12. The bank in charge of the loan system has agreed to endorse the project, and a construction company has already signed the contract. The construction should thus have started in January 2016, but all these measures had been taken before the worsening of Brazil's political crisis during the summer of 2015. Of the 1500 flats to be built on the site of Projeto Arcadia, less than 300 will be allocated to the invaders, who will not be allowed to decide and choose whom among them will be allocated a flat in the complex. Moreover, the land will have to be fully vacated for the building work to commence.

13. (see above, page 198).

14. (see above, page 198).

15. Long seen as emblematic examples of pristine wilderness, Amazonia's forests are understood today as resilient and evolving legacies of both nature and culture. See Balée (2013) and Rival (2016).

16. In extractive reserves, biological diversity depends on the productive protection afforded by a certain type of anthropogenisation through agroforestry. Like in the areas cultivated by native Amazonians (see chapter by Manuela Carneiro da Cunha), biological diversity varies in correlation with cultural diversity.

17. For Gregory (2005), these processes are accessible only by theoretically informed fieldwork. Anthropologists must thus continue to historicise their central concepts from the perspective of the contemporary global disjuncture in which we all live (Gregory 2005).

REFERENCES

Altieri, M., and V.M. Toledo. 2011. The Agroecological Revolution in Latin America: Rescuing Nature, Ensuring Food Sovereignty and Empowering Peasants. *The Journal of Peasant Studies* 38 (3): 587–612.

Balée, W. 2013. *Cultural Forests of the Amazon. A Historical Ecology of People and Their Landscapes*. Tuscaloosa: University of Alabama Press.

Gregory, C. 2005. *Adaptation, Commodification and Sustainability: Lessons from Monsoon Asia*. Conference Paper Presented at the Conference Ecological Threats and New Promises of Sustainability for the 21st Century, University of Oxford, July 3–5.

Martinez-Alier, J., I. Anguelovski, P. Bond, et al. 2014. Between Activism and Science: Grassroots Concepts for Sustainability Coined by Environmental Justice Organizations. *Journal of Political Ecology* 21: 19–60.

Rival, L. 2009. The Resilience of Indigenous Intelligence. In *The Question of Resilience. Social Responses to Climate Change*, ed. K. Hastrup, 293–313. Copenhagen: The Royal Danish Academy of Sciences and Letters.

———. 2012. *Sustainable Development Through Policy Integration in Latin America: A Comparative Approach*. UNRISD, Occasional Paper Seven, Social Dimensions of Green Economy and Sustainable Development. April. ISBN 978-9-29-085087-8.

———. 2014. Encountering Nature Through Fieldwork Experiments: Indigenous Knowledge, Local Creativity and Modes of Reasoning. *Journal of the Royal Anthropological Institute (JRAI)* 20 (2): 218–236.

———. 2016. *Huaorani Transformations in 21st Century Ecuador*. Tucson: University of Arizona Press.

Ruiz Murrieta, M., and R. Pinzón Rueda, eds. 1995. *Extractive Reserves*. Gland: IUCN.

Sachs, J. 2015. *The Age of Sustainable Development*. New York: Columbia University Press.

Wezel, A., S. Bellon, T. Doré, C. Francis, D. Vallod, and C. David. 2009. Agroecology as a Science, a Movement and a Practice: A Review. *Agronomy for Sustainable Development* 29: 503–515.

CHAPTER 12

The Gaia Complex: Ethical Challenges to an Anthropocentric 'Common Future'

Veronica Strang

INTRODUCTION

If there is a core issue for an anthropology of sustainability to tackle, it is perhaps the major, though often elided, contradiction between the stated aims of current environmental management (sustainability) and the dominant ideas and values that actually direct human–environmental relations (development). Illich has suggested that these are fundamentally contradictory, and as long as notions of development and growth are conflated and biophysical limits are ignored, this is clearly the case. Highlighting the Promethean hubris of transgressing 'the boundaries of the human condition', he observes that 'sustainable' is the language of balance and limits, and 'development' is the language of the expectation of more. 'Now Everyman has become Prometheus and Nemesis has become endemic; it is the backlash of progress. We are hostage to a lifestyle that provokes doom' (1999: 14).

There is a similar internal contradiction between hand-wringing over species extinctions and assumptions about human dominion. At a

---

V. Strang (✉)
Institute of Advanced Study, Durham University, Durham, UK

Department of Anthropology, Durham University, Durham, UK

© The Author(s) 2017
M. Brightman, J. Lewis (eds.), *The Anthropology of Sustainability*,
Palgrave Studies in Anthropology of Sustainability,
DOI 10.1057/978-1-137-56636-2_12

fundamental level—despite multiple critiques from anthropologists, ethicists, indigenous communities, feminists, environmental countermovements etc.—dominant discourses continue to position humankind as separate from and superior to the non-human, and thus to confer upon them rights to own, control and make use of non-human species and things in accord with human interests. This underlying assumption has become so entrenched as to be normalised and continues to drive ultimately unsustainable practices (Descola and Palsson 1996; Escobar 1999; Ingold and Palsson 2013).

An intrinsically managerial perspective appears to have become more intractably embedded in the last century or so, as burgeoning confidence in human instrumentalism has grown alongside technological advances. In coining the phrase 'The Anthropocene', Crutzen and Stoermer (2000) suggest that the industrial revolution and the invention of the steam engine were key turning points. There are other likely factors: the rapid technological advances initiated by two world wars in this century have clearly played a role, as has the extreme vision of free-market competition globalised in the 1980s. A related and critical factor has been the emergence of multi-national corporations and their capacities to undermine and/or replace the more collective governance of the State (Strang 2011, 2016a).[1] But instrumentalism has much deeper historical roots (Plumwood 1993, 2002; Strang 2014a) most particularly in societies that have taken particular developmental tangents, so it may be more useful to recognise this as a continuous (and accelerating) process with significant cumulative effects.[2]

The decades leading into the 1980s brought greater recognition that increasingly intensive instrumentalism has created a range of problems not only for less powerful human groups, but also for non-human species and the material environment. When such anxieties about sustainability and ecological well-being began to coalesce, *The Brundtland Report – Our Common Future*, published in 1987, initiated a major international conversation about 'sustainability'. At the time, when I was asked to help write the Canadian contribution to the report, this seemed promising. Humankind would, collectively, invent a way forward that would save the planet and all of its inhabitants, and ensure social and ecological justice for all. Thus, the *Report* attempted to establish a vision of 'sustainable development' in which humankind would continue to 'progress' while simultaneously finding ways of engaging with non-humans and material systems that would not destroy these, allowing them, instead, to replenish themselves at a rate similar to or even faster than the speed at which societies were making use of them.

To some extent, this simple definition of sustainability, as a balance of use and material reproduction, has proved to be quite robust. As I have noted elsewhere, sustainability remains an ineluctably material matter, dependent upon the extent to which the material flows required by all species and environments are maintained sufficiently to sustain their well-being over time, rather than being redirected into purely human purposes/processes of consumption (Strang 2014b). However, although a principle of distributive justice is potentially implicit in the sharing of resources equitably among species (Baxter 2005; Chen et al. 2013), the *Brundtland Report* was more self-interested in its intent, arguing from a primarily Euro-American policy perspective that maintaining uncompromised ecosystems is a practical necessity in ensuring human well-being (see Dobson 1998 and Signe Howell, Chap. 8).

A Disappearing Other World

Since *The Brundtland Report* was published, the realities of a primary focus on human interests have become more apparent, as market-based, growth-based economies have intensified resource use around the world, externalising the costs to non-human species and environments. The result has been the emergence of an anthropogenic mass extinction event, in which a 'normal' rate of species extinction has spiked at a speed previously matched only by massive global catastrophes. In the last 500 years, but most particularly in the last half-century, thousands of species have been pushed into oblivion, and the International Union for the Conservation of Nature (IUCN) predicts an even more accelerated rate of disappearance on the immediate horizon (Caldararo 2004; Diamond 2005; IUCN 2015; Kopnina and Shoreman-Ouimet 2015; Strang 2016b) (Fig. 12.1).

While major attention has been drawn to the overarching problem of climate change, most of these extinctions—and climate change itself—are more immediately due to ongoing habitat destruction, as human societies redirect freshwater into irrigation; consume fish stocks; destroy forests and wetlands; and extend the land areas cleared, drained and used for agricultural and other purposes. Of course non-human species have not been the only casualties: as anthropologists are keenly aware, many small, or less powerful, human communities have also absorbed the costs of 'developments' geared towards the interests of more powerful groups.

Fig. 12.1   Seal pup, New Zealand

Obviously there are many factors that have led to such unsustainable practices, but one of the most central of these is a widespread inability to detach from progressive notions of development the idea that this requires continual growth. These concepts are not necessarily conflated: it is theoretically feasible to have concepts of development based entirely on other criteria. For example, some of us might consider that real development would be to achieve the wider adoption of more civilised and collaborative practices between human groups, and between humankind and other species. A pretty thought. But Western societies have, at this stage, so thoroughly globalised capitalist ideologies of growth that it is now extremely difficult for alternative ideas, such as those promoting 'Degrowth Economics', to get a hearing at all. Thus, the extent to which the Barcelona Declaration on Degrowth in 2010[3] has entered mainstream debates is very limited. And, similarly, the 'pluriverse' of alternate lifeways described by ethnographers around the world which, as Escobar (1999) observes can provide exemplary models of sustainability, are simultaneously ignored and overridden (Fig. 12.2).

Fig. 12.2 Guadiana dam, Portugal

A second key factor is the ingrained assumption that humankind has, by right, directive control of the world. In the same year that *The Brundtland Report* was published, James Lovelock's book *Gaia: A new look at life on earth* was re-issued, having first been published in 1979. Although it built on earlier ideas—in particular Vladimir Vernadsky's work in the 1920s, which introduced the notion of the Earth as a whole biosphere—Lovelock's ideas achieved prominence in conjunction with *The Brundtland Report* because they promoted a psychologically positive whole-system vision of the Earth as a living being: the goddess Gaia. At a time when anxieties about humankind's alienation from nature were rising, this vision of reunion with Gaia's motherly embrace was especially appealing.

Such an integrative view, as Bruno Latour points out (2015), challenges an assumed nature–culture divide and foregrounds the power of nature. However, I would argue that Lovelock's purportedly integrative notion of Gaia was not only anthropomorphic, but problematically anthropocentric. While it acknowledged the role of all living organisms in regulating the planetary 'system', it implied that with the advantage of reflexive consciousness and intentionality humans had an agentive lead. Giving a lecture in

Oxford a few years later, Lovelock referred to humankind as the 'brains of the planet'. While he was dubious about our capacity to provide 'responsible stewardship' of Gaia,[4] this served to entrench a broader prevailing idea that, as the 'head', as the conscious mind/ego of this presumably unconscious/id and subaltern metaphorical body, humankind could and should assume the direction of planetary events 'for the good of the whole'.

These debates did encourage a moral imperative for stewardship which continues to underpin multiple efforts towards recycling, energy efficiencies, and so forth. But, at the same time, human resource use and environmental destruction have continued to expand so rapidly that such mitigative efforts look dangerously like fiddling while Rome burns. More fundamental changes are clearly needed, but these cannot be achieved without paradigmatic changes in the thinking that underlies human relationships with non-human and material worlds.

Possibly the egocentric, anthropocentric belief that humans are the 'brains of the planet' lies at the heart of the problem. Managerial control carries with it key assumptions about elite managerial rights and ownership, and it is perhaps no coincidence that these ideas came to prominence in the midst of a neo-liberal economic boom promoting a vision of Mankind as the proprietary 'Masters of the Universe'. A globalising wave of marketised neo-colonialism followed and it is worth noting that—as the language suggests—this, like earlier colonial hegemonies, was an intensely masculinised endeavour.

Thus we see—growing from deep historical roots in Biblical concepts of patriarchal 'dominion'—the flowering of terms such as 'ecosystem services' or 'environmental services': the idea that other species and the material world are there simply to serve and provide for humankind. Such a superior anthropocentric view naturally encourages the assumption that the needs and interests of other species and ecosystems are intrinsically secondary and can be sacrificed to short-term human interests. It is this central flaw that an anthropology of sustainability needs to address, by providing new theories that can generate new practices.

Some good work has already been done. Anthropologists have long been providing ethnographic accounts of subaltern worldviews that adhere to more genuinely sustainable ideas and practices, and which are implicitly and sometimes—political freedom permitting—explicitly critical of dominant models and their appropriative aims. There are multiple mini-Zomias (Scott 2009): colonised communities trying to evade the heavy hand of the State and its practices in order to retain their own lifeways and values.

The flows of ideas and values through international networks of these groups, overlapping with the critiques emerging from environmental and social countermovements, are the groundswell of a potential new wave.

A willingness to learn from alternate ways of thinking, coupled with growing concern about human hubris, has led scholars to present ethical challenges promoting the interests of the non-human or 'more than human', and calling for relational theorisations of human–non-human engagements.[5] As Escobar observes (Chap. 14), such theorisations are theoretically robust in that 'nothing pre-exists the relations that constitute it'. Still, such ethical perspectives have raised some anxieties: there are concerns about faux animism (Pels 1998); there is the risk that such models, and their valorisation of non-human agency, may encourage human societies to evade responsibility for major abuses of power. There are concerns that such perspectives may replace culture with ontology. Escobar notes— rightly—that humans do not act homogenously as a physical force upon the planet: they have highly diverse capacities to do so, as well as differential vulnerability to the consequences of human action.

But, while cognisant of the 'creative force' of things, to use Escobar's phrase (2015), such ethical perspectives do not assume that agency equals animism; nor do they elide differentials in power relations: on the contrary, they consider carefully how different agencies and interests are negotiated. Nor are they oblivious to cultural diversity: they simply extend this to non-human kinds, recognising that (while levels of consciousness and reflexivity vary widely) all living species have social relations, and some normative behavioural rules. I would argue, therefore, that such theories don't, in fact, throw the baby out with the ontological bathwater. In a sense, these more inclusive models readily complement earlier insightful anthropological explorations of human–animal relations[6]; the lively debates about material things and their agentive capacities[7]; and overarching views of the networks of relations or 'assemblages' that connect these.[8]

Thus, there has been a florescence of theories—employed in many of the papers at the CAOS conference—that propose more inclusive and ethical visions of human–non-human relations. While it may be difficult for a discipline that focuses so intensely on human societies to 'de-anthropocentrise', as Escobar observes (Chap. 14), cultural diversity and biodiversity are interdependent, and the need to valorise pluriverses cannot be confined to human perspectives. All disciplines, including our own, need to seek a cure from the Gaia complex.

How can we carry these new ways of thinking into an 'anthropology of sustainability'?

Let us suggest, for a start, that if we want a radical change of direction, a conscious effort needs to be made not to put humankind in the driving seat in the first place, or at least not the self-appointed Masters of the Universe. This points to a need for a major political shift away from competition towards collaboration. While neo-liberal elites have successfully evangelised a belief that competition is a literally fundamental drive for humans and other species, it is equally reasonable to consider evolution in terms of inter-relationality. Gregory Bateson recommended just such a shift, with his acknowledgement of the agency of context and a prescient view of the symbiotic relations between species and material environments:

> All directional change, even in biological evolution and phylogeny, might—or must—be due to progressive interaction between organisms. Under natural selection, such change in relationships would favor progressive change in anatomy and physiology... The evolution of the horse from *Eohip pus* was not a one-sided adjustment to life on grassy plains. Surely the grassy plains themselves were evolved *pari passe* with the evolution of the teeth and hooves of the horses and other ungulates. Turf was the evolving response of the vegetation to the evolution of the horse. (1987: 163–164)

A successful push to give greater influence to relationality and collaboration would open up a different set of social and economic possibilities, not just for human societies, but also for their relationships with the non-human. And with a more balanced relational view, the interests of the non-human would cease to be automatically secondary or expendable.

A Non-anthropocentric Anthropology?

What does a greater encompassment of non-human interests mean for a discipline such as anthropology? There are obvious problems in aligning with conservation organisations. With considerable frequency, in considering such groups' efforts to protect non-human species and environments, anthropologists have found themselves critiquing interventions that ignore the ideas, the knowledges, needs and indeed the rights of indigenous communities. Katherine Homewood's research (Chap. 6) expresses this clearly, drawing attention to the way that imposed notions of 'sustainability', formed via UN Sustainable Goals, can play out at a local level, encouraging appropriation and/or commodification of the commons and the loss of customary lifeways (see also Adams Chap. 7; Rockström et al. 2009).

There are more subtle issues, too, about the recursive effects of local communities' intellectual engagement with conservation organisations. My own ethnographic research provides an example, describing the efforts of Aboriginal Rangers in Cape York, Australia, to 'walk the walk and talk the talk' with conservation groups and government environmental agencies (Strang 1998). While this was and remains politically necessary, such engagement has introduced into local belief systems a fundamentally instrumentalist managerial approach, which presents an inevitable challenge to long-term beliefs and values framing human–environmental relations in terms of collaborative partnership with the non-human. There are resonances here with Moore's observation (Chap. 4), that Euro-American ideas about sustainability also pose an intellectual challenge to worldviews that are presentist, requiring the adoption of ideas about a 'future conditional world'.

As this implies, and as writers such as Escobar (Chap. 14) and Bird-David (1999) have shown, indigenous worldviews often contain models that are intrinsically relational. Howell (Chap. 8) questions whether knowledges from other lifeways are transferable. I have argued that anthropological theories are co-produced via collaboration with people having a diverse range of worldviews, and therefore depend heavily on precisely such an exchange of knowledges (Strang 2006). But the wider question—can societies as a whole adopt ideas and values from subaltern perspectives—is a trickier one: clearly beliefs about totemic ancestral beings, immanent forces etc. do not translate readily. But broader concepts and values about relationality and positionality, and about affective relations with the non-human, are a different matter. Here there is indeed creative scope for conceptual exchange or what Strathern calls 'borrowing' (2011). International debates about the 'ontological turn', and the emergence of post-human ideas demonstrate that some considerable borrowing of this kind has already taken place. This suggests that it is indeed possible to continue to critique the imposition of dominant models of 'sustainability', while simultaneously composing an anthropology of sustainability that makes use of new ethical thinking about human–non-human relations.

Putting Theory into Practice

As Tsing's exemplary study of fungi and feral biologies (Chap. 3) illustrates, there are many complex issues to encompass when considering the engagements between humans and even a single species. Extending the in-depth approaches of ethnography to the multiplicity of non-human species and materialities with which human communities interact, their diverse forms of being and the massive range of temporal and spatial scales upon which they exist, poses a major practical challenge to researchers. Even a general sketch of these relations depends on some broad knowledge about non-human species and the processes through which these live and reproduce. Much such knowledge can be gleaned from local communities: working with hunter-gatherers assures an excellent education in the behaviour of non-human species and in the hydrological and biological processes of the local environment. But while a grassroots view of human–non-human relations may be ethical, sustainable and deeply informed by long-term knowledge traditions, there remains a need to translate it into meta-discursive models that can be communicated across international scholarly networks. As Kirsten Hastrup notes (Chap. 9), there is no such thing as a closed system: on a planetary scale, sustainability depends on the adoption of better ideas and practices worldwide (Fig. 12.3).

An anthropology of sustainability therefore requires more than anthropology. What I would like to suggest is a more permeable, more interdisciplinary approach to sustainability, in which we work collaboratively with other disciplinary areas—that is, those whose expertise is focused more specifically on other species and material processes. Many environmental (or for that matter medical and other) anthropologists already do interdisciplinary work with natural scientists. For example, in conducting ethnographic research in river catchment areas, I have often collaborated with ecologists, biologists and hydrologists to include non-human factors in analyses of water use and management. But there is a quantum difference between a general sharing/borrowing of ideas and working in genuinely interdisciplinary ways, to bring multiple perspectives into a more fully integrated view.

In essence, this suggests a return to a more holistic, less siloed vision of the Academy.[9] The anxieties of social scientists to escape biological determinism have led to an intellectual separation which leaves many cross-cutting nature–culture issues peculiarly fragmented (Strathern 1992). I would concur with Palsson, Ingold and others in arguing that this is both

Fig. 12.3 Human–animal relations (Photo: Sally Johns)

theoretically and practically insufficient. Rapprochement between social and biological anthropology has been difficult in the past: but finding new ways of working together is overdue. I would go further and add that there is also much to be gained by engaging much more fully with the work of our natural science colleagues. I am not alone in thinking that this is helpful. Helmreich's work has benefited considerably from collaboration with microbiologists (2009). And, in Chap. 3, Tsing notes how understanding feral biologies requires knowledge about industrial agriculture (see also Tsing 2015). Carneiro da Cunha suggests that thinking about matter, energy and entropy can illuminate understandings of sustainability. And Hastrup notes that social and natural histories are inextricably entangled (Fig. 12.4).

It is challenging, but also usefully broadening to work in concert with more directly material perspectives. As noted at the outset, the most robust definitions of sustainability fundamentally ground it in materiality. Looking through a natural science lens, it is not difficult to see that at the most basic level all ecosystems depend on certain flows of matter: all living organisms require hydration and nutrition, as well as effective waste removal systems. They need environments that are sufficiently safe and stable in their

Fig. 12.4 Glacier, South Island, New Zealand

conditions so that they can reproduce. In order for them to have these things, hydrological and meteorological systems need to function so that glaciers provide storage for freshwater; aquifers are replenished; oceans and lakes maintain chemical and temperature balance; and water courses maintain sufficient flow (and sufficiently uncompromised water quality) to hydrate multiple habitats and their inhabitants, carry nutrients, deposit silt, and so forth.

These basic flows of matter are vital on all, micro-cosmic and macrocosmic, scales. Left to their own devices, systems move matter around in patterns of flow that have evolved over deep time, with multiple species adapting and contributing to these movements over similarly lengthy periods. The imposition of human agency, overriding the directive capacities of other species and things, may be said to redirect flows into human interests. More often than not, this entails appropriating the water, nutrients, soils, plants etc. that previously supplied the needs of, or provided habitat for, other species, and/or using finite resources at rates that are unsustainable (Fig. 12.5).

Fig. 12.5   Irrigation channel, North Queensland

Understanding these material effects is critical. So, we need to consider, simultaneously, how humans redirect resources and appropriate materials *and* how these movements of matter affect non-human species, environments and systems. There is some useful work on water, considering how it is redirected from the broader needs of ecosystems and their dependent species and virtually 'embodied' in crops and artefacts. Thus—drawing on earlier ideas about life-cycle analysis—researchers have begun measuring how much water it takes to produce things—beef, jeans, wine, whatever—and how much it takes to send these things to distant markets (Allan 2011; Strang 2014b). They have begun to look at the vast 'water footprints' made by specific patterns of consumption, for example, demonstrating that German consumers create a water footprint across 400 different countries

(Meissner 2012). Similar work is being done on oil and other resource flows (e.g. Weszkalnys and Richardson 2014). There is also smaller-scale work, within ecosystems, considering how the redirection of water through dams and irrigation schemes affects riverbanks and their inhabitants, aquatic plant and animal species, soil microbes and structures, coastal marine areas and their ecologies. This focus on the material allows us to connect natural science research on flows of matter with ethnographic research about how humans, non-humans and things interact.

A similar broadening of focus is possible in work on interspecies relations, which has begun to move beyond thinking about how humans relate to animals (Fuentes and Wolfe 2002; Fuentes 2010; Noske 1989, 1997). Scholars are increasingly making imaginative leaps into non-human worlds, sometimes with the help of natural scientists. Thus we have Helmreich's writing on microbes, in collaboration with microbiologist Ed de Long (Helmreich 2009). We have Hayward's account of finger-eye corals and how they experience the world (2010); Head and Atchison's exploration of plants and their symbiotic abilities (2009), Lowe's thinking about viral clouds (2010) and Tsing's work on fungi (2015 and Chap. 3). What differentiates this work is that it deliberately steps away from the human perspective to imagine non-human experiences, thus providing a less anthropocentric view of relationships between species and things. And this is often assisted by different kinds of disciplinary expertise, from biology, zoology, ecology.

It is obvious where I am heading with this: I am suggesting, fundamentally, that an anthropology of sustainability requires us to climb out of a safe disciplinary silo and to engage wholeheartedly with other areas of disciplinary knowledge. A more balanced and integrated vision of human–non-human relations necessitates a more genuinely interdisciplinary perspective. Many anthropologists are wary of such collaborative endeavours. There are anxieties about the token inclusion of social issues; the unwillingness of others to engage with social theory; intellectual pollution; the compromising of 'real ethnography' and so on. However, the Institute of Advanced Study in Durham has gained some experience in facilitating cross-disciplinary collaboration, and this has produced some interesting results as well as some guidelines on how to make it work and avoid the pitfalls (Strang and Bell 2013; Strang and McLeish 2015). More broadly, the academy is beginning to see the need for genuinely interdisciplinary approaches to complex issues, including environmental change, and there are new opportunities for anthropologists not only to take part in these, but to take the lead in composing coherent, integrated research that, as well as making use of the social and natural sciences, might also encourage changes in social and material practices and enable more sustainable ways of life.

This draws attention to some unrealised potentials of our discipline. One of the major problems with many interdisciplinary projects is that, led by natural scientists, they have tended to rely on reductive models that do not encompass social issues. Anthropology, of course, has large, inclusive models which approach specific contexts holistically; which encompass multiple and diverse perspectives; and which—in collecting data in multiple areas—overlap readily with a whole range of more specialised disciplinary approaches. If we put our ethical theoretical developments together with a disciplinary commitment to the holistic collection of data, it is possible to conceive of a model that (a) repositions humankind more equitably in relation to non-human species and things and (b) readily engages inclusively with other areas of disciplinary expertise. Add to this the additional advantage of anthropological skills in cross-cultural—and thus cross-disciplinary—translation, and an obvious conclusion is that, rather than being a peripheral tag-on, anthropologists should be taking the initiative in interdisciplinary projects, including the anthropology of sustainability.

RE-IMAGINED COMMUNITIES

How might this play out in practice? How might one, for example, approach issues of sustainability in a river catchment area? I think there is potential for a new approach (Strang 2017). Having conducted ethnographies along rivers such as the Mitchell River in north Queensland, and the River Stour in Dorset, I have considered the various human communities in the catchment area; their social relations; their economic activities and their beliefs, values and practices. Such work requires a long-term view of the history of human occupation in the area, and consideration of how communities' activities have changed over time. In general, I have tried to incorporate into these accounts a sense of the material and non-human worlds that the river catchment areas contain (Fig. 12.6).

But this could go further: why not consider, equally, a range of non-human inhabitants of the watershed, conducting research on soil microbes, aquatic species, amphibians, birds, and mammals, including domesticated species such as sheep and cattle. Why not investigate the plant life within the catchment area, again seeking an indicative—wild and domesticated—range of species? It is quite possible to consider the needs and interests of these non-human species, and the effects of human activities

Fig. 12.6 Stream in Finse, Norway

upon them, as well as their own agentive capacities to act upon human communities, each other, and the material environment.

Similarly, it would be helpful to consider more closely the particular material elements and processes of that environment: its topology and topography, its distributions of flora and fauna, its hydrology, and—as with living kinds—what is needed to sustain these elements and their various processes, what human and non-human activities impinge upon them, and how. What are *their* agentive effects? How do their particular properties and characteristics, their processes, act upon the human and non-human species in the catchment area: how, in Bateson's terms, does the turf affect the horse and its adaptations over time?

One of the challenges of such a project is that it would produce multiple—quantitative and qualitative—kinds of data. How can one bring these together in such a way that it is possible to discern the relationships between them and their material effects upon each other? Previous efforts in projects bringing anthropology and archaeology together—such as Chris Gosden's work (2013)—have made use of GPS mapping. For a wider interdisciplinary project, this would not be sufficient in and of itself (and there is no room in such collaborative work for methodological fascism) but it does provide a potential way to consider the layers of human and non-human experience systematically, and to enable the various project participants to have a common mode of explanation through which they can talk to each other.

Such methodology could also address the issue of scale: clearly there would be a range of spatial and temporal scales to encompass and integrate: geological changes—the production of soils and microbes—require large temporal scales. The movements of water take place at a large meteorological level, at a localised hydrological level, and at microscopic levels of hydration. Human activities, while enacted within the catchment area, link with wider social and economic systems and processes. Thus, mapping the flows between multiple components of these systems requires methods that can focus on micro-processes, while also being able to extend outwards to consider how these connect with much larger movements of things and persons. But the key point is that a levelling methodology, encompassing different scales, takes seriously the reality that all human and non-human elements in the river catchment have needs and interests to be met. As such, it would also make very visible the inequalities in relations, and the extent to which various agencies are expressed and/or overridden.

Conclusion

This kind of approach presents an optimistic vision of a complete, ethically balanced picture of human and non-human interactions and the ways in which they act upon each other. Such an explication of agencies and effects has the potential to highlight where these are dysfunctional, that is, unsustainable. What I would hope might be gained by heading in this direction is threefold. First, it has the potential for applying, in practice, an ethical theoretical model which rejects the hubris of the Gaia complex and fully reintegrates human communities into the living systems we inhabit. Second, it offers the possibility of genuinely interdisciplinary environmental research that is intellectually and strategically beneficial for anthropology and for the academy as a whole. Third, it provides an avenue towards collaborative research methods that will help to illuminate issues of sustainability. This is what I think an anthropology of sustainability could achieve.

NOTES

1. As Keith Hart noted at the CAOS conference that initiated this volume, the efforts of corporations to present themselves as persons with rights rings an alarm about some of the potential pitfalls of dissolving human–non-human divides.
2. This resonates with Thomas Hylland Eriksen's notion of 'overheating' (2013).
3. The first conference on Degrowth took place in Paris in 2008.
4. Lovelock commented rather caustically in his later book on planetary medicine that he 'would sooner expect a goat to succeed as a gardener than expect humans to become responsible stewards of the Earth' (1991: 186).
5. For example, Baxter (2005), Dobson (1998), Haraway (2008), Kirksey and Helmreich (2010), Ritvo (1987), Serpell (1996).
6. For example, Serpell (1996).
7. For example, Bakker and Bridge (2006), Bennett (2009), Boivin (2008), Chen et al. (2013), Coole and Frost (2010), Gell (1998), Ingold (2012), Knappett and Malafouris (2008), Strang (2014b), Tsing (2004, 2015 and Chap. 3).
8. For example, Latour (2005), Mol and Law (1994).
9. This is something that anthropology's ancestral figures didn't find odd at all: Kirksey and Helmreich, for example, note Lewis Henry Morgan's work on beavers in the 1860s, and the openness to multi-species thinking that pertained at that time (2010). And Bateson, as cited in this chapter, appears to have been extremely comfortable in crossing disciplinary boundaries (1972).

REFERENCES

Allan, A. 2011. *Virtual Water: Tackling the Threat To Our Planet's Most Precious Resource.* London: I.B. Tauris.

Bakker, K., and G. Bridge. 2006. Material Worlds? Resource Geographies and the "Matter of Nature". *Progress in Human Geography* 30: 5–27.

Bateson, G. 1987 [1972]. *Steps to an Ecology of Mind: Collected Essays in Anthropology, Psychiatry, Evolution and Epistemology.* London/Northvale/New Jersey: Jason Aronson Inc.

Baxter, B. 2005. *A Theory of Ecological Justice.* London/New York: Routledge.

Bennett, J. 2009. *Vibrant Matter: A Political Ecology of Things.* Durham: Duke University Press.

Bird-David, N. 1999. 'Animism' Revisited: Personhood, Environment and Relational Epistemology. *Current Anthropology* 40 (Supplement): 67–91.

Boivin, N. 2008. *Material Cultures, Material Minds: The Impact of Things on Human Thought, Society, and Evolution.* Cambridge/New York: Cambridge University Press.

Caldararo, N. 2004. *Sustainability, Human Ecology, and the Collapse of Complex Societies: Economic Anthropology and a 21st Century Adaptation.* New York/London: Edwin Mellen Press.

Chen, C., J. Macleod, and A. Neimanis, eds. 2013. *Thinking With Water.* Montreal: McGill-Queens University Press.

Coole, D., and S. Frost. 2010. *New Materialisms: Ontology, Agency and Politics.* Durham/London: Duke University Press.

Crutzen, P., and E. Stoermer 2000. The "Anthropocene". In *Global Change Newsletter*, 41. The International Geosphere–Biosphere Programme (IGBP): A Study of Global Change, International Council for Science (ICSU). 17–18. http://www.igbp.net/download/18.316f18321323470177580001401/NL41.pdf. Accessed 26 Apr 15.

Descola, P., and G. Palsson, eds. 1996. *Nature and Society: Anthropological Perspectives.* London/New York: Routledge.

Diamond, J. 2005. *Collapse: How Societies Choose to Fail or Succeed.* New York: Penguin.

Dobson, A. 1998. *Justice and the Environment: Conceptions of Environmental Sustainability and Theories of Distributive Justice.* Oxford: Oxford University Press.

Eriksen, T. 2013. Deep and Shallow Time in Social Change. In *Regimes of Temporality: Investigating the Plurality and Order of Times Across Histories, Cultures, Technologies, Materialities and Media.* International Conference, University of Oslo, June 5–7, 2013.

Escobar, A. 1999. After Nature: steps to an anti-essentialist political ecology. *Current Anthropology* 40 (1): 1–16.

Fuentes, A. 2010. Naturalcultural Encounters in Bali: Monkeys, Temples, Tourists and Ethnoprimatology. *Cultural Anthropology* 25 (4): 600–624.

Fuentes, A., and L. Wolfe, eds. 2002. *Primates Face to Face: Conservation Implications of Human and Nonhuman Primate Interconnections.* Cambridge/New York: Cambridge University Press.

Gell, A. 1998. *Art and Agency. An Anthropological Theory.* Oxford/New York: Berg.

Gosden, C. 2013. Time and Nationhood: Beyond the Invention of Tradition and Imagined Communities. In *About Time.* Lecture Series, Institute of Advanced Study, Durham, May 13, 2013.

Haraway, D. 2008. *When Species Meet.* Minneapolis: University of Minnesota Press.

Hayward, E. 2010. Fingereyes: impressions of cup corals. *Cultural Anthropology* 25 (4): 577–599.

Head, L., and J. Atchison. 2009. Cultural ecology: emerging human-plant geographies. *Progress in Human Geography* 33: 236–245.

Helmreich, S. 2009. *Alien Ocean: Anthropological Voyages in Microbial Seas.* Berkeley: University of California Press.

Illich, I. 1999. The shadow our future throws. *New Perspectives Quarterly* 16 (2): 14–18.

Ingold, T. 2012. Towards an ecology of materials. *Annual Review of Anthropology* 41: 427–442.

Ingold, T., and G. Palsson, eds. 2013. *Biosocial Becomings: Integrating Social and Biological Anthropology.* Cambridge: Cambridge University Press.

International Union for the Conservation of Nature. 2015. *Species Extinction: The Facts.* http://cmsdata.iucn.org/downloads/species_extinction_05_2007.pdf. Accessed 26 Apr 15.

Kirksey, S., and S. Helmreich. 2010. The Emergence of Multispecies Ethnography. *Cultural Anthropology* 25 (4): 545–576.

Knappett, C., and L. Malafouris, eds. 2008. *Material Agency: Towards a Non-anthropocentric Approach.* New York: Springer.

Kopnina, H., and E. Shoreman-Ouimet. 2015. *Culture and Conservation: Beyond Anthropocentrism.* London/New York: Routledge.

Latour, B. 2005. *Reassembling the Social: An Introduction to Actor-Network-Theory.* Oxford: Oxford University Press.

Lovelock, J. 1987 [1979]. *Gaia: A New Look at Life on Earth.* Oxford: Oxford University Press.

———. 1991. *Gaia: The Practical Science of Planetary Medicine.* London: Gaia Books.

Lowe, C. 2010. Viral Clouds: Becoming H5N1 in Indonesia. *Cultural Anthropology* 25 (4): 625–649.

Meissner, S. 2012. Virtual Water and Water Footprints. Global Supply and Production Chains and Their Impacts on Freshwater Resources. In *People at the Well.*

Kinds, Usages and Meanings of Water in a Global Perspective, ed. P. Hahn, K. Cless, and J. Soentgen, 44–64. Chicago: University of Chicago Press.

Mol, A., and J. Law. 1994. Regions, Networks and Fluids: Anaemia and Social Topology. *Social Studies of Science* 24 (4): 641–671.

Noske, B. 1989. *Humans and Other Animals*. London: Pluto Press.

———. 1997. *Beyond Boundaries: Humans and Animals*. Montreal/London: Black Rose.

Pels, P. 1998. The Spirit of Matter. On Fetish, Rarity, Fact and Fancy. In *Border Fetishism. Material Objects in Unstable Spaces*, ed. P. Spyer, 91–121. London/New York: Routledge.

Plumwood, V. 1993. *Feminism and the Mastery of Nature*. London/New York: Routledge.

———. 2002. *Environmental Culture: The Ecological Crisis of Reason*. London/New York: Routledge.

Ritvo, H. 1987. *The Animal Estate: The English and Other Creatures in the Victorian Age*. Cambridge, MA: Harvard University Press.

Rockström, J., W. Steffen, K. Noone, Å. Persson, F. Stuart Chapin, E. Lambin, T. Lenton, M. Scheffer, C. Folke, H. Schellnhuber, B. Nykvist, C. de Wit, T. Hughes, S. van der Leeuw, H. Rodhe, S. Sörlin, P. Snyder, R. Costanza, U. Svedin, M. Falkenmark, L. Karlberg, R. Corell, V. Fabry, J. Hansen, B. Walker, D. Liverman, K. Richardson, P. Crutzen, and J. Foley. 2009. A Safe Operating Space for Humanity. *Nature* 461 (7263): 472–475.

Scott, J. 2009. *The Art of Not Being Governed: An Anarchist History of Upland Southeast Asia*. New Haven/London: Yale University Press.

Serpell, J. 1996. *In the Company of Animals: A Study of Human-animal Relationships, Cambridge*. New York: Cambridge University Press.

Strang, V. 1998. The Strong Arm of the Law: Aboriginal Rangers and Anthropology. *Australian Archaeology* 47: 20–29.

———. 2006. A happy Coincidence? Symbiosis and Synthesis in Anthropological and Indigenous Knowledges. *Current Anthropology.* 47 (6): 981–1008.

———. 2011. Fluid Forms: Owning Water in Australia. In *Ownership and Appropriation*, ed. V. Strang and M. Busse, 171–195. Oxford/New York: ASA Monograph/Berg.

———. 2014a. Lording It Over the Goddess: Water, Gender and Human-Environmental Relations. *Journal of Feminist Studies in Religion* 30 (1): 83–107.

———. 2014b. Fluid Consistencies: Meaning and Materiality in Human Engagements With Water. *Archaeological Dialogues.* Cambridge University Press 21 (2): 133–150.

———. 2016a. Infrastructural Relations: Water, Political Power and the Rise of a New 'Despotic Regime'. *Water Alternatives,* Special Issue. *Water, Infrastructure and Political Rule.* 9 (2): 292–318.

————. 2016b. Justice for All: Inconvenient Truths and Reconciliation in Human-Non-Human Relations. In *Major Works in Anthropology: Environmental Anthropology*. Vol. 2, 263–278. London: Taylor and Francis. Reprinted from H. Kopnina and E. Shoreman-Ouimet, eds. 2016. *Routledge International Handbook of Environmental Anthropology*. Abingdon/New York: Routledge. 263–278.

————. 2017. Re-imagined Communities: A New Ethical Approach to Water Policy. In *The Oxford Handbook on Water Politics and Policy*, ed. K. Conca and E. Weinthal. Oxford/New York: Oxford University Press.

Strang, V., and S. Bell. 2013. *Navigating Interdisciplinarity*. Durham: Institute of Advanced Study, Durham University.

Strang, V., and T. McLeish. 2015. *Evaluating Interdisciplinary Research: A Practical Guide*. Durham: Durham University, Institute of Advanced Study.

Strathern, M. 1992. *After Nature: English Kinship in the Late Twentieth Century*. Cambridge: Cambridge University Press.

————. 2011. Sharing, Stealing and Borrowing Simultaneously. In *Ownership and Appropriation*, ed. V. Strang and M. Busse, 23–41. Oxford/New York: Berg.

Tsing, A. 2004. *Friction: An Ethnography of Global Connections*. Princeton: Princeton University Press.

————. 2015. *In the Midst of Disturbance: Symbiosis, Coordination, History, Landscape*. Firth Lecture, ASA Conference, Symbiotic Anthropologies: Theoretical Commensalities and Methodological Mutualisms, Exeter University, April 13–16, 2015.

Vernadsky, V. 1986 [1920]. *The Biosphere*. Santa Fe: Synergetic Press.

Weszkalnys, G., and T. Richardson, eds. 2014. Resource Materialities: New Anthropological Perspectives on Natural Resource Environments. Special Issue. *Anthropological Quarterly* 87 (1): 5–30.

World Commission on Environment and Development. 1987. *Our Common Future, The World Commission on Environment and Development, [The Brundtland Report]*. Oxford/New York: Oxford University Press.

CHAPTER 13

Interlude: Performing Gaia

Frédérique Aït-Touati and Bruno Latour

In an article published in 2009 in the journal *Alternatives Théâtrales*, we tried to overcome some sticking points in the theatre of science.

CHARACTER 1   You are terribly out of date. You keep bringing these miserable humans onto the stage, despite the fact that the scenography of the sciences has many other resources – show them! It really is pitiful, your anthropocentric theatre! (...)

Presenting a dialogue between two fictional characters, the first a scholar of science studies and the second a grumpy defender of the separation between the arts and the sciences, the article brought their sterile debate to a close with Gaia's entrance onstage.

F. Aït-Touati (✉)
CNRS and EHESS, Paris, France

B. Latour
Sciences Po, Paris, France

© The Author(s) 2017   229
M. Brightman, J. Lewis (eds.), *The Anthropology of Sustainability*,
Palgrave Studies in Anthropology of Sustainability,
DOI 10.1057/978-1-137-56636-2_13

CHARACTER 2   'Other times, other customs'. Today, things really aren't the same. Science and literature sleep in separate beds, you can't do anything about it.

CHARACTER 3   It's a good thing too, they would give birth to monsters!

CHARACTER 1   We're back in the 16th century! We've gone back in time. And not in order to perform a play in period costume. We need another kind of theatre and another kind of science, because the beings that are going to land upon us, they aren't anthropomorphic at all. They won't be content with acting as accessories or as an excuse for our petty human affairs.

CHARACTER 2   (*ironically*). Are you, by any chance, thinking of Gaia?

CHARACTER 3   Gaia? But she's a goddess, what could be more anthropomorphic! What is she doing here?

CHARACTER 1   (*dramatically*) Here, Gaia solemnly makes her entrance....

Taking stock of the limits of an anthropocentric theatre, the article called for a theatre capable of taking on questions that exceed those of the human comedy. The show *Gaia Global Circus* is in a way the attempt to respond to the challenge that we set ourselves: to experiment with theatre as a heuristic tool to reflect upon the consequences of Gaia's entry on stage. The process we went through, the problems, how we felt our way, and the experiments that were necessary may equip us to shed a little light upon this attempt at a 'sensory knowledge' that we have been developing together for about ten years,[1] and sharing with a growing number of researchers and artists.[2]

The creation of the show took place between April 2010 and September 2013, the date of the première at Toulouse. During the first phase of the project, three of us worked together, Bruno, Frédérique and Chloé, resulting in the writing of a first text entitled *Cosmocolosse*.[3] From September 2011, we chose to develop the subject, together with four actors, through a writing and improvisation workshop which took place during several periods of residence at the Chartreuse de Villeneuve lez Avignon and at the Comédie de Reims. During this three-year period, we developed an original creative process, involving a philosopher and a theatre company[4] in a field project that brought us to the Plateau de Saclay (also known as the European Silicon Valley) to meet climatologists in a laboratory of dynamic meteorology, then at the ENS to meet experts in climate modelling, then in a sediment core preservation chamber of the CNRS. We met numerous researchers, climatologists, philosophers and historians of science and asked them to react to the work in progress; Clive Hamilton on geo-engineering, Paul Edwards on the concept of a climate machine, Valérie Masson-Delmotte on recent developments in climatology, Naomi Oreskes on the 'merchants of doubt' and the false climate controversy, Marie Farge on questions of modelling. This journey, which borrowed exploratory methods from documentary theatre and the theatre of inquiry, allowed us to capture the diversity of opinions, of comments, and of languages that graft themselves around the question of the responsibility of man for the ecological crisis, and more generally around discussions of the Anthropocene. It was thus less a question of staging an already constructed theory (the famous 'Gaia hypothesis' of James Lovelock) than of working, with the tools of theatre and of philosophy, on the elaboration and elucidation of a common question: how to capture, understand, feel and represent to oneself the irruption of the new character of Gaia. The collective writing of the show imposed itself as a way of expressing the state of disarray into which our research on the question threw us.

From the beginning of the project, it seemed to us that theatre constituted a particularly suitable medium for expressing the special sort of passions raised by the new climatic regime: alarm, stupefaction, incredulity, resistance, anger, but also fear, disarray or despair. On the stage, four actors ask themselves about this event of which scientists are warning us all, and which they call, according to context: the ecological crisis, global warming, the Anthropocene. These actors try, through a series of experimental scenarios and situations, to understand what is happening to us. Very quickly, we saw two pitfalls emerging: *discourse*—the pedagogical form of conceptual theatre—and *lamento*—a form that is very fashionable in current cinematographic productions dealing with political ecology, felt by many to be the heirs of disaster movies (throbbing and grandiose music, consensual lyricism, imprecatory voice over, direct addresses). Against this dystopian aesthetic, we developed a burlesque imaginary, willingly comical, and inspired by comics as much as by Shakespeare's *Tempest* or Greek tragedy. This is a world in which Noah is refused a loan to make a new Ark, and where climatologists become activists in order to be heard, a world in which Cassandra and apocalyptic prophets make an appearance on stage and we can't decide whether they are ridiculous or scary (probably a bit of both, as this is a tragi-comedy). If ecological films can exploit the beautiful image that engages the viewer in marvellous contemplation (sublime landscapes, moving testimonies on the richness of cultures and species), theatre must innovate on a different aesthetic terrain: the kaleidoscopic text written by Pierre Daubigny[5] based on the workshops and the actors' improvisations seeks to produce a 'shower of voices' that captures the uncertainty of the reactions and emotions, their extreme variability, and forbids any univocality. The changes in register (from the scientific language of the experts, to the technical or fine language of politicians, to the language of almost biblical resonance of poetic figures) are made perceptible by the art of the actors. These inversions that trouble the characters, and these passages from a discursive to a playful register, create dramatic ruptures that the production accentuates rather than hiding them.

The play thus interrogates the modes in which we construct knowledge: our bodies, our senses, our tools, our instruments, and all that allows us more generally to capture and assimilate the world. It is because science is envisaged here as a sensory activity, aesthetic in the primary sense of the word, that it can be the subject of a theatrical production. The theatre continues this effort of sensitivity on the part of the tools of science by putting its own tools into action: brusque or progressive passages from one atmosphere to another—from one *climate* to another. The theatrical space, with its artifice, allows one to experiment with the space we inhabit and the agents who populate the world. But it is not enough to make the human cacophony heard. Gaia does not speak the same language as us. We are not used to listening to her. How can her voice be made audible? How to make entities (humans, objects, categories) exist by speaking in their name?[6] This is the domain of science, whose descriptions and inscriptions give rise to new entities. It is also what theatre does, in its own way, by putting gods, ghosts and beings of nature on the stage. But the parallelism stops there. Science and theatre, of course, do not make the beings of nature speak in the same way. During the rehearsals and writing workshops, we worked with the visual and conceptual material of climate science, in order at last only to maintain one element: the model. Of science, we did not use the data (contours and digits) but a method, not the content but a process. Modelling seemed to us an essential point of contact between the climate question and the theatre. The central element of the play is a model, not a scientific one but a theatrical one: a theatrical apparatus (a stage machine) that perturbs and inflects the course of the human comedy. This model, that we called the 'marquee' or the 'canopy', a white canvas suspended above the stage and the public using helium balloons, is both a naïve and effective modelling of Gaia.

We attempt with this model to clarify two important points: the interior/exterior articulation (Gaia is not a globe, it is more of an envelope), and the reversal of the Copernican revolution. In other words, the surprising return of man to the centre expressed in the notion of the Anthropocene. He is no longer at the centre in the sense of the pre-Copernican cosmology, but he is at the centre because he is responsible, and must take charge of the world that he himself has created. This explains the pertinence in our view of constructing a theatrical model that re-enact the process of scientific modelling albeit without imitating climatic models. Sampling, collection, measuring, analysis, transformation, styling: such are a few of the gestures that we have drawn from the scientific work of modelling, to bring them to our

medium. In doing so, our theatrical model becomes an apparatus of negotiation and translation: an object of discussion around which actors gather,
discuss, plan, argue, struggle and negotiate. The question of translation is at
the heart of the play: how to translate Gaia through science? How to
translate scientific speech through the media? How to translate scientific
speech through a political decision? The play shows multiple ruptures of
translation, and plays on different modes of translation: a political discourse
translated by a comical sign language that makes political speech grate; a
Beatles song translated by an angry teenager, who becomes a derisory and
comical allegory of a misunderstood Gaia. Using fictional scenes and multiple scenarios, Daubigny's play allowed us to explore the variety of stand-
points in the face of climate crisis, and to take them all the way to their
extreme consequences.

It is a matter of *performing Gaia*, then, in all senses of the phrase: in
trying to bring this new actor to the stage using the powerful and simple
means of the stage, but also to become sensitive to the performances, in the
semiotic and theatrical senses of the term, of Gaia. It was indeed a case of
testing Gaia's agentivity by means of the theatre. Usually, when speaking of
the Earth as a whole, one is satisfied with general or empty formulas: Earth is
alive, the planet has a history, all is connected, we should be one with it, etc.
And, for scientists and for non-scientists, the question of the Earth's power
to act remains an enigma. It was therefore not a matter of *transmitting* a
message about her activity. The great opportunity to speak about the new
climatic regime at the theatre is that activists, artists, amateurs intervene at
the same time as researchers who discover with amazement the rhythms,
reactions and tremblings of the planet. We are therefore not in the usual
pedagogical situation, so perilous for all aspiringly scientific theatre, because
the kind of power to act is not known to anyone. How can we prepare
ourselves to face such an active and reactive Gaia? By transforming our very
relationship to the stage, by bringing to the foreground the décor that used
to be left to the background to deal with human affairs. Hence the idea of a
décor-actor interacting with the actors on stage. During the work of
rehearsal and creation, we very concretely experienced the power to act of
this immense puppet that we had constructed but whose presence and
movements occupied an essential place, that of an actant, and even, literally,
of an overwhelming fifth actor. *Gaia Global Circus* stages the consequences
and the passions raised by this inversion of the hierarchy of agents. We were
struck by the emotion of certain researchers who saw the play: although
nothing in the content resembled what they did, they saw in the agitations

of this canopy the representation, at last living and realist, of their problems of method, despite or perhaps because of this lack of realism.

What interests us in this reprise by theatre of research questions—or reprise by research of inventions produced on the stage—is that it is possible to invent a form of collaboration between scientists and artists but also with activists. What a pleasure to see members of the audience at wonderful 'aftershows' who find themselves reassured to have finally seen their own conflicts dramatised. On all ecological questions we are all divided. However public discourse assumes a sort of general consent (or stubborn opposition). The power of theatre consists of being able to dramatise disagreements by putting them on stage and, in this way, to de-dramatise them by making possible a discussion that was impossible before. This cathartic effect is of great importance for all climate politics.

NOTES

1. For an archive and news on our joint projects, see www.zonecritique.org. In addition to the performances and shows, the experimental programme in political arts (programme expérimental en arts politiques, SPEAP), founded by Bruno Latour and directed by Frédérique Aït-Touati, is one of the key centres for this profoundly pragmatist research (Aït-Touati and Latour 2009).

2. For example, the historian Guillaume Mazeau whose work with theatrical director Joël Pommerat for the show 'Ça ira (1). Fin de Louis' has deeply transformed his way of conceiving his practice as an historian; the philosopher Vinciane Despret who constructed his inquiry into the Dead following a 'path of obedience' in the manner of Sophie Calle; or Baptiste Morizot and his "fieldwork" philosophy, in which he makes tracking wolves an essential component of his reflections.

3. The text of *Cosmocolosse* is available on various sites: zonecritique.org, brunolatour.fr. The text has been adapted twice for radio, once in German on Bavarian Radio (2014), and again in French for France Culture (2016).

4. *Gaia Global Circus*, a play by Pierre Daubigny following a project by Bruno Latour, directed by Frédérique Aït-Touati and Chloé Latour, with Claire Astruc, Luigi Cerri, Jade Collinet, Matthieu Protin, machines and optic effects by Olivier Vallet, lights by Benoît Aubry, costumes by Elsa Blin.

5. The entire text of the play *Gaïa Global Circus* is available in French and English on: zonecritique.org.

6. We addressed this question in another performative form that we conceived in May 2015, entitled 'Make it Work, the Theatre of Negotiations': for one week, 200 students from all over the world gathered in the theatre of

Nanterre-Amandiers to simulate an international negotiation on the climate or COP (Conference of the Parties) of a new kind, in which the soils, the oceans, the forests, Amazonia, businesses, young people, the 'oil in the ground' and many other territories and non-human collectives were invited to the negotiation table as well as the usual state delegations.

Reference

Aït-Touati, F., and B. Latour. 2009. De la paillasse aux planches. Entretien (sans conclusion) sur le théâtre de l'expérience. *Alternatives Théâtrales* 102–103: 42–45.

CHAPTER 14

Sustaining the Pluriverse: The Political Ontology of Territorial Struggles in Latin America

Arturo Escobar

We, Afrodescendant women of Northern Cauca, understand the ancestral value of our territories. Our ancestors taught us that we should guarantee our descendants (renacientes) permanence in our territories.... Our territories have been defined by life, joy, and peace.... Because our love for life is stronger than our fear of death! Territories and Life are not sold—they are loved and defended [Communiqué of the Mobilization of Afrodescendant Women for the Caring of Life and the Ancestral Territory, November 25, 2015].[1]

A. Escobar (✉)
Department of Anthropology, University of North Carolina, Chapel Hill, NC, USA

Research Associate with the Culture, Memory, and Nation group, Universidad del Valle, Cali, Colombia

© The Author(s) 2017   237
M. Brightman, J. Lewis (eds.), *The Anthropology of Sustainability*,
Palgrave Studies in Anthropology of Sustainability,
DOI 10.1057/978-1-137-56636-2_14

INTRODUCTION: FROM WAR TO AUTONOMY, AND FROM UNSUSTAINABILITY TO SUSTAINMENT

From November 17 to 27, a group of 22 women marched from the predominantly Afrodescendant town of La Toma in the Norte del Cauca region in Colombia's southwest to Bogotá, a distance of 440 km, to protest the illegal and destructive gold mining going on in their ancestral territories. They were accompanied by a group of young men, the *guardia cimarrona* (maroon guard), organized on the model of *guardia indígena*, an unarmed practice of self-protection of the neighboring Nasa *pueblo* (people). Many people joined in along the way, or offered solidarity, in small towns and larger cities such as Cali and Ibagué. Upon arrival to the cold Andean *sabana* (plateau) where Bogotá is located, and faced with the indifference and dilatory tactics of the bureaucrats of the Minister of the Interior, the women decided to occupy the building, which they proceeded to do for close to two weeks, despite threats of forced eviction and the intense *frío sabanero*, or the region's cold, until finally reaching a signed agreement with the government. The agreement called, among other things, for the removal of all the *retroexcavadoras* (large backhoe excavating machines) used for gold extraction and the drafting of a protection plan for the communities from threats by backhoe owners and other armed actors. By mid-January, however, and despite timid attempts by various government agencies to show presence in the territory, it was clear that the agreements were not going to be fulfilled. By mid-April, Francia Márquez, one of the main leaders of the March, had already penned two amazingly brave and lucid open letters to the government and the public at large. 'I do not cease to ask myself', she asked in the first letter of April 18, 'Do the lives of black and indigenous people and peasants have any worth in this country?' And she goes on to say: 'Everything we have lived has been for the love we have known in our territories, the love we feel when we see the plantain germinate, when we have a sunny fishing day, of knowing your family is close by . . . our land is the place where we dream of our future with dignity. Perhaps that's why they [armed actors, including the army, paramilitaries, and guerrillas] persecute us, because we want a life of autonomy and not of dependency'.[2]

Written in the context of the tense peace negotiation between the government and the FARC guerillas, the letter also contained a direct indictment of the government's national development plan, one of whose pillars or *locomotoras* (locomotives) is precisely mining. For Márquez, this model can only generate hunger, misery, and war. The implication is clear: without transforming radically this model, and without obtaining the conditions of autonomy for the territories, peace will be illusory. There can never be peace, she added in her second letter, 'if the government is not able to create the conditions to take care of life, if it does not privilege the life of all beings above all private interests and the interests of the transnationals'. As she reminded everybody in her second letter, less than a week later, 'we started on this march to let you all know that illegal mining is leaving us without our families, robbing us from the possibility of continuing to live in the territory where our umbilical cords are buried'.[3] Addressed 'To those women that take care of their territories as if it were their daughters and sons. To the women and men who care for a Dignified, Simple, and Solidary Life', the letter ended with the March's slogan: *Territories and Life are not sold – they are loved and defended.*

This chapter takes the defense of territories, as evidenced in the case of the black communities in Northern Cauca, as a point of departure to raise some questions about the concept of sustainability in anthropology, geography, and political ecology. The movements for the defense of territories against the onslaught by globalized capital, extractivist forms of development, and modernist discourses of progress, growth, value, and order provide an excellent grounding for rethinking sustainability. Anchored on this grounding, and in tandem with certain critical trends in the academy associated with the 'ontological turn', the argument I develop here can be stated as follows: Most frameworks and practices associated with 'sustainability' at present amount at best to reducing unsustainability, while keeping the underlying world order and vision in place—what activists often call the 'globalized civilizational model' and scholars refer to as 'the One-World World' (OWW) model (Law 2011). From activists perspectives, however, what needs to be sustained, on the contrary, is the pluriverse or, to use the wise Zapatista formula, 'a world where many worlds fit'. In this sense, many territorial struggles (by Afrodescendants, indigenous peoples, peasant, and often times poor urban dwellers) can be seen as ontological struggles; they interrupt the globalizing project of fitting many worlds into one. These struggles are important contributions to ecological and cultural transitions toward the pluriverse. As such, the knowledges they produce might be particularly relevant for the search for post-capitalist, sustainable plural models of life. To see them in this way, however, requires that we situate them within a twofold context: the search for transitions, which can be gleaned from transition movements and visionaries in many parts of the

Global South and the Global North; and a renewed understanding of the self-organizing dynamics of the Earth.

Part I of this chapter starts with some very brief remarks about political ecology (PE), situating the emergent field of political ontology with PE's genealogy. Part II summarizes the ontological approach to territorial struggles, highlighting the central role of relational worlds or ontologies in this onto-epistemic political field. Part III highlights the need for going back to a profound understanding of the Earth as some indigenous activists and ecological visionaries do at present, in order to ascertain the farsighted character of the thought being produced by these actors, largely outside of the academy, and to rethink sustainability. The conclusion, finally, underlies the crucial role of knowledges produced in territorial struggles for transitions to the pluriverse. It also makes an initial foray into the notion of design for transitions or, as some design thinkers call it, for moving toward an Age of Sustainment. I should note that each part is very sketchily developed given space limitations. By outlining the argument as a whole, however, I hope to lay down the bare rudiments of a political ontology approach to sustainability.

FROM POLITICAL ECOLOGY TO POLITICAL ONTOLOGY

There are many ways to tell the genealogy of political ecology.[4] There is broad agreement about its starting point in the 1970s, when a number of social scientists began to analyze the relation between society, or capitalism, and the environment by combining ecological frameworks (largely from the cultural and human ecology of the 1950s–1970s) with social theory frameworks, particularly Marxism (yet from other perspectives as well, such as systems theory). Some of the early critiques of sustainability were influenced by this early political ecology.[5] Since then, the field has remained intensely interdisciplinary, with geography, anthropology, sociology, ecological economics, and environmental history perhaps playing the most prominent roles. Since the 1990s, post-structuralism favored a shift in focus toward the various regimes of representation and power (discourses, science, patriarchy, whiteness, and colonial narratives) through which 'nature' has been culturally constructed, historically and in place. In general terms, what came out of these two very productive phases was an understanding of political ecology as the field that studies the multiple intersections between nature, culture, power, and history. Emphases oscillated between 'the social production of nature' (more prevalent in Marxist geography) to 'the cultural construction of nature' (in post-structuralist-inflected anthropology). Ecological economics maintained a relatively unique path for a time, centered on reframing economics through various material-energetic analyses and questions of valuation. It became linked with political ecology explicitly through a concern with environmental struggles, for instance, in terms of what Martínez-Alier called 'ecological distribution conflicts' (2002; see also Healy et al. 2013).

These approaches or phases overlap today in the work of many authors; a certain theoretical eclecticism characterizes political ecology. The current moment can nevertheless be considered a distinct, third phase. This phase can broadly be described as post-constructivist and neo-materialist. While it incorporates many of the insights of the constructivist moment (nature is historically and culturally constructed) and continues to pay attention to the social production of nature by capital under globalizing conditions, the center of attention now is on an entire range of aspects that were largely bypassed by the social and human sciences as a whole. The category that perhaps most aptly harbors these diverse tendencies is the 'ontological turn'; it has become salient in geography, anthropology, and political theory during the past decade. What defines this turn is the attention to a host of factors that deeply shape what we come to know as 'reality' but which the academy rarely tackled—things like objects and 'things', non-humans, matter and materiality (soil, energy, infrastructures, weather, bytes), emotions, spirituality, feelings, and so forth. What brings together these very disparate list of items is the attempt to break away from the normative divides, central to the modern regime of truth, between subject and object, mind and body, reason and emotion, living and inanimate, human and non-human, organic and inorganic, and so forth. This is why this set of perspectives can be properly called post-dualist. More colloquially, it can be said that what we are witnessing with post-dualist, neo-materialist critical theories is the return of the repressed side of the dualisms—the forceful emergence of the subordinated and often feminized and racialized side of all the above binaries.

The most important target of post-dualist political ecology is the divide between nature and culture and the idea that there is a 'single nature' to which there correspond 'many cultures'. The deconstruction of the first divide started in the 1980s, with the works of Ingold, Strathern, Descola, Haraway, Law and Latour (and many others, including in other parts of the world). The recent scholarship, however, makes a concerted effort at re-connecting nature and culture, and humans and non-humans, through a rich variety of theoretical and ethnographic proposals and investigations. Re-connection may take the form of visualizing networks, assemblages, naturecultures or socionatures, or compositions or 'more-than-human' worlds always in the process of being created by all kinds of actors and processes. 'Distributed agency' (e.g., Bennett 2010) and 'relational ontologies' are key concepts here. Whether these post-dualist trends finally manage to leave behind the anthropocentric and Eurocentric features of modern social theory and their particular accentuation in the Anglo-American academy is still a matter of debate. In the remainder of this section, I discuss two lines of work that are tackling this problematic: feminist political ecology and political ontology.

It is not a coincidence that much of the most interesting work being done at the interface of the ontological turn and political ecology is being done by feminist geographers, anthropologists, and political theorists.[6] Perhaps it could be said that they are the 'most consistently relational' among the academics working across the nature/culture divide, while being mindful of not 're-worlding everything into one lens', as Paige West put it (as many of us, academics, are prone to do).[7] Though not strictly located within political ecology or feminist political ecology (although see Harcourt and Nelson 2015), the relational writings of feminists from the Global South are very important for radicalizing the insights of post-dualist feminist political ecology. Carolyn Shaw (2014) proposes the African feminist notion of 'negofeminism' —a feminism that is non-ego based—as a basis for relational thinking and writing, a notion that recalls that of the 'expanded ecological self' of deep ecology. Something similar can be said of the potential contributions to feminist political ecology and post-dualist political ecology by decolonial Latin American feminists, for whom an essential part of any feminist work is the deconstruction of the colonial divide (the 'us' vs. 'them' divide instaurated since the Conquest of America, slavery and colonialism and that is alive and well today with modernizing globalization and development; see Espinosa et al. 2014). Of course, feminists have a strong living genealogy on which to construct their theoretical-political projects on a 'high relationality' mode, from questions about the situatedness of knowledge, the historicity of the body, and the salience of emotions and affect to the relevance of women's voices from the Global South. This heritage is reflected today in the feminist commitment and creativity to exploring other ways of worlding, including new insights about what keeps the dominating ontologies in place. Feminist political ecology today can be said to be a transnational practiced space of understanding and healing (e.g., Baksh and Harcourt 2015). They suggest that attachments (to body, place, and 'nature') have ontological status. In some versions, there is an explicit aim to build effective bridges across worlds by revisioning community, spirituality, and place intimacy, as a way to repair the damages inflicted by the ontology of disconnection. Anzaldúa's powerful call on all us, humans, to be *nepantleras*, bridge builders and re-weavers of relationality, is shared by some of these new orientations (Anzaldúa 2002).

Along with decolonial feminist political ecology, political ontology can be said to be an ontological-political strategy to re-weave life and community with the many territorial struggles of today. The deconstruction of the colonial divide is also central to political ontology. The term 'political ontology' was coined by anthropologist Mario Blaser (2009, 2010, 2013) and continues to be developed by this author along with de la Cadena and Escobar (e.g., Blaser 2013; de la Cadena 2010, 2015; Escobar 2014; Blaser et al. 2014). The emphasis is on worlds and worlding in two senses: on the one hand, political ontology refers to the power-laden practices involved in bringing into being a particular world or ontology; on the other hand, it refers to a field of study that focuses on the inter-relations among worlds, including the conflicts that ensue as different ontologies strive to sustain their own existence in their interaction with other worlds. It should be emphasized that political ontology situates itself simultaneously within critical trends in the academy and within ongoing struggles for the defense of territories and worlds. It is this active and profound commitment to thinking from the space of struggles involving ecological-ontological conflicts that gives political ontology its specificity at present. 'Ontological struggles', in this context, as we shall see in the next section, also signal a problematization of the universalizing ontology of the dominant forms of modernity—what John Law (2011) has descriptively called 'The One-World World'. Political ontology is also intended to make visible the ontological dimension of the accumulation by dispossession that is going on today in many parts of the world with extractivist development models, principally large-scale mining, agro-fuels, and land grabbing linked to commercial agriculture (McMichael 2013). Against the will to render the world into one, political ontology asserts the importance of enhancing the pluriverse.

While political ontology is very much influenced by the 'more-than-human' trend of late, and also seeks to scrutinize human-centered assemblages, by placing itself deeply (ethnographically and politically) within worlds that are not constructed solely on the basis of the nature/culture divide, even if pushed to become partially connected with the OWW and hence to make themselves also in terms of the divide, political ontology advocates hope to render visible those heterogeneous assemblages of life that enact non-dualist, relational worlds. Political ontology also has a decidedly decolonial orientation in that it rearticulates the colonial difference (the hierarchies of differences created historically by the effects of the OWW's domineering ontology on other worlds and knowledges), and the OWW's epistemic inability to recognize that which exceeds it, into a vision of relational onto-epistemic formations in movement that renovates our understanding of 'the human' and of what exists in general. The historicity of political ontology at the present moment, lastly, is given by the utter necessity, as gleaned from many indigenous, Afrodescendant, and peasant mobilizations in Latin America, of defending relational territories-worlds from the ravages of large-scale extractivist operations, such as mining and agro-fuels (e.g., Gudynas 2015). Against the ontological occupation and destruction of worlds effected by the globalization project, political ontology emphasizes the importance of thinking from, and within, those configurations of life that, while partially connected with the globalizing worlds, also remain unoccupied by them (de la Cadena 2015).

THE POLITICAL ONTOLOGY OF TERRITORIAL STRUGGLES IN LATIN AMERICA

Elders and young activists in many territorial communities worldwide (including increasingly in urban areas) eloquently express why they defend their worlds even at the price of their lives. In the words of the same activist from the Afrodescendant community of La Toma already mentioned, '*It is patently clear to us that we are confronting monsters such as transnational corporations and the State. Yet nobody is willing to leave her/his territory; I might get killed here but I am not leaving*'.[8] Such resistance takes place within a long history of domination and resistance, and this is essential for understanding territorial defense as an ontological-political practice. La Toma communities have knowledge of their continued presence in the territory since the first half of the XVII century. It's an eloquent example of what activists call 'ancestrality', referring to the ancestral mandate that inspires today's struggles and that persists in the memory of the elders, amply documented by oral history and scholars (Lisifrey et al. 2013). This mandate is joyfully celebrated in oral poetry and song: *Del Africa llegamos con un legado ancestral; la memoria del mundo debemos recuperar* ('From Africa we arrived with an ancestral legacy; we must recover the world's memory').[9] Far from an intransigent attachment to the past, ancestrality stems from a living memory that orients itself to the ability to envision a different future—a sort of 'futurality' that imagines, and struggles for, the conditions that will allow them to persevere as a distinct world.[10]

Within relational worlds, the defense of territory, life, and the commons are one and the same. To this extent, this chapter's argument can be restated as follows: The perseverance of communities, commons, and the struggles for their defense and reconstitution—particularly, but not only, those that incorporate explicitly ethno-territorial dimensions—involves resistance and the defense and affirmation of territories that, at their best and most radical, can be described as pluriversal, that is, as fostering the co-existence of multiple worlds. Conversely, whereas the occupation of territories by capital and the State implies economic, technological, cultural, ecological, and often armed aspects, its most fundamental dimension is ontological. From this perspective, what occupies territories is a particular ontology, that of individuals, expert knowledge, and markets. By resisting the neoliberal globalizing project, many indigenous, Afrodescendant, peasant, and poor urban communities are advancing *ontological struggles*. The struggle to maintain multiple worlds—the pluriverse—is best embodied by the Zapatista dictum, *un mundo donde quepan muchos mundos*, a world where many worlds fit. Many of these worlds can thus be seen as engaged in struggles for the perseverance and enhancement of the pluriverse.

Another clear case of ontological occupation of territories comes from the southernmost area of the Colombian Pacific, around the port city of Tumaco. Here, since the early 1980s, the mangrove and humid forests have been destroyed and communities displaced to give way to oil palm plantations and industrial shrimp cultivation. Inexistent in the 1970s, by the mid-1990s oil palm had expanded to over 30,000 hectares, and the industry's projection was to double the area in a few years. The monotony of the plantation—row after row of palm as far as you can see, a green desert of sorts—has replaced the diverse, heterogeneous, and entangled worlds of forest and communities. There are two important aspects to remark from this dramatic change: first, the 'plantation form' effaces the relations maintained with and by the forest-world; emerging from a dualist ontology of human dominance over so-called 'nature' understood as 'inert space' or 'resources' to be had, the plantation is one of the most effective means to bring about the ontological occupation of local relational worlds. In fact, plantations arc unthinkable from the relational perspective of forest-worlds; within these worlds, forest utilization practices take on an entirely different form that ecologists describe in terms of agro-ecology and agro-forestry; even the landscape, of course, is entirely different. Not far from the oil palm plantations, industrial shrimp companies were also busy in the 1980s and 1990s transforming the mangrove-world into disciplined succession of rectangular pools, 'scientifically' controlled. A very polluting and destructive industry especially when constructed on mangrove swamps, this type of shrimp farming constitutes another clear example of ontological occupation and politics at play (Escobar 2008, 2014).

Mangrove forests are primary examples of what here is called a 'relational ontology'. The mangrove-world is enacted minute by minute, day by day, through an infinite set of practices carried out by a multiplicity of beings and life forms, involving a complex organic and inorganic material weaving of water, minerals, degrees of salinity, forms of energy (sun, tides, moon, relations of force), human activity, spiritual beings, and so forth. There is a rhizome 'logic' to these entanglements, a 'logic' that is impossible to follow in any simple way, and very difficult to map and measure, if at all; this logic reveals an altogether different way of being and becoming in territory and place.[11] These experiences constitute relational worlds or ontologies. To put it abstractly, a relational ontology of this sort can be defined as one in which *nothing preexists the relations that constitute it.* Said otherwise, things and beings *are* their relations, they do not exist prior to them.

As the anthropologist Tim Ingold says (2011: 131), these 'worlds without objects' are always in movement, made up of materials in motion, flux and becoming; in these worlds, living beings of all kinds constitute each other's conditions for existence; they 'interweave to form an immense and continually evolving tapestry' (p. 10). These worlds do not require the divide between nature and culture in order to exist—in fact, they exist as such only because they are enacted by practices that do not rely on such divide. In a relational ontology, 'beings do not simply occupy the world, they *inhabit* it, and in so doing – in threading their own paths through the meshwork – they contribute to their ever evolving weave' (p. 71). Commons exist in these relational worlds, not in worlds that are imagined as inert and waiting to be occupied.

Even if the relations that ceaselessly enact the mangrove-world are always changing, to significantly mess them up often results in the degradation of such worlds. Such is the case with industrial shrimp farming schemes and oil palm plantations for agro-fuels, already mentioned, often built with the avowed aim to transform them from 'worthless swamp' to agro-industrial complexes (Ogden 2010). Here, of course, we find many of the operations of the OWW at play: the conversion of everything that exists in the mangrove-world into mixes of 'nature' and 'resources'; the effacing of the life-enabling materiality of the inorganic and the non-human, and their treatment as 'objects' to be extracted, eradicated, or destroyed; and linking the forest-worlds so transformed to 'world markets' for profit. In these cases, the insatiable appetite of the OWW spells out the progressive destruction of the mangrove-world, its ontological capture and reconversion by capital and the State (Deleuze and Guattari 1987; Escobar 2008). The OWW, in short, denies the mangrove-world its possibility of existing as such. Local struggles constitute attempts to re-establish some degree of symmetry to the partial connections that the mangrove-worlds maintain with the OWW.

THINKING-FEELING WITH THE EARTH

There are many signs that suggest that the One-World doctrine is unraveling, and political ontology helps us understand this process. The ubiquity of the language of crisis to refer to the planetary ecological and social conditions (chiefly, but well beyond, climate change) heralds this unraveling. The growing visibility of struggles to defend mountains, landscapes, forests, territories, and so forth by appealing to a relational (non-dualist) and pluri-ontological understanding of life is another manifestation of the OWW's crisis.

The unraveling of the OWW fosters momentous questions for both social theory and political activism on behalf of territories: How did the OWW become so powerful? How does it work today? How is it made and unmade? Can it be rearticulated in terms of a plurality of worlds? (Law 2004, 2011; Law and Lien 2012; Blaser et al. 2014). This conjuncture and questions define a rich context for political ontology and pluriversal studies: on the one hand, the need to understand the conditions by which the OWW continues to maintain its dominance; on the other, the emergence of projects based on different ontological commitments and ways of worlding, including commoning (e.g., Nonini 2007; Bollier 2014; Bollier and Helfrich 2012), and how they struggle to weaken the one-world project while widening their spaces of re-existence.

The 'pluriverse' is a way of looking at reality that contrasts with the OWW assumption that there is a single reality to which there correspond multiple cultures, perspectives, or subjective representations. For the pluriverse proposal, there are multiple reals; however, the proposal is not intended to 'correct' the view of a single real on the grounds of being a truer account of 'reality'. The pluriverse is a tool to first, make alternatives to the one world plausible to one-worlders, and, second, provide resonance to those other worlds that interrupt the one-world story (Blaser et al. 2014). Displacing the centrality of this dualist ontology, while broadening the space for non-dualist ontologies, is a sine qua non for breaking away from the one-world story. This implies a transition from concepts such as 'globalization' and 'global studies' to concepts centered on the pluriverse as made up of a multiplicity of mutually entangled and co-constituting but distinct worlds.

As it was mentioned in the introduction, knowledges produced in the struggles for the defense of relational worlds might be more farsighted and appropriate to the conjuncture of modern problems without modern solutions (Santos 2014) than its academic counterparts. To substantiate this claim fully requires that we locate these knowledges within a twofold context: that of the need for civilizational transitions, on the one hand, and the planetary dynamics brought to the fore by global climate change, the destruction of biodiversity, and the anthropocene. The first context involves a consideration of the multiplication of discourses of transition over the past decade; the second, the pressing historical need to become attuned again to what the North Carolina ecologist and theologian Thomas Berry (1988, 1999) has poetically called 'the dream of the Earth' (Berry 1988, 1999). Territorial struggles, as it will be argued in this last section, are producing among the most insightful knowledges for the cultural and ecological transitions seen as necessary to face the crisis; these knowledges are also profoundly attuned to the self-organizing dynamics of the Earth. Only the second of these factors, however, will be discussed here (see Escobar 2015 for a discussion of transition discourses).

There are many non-dualist philosophies (more often known as cosmovisions) that reflect a deeply relational understanding of life, such as Muntu and Ubuntu in parts of Africa[12]; the Pachamama or Mama Kiwe among South American indigenous peoples; US and Canadian American Indian cosmologies[13]; the Buddhist philosophy of mind; and non-dualist cosmogonies from various historical civilizations. Non-dualist traditions also exist within the West, as alternative Wests or non-dominant forms of modernity (see, e.g., Santos 2014; Dreyfus and Kelly 2011; Goodwin 2007). These are expressions of the fact that, like every other living being, humans and non-humans alike are an expression of the creative force of the earth, of its self-organization and constant emergence; simply put, every living being is implicated in the existence and co-arising of all living beings on the planet. One of the most compelling visions in this regard has been proposed by Berry. For Berry, 'the deepest cause of the present devastation is found in a mode of consciousness that has established a radical discontinuity between the human and other modes of being and the bestowal of all rights on the humans' (1999: 4). He identifies governments, corporations, universities, and religions as the fundamental establishments that keep this state of affairs in place. We, moderns, have lost our integral relation with the universe, and must restore it by bringing about a new intimacy with the Earth. As the first 'radically anthropocentric society' (1988: 202), we have become rational, dreamless people.

Given that we cannot be intimate with the Earth within a mechanistic paradigm, we are in dire need of a New Story that might enable us to reunite the sacred and the universe, the human, and the non-human. The wisdom traditions, including those of indigenous peoples, are a partial guide toward this goal of re-embedding ourselves within the Earth. Within these traditions, humans are embedded within the earth, not an individual consciousness existing in an inert world. As a Nasa indigenous leader from Southwest Colombia put it, *somos la continuidad de la tierra, miremos desde el corazón de la tierra* ('we are the extension of the earth, let us think from the earth's heart'). Most Western intellectual traditions have been inimical to this profound realization.[14]

Given that the humans have become a planetary force, however (what is now called the anthropocene), we (all humans, but particularly moderns) need to formulate a more explicit project of transformation and transition. Berry seeks to give shape to this project by calling for a transition from 'the terminal Cenozoic to the emerging Ecozoic era', or 'from the period when humans were a disruptive force on the planet Earth to the period when humans become present to the planet in a manner that is mutually enhancing' (199: 7, 11). Above all, we need to recognize that modern culture provides insufficient guidance for the Ecozoic era, and that hence we need to go back to the Earth as a source of insight for action—which is precisely what many relational struggles in defense of the territories and the earth are doing.[15] This mandate has significant implications for how we think about sustainability.

Activists at the forefront of these struggles will easily recognize Berry's dictum that 'Earth is a communion of subjects, not a collection of objects' (2013: 4). Ecology, in this sense, becomes 'a functional cosmology' (I should emphasize that these statements by Berry stem from a biocentric, not anthropocentric, vision; they do not rely on an epistemology and ontology of subjects and objects). Again, we can think here of the many functional cosmologies maintained by many peoples throughout history, including in the alternative Wests themselves. The new stories seek to reunite the sacred and the universe. While indigenous traditions have an important role to play in this endeavor, so does a transformed understanding of science, one which would help humans reinterpret their place at the species level within a new universe story. By placing it within a reinterpreted cosmology, science would move beyond the dominant technical and instrumental comprehension of the world to be reintegrated with the phenomenal world and so it would contribute to humans' reencounter with the numinous universe.

CONCLUSION

That Berry calls for a necessary restructuring of our civilization is perfectly understood by many activists of territorial struggles and transition activists worldwide. They can be said to be engaged in the sociology and political ontology of emergences that characterize the pluriverse (Santos 2014; Escobar 2014). In the Global North, emphases on the relocalization of food, energy, and economy, as in the Transition Town Initiative, for instance (Hopkins 2011), and the degrowth (e.g., D'Alisa et al. 2014) and commons (Bollier and Helfrich 2012; Bollier 2014) movements are also part of this emergence; they emphasize the historical re-communalization of social life and its reconnection with the Earth (e.g., Macy and Johnstone 2012). Here again, we find the idea of the farsighted character of the knowledge produced by transition forms of activism, and I want to mention some of the knowledges created by territorial struggles in ending. This character can be gleaned from the following aspects of such knowledges: they evince a profound understanding about life and the Earth; they articulate a farsighted political strategy vis-à-vis capitalism and the State; they include forms of knowing that operate through relation and experience, as well as embodied and embedded reflexivity; they exhibit an acute consciousness of the planetary conjuncture; and they envision realizable utopias for the construction and entanglement of worlds toward the pluriverse, such as the visions of Buen Vivir (well-being) and rights of nature currently being spearhead by movements and dissenting intellectuals in South America (e.g., Acosta and Martinez 2009; Gudynas 2014, 2015). Transition knowledges problematize the teleology, outcome orientation, economism, and instrumentalism of expert knowledge, development, and conventional design.

The academy has not been auspicious to relationality; indeed, from the perspective of this chapter it could be said that the academy, taken as whole, has been part of the occupying ontology. We, academics, often ignore living knowledges, communal and spiritual knowledge, art, even other 'non-academic' literatures that would be relevant for our inquiries (for instance, the growing field of spiritual ecology, of which Berry is a central figure, which would be so relevant to rethinking sustainability). Unsustainability cannot be addressed only theoretically, even if theory of course will be important in the transitions debate. To take seriously the profound insights of relationality implies that we need to partially move beyond the logos to practice and experience; that we give up the *individual* idea of what it means to be radical; and willingness on our part to transform our academic and knowledge practices accordingly, in order to welcome a much larger collective of humans and non-humans into our conversations that we have done thus far. In short, it calls on us *to re-learn to walk the world as living beings.*[16] This is the imaginary that feminist and decolonial political ontologies are attempting to build, as practiced spaces for understanding and healing, and as pluriversal pedagogies for re-weaving co-creating worlds with others.

While I can barely hint at this aspect of transitions here, I would like to end by making a brief reference to an emerging notion of design from ontological perspectives. The basic insight is straightforward: in designing tools (broadly speaking, objects, services, structures, and interventions), we are designing ways of being (Winograd and Flores 1986). Design generates our structures of possibility—it creates a 'world-within-the-world' (Fry 2012)—that contributes to unsustainability and defuturing (destruction of futures). We design the world and it designs us back. The key question is: Can relationality furnish the elements for a new foundation for design? There are multiple sources for thinking that this indeed can be, or is actually, the case. Australian designer Tony Fry speaks of ontological design as a strategy for a transition from Enlightenment to Sustainment. So understood, design would challenge the unsustainability intensified by capitalist modernity. In some approaches, the visions of transition become the basis for new design practices, indeed to the very thought of design for transitions.[17]

By re-positioning the human among earth beings, vibrant things, and spirituality and the sacred, these novel design orientations might contribute to reinvent the 'human' in non-dualist, post-humanist ways.

According to this new orientation, too, there are design traditions all over the world and in all cultures, in that every community, in some sense—and in increasingly explicit ways—practices the design of itself. Although this is more a hypothesis for now than a cogent framework, it can be said that one of the greater challenges for sustainability thinking today is to come up with ways in which communities can design their worlds from a space of autonomy, thus contributing to enhancing the pluriverse. Ontologically understood, design could become a powerful critique of, and an alternative to, development, endless growth, unsustainability, and defuturing, a way of healing territories, life, and the Earth. This, too, is the meaning of the principle of La Toma women's march with which this chapter started: *Territories and Life are not sold – they are loved and defended.* Far from merely reducing unsustainability, the thrust of this thought is the sustainability of the pluriverse.

NOTES

1. Translated from the Spanish in: http://afrocolombian.org/2014/11/25/peace-without-ancestral-afrodescendant-territories-not-for-the-black-women-of-northern-cauca/. Accessed 25 May 2015.
2. Francia Márquez, 'Situación que carcome mis entrañas. A propósito de la orden de bombardear el Cauca', open letter, April 18, 2015 (this an all other translations are mine).
3. Francia Márquez, 'A las mujeres que cuidan de sus territorios como a sus hijas e hijos. A las cuidadores y cuidadores de la Vida Digna, Sencilla y Solidaria', open letter, April 14, 2015. I should note that the reference to the umbilical cord refers to the long-standing practice among rural and forest Afrodescendant communities to bury the placenta and umbilical cord in order to create an indissoluble link with the territory, so that humans become an integral part of it, and a bit more than human, too.
4. This is not a comprehensive review by any means. I want to highlight some elements of the political ecology genealogy of importance for political ontology. There are many schools of political ecology (sometimes not earmarked as such) in many parts of the world going back to the 1970s, including Latin America and South Asia, Catalunya, France, Germany, and Scandinavia. This complete genealogy is still to be told in English, given that most reviews to date focus in the Anglo-American traditions. See Escobar (2010) for

additional references, and Bryant, ed. (2015) for an excellent comprehensive collection on contemporary political ecology. See also Dove et al., eds. (2011); Harcourt and Nelson, eds. (2015).

5. For instance, by Redclift (1987) and Leff (1986).

6. Thinks, for instance, about Dianne Rocheleau, Paige West, Laura Ogden, Wendy Harcourt, Sarah Whatmore, Anna Tsing, Gibson-Graham, and Jane Bennett, among others. While not all of these scholars construct their work explicitly as feminist, a feminist sensibility to relation and multiplicity is always present.

7. Remarks at the AAA Annual Meeting, Washington, DC, December 2014.

8. Statement by Francia Márquez of the Community Council of La Toma, taken from the documentary La Toma, by Paula Mendoza, http://www.youtube.com/watch?v=BrgVcdnwU0M, accessed May 20, 2013. Most of this brief section on La Toma comes from meetings in which I have participated with La Toma leaders in 2009, 2012, 2014, and 2015, as well as campaigns to stop illegal mining in this ancestral territory and accounts of the March to Bogotá of November 2014.

9. From the documentary by Mendoza cited above.

10. I borrow the term futurality from Australian designer Tony Fry (2012).

11. I have in mind here, of course, Deleuze and Guattari's discussion of rhizomes (1987), and Laura Ogden's (2010) remarkable extension of this concept to the human/non-human assemblages in the Florida Everglades.

12. Archbishop Desmond Tutu ventured an extension of the *Ubuntu* principle—usually explained as 'I exist because you exist'—to the entire realm of the living (cited in Bassey 2012: 9).

13. See the excellent collection of writings on the Idle No More movement (Kino-nda-niimi Collective 2014). Many of the articles, stories, and poems can be read on an ontological register.

14. Statement by Marcus Yule, gobernador Nasa, at the congress, 'Política Rural: Retos, Riesgos y Perspectivas', Bogotá, October 28–30, 2013.

15. Berry had developed a well worked out statement on the anthropocene well before the term was officially coined. As he put it in *The Dream of the Earth*, 'We are acting on a geological and biological order of magnitude. ... the anthropogenic shock that is overwhelming the earth is of an order of magnitude beyond anything previously known in human historical and cultural development. As we have indicated, only those geological and biological changes of the past that have taken hundreds of millions of years for their accomplishment can be referred to as having any comparable order of magnitude' (1988: 206, 211). Or, from his last published book, 'So now we awaken to a period of extensive disarray in the biological structure and functioning of the planet .... [we are] dealing with the disruption and even the termination of a geobiological period that has governed the functioning

of the planet for some 67 million years' (1999: 3). One can read his proposal of the Ecozoic era as a purposive response to the anthropocene.

16. *Aprender a caminar el mundo come seres vivos es el punto de partida para re-aprender la vida*, remark made by Adriana Paredes Pinda, Mapuche *machi* and poet, Chapel Hill, October 30, 2014.

17. Various types of 'design for transitions' are emerging in the academy as well, for instance, at Schumacher College in southern England, and at Carnegie Mellon University, where a new PhD program in Transition Design has been created (led by Terry Irwin, Gideon Kossoff, with the collaboration of Damian White, Ezio Manzini, and other design thinkers). See (Irwin 2015; Tonkinwise 2015; Manzini 2015), and http://design.cmu.edu/con tent/doctoral-research-foci

REFERENCES

Acosta, A., and E. Martínez, eds. 2009. *El buen vivir. Una vía para el desarrollo.* Quito: Abya-Yala.

Anzaldúa, G. 2002. Now Let Us Shift. ... The Path of Conocimiento.... Inner Work, Public Acts. In *This Bridge We Call Home. Radical Visions for Social Transformation*, ed. Gloria Anzaldúa and Analouise Keatin, 540–578. New York: Routledge.

Baksh, R., and W. Harcourt, eds. 2015. *The Oxford Handbook of Transnational Feminist Movements.* Oxford: Oxford University Press.

Bassey, N. 2012. *To Cook a Continent. Destructive Extraction and the Climate Crisis in Africa.* Cape Town: University of Kwa Zulu Natal Press.

Bennett, J. 2010. *Vibrant Matter. A Political Ecology of Things.* Durham: Duke University Press.

Berry, T. 1988. *The Dream of the Earth*, 194–215. San Francisco: Sierra Club Books.

———. 1999. *The Great Work: Our Way Into the Future.* New York: Bell Tower.

———. 2013. The Determining Features of the Ecozoic Era. *The Ecozoic* 3: 4–6.

Blaser, M. 2009. The Political Ontology of a Sustainable Hunting Program. *American Anthropologist* 111 (1): 10–20.

———. 2010. *Storytelling Globalization from the Chaco and Beyond.* Durham/Gabriola Island: Duke University Press/New Society Publishers.

———. 2013. Ontological Conflicts and the Stories of Peoples in Spite of Europe: Towards a Conversation on Political Ontology. *Current Anthropology* 54 (5): 547–568.

Blaser, M., M. de la Cadena, and A. Escobar. 2014. The Anthropocene and the One World. Introduction to *Pluriversal Studies Reader.* Unpublished manuscript.

Bollier, D. 2014. *Think like a Commoner. A Short Introduction to the Life of the Commons.* Gabriola: New Society Publishers.

Bollier, D., and S. Helfrich, eds. 2012. *The Wealth of the Commons: A World beyond Market and the State.* Amherst: Leveller Press.

Bryant, R., ed. 2015. *The International Handbook of Political Ecology.* Cheltenham: Elgar.

de la Cadena, M. 2010. Indigenous Cosmopolitics in the Andes: Conceptual Reflections Beyond Politics. *Cultural Anthropology* 25 (2): 334–370.

———. 2015. *Earth Beings: Ecologies of Practice Across Andean Worlds.* Durham: Duke University Press.

D'Alissa, G., F. Demaria, and G. Kallis, eds. 2014. *Degrowth: A Vocabulary for a New Era.* London: Routledge. Introduction.

Deleuze, G., and F. Guattari. 1987. *Mil mesetas. Capitalismo y esquizofrenia.* Valencia: Pre-Textos.

Dove, M., P. Sajise, and A. Dolittle, eds. 2011. *Beyond the Sacred Forest. Complicating Conservation in South East Asia.* Durham: Duke University Press.

Dreyfus, H., and S. Kelly. 2011. *All Things Shining. Reading the Western Classics to Find Meaning in a Secular Age.* New York: Free Press.

Escobar, A. 2008. *Territories of Difference: Place~Movements~Life~Redes.* Durham: Duke University Press.

———. 2010. Postconstructivist Political Ecologies. In *International Handbook of Environmental Sociology,* ed. M. Redclift and G. Woodgate, 2nd ed., 91–105. Cheltenham: Elgar.

———. 2014. *Sentipensar con la Tierra: Postdesarrollo y Diferencia Radical.* Medellín: Universidad Autónoma Latinoamericana.

———. 2015. Degrowth, Postdevelopment, and Transitions: A Preliminary Conversation. *Sustainability Science.* doi:10.1007/s11625-015-0297-5

Espinosa, Y., D. Gómez, and K. Ochoa, eds. 2014. *Tejiendo de otro modo. Feminismo, epistemología y apuestas decoloniales en Abya Yala.* Popayán: Universidad del Cauca.

Fry, T. 2012. *Becoming Human by Design.* London: Berg.

Goodwin, B. 2007. *Nature's Due: Healing Our Fragmented Culture.* Edinburgh: Floris Books.

Gudynas, E. 2014. *Derechos de la naturaleza/Etica bicentrica y políticas ambientales.* Lima: PDTG/redGE/CLAES.

———. 2015. *Extractivismos. Economía, ecología y política de un modo de entender el desarrollo y la naturaleza.* Cochabamba: CEDIB/CLAES.

Harcourt, W., and I. Nelson, eds. 2015. *Practicing Feminist Political Ecology.* London: Zed Books.

Healy, H., J. Martínez-Alier, L. Temper, M. Walter, and J.-F. Gerber, eds. 2013. *Ecological Economics from the Ground Up.* London: Routledge.

Hopkins, R. 2011. *The Transition Companion. Making Your Community More Resilient in Uncertain Times.* White River Junction: Chelsea Green Publishing.

Ingold, T. 2011. *Being Alive. Essays on Movement, Knowledge, and Description.* New York: Routledge.

Irwin, T. 2015. Transition Design: A Proposal for a New Area of Design Practice, Study, and Research. *Design and Culture* 7 (2): 229–246.

Kino-nda-niimi Collective. 2014. *The Winter We danced. Voices from the Past, the Future, and the Idle No More Movement.* Winnipeg: Arp Books.

Law, J. 2004. *After Method: Mess in Social Science Research.* London: Routledge.

———. 2011. *What's Wrong with a One-World World.* Presented to the Center for the Humanities, Wesleyan University, September 19. www.heterogeneities.net/publications/Law2111WhatsWrongWithAOneWprldWorld.pdf

Law, J., and M. Lien. 2012. Denaturalizing Nature. Unpublished manuscript.

Leff, E. 1986. *Ecología y capital.* México: Siglo XXI.

Lisifrey, A., L.A. Vargas, E. Mina, A. Rojas, A.M. Solarte, G. Vanegas, and A. Vega. 2013. *La Toma. Historias de territorio, resistencia y autonomía en la cuenca del Alto Cauca.* Bogotá: Universidad Javeriana y Consejo Comunitario de La Toma.

Macy, J., and C. Johnstone. 2012. *Active Hope: How to Face the Mess We're in Without Going Crazy.* Novato: New World Library.

Manzini, E. 2015. *Design, When Everybody Designs.* Cambridge: MIT Press.

Martínez Alier, J. 2002. *The Environmentalism of the Poor. A Study of Ecological Conflicts and Valuation.* London: Elgar.

McMichael, P. 2013. Rethinking Land Grab Ontology. *Rural Sociology* 79 (1): 34–55.

Nonini, D., ed. 2007. *The Global Idea of The Commons.* New York: Berghahn Books.

Ogden, L. 2010. Swamplife. In *People, Gators, and Mangroves Entangled in the Everglades.* Minneapolis: University of Minnesota Press.

Redclift, M. 1987. *Sustainable Development: Exploring the Contradictions.* London: Routledge.

Santos, B. 2014. *Epistemologies of the South. Justice against Epistemicide.* Boulder: Paradigm Publishers.

Shaw, C. 2014. *Productive Borders: African-American and African Feminist Interventions, a Personal Journey.* Presented at the Panel on "Decolonial Feminism/World Anthropologies". American Anthropological Association Annual Meeting, Washington, December 6.

Tonkinwise, C. 2015. *Transition Design as Postindustrial Interaction Design?* https://medium.com/@camerontw/transition-design-as-postindustrialinteraction-design-6c8668055e8d. Accessed 3 June 2015.

Winograd, T., and F. Flores. 1986. *Understanding Computers and Cognition. A New Foundation for Design.* Norwood: Ablex Publishing Corporation.

CHAPTER 15

Traditional People, Collectors of Diversity

Manuela Carneiro da Cunha

What is needed for life? Nicholas Georgescu-Roegen (1986),[1] claiming roots in Ludwig Boltzmann and Erwin Schrodinger, asserted that life needs three basic things: first, matter (such as natural resources); second, energy; the third and more mysteriously is diversity, also known as low or negative entropy. Let's start, as does Georgescu, with energy. Energy, in the 1970s, following the oil crisis of 1973–1974, became (and still is) the focus of much concern and attention. A fad even suggested that energetic economics could adequately represent the whole of economic processes. Hence, everything should be explained by energy measures. In anthropol-

---

This chapter relies on and dialogues with texts presented by Mauro W.B. Almeida in symposia held in 2014 and 2016, "Desenvolvimento Entrópico e a Alternativa da Diversidade" and "Metafísicas do Fim do Mundo e Encontros Pragmáticos com Entropia" (see References).

M.C. da Cunha (✉)
Department of Anthropology, University of Chicago, Chicago, IL, USA

University of São Paulo, State of São Paulo, Brazil

© The Author(s) 2017
M. Brightman, J. Lewis (eds.), *The Anthropology of Sustainability*,
Palgrave Studies in Anthropology of Sustainability,
DOI 10.1057/978-1-137-56636-2_15

ogy, we had our own versions of the same trend notably with the so-called
ecological anthropology, which posited available protein intake as the foundation of "cultural development," whatever that was supposed to mean.[2] A
necessary condition for life is thus energy, but not just any energy (of which
there is plenty in the Universe) but rather, as Lord Kelvin famously
established, *energy available to us.* Energy in the Universe is never lost,
but it does transform itself; yet some forms of energy are not available for
our usage, that is, for conversion into work. To be usable, there must be
some difference between two states, such as a temperature difference for
a steam engine, or an altitude difference in a river for generating
electricity.

This is why life needs low entropy as well as energy. Entropy can be
envisioned as a measure of homogeneity present in a given set. Entropy is
low[3] when internal diversity is high. It grows as diversity decreases. It is low
entropy (differences) that allows for available energy. Entropy is the subject
of the disturbing second law of thermodynamics. It is disturbing because it
introduced irreversibility in an otherwise perfectly reversible physicist's
world. The issue is that those differences in states that make energy available
to us can only be used once. One cannot expect that they would spontane-
ously, that is, by themselves and with no work involved, revert to their
previous form. If you put milk into your coffee, you do not expect milk and
coffee to separate again. Differences irreversibly degrade into homogeneity.
And perfect homogeneity, as for instance full temperature equilibrium
between liquids that started off at different temperatures is devoid of any
motion, is inert. Thermodynamic equilibrium is death (Schrodinger 1944:
71–2). Yet everything evolves in that direction, entropy grows and does not
decrease. Differences are erased over time. That being the case, how are
living beings able to maintain (to a certain extent) the functioning of their
organs, and how are they able to delay death?

Low entropy thus means differences, distinctions, or "order" as
Schrodinger (following Boltzmann) calls it. It is *diversity.* High entropy,
in contrast, is paucity of internal distinctions. The term disorder in this
vocabulary may seem counterintuitive to a totalitarian regime, whose idea
of order is that of uniformity. Here, in contrast, it is disorder that stands for
uniformity, while order stands for heterogeneity. And the second law of
thermodynamics "one of the rules of the world," as Richard Feynman puts
it, "is that a thing goes from an ordered condition to a disordered" (Feynman 1965: 113). Low entropy is always degraded into higher entropy.
Diversity irrevocably turns into homogeneity.

How then can organization, that is life, persist when time conspires against it? How can life resist such a rule of the world? Well, as Schrodinger puts it, *organization is maintained by extracting "order" from the environment* (p. 73), and by environment he means something external to the system. So for organization to persist (the second law notwithstanding), it needs to feed on order, that is, low entropy, in short, diversity.

Georgescu sums up the process in these terms: *a living organism does not need just energy but low entropy, which it sucks from the environment and degrades into high entropy (waste). This continuous flow of low entropy maintains the biological body in good order and also supports all activities of the organism.* And he goes on to say that low entropy is a necessary (although not sufficient) condition for a thing to have value for us.

In his 1986 paper, Georgescu calls attention to a third element necessary for life, and that is, matter (matter in bulk, he writes, as distinguished from microscopic matter). Matter, just like energy, might be present in either available or unavailable form to us. But "the point is," he writes, "that both available energy and available matter are irrevocably degraded into unavailable states." In other words, life needs matter, energy, and low entropy: matter, energy, and diversity. As is well known, the conclusion Georgescu reaches is that growth cannot be unlimited, for steady work cannot be continued indefinitely without a continuous supply of matter, energy, and low entropy.

Claude Lévi-Strauss was the one anthropologist who applied the concept of entropy to cultures. He lamented the loss of cultural diversity and sadly anticipated a growingly homogeneous world.[4] Limiting economic growth and maximizing leisure rather than maximizing material goods were powerful ideas in the late 1960s and the 1970s.[5] Had these ideas prevailed in mainstream economics, the current debate on the End of the World would have been quite different. I submit that a sustainable future hinges on diversity in every domain, and that people's diversity is a formidable contribution to that end.

An Example: Agrobiodiversity

I seize this cue for turning to a quite literal example of how diversity is essential to life and how traditional people contribute to it. I take my example from agricultural biodiversity, domesticated or semi-domesticated plant diversity, also known as agrobiodiversity. Today, there exist 250,000 globally identified plant species with numerous varieties, and 7000 crops exist that were used for food by humans along history. Of these, there are merely 12 crops and 5 animal species that provide three-fourths of human food today (Twiller 2014). These crops and animals have been domesticated in different parts of the world (such as Mesopotamia for wheat, India and China for rice, Mexico for Maize and so on) where they retain a (relatively) high diversity of varieties. As is widely known, the Green Revolution, after World War II, focused on maximizing agricultural production and thus selected plant varieties with a maximum yield. While very successful on that respect, it produced, however, what in spy movies is called, "collateral damages." Food sovereignty and agricultural diversity were among those damages. Great numbers of varieties of maize, rice, wheat and many other basic foodstuffs were lost.

Diversity of varieties is a matter of food security. The example that is regularly quoted is that of the great Irish famine (1845–1849). Because it relied on too few potato varieties, Irish agriculture did not resist potato blight attacks on its crops. This disaster was compounded with the British government's indifference to Irish predicament (Sen 1981), and one million people died while another million emigrated.

Potatoes originated and were domesticated in the Andes some 6000 years ago. More than 1000 varieties were selected by Andean peasants. A secondary center of potato diversity is the island of Chiloe, in southern Chile, where some 400 potato varieties were bred. Spaniards introduced potatoes in Europe by the end of the sixteenth century. Potatoes were slowly and cautiously adopted in different European countries, but by the eighteenth century it had become a major foodstuff; the rise of population during the Industrial Revolution is often credited to its adoption. The Irish relied mainly on a very productive Chiloe variety, which was devastated by potato blight.

Genetic diversity of cultivated plants is essential for food security, since some varieties can be resistant to biotic attacks (such as fungi, virus, parasites, and pests in general) and abiotic (such as climate) changes. The very father of the Green Revolution that dramatically reduced plant diversity, Norman Borlaug, launched in 1971 the CGIAR (Consultative Group on International Agricultural Research) initiative. Its mission was to set up gene banks of agricultural varieties for the most basic crops and conserve in ideal conditions the maximum number of varieties available. Gene banks however are not enough: living beings coevolve with their habitat and adapt to climate change as well as to diseases and parasites. In a gene bank, no such evolution occurs; hence conservation in situ and more specifically *on-farm* conservation are important.[6] That kind of dynamic conservation can be provided by technicians in controlled plots, but it is also freely provided by local agriculturalists, particularly in areas of origin or in areas of diversification of such crops. Hence, the importance of on-farm conservation was felt. The crucial contribution of on-farm conservation was recognized in 1996 at the Leipzig Conference and further included in the 2001 UN International Treaty on Plant Genetic Resources for Food and Agriculture.

WHO PRODUCES DOMESTICATED DIVERSITY?

There are several ways to produce diversity and several ways to conserve it.

More than half of Amazonian plants, even those that are hermaphrodite, have cross fertilization (Kerr 1987: 160). Cross fertilization, which is sex with a different individual, is key for producing diversity. Vegetative reproduction, on the other hand, is a great way to conserve varieties and is quite common in the Amazon. Bulbs, rhizomes, and manioc stem cuttings, for example, conserve varieties as clones. Building on those two mechanisms, aboriginal societies in the Amazon have produced and selected a great diversity of fruit trees and crops (Kerr 1987).

Selection practices, however, may not necessarily be consistent with the conservation of diversity. Plant breeders usually opt for what are considered, under whatever criteria—be it taste, size, productivity, resistance, etc.—the most desirable varieties and allow many other varieties to die out.

In contrast, there are examples among Amazonian aboriginal societies of the coexistence of pursuing both selection and diversity. Two examples from the Rio Negro basin will be presented. The whole of the Rio Negro basin is known for a high diversity of at least two species: a specific pepper species (*Capsicum chinense* Jacq.) on the Içana river and manioc (*Manihot esculenta* Crantz) on the upper Uaupés and middle and upper Rio Negro. In both cases, women agriculturalists engage in the selection of new varieties. Starting with *Capsicum spp.*, a total of 78 varieties were found in 40 Içana villages (roughly half of the total number of villages). A Capsicum census was conducted in 17 Baniwa villages: out of an average of 32 different cultivated plants per garden, there were 5,46 varieties of *Capsicum spp.* and a maximum of 14 varieties in some particularly motivated women's gardens. Ninety percent of these varieties are from *Capsicum chinense* Jacq. This species, though self-pollinating, is also prone to cross pollination

(Costa et al. 2008). This ability, the fact that different varieties are planted close by and the active circulation of varieties in the region, accounts for the continuous creation of new varieties. These new varieties are carefully observed and selected by women and enter the family pool of varieties (Adeilson Silva, pers. comm.; ISA, FOIRN et al. 2007–2009).

Women agriculturalists of the upper and middle Rio Negro have an even more striking role in ensuring a high diversity of manioc (*Manihot esculenta* Crantz) varieties. Traditional practices imply not only selection of naturally occurring new varieties, but they actually favor the creation of such varieties and their conservation.[7]

Bitter manioc is the staple dietary crop, and manioc is replanted from stem cuttings, which entails that individual plants are nothing but clones from the plants that originated them. Yet, manioc (as well as potatoes which like manioc have vegetative reproduction) has retained sexual reproduction capabilities. Manioc has flowers and produces seeds. Those seeds have a sweet appendix that makes them attractive to ants. Consequently, ants will collect and bury them. Those seeds are dormant and will only germinate provided the area is subject to fire. They will stay in the ground for the whole fallow period until the plot is burnt and cultivated again.

A number of traditional practices in Rio Negro favor the multiplication of new varieties. I will describe four of them.[8] Gardening is a women's domain on the Rio Negro basin. Much like the Achuar women described by Anne-Christine Taylor and Philippe Descola (1986), gardening is their source of pride and value. Gardens bear witness to their mistress' diligence, abilities, and social prestige. Manioc plants are overly tended for, and other plants will be there to serve them. Some will play drums for them to dance and rejoice, others will comb them, still others will protect them. An index of gardening success for a Rio Negro woman is the sheer number of different species and varieties she cultivates. That number, in turn, relies on her social network and prestige, as a number of different varieties were gifts from women relatives and friends.[9] Any visit or festivity attended in a different community from one's own seems to be the welcome occasion for obtaining new varieties. Among the people of the Uaupés River, on the upper Rio Negro basin, manioc diversity has marriage rules as one of its sources. Language exogamy and virilocality rules entail that a woman will start her own garden in her husband's village (Chernela 1986). Her mother will give her manioc stem cuttings before she leaves her maiden village, and so will her mother-in-law once she moves to her husband's village.

Moreover, several married women from different linguistic groups will usually be living in the same village, favoring a greater circulation of varieties.

People will maintain a minimum of three gardens at once, each in a different stage. After three years, a plot is reverted to fallow and manioc cuts will be transferred to a recently opened garden. Those stem cuts will normally exceed the necessities of the new garden. However, one is never supposed to discard manioc stem cuttings. The cuttings in excess will be roughly planted all together on the perimeter of the old garden and left there to survive and possibly sexually reproduce. Then there is the burning of old gardens, after an adequate period of fallow, which allows for the dormant seeds (the ones that resulted from sexual reproduction) to germinate. Note, in passing, how this process shows a remarkable "fit" of much denigrated slash and burn agricultural techniques to manioc. This is when seedlings will emerge. On the Rio Negro, they will be preserved and tended. They are understood as both coming from and belonging to "the old folk" (os antigos) and paradoxically (since they are result of sexual reproduction) as orphans.[10] Women will attentively observe the new-comers. They will separate spots for them and they will be experimented upon for at least two or three years. Their first year tubers–one single conical tuber per individual–will be unique and distinct from subsequent years' tubers. Only when they are replanted from stem cuttings will they show their true colors, qualities, or specificities.

Manioc cultivars have the capacity of staying in the ground without rotting for a time that will reach, in some cases, up to two years. Hence, there is no problem with storage of manioc. Different varieties will be ripe at different moments. The earlier ones can be harvested after just six months. This is no doubt a practical reason for planting different varieties in a single garden. But it can hardly explain the excess that certain women indulge in, of cultivating up to 40 varieties in their gardens (Emperaire et al. 1998). What is remarkable about the collections of varieties that result from these practices is that there seems to be no organoleptic reason given for them. And yet there are dozens of recipes for both food and beverages made out of manioc. Bitter manioc, that is, poisonous manioc, is locally classified in just two basic categories: yellow manioc and white manioc. Every recipe will distinguish those two kinds of bitter manioc, which may be used alone or mixed. White manioc will contain more starch, yellow manioc produces more flour. On the Rio Negro, manioc flour is usually made out of a mix of white and yellow manioc. While recipes that include immersion for three days in running water will specifically call for drier varieties, no recipe will normally specify a variety within each of these two categories, and a specific taste of a variety is not mentioned.[11]

There is also a moral imperative related to manioc diversity. As much as one is not supposed to discard manioc stems, one should not ignore any variety. That rule is linked to São Tomé (Saint Thomas), one of the 12 apostles and the patron of manioc. It is to this saint that one lights up a candle when grasshoppers or ants attack one's garden, or when deer start eating young leaves of manioc. A story I heard in 2007 from an elderly lady on the mid-Rio Negro tells of São Tomé despising a yellow variety of manioc and being reprimanded by the tuber itself. What I am trying to point out is that there is no obvious practical reason for such a wide diversity in manioc varieties. A taste, a passion for diversity, seems to be a good enough reason.[12]

A PASSION FOR DIVERSITY

Anthropologists, often in ignorance of similar findings by human geographers and natural scientists, have gathered a wealth of evidence that suggests a nexus between traditional people and what could be called a *penchant* for diversity in many domains. Charles Darwin, in his 1859 "On the Origin of Species," pays great attention to what he calls "artificial selection," that is, "selection by man." He even confesses to have endeavored to become an amateur pigeon breeder himself. He more than once stresses and praises the outstanding ability and expertise required for the job: one has to be able to notice small differences, "differences absolutely inappreciable by an uneducated eye – differences that I for one have vainly attempted to appreciate. Not one man in a thousand has the accuracy of eye and judgment sufficient to become an eminent breeder" (Darwin 1859: 32). And in his *Variations of Animals and Plants under Domestication* (1868, p. 177), Darwin states on the same ability: "Indomitable patience, the finest powers of discrimination, and sound judgment must be exercised during many years." The first chapter of *The Savage Mind* (Levi-Strauss 1962) enumerates a plethora of examples of diversity, starting with Harold Conklin's findings among the Hanunoo in the Philippines, to which many more contemporary examples could be added.

I contend that Indigenous and local societies seem to overwhelmingly *value diversity per se,* for its own sake.[13] This includes varieties of living species and of landscapes. Accordingly, they pay attention to minute characteristics and tend to have extensive classification systems.

Thus, Baniwa of the upper Rio Negro in Brazil, in a short conversation with Geraldo Andrello, listed 53 categories of vegetation named after their dominant tree species (Cabalzar and Ricardo 2006: 65). The Matses in Peru distinguish 47 habitats according to geomorphological and ecological criteria (Fleck 1997). The Matsiguenga, also in the Peruvian Amazon, distinguish 69 habitats along topographic, hydrologic, geologic and type of perturbation criteria (Shepard et al. 2001). Ghillean Prance was the author of the first major quantitative botanical research, published in 1987, in tropical America. He wrote that Kayapó from Pará, in the Brazilian Amazon, use 76 forest species out of the 99 that were found (Prance et al. 1987). Riverine peasants in the Peruvian Amazon use 131 forest species (Pinedo-Vasquez et al. 1990). Tapajós National Forest dwellers, in Pará as well, use 120 forest species, and they recognize and have names for 439 plant morphotypes (Couly 2009). Turning to bees, Enawene-Nawe Indians living in the southern Brazilian Amazon name 48 stingless bee species and describe their ecologic characteristics (Mendes dos Santos and Yasmine Antonini 2008). Studies among the *Guarani-mbyá* indigenous peoples showed the existence of a diversified knowledge of the people about bees and wasps, distinguishing 25 ethno species divided into these two groups of insects. Cultivated plants are a major example of what one could call a passion for diversity. Anna Tsing aptly writes "to appreciate Meratus Dayak pleasures in biodiversity, the swidden field is an important site" (2005: 165).

One can find high diversity in cultivated species, as the following example illustrates: in two communities close to Cruzeiro do Sul, on the upper Juruá, Acre, Brazil, where 52 agriculturalists were interviewed, 338 morphotypes corresponding to 269 botanical species were found (Emperaire et al. submitted 2014).

But one also very often finds high diversity within the most important staple food species. We have already seen the example of manioc on the Rio Negro.

Infra-species diversity of manioc has been widely documented in Amazonian indigenous societies. To restrict ourselves to the most staggering numbers, Amuesha people in Peru may boast of 204 manioc varieties, half of which are "sweet manioc" (Salick et al. 1997: 7); Huambisa, some 100 (Boster 1983: 61), roughly the same number found in a Tatuyo village (Dufour 1993: 51) and Piaroa (Heckler and Zent); 89 among Tukano/

Desana of the Uaupés River (Rio Negro) (Emperaire 2000) and more than a hundred, as we just saw, on the middle Rio Negro (Emperaire et al. 2008); 77 in a mixed Makushi and Wapishana village in southwest Guiana (Elias et al. 2000). Similar results have been underscored, particularly since the 1980s, for several other crops, and Stephen Brush, a pioneer on the subject among anthropologists, was able to publish in 1995 a first review on the topic (see Brush 1991, 1995).

As more research is carried out in the Amazon, astonishing results continue to emerge. The Kuikuru of the upper Xingu plants 15 morphotypes of pequi (Caryocar sp.) and recognizes two others: one being the forest "grand-father" of all pequis and the other whose seeds are dispersed by animals (Smith 2013: 153 ss.)

A research conducted in 2008 in a Mebêngôkre-Kayapó village in Pará, Brazil, showed that women knew and named 49 varieties of sweet potatoes (*Ipanoea batata* Lam.) of which 28 were under cultivation that year; 36 kinds of yams (*Dioscorea* spp.) 25 of which were present in the gardens that year; and 26 varieties of bananas (*Musa paradisiaca*), 18 of which were being cultivated in 2008 (Robert et al. 2012). These numbers were consistent with results Warwick Kerr had obtained in 1986, 22 years earlier (Kerr 1987). It is worth mentioning that women would be cultivating some 40 plants in each of the total number of plants (Robert et al. 2012). Note that the Mebêngôkre-Kayapó speak of "beautiful gardens" in one more instantiation of the aesthetic dimension of diversity (Tsing 2005).

I have looked for examples in the Amazon region, but we are sure to find similar cases elsewhere. In Melanesia, Caillon et al. (2006) report that Vanuatu growers identified 96 morphotypes of taro (*Colocasia esculenta* (L.) Schott); nearly 200 fig tree varieties in Morocco alone (Achtak et al. 2010); over a thousand olive cultivars in the Mediterranean region (Bartolini et al. 1998); as many potato varieties in the Andes; and the list is extensive.

PUTTING IN A GOOD WORD FOR SWIDDEN OR SHIFTING AGRICULTURE

Anna Tsing (2005: 165) recalls that since Conklin's seminal work (1954, 1962), shifting cultivation is known for its high diversity in cultivated plants as well as in plant varieties.[14] Shifting cultivation or swidden agriculture, as practiced by Amazonian indigenous societies such as the Kaapor, seems to preserve forest biodiversity itself. W. Balee has shown that secondary forests derived from agricultural practices, while exhibiting a specific mix of tree species, are not however less biodiverse than primary forests (Balee 1993: 389–390). Yet swidden agriculture and its use of fire have had a bad press for quite a while, despite several attempts at showing its "rationality." Traditional swidden agriculturalists all over the world, particularly in South East Asia, have been subject to intensive pressures to turn to cash-crop monocultures (Padoch et al. 2008). The costs of such a move in regard to food security and genetic erosion have only recently been taken into account by FAO (AIPP and IWGIA 2014), on the initiative of the Asian Indigenous People Pact. Yet it looks like recommendations for productivity at all costs have won the minds of decision-makers in developing countries. Their rejection of swidden cultivation is a by-product of their deeply ingrained belief in what counts as "development."

Here is a telling example. In November 2010, the traditional agricultural system of the Rio Negro, described above, was declared Intangible Heritage of Brazil (Emperaire et al. 2010). Diversity was a foundational argument for such acceptance. Yet, two and a half years later, in April 2013, the government of the state of Amazonas decided to promote manioc production in the region, on Green Revolution mode. To counteract such a policy, our group of researchers, who had submitted the Heritage case, organized an in situ course with classes taught by traditional indigenous agriculturalists and supported by highly respected agricultural researchers working in state of the art federal institutions. To attend the course, the Amazonas government only sent indigenous people who had been trained as agricultural counselors. After listening to the classes, these trained specialists declared that they had previous knowledge of what had been taught: after all, their own parents had always used similar practices and technology, but that those practices were precisely what they, as counselors, had been taught to abandon.

Swidden agriculture is also subject to attacks coming from a very different source. Some conservation NGOs object to any use of fire, however controlled and irrespective of the scale involved, in the preparation of fields. Recent publications and findings are now questioning the wisdom of such across the board fire prohibition (e.g., Adams et al. 2013).

CONCLUSION: PRODUCING AND COLLECTING DIVERSITY

Traditional people have been shown to be partial to diversity in its many forms, and there is an aesthetic dimension to their taste. Although they partake in the qualities Charles Darwin described for breeders in general, traditional practitioners seem to favor collections over selection.[15] They significantly differ from selectors in that they do not discard varieties. Their practices are not only central to the conservation of biodiversity, as the Convention for Biological Diversity recognizes (art.8j), but they actually may even *produce biodiversity*. This is but a particular case, I suspect, of a much more general law, one that demands diversity in every domain, societies included, for life to go on.

NOTES

1. Georgescu's argument goes back nearly 50 years to his essay Analytical Economics, published in 1966.
2. See for instance Daniel Gross's telling title: Protein Capture and Cultural Development in the Amazon Basin 1975 American Anthropological Association American Anthropologist Volume 77, Issue 3, pages 526–549, September 1975. An earlier version of this paper was read at the 38th Annual Meeting of the Society for American Archaeology in May 1973 in San Francisco. It was part of a symposium entitled "Ecological Anthropology," which received support from the Wenner-Gren Foundation. For a masterly rebuttal of a similar argument by Marvin Harris, see Marshall Sahlins.
3. Schrodinger uses the expression negative entropy rather than low entropy, but to avoid the *negative* ring to it, other writers such as Georgescu prefer low entropy.
4. For a remarkable analysis of that aspect of Levi-Strauss' ideas, see Barbosa de Almeida (1990).
5. Anthropology made a major contribution to this trend with the groundbreaking essay published by Marshall Sahlins (1972) on the First affluent societies. So-called primitive societies were no longer limited in their so-called development by protein availability or other scarce energy source.
6. See for example the 2015 conclusions of Commission on Genetic Resources for Food and Agriculture of FAO, an intergovernmental forum for the discussion and development of knowledge and policies relevant to biodiversity for future use of genetic resources for food and agriculture (L. Collette et al. 2015).
7. Research on the Rio Negro was conducted by Project PACTA2 jointly sponsored by CNPq (Brazil) and IRD-UMR 208 (France), n° 490826/

2008-3, led by M. Almeida and L. Emperaire and by the Project *Effects of intellectual and rights protection on traditional people and traditional knowledge. Case studies in Brazil* led by M. Carneiro da Cunha, sponsored by the Ford Foundation. Authorization CGEN n° 139, DOU (April 4, 2006).

8. Laura Rival and Doyle McKey (2008) provide a much more detailed description of the biological foundations of a very similar process of manioc diversification among the Macushi Indians. Their article calls for further research in other Amerindian societies, which the present paper should contribute to.

9. For a closer analysis on factors affecting diversity of varieties, see Kawa et al. (2013).

10. This seeming paradox is easily elucidated. As these seedlings were not planted by humans, they start life lacking a mother to tend them. It points to the Amazonian understanding that the relationship between a woman and her plants is one of dedicated motherhood (Descola 1996) and that parenthood is eminently social rather than biological.

11. "Mandioca d'água" could possibly be the only exception to this general rule (L. Emperaire, pers. comm.).

12. Anna Tsing (2005) mentions an aesthetic dimension, which is congruent to what I call a taste for diversity, since such a taste implies aesthetic pleasure. And indeed there is a manifest aesthetic pleasure in a woman's appreciation of her diverse garden.

13. For a similar point, see Rival and McKey (2008).

14. One should point out that shifting cultivation presently is a more acceptable name for what was previously known as slash and burn agriculture.

15. A similar point was suggested by Emeraire et al. (2008: 8).

References

Achtak, H., M. Ater, A. Oukabli, S. Santoni, F. Kjellberg, and B. Khadari. 2010. Traditional Agroecosystems as Conservatories and Incubators of Cultivated Plant Varietal Diversity: The Case of Fig (Ficus carica L.) in Morocco. *BMC Plant Biology* 10: 28.

Adams, C., L. Munari, N. Van Vliet, et al. 2013. Diversifying Incomes and Losing Landscape Complexity in Quilombola Shifting Cultivation Communities of the Atlantic Rainforest (Brazil). *Human Ecology* 41 (1): 119–137.

AIPP (Asia Indigenous People Pact) and IWGIA. 2014. *Shifting Cultivation, Livelihood and Food Security.* www.aippnet.org: www.iwgia.org

Balée, W. 1993. Biodiversidade e os índios Amazônicos. In *Amazônia: Etnologia e História Indígena*, ed. E. Viveiros de Castro and M. Carneiro da Cunha, 385–395. São Paulo: FAPESP/NHII/USP.

Barbosa de Almeida, M. 1990. Symmetry and Entropy: Mathematical Metaphors in the Work Of Lévi-Strauss. *Current Anthropology* 31 (4): 367–385.

———. 2014. *Metafísicas do Fim do Mundo e Encontros Pragmáticos com Entropia.* Paper presented to the Symposium Os Mil Nomes de Gaia: Do Antropoceno à Idade da Terra, held in Rio de Janeiro, September 15–19, 2014, ms.

———. 2016. Desenvolvimento antrópico e a alternativa de diversidade. *Ruris* 10 (1): 19–39.

Bartolini, G., G. Prevost, C. Messeri, G. Carignani, and U. Menini. 1998. *Olive Germplasm. Cultivars and World-Wide Collections.* Rome: FAO.

Boster, J.S. 1983. A Comparison of the Diversity of Jivaroan Gardens with That of the Tropical Forest. *Human Ecology* 2 (1): 47–67.

Brush, S.B. 1991. A Farmer Based Approach to Conserving Crop Germplasm. *Economic Botany* 45: 153–165.

———. 1995. *In Situ* Conservation of Landraces in Centers of Crop Diversity. *Crop Science* 35: 346–354.

Cabalzar, A., and B. Ricardo, eds. 2006. *Mapa-Livro Povos Indígenas do Rio Negro.* 3rd ed. São Paulo: ISA & FOIRN.

Caillon, S., J. Quero-Garcia, J.-P. Lescure, and V. Lebot. 2006. Nature of taro (Colocasia esculenta (L.) Schott) Genetic Diversity Prevalent in a Pacific Ocean Island, Vanua Lava, Vanuatu. *Genetic Resources and Crop Evolution* 53 (6): 1273–1289.

Chernela, J. 1986. Os Cultivares de Mandioca na Área do Uaupés (Tukâno). In *Suma Etnológica Brasileira 1, Etnobiologia,* ed. D. Ribeiro, 151–158. Vozes: Petrópolis.

Collette, L., D. Luchetti, D. Pilling, A. Asfaw, and A. Fonteneau. 2015. Main Conclusions and Opportunities. In *Coping with Climate Change – The Roles of Genetic Resources for Food and Agriculture,* 101–112. Rome: FAO.

Conklin, Harold C. 1954. The Relation of Hanunóo Culture to the Plant World. MS. Thesis, Yale University.

———. 1962. Lexicographical Treatment of Folk Taxonomies. *International Journal of American Linguistics* 28 (2), IV: 119–141.

Costa, L. Vilagelim, M.T. Gomes Lopes, R. Lopes, and S.R.M. Alves. 2008. Polinização e fixação de frutos em *Capsicum chinense* Jacq. *Acta Amazonica* 38 (2): 361–364.

Couly, C. 2009. Savoirs locaux, usages et gestion de la biodiversité agricole et forestière en Amazonie brésilienne: cas des Ribeirinhos de la Forêt nationale du Tapajós (Pará). PhD dissertation, UnB et Museum National d'Histoire Naturelle.

Darwin, Charles. 1859. *On the Origin of Species.* London: John Murray.

———. 1868. *Variations of Animals and Plants under Domestication.* London: John Murray.

Descola, P. 1986. *La Nature domestique. Symbolisme et praxis dans l'écologie des Achuar*. Paris: Editions de la Maison des Sciences de l'Homme.

———. 1996. Constructing Natures: Symbolic Ecology and Social Practice. In *Nature and society: Anthropological Perspectives*, ed. P. Descola and G. Pálsson, 82–102. New York: Routledge.

Dufour, D.L. 1993. Uso de la Selva Tropical por los indígenas Tukano del Vaupés. In *La Selva Humanizada*, ed. F. Correa, 47–62. Bogotá: Instituto Colombiano de Antropologia.

Elias, M., L. Rival, and D. Mc Key. 2000. Perception and Management of Cassava Diversity Among Macushi Amerindians of Guyana. *Journal of Ethnobiology* 20 (2): 239–265.

Emperaire, L. 2000. Approche ethnologique et socioeconomique dela gestion de la diversité variétale du manioc, haut Rio Negro (Yauareté). Rapport de mission, IRD et ISA, ms 20pp.

Emperaire, L., F. Pinton, and G. Second. 1998. Gestion dynamique de la diversité variétale du manioc (Manihot esculenta) en Amazonie du Nord-Ouest. *Natures, Sciences et Sociétés* 6 (2): 27–42.

Emperaire, L., P. Robert, J. Santilli, L. Eloy, E. Katz, C.L. López Garces, A.-E. Laques, M.C. Cunha, and M. Almeida. 2008. Diversité agricole et patrimoine dans le moyen Rio Negro. *Les Actes du BRG* 7: 139–153.

Emperaire, L. (ed.), L. van Velthem, A.G. de Oliveira, J. Santilli, M. Carneiro da Cunha, and E. Katz. 2010. *Dossiê de registro do sistema agrícola tradicional do Rio Negro*. Brasília: ACIMRN/IRD/IPHAN/Unicamp-CNPq. 235p. http://portal.iphan.gov.br/uploads/ckfinder/arquivos/Dossie_sistema_agricola_rio_negro.pdf

Emperaire, L., L. Eloy, and A.C. Seixas. 2014. *Quando a agrobiodiversidade cruza a BR, Agrobiodiversidade na região de Cruzeiro do Sul*, Acre.

Feynman, Richard. 1965. *The Character of Physical Laws*. Modern Library.

Fleck, D.W. 1997. Mammalian Diversity in Rainforest Habitats as Recognized by Matses Indians in Peruvian Amazon. MS. Thesis, The Ohio State University, Columbus.

ISA, FOIRN et al. 2007–2009. (Instituto Socioambiental (ISA); Federação das Organizações Indígenas do Rio Negro (FOIRN); Organização Indígena da Bacia do Içana (OIBI); Escola Indígena Baniwa e Coripaco (EIBC-Pamáali); Escola Indígena Paraattana (EIBP); Escola Indígena Mádzeero; Escola Indígena Walipere-Dakenai; Escola Indígena Eenawi). *Base de Dados do Projeto de Pesquisa "Pimentas na Bacia do Içana-Ayari: bases para a sustentabilidade da produção e comercialização"* (database).

Kawa, N.C., C. Mccarty, and C.R. Clement. 2013. Manioc Varietal Diversity, Social Networks, and Distribution Constraints in Rural Amazonia. *Current Anthropology* 54: 764–770.

Kerr, W. 1987. Agricultura e Seleçãogenética de Plantas. In *Etnobiolgyia*, vol. 1 of *Suma Etnologica Brasileira*, ed. B. Ribeiro, 159–72. Petrópolis: FINEP and Vozes.

Lévi-Strauss, C. 1962. *La Pensée Sauvage*. Paris: Plon.

Mendes dos Santos, G., and Y. Antonini. 2008. The Traditional Knowledge on Stingless Bees (Apidae: Meliponina) Used by the Enawene-Nawe Tribe in Western Brazil. *Journal of Ethnobiology and Ethnomedicine* 4: 19.

Nicholas, Georgescu-Roegen. 1986. The Entropy Law and the Economic Process in Retrospect. *Eastern Economic Journal* 12 (1): 475–497.

Padoch, C., E. Brondizio, S. Costa, M. Pinedo-Vasquez, R.R. Sears, and A. Siqueira. 2008. Urban Forest and Rural Cities: Multi-Sited Households, Consumption Patterns, and Forest Resources in Amazonia. *Ecology and Society* 13 (2): 2.

Pinedo-Vasquez, M., M. Zarin, D. Jipp, and J. Chota-Inuma. 1990. Use-Values of Tree Species in a Communal Forest Reserve in Northeast Peru. *Conservation Biology* 4 (4): 405–417.

Prance, G.T., W. Balée, B. Boom, and R. Carneiro. 1987. Quantitative Ethnobotany and the Case for Conservation in the Amazon. *Conservation Biology* 1 (4): 296–310.

Rival, L., and D. McKey. 2008. Domestication and Diversity in Manioc (*Manihot esculenta* Crantz ssp. *esculenta*, Euphorbiaceae). *Current Anthropology* 49 (6): 1119–1128.

Robert, P., C. López Garcés, A.-E. Laques, and M. Coelho-Ferreira. 2012. A beleza das roças: agrobiodiversidade Mebêngôkre-Kayapó em tempos de globalização. *Boletim do Museu Paraense Emílio Goeldi Ciências Humanas* 7: 339–369.

Sahlins, M. 1972. The Original Affluent Society. In *Stone Age Economics*, 1–39.

Salick, J., N. Cellinese, and S. Knapp. 1997. Indigenous Diversity of Cassava: Generation, Maintenance Use and Loss Among the Amuesha, Peruvian Upper Amazon. *Economic Botany* 51 (1): 6–19.

Schrodinger, E. 1967 [1944]. *What is Life?* Cambridge: Cambridge University Press.

Sen, A. 1981. *Poverty and Famines: An Essay on Entitlement and Deprivation*. Oxford: Oxford University Press.

Shepard, G.H., W. Douglas, L.M. Yu, and M. Italiano. 2001. Rainforest Habitat Classification Among the Matsigenka of the Peruvian Amazon. *Journal of Ethnobiology* 21 (1): 1–38.

Smith, M. 2013. Árvores de Cultura: Cultivo e Uso do Pequi (Caryocar sp., Caryocaraceae) entre os Kuikuro do Alto Xingu, MT. PhD dissertation, University of Brasília.

Tsing, A.L. 2005. *Friction: An Ethnography of Global Connections*. Princeton: Princeton University Press.

Twiller, A. 2014. Agricultural Biodiversity: The Foundation of Resilient Family Farms. *Rural 21* 48: 24–26.

CHAPTER 16

Local Struggles with Entropy: Caipora and Other Demons

Mauro W. Barbosa de Almeida

THE THERMODYNAMIC CRITIQUE OF DEVELOPMENT

Energy has been a measure of progress throughout the last century. The German physicist Ludwig Boltzmann, who considered his own views of the Second Law of Thermodynamics as the physical equivalent of Darwin's principle of evolution, proposed that:

> ...the general law of the struggle for existence of living beings is not a struggle for raw matter – the raw matter of all organisms is available in air, water and soil in excess –, and neither is it a struggle for energy, which is abundantly contained in the form of heat in every body; it is struggle for [low] entropy, which becomes available through the transition of energy from the hot sun to the cold earth. (Boltzmann 1919[1906]: 40)

Leslie White, borrowing from Wilhelm Ostwald's assertion that "all life is a struggle for *free energy*" (White 1949: 113–117, 367 ss.), defined

M.W. Barbosa de Almeida (✉)
Campinas State University, Campinas, Brazil

© The Author(s) 2017   273
M. Brightman, J. Lewis (eds.), *The Anthropology of Sustainability*,
Palgrave Studies in Anthropology of Sustainability,
DOI 10.1057/978-1-137-56636-2_16

"the amount of *energy* harnessed per capita per year" as a measure of the "degree of cultural development" (White 1959: 41). However, in so doing Leslie White and other representatives of the evolutionary history based on energy maximization left behind the crucial distinction between *energy* and *free energy*. The discarded distinction is crucial because while *energy* is never lost—and this is the content of the First Law of Thermo-dynamics—*free energy* can only decrease through time.[1] Thus, Earth's deposits of carbon, oil, and gas (Kümmel 2011: 10–6), which are storages of low-entropy energy captured by plants and stored in fossil deposits in "unstable equilibrium" (Brillouin 1990: 95), can only be degraded by human action. Had Leslie White kept his view of "evolution" in harmony with Boltzmann's "struggle for free energy" ("struggle for [low] entropy"), he could have anticipated Georgescu-Roegen's thesis: that the economic process is necessarily an *increase* of entropy (Georgescu-Roegen 1986; cf. Boltzmann 1919: 40; Hornborg 2001 and Kümmel 2011).

More energy per capita is not just represented by food calories; it consists of more cell phones and laptops, more cars and travel. If measured in horse-power, or labor-power, increasing energy per capita amounts to having more and more "energy slaves" at our disposal to convert heat into work (Kümmel 2011). Thus defined, infinite progress is a race toward an unattainable goal, a point made two millennia ago by Aristotle in reference to the accumulation of wealth for its own sake. The First Law of Thermo-dynamics, the science born of the study of industrial heat machines, states that energy is never lost. This statement suggests that perhaps technological progress could indefinitely increase the efficiency in the use of energy, thus providing more and more energy per capita forever.[2] The metaphysics of economic growth echoes the dream of perpetual-motion machines in the form of continued and increasing growth of economic systems.[3] However, Sadi Carnot, a young French engineer, proved in 1824 that there is an insurmountable barrier to the efficiency of any heat machine: every thermal machine, using any fuel or mechanism whatsoever, can only convert heat into work as long as there is a *difference* of temperature in the working fuel, and this difference can only decrease, or at most remain constant, along a working cycle (Carnot 1824). This means that any thermal machine must dissipate energy available to do work in the form of heat and waste. Clausius, from whom the elusive concept of entropy derives, phrased this idea like a haiku:

The energy of the world is zero-sum.
The entropy of the world runs
towards a maximum.[4]

The sobering implication of this message for economic systems was ignored until Georgescu-Roegen called attention to it, asserting famously that every economic process is based on the production of entropy (Georgescu-Roegen 1971, 1986).[5] In Georgescu-Roegen's description, the economic process is seen as a giant thermal machine converting low-entropy energy stored in Earth's natural reserves (due to the activity of photosynthetic cells) into manufactured products, generating low-quality energy, or heat and waste, in the process. Carnot's thermal machine was thus metaphorically amplified to the scale of the world economy; or alternatively Clausius universe was telescoped to the scale of the Earth. In either case, the message was that nature's laws had to be taken into account by human economics.

Georgescu-Roegen's book (1971, 1986) had a less immediate impact than the Club of Rome report (Meadows et al. 1972) on public concern over the limits to natural resources (cf. also WCED 1987), but his message fared better with the passage of years, resulting in a whole branch of science known as "ecological economics", concerned with the exhaustion of resources and global pollution.[6] The resulting fusion of thermodynamic language with economic theory (Martinez Alier and Schlüpmann, 1990) originated a version of "unequal exchange" theory as the appropriation of high-quality energy ("exergy") by the world centers from the peripheral countries, in exchange of waste or "anergy" (Frank 1966; Wallerstein 1974; Hornborg 1992, 2001). Rosa Luxemburg argued early in the twentieth century something similar: against Marx's circular, self-contained "enlarged accumulation" schemes, she countered that capital growth demanded a continuous inflow of non-produced natural resources and the continued incorporation of non-capitalist societies into the world market of consumption and labor (Luxemburg 1951). She called these twin processes of the destruction of natural resources and of the "annihilation" of non-capitalist societies a "struggle against natural economy" waged by capitalism at its expanding frontiers (Luxemburg 1951).[7]

DEVELOPMENT AS LOSS OF DIVERSITY

The elusive notion of entropy took a turn by 1949, when it started to be widely recognized as a concept linked not only with the physics of heat, but also with information and communication (Schrödinger 1944; Wiener 1948; Shannon 1949; Brillouin 1990[1949]). The notion of entropy as a measure related both to energy degradation and to information was invoked by Lévi-Strauss to express a melancholy view of human progress: in his usage, "entropy" was a degree of "inertia"—a metaphorical usage which goes from the impossibility of doing work where there is no temperature difference (physical maximum entropy) to cultural "inertia" where there is no cultural difference and therefore no cultural change (Lévi-Strauss 1973; Barbosa de Almeida 1990). In *Race and History*, Lévi-Strauss had criticized Leslie White's notion of social evolution as the increase of energy per capita (Lévi-Strauss 1973[1952]), offering in its place the notion of increase of cultural diversity based on communication between distinct societies. In this sense, "cultural progress", in Lévi-Strauss' analogy—this time inspired in the theory of games—resulted from a coalition between cultures through which there would be the interchange of random variations contributed by each player (Lévi-Strauss 1973[1952]). This analogy implies however that in the long term, the exchange of information would lead to the "homogenization of the resources of each player": ". . . if diversity is an initial condition, it must be recognized that the chances of gaining [benefiting from the interchange] become weaker as the game goes on" (Lévi-Strauss 1973[1955]: 418).[8] In the end, he writes,

> *Every exchanged word, every line printed, establishes a communication between two interlocutors, thus creating evenness on a level where before there was an information gap and consequently a greater degree of organization. Anthropology could be instead named 'entropology', as the name of the science of the highest manifestations of this process of disintegration.* (Lévi-Strauss 1973[1952]: 543, 1973[1955]: 447–48)[9]

Lévi-Strauss is here mixing Clausius' sentence of "heat death" for the universe—in the sense of increasing thermodynamic entropy—with the information theory concept of the loss of "an information gap".[10] But thermodynamic entropy and informational entropy carry different implications. To illustrate this point, let us consider 1 hectare of tropical forest containing circa 500 individuals and 280 tree species per hectare (Silveira et al. 2002: 73): Shannon's information measure ("entropy", corresponding to Wiener's "neguentropy") would then be 8.1 bits: the amount of information obtained from picking at random one tree from a plot of 1 hectare, assuming that all 280 different species were equally abundant and spread at random. On the other hand, we estimate the abundance of rubber trees (*Hevea brasiliensis*) in the upper Jurua forest as nearly one individual per hectare (Emperaire and Barbosa de Almeida 2002: 285–309; Barbosa de Almeida et al. 2016). This means that in order to tap 400 rubber trees in a day's journey, a rubber tapper extracting rubber from wild trees would have to traverse 400 hectares of forest, while in a typical rubber plantation, 1 hectare contains 400 genetically identical rubber trees. Shannon's information measure is zero in the plantation, while economic productivity per hectare is hugely higher in the plantation. If we compare the extractive economy with the plantation economy in terms of diversity, the extractive economy conserves a maximum of diversity—8.1 bits in the forest economy against 0 bits in the plantation economy. Notwithstanding, the plantation not only has the same thermodynamic free energy as the wild forest, but captures the same amount of carbon from the atmosphere. Or, to use a more outrageous comparison to force the point, consider the whole content of the British Library, or the Kew Gardens collections, and an equal biomass of a plantation timber: all three quantities should have about the same thermodynamic free energy (in a loose sense, "low entropy"), and the plantation has in this case the advantage of acting as a carbon sink and making a profit while doing it, while the British Library or Kew Gardens contributes to atmospheric heating with its carbon emissions due to heating requirements, and economically requires government subsidies, failing the tests of thermodynamic and economic sustainability. Biological diversity is associated with cultural diversity. Laure Emperaire found over 120 varieties of cassava cultivated by indigenous women along the middle Negro River in a limited area. If we contrast this variety with the cultivated biomass in commercial agriculture, the same contrast between informational entropy and thermodynamic entropy is obtained (Emperaire and Peroni 2007; Rival and McKey 2008; Heckler and Zent 2008).

SUSTAINABILITY OF DIVERSITY, NOT JUST OF ENERGY CONSUMPTION

In fact, the best way for anthropologists to support "sustained development" in the usual economic-energetic sense is supporting diversity of practice and knowledge associated with ontological diversity in the widest possible sense, that is, encompassing nature and culture (Viveiros de Castro 2005). Contemporary ecological economics was fertilized by physics and biology, resulting in its concern with pollution and with "sustained extraction". Anthropology entered this discussion by a tortuous path: while ecological economics was pointing to the failures of the "invisible hand" to guide the use of natural resources and to evaluate the costs of pollution, biologist Garrett Hardin's "tragedy of the Commons" parable (Hardin 1968) shifted the blame to the absence of property rights and of state action over the so-called commons. Although Hardin's examples were "cattlemen leasing national land on the western ranges", whaling by maritime nations, and National Parks "open to all, without limit" (Hardin 1968: 1245), environmentalists read his paper as an indictment of peasants who share common resources. In fact, in many cases, rules at the community level provide a basis for sustainable management of resources (McCay and Acheson 1990; Ostrom et al. 1997; Berkes and Folke 1998; Gibson et al. 2000; Dietz et al. 2003). From this perspective, the "tragedy of the commons" is the erosion of local institutions brought about by the ongoing "struggle for the commons" (Dietz et al. 2003): the tragedy is the erosion of diversity of biodiversity, of cultural practices, and of worldviews. The task at hand for anthropologists is then to sustain diversity—from myths to cultivated plants to kinship systems to ontologies to "the management of the world" (Cabalzar 2010; Andrello 2012; Kopenawa and Albert 2013[2010]). This means a shift from the sustainable production mantra to sustained ontologies. This stance may be compared with the anti-commensurability arguments of Elizabeth Povinelli (2001) and with the defense of marginality as a counter-development strategy defended by Anna Tsing (1994), and also with the ontological pluralism defended by Sahlins (2014).

DEMONS AGAINST THE SECOND LAW

How this could be done? Let me pursue the link between information and entropy, which was discovered by James Maxwell. Maxwell, the inventor of statistical physics, announced to this friend Tait that he had "picked a hole in the Second Law". As Maxwell put it, a "neat-fingered and intelligent being", who could see individual molecules, would be able to stop and revert entropy increases using information[11]: in other words, an "intelligent being" could revert the Second Law (Leff and Rex 1990, 2003; Cápek and Sheehan 2005). The "intelligent being" was baptized as a "Maxwell Demon" by "a friend", i.e. by Tait. And the important point is that a Maxwell Demon should be capable of keeping entropy increase at bay— by controlling the exchange of things across a boundary by means of a judicious usage of information. In other words, Maxwell Demons counter-act the trend toward increasing entropy or "evenness" by obtaining infor-mation on what approaches the frontier and using it to close or to open a door. "Maxwell Demons" have been compared with local opposition to "the tragedy of the commons" (Barbosa de Almeida 1993: chap. 10).

The "Maxwell Demons" metaphor has a disturbing implication. Such "demons" act by controlling frontiers, that is to say, by controlling in-flows and out-flows of things and symbols, and, in so doing, maintaining differ-ences. However, such "demons"—if understood as local leaders, represen-tatives, middlemen, and so on—are themselves subjects of the disaggregating effects of "cultural entropy". In other words, these brokers tend to lose their ability to discriminate as they exchange matter and information with the exterior, thus becoming victims of the entropy effects they were supposed to control. Lévi-Strauss' paradox of communication emerges again: the exchange of information upon which Maxwell's Demons rely in order to decide whether to open or to close a door leads ultimately to the loss of discrimination. The Demons start to fluctuate at random. Although there is no absolute remedy, the analogy suggests that local demons acting at the boundaries must be fed with external sources of energy in order to remain cool. In other words, those local gatekeepers of local-global exchanges, such as collectives, shamans, or native brokers, must themselves be partners in wider coalitions (Barbosa de Almeida 1993).

CAIPORA

Caipora, among Amazonian caboclo and Indians, is a sexually ambiguous forest entity, a *caboclo* hybrid version of Masters of Game who inhabit Amazonian indigenous worlds. Caipora is a herdsman of some wild animals, those treated as *game* for humans, and he intermediates in the encounters between human predators and wild prey. He demands respect for dead animals, and one major concern of hunters is not to insult the bodies of Caipora animals. *Insultar, to insult,* is the Portuguese word for it. *Insult* can happen at any moment since the dead body of the prey is found in the forest and carried back home to the house's kitchen and delivered to the care of women.[12] From the moment the animal's body is delivered to women's care in the house's kitchen, another complex set of etiquette rules. Ashes must not be mixed up with blood in the oven; bones must not be mixed up with blood. Women carefully dispose of bones so they will not be put in contact with menstrual, or feminine, blood.

This is one of the consequences: Caipora places a barrier to the existence of a closed consumption circle that excludes the commercialization of meat. In this sense, Caipora is a Maxwellian Demon, counteracting the destruction of diversity of human–animal social systems. Caipora existence is a consequence of caboclo ontologies, one among many non-modern ontologies, that is to say: worlds inhabited by beings whose existence we "westerns" deny, while affirming the existence of many other beings that are not seen in Caipora societies such as interest rates and futures markets.

An alliance between Caipora communities of humans, animals and invisible beings and scientific communities is possible under certain circumstances. By the 1990s, the "sustainable extraction" model was hegemonic in conservationist conferences dealing with wildlife (Robinson and Redford 1991). The Caipora ethics was indifferent to quotas and sustainable rates of catch. It was concerned with giving away the catch along a circle of neighbors, with protecting the animal body from insult, and keeping it out of the market. Vitally, Caipora demanded refuges for the healing and reproduction of animals. Caipora ontology can in some cases converge in its pragmatic consequences with scientific ontologies (Barbosa de Almeida 2013).

In the 1990s, another conservation paradigm emerged, in which instead of "sustainable catch rates" the notion of "sink and source" partition of a territory was central. As long as a sufficient portion of the territory was not hunted, the interaction between predators and prey would be stable. Both Caipora and sink and source ontologies agreed on their ethical commands: leave a part of the forest alone. But this was not all, because from the point of view of the local hunters, catch returns of deer and wild pigs were not only "sustainable", but they were growing: the data indicated that the yields for hunting efforts for game were increasing in the recent history. They attributed this to their new hunting rules which (since the creation of the Extractive Reserve in the 1990s) prohibited the use of *paulista* dogs. They are called Paulista because they are supposed to come from the city of São Paulo which is also imagined as the origin of all merchandise. *Paulista* dogs ravaged forests and scared deer when not killing them. But only richer hunters or member of big families could purchase *paulista* dogs. Thus, the introduction of "dogs as a means of production", as predatory weapons, was distorting the equal access to game. The prohibition of *paulista* dogs was from their point of view a success. It was a case of local justice based on local sociological wisdom, connected to the older ontologies whose protagonist was the Master of Game, and of which Caipora is a hybrid descendant (Barbosa de Almeida and Pantoja 2004).

Caipora worlds are my familiar example of indigenous and hybrid ontologies acting as barriers against the generalized dominance of Capitalocenic order. I would add to this a point based on the recent work of Erika Mesquita on the indigenous perceptions of climatic changes in the same area (Mesquita 2013). Birds and several other animal groups are described by Cashinahua as the masters who instruct humans about incoming changes in rains, temperature, winds, and so on. And now Cashinahua say that birds are getting confused by irregular rising waters, decreasing cold spells, and progressive heat. They are losing the ability to instruct humans, and humans in their turn are losing the capacity to predict when waters will rise. Maybe this is because, as the older Ashaninca told her, the Sun is returning to the Earth, making it consequently hotter and hotter; maybe, as the younger say, it is because humans are transforming forest into grazing land and the Earth itself is becoming hotter under the action of the sun.

The Ashaninca have allied themselves with the descendants of rubber tappers, planning to reoccupy degraded territory with forest. These alliances could perhaps be seen as other cases of coalition among humans, which include the active role of invisible beings such as Caipora and the *Iushin* of Cashinahua ontologies. Antonio Alves, an Amazonian-based writer and cosmological activist, has coined an apt word for a generalized program of commonwealth including multiple kinds of beings human and non-human. "Forestzenship" is more than citizenship for biological beings, because it is intended to encompass rights of rivers and of stones together with rights of trees and non-human animals (Alves 2004: 51, 94, 117). Many other examples of Amazonian-Andean social-ontological barriers against the generalized hegemony of Capitalocenic value-ontologies could be listed, including recent Mapuche politico-theological writings (Quidel Lincoleo 2012).

GAIA STRATEGY AND ANT–PEOPLE ALLIANCES

In 1965, James Schmitz described in a science fiction tale an alliance of humans and nature as the strategy of the planet Wrake, a reserve of "diamond wood natural resources", to defend itself against humans.

> The organism that was the diamond wood forest grew quiet again. The quiet spread back to its central mind unit in the Queen Grove, and the unit began to relax towards somnolence. A crisis had been passed—perhaps the last of the many it had foreseen when human beings first arrived on the world of Wrake. (Schmitz 1965)

The narrative goes on, using the indirect free discourse to express Wrake's point of view:

> The only defense against Man was Man. Understanding that, it had laid its plans. On a world now owned by Man, it adopted Man, brought him into its ecology, and its ecology into a new and again successful balance. This had been a final flurry. A dangerous attack by dangerous humans. But the period of danger was nearly over, would soon be for good a thing of the past. It had planned well, the central mind unit told itself drowsily. But now, since there was no further need to think today, it would stop thinking. (Schmitz 1965)

Wrake-Gaia is an entity able to react against external disturbances, in a moment of danger, only to go back to the mode of immanence (cf. Kohn 2013). On the other hand, *Man* contains ambiguously the reference to "dangerous humans"—enterprises intent to exploit Wrake's natural resources for profit—and those friendly humans who were "adopted in the ecology", children and cooperative communities bound to Wrake by pacts and kinship bonds. Wrake does not hesitate to exterminate the harmful variety of humans, and sustain the beneficial parasitic human varieties. Wrake-Gaia adopts some human communities connected by kinship and cooperation, as part of a balanced parasitic cooperation. The struggle between Wrake-Gaia supported by Humans and Human corporations intending to exploit Wrake as a source of natural resources parallels the argument of Deborah Danowski and Eduardo Viveiros de Castro: the fate of Earth-Gaia is tied up to the struggle between the people of Gaia or Terrans and the collective corporations represented by banks and governments (Danowski and Viveiros de Castro 2014: 315 ff.). This view offers the possibility of non-condescending anthropological activism; for instance, alliances between biological-human communities against capital accumulation read as the destruction of natural resources and of the diversity of non-capitalist human organizations.

Using the language of "Maxwell Demons", these strategies would amount to resistance against territorial expropriation, against institutional disaggregation, and against ontological erosion. The fight against the erosion of differences is the action of "Maxwell Demons" opposing the homogenizing push of industrial civilization. This struggle is not tied up to any particular form or concept of humankind, and might therefore be described as an anarchistic opposition to modernist civilization.

ANOTHER SINGULARITY

Finally, I offer an anti-accelerationist proposal suggested by bio-politics (Farage 2013; Foucault 1976). This is the proposed anti-singularity: the point at which we will think/sense/imagine together with animals and plants—with the support of machines. Biocentric politics means extending human rights to animals. Against the objection which says that animals cannot be subjects of rights because they have no responsibility nor voice, there are two answers: first, non-human animals express their will by resisting or trying to escape—the lobster struggles to crawl out of a scalding pan, and the cow tries to flee the death corridor when it smells death.[13] The second argument is that at the approaching zoo-centric singularity, human and animal brains will be connected to multi-specific bodies and sensing apparatuses—a horizon beyond which chemo-sensing, image-thinking, and emotional intelligence will be fused and where the usual ethical rules will be deeply transformed. Scientists, humans, and shamans will debate about forestzenship and zoo-citizenship, in fora where animals and possibly plants will be self-represented in collective networks. This bio-singularity may be called the Great Leap Out of the Box—by means of which the proverbial Schrödinger's cat will be able to engage his experimentalist masters and fight for existence—a truly ontological war.

To conclude, in James Schmitz's Balanced Ecology tale, a whole ecosystem—a living forest—allies with good humans organized in cooperatives in a struggle against bad humans, because *the only weapon against humans are humans*. Good humans are Terrans (Danowsky and Viveiros de Castro): those humans who ally themselves to indigenous peoples and to their fights against the suicide of Gaia by global warming or thermodynamic entropy, while sustaining the diversity that distinguishes the good life from mere subsistence.

NOTES

1. Free energy is sometimes referred to as *exergy*. Increases in entropy correspond to a decrease in *free energy* and less *exergy* (Lemons 2013: 20; Van Wylen et al. 2017).

2. This insane hope was ingrained in Leslie White's equation "E × T → C", where "C represents the degree of cultural development, E the amount of energy harnessed per capita per year, and T, the quality of efficiency of the tools employed in the expenditure of the energy" (White 1949: 368, 1959: 43).

3. The idea of a circular economic process is common to both classical and neoclassical economic systems (Sraffa 1960; Solow 1974).

4. *Die Energie der Welt is konstant. Die Entropy der Welt strebt einem Maximum zu.*

5. The question of *where* all this diminishing low entropy came from in the first place has had the following answer in a standard thermodynamics handbook: "*The author has found that the second law tends to increase his conviction that there is a Creator who has the answer for the future destiny of man and the universe*". The same credo appears, with "the author" replaced with "the authors", in the augmented 4th edition of 1994 of van Wylen et al. 2011: 196.

6. Against Georgescu-Roegen's, Robert Solow, the neoclassical apostle of indefinite economic growth, argues that, for example, if the marginal profit of copper extraction exceeds the interest rate in the capital market, technological advances substitute another item for copper, and therefore markets correct any trend to exhaust resources (Solow 1974; Dasgupta and Heal 1979: 224; Brown et al. 2003). This is called the *golden rule*, which however, when applied to the whale fishing industry leads to the conclusion that "... an annual discount rate $i > 21$ percent would suffice to cause the whalers to prefer extinction to conservation of the whales" (Clark 1973:958).

7. "Since the traditional social relationships of the natives are the strongest defensive wall of their society as well as of its material basis of existence, there follows, as the introductory methods of capital, the systematic and planned destruction and annihilation of non-capitalistic social relationships that it encounters in its expansion. Here we have no longer to do with primitive accumulation; the process goes on until the present day" (Luxemburg 1951:370).

8. "The world began without man and will end without him. (...) far from [man's part] being opposed to universal decline, he himself appears as perhaps the most effective agent working towards the disintegration of the original order of things and hurrying on powerfully organized matter towards ever greater inertia (...) Thus it is that civilization, taken as a whole, can be described as an extraordinarily complex mechanism, which

we might be tempted to see as offering an opportunity of survival for the human world, if its function were not to produce what physicists call entropy, that is inertia" (Lévi-Strauss 1973: 542–43, 447–48; Barbosa de Almeida 1990: 373–374; cf. Boltzmann 1995[1896–98]: 447).

9. Cf. Clausius' early phrasing of entropy as "disgregation" (Pellegrino et al. 2015).

10. In defense of the link between the two "entropies", see Brillouin 1990 [1949], and Jaynes 1957; against it, Atkins 1984 and Georgescu-Roegen 1971.

11. "... if we conceive a being whose faculties are so sharpened that he can follow every molecule in its course, such a being, whose attributes are still as essentially finite as our own, would be able to do what is at present impossible to us" (Leff and Rex 1990: 4–6, 34; Leff and Rex 2003: 179).

12. A deer, a peccary, or a cutia (Dasyprocta sp.) must be carried back home, usually being tied up using *envira* (tree bark). Placing the body at one's left elbow is not the same as placing it as one's right elbow; carrying it with the right hand is not the same as carrying with the left hand. In one case, the animal body is "insulted". Urinating around the dead body of the prey "insults" her/him. Hunters do not claim to have complete knowledge of what *insults* the game. A common practice is to keep parts of the prey (tails, "hair", *apples* = balls of hair) and using them to conciliate Caipora.

13. On voice and exit, see Hirschman 1970; on lobsters see Wallace 2007; on animal communication, Grandin and Johnson 2005.

REFERENCES

Alves, A. 2004. *Artigos em Geral.* Rio Branco (Acre).

Andrello, G., ed. 2012. *Rotas de Criação e Transformação. Narrativas de origem dos povos indígenas do Rio Negro.* São Paulo/São Gabriel da Cachoeira (Amazonas): ISA (Instituto Socioambiental) and FOIRN (Federation of Indigenous Organizations of Rio Negro).

Atkins, P.W. 1984. *The Second Law.* New York: Scientific American Books.

Berkes, F., and C. Folke, eds. 1998. *Linking Social and Ecological Systems. Management Practices and Social Mechanisms for Building Resilience.* Cambridge: Cambridge University Press.

Boltzmann, L. 1919 [1906]. *Populäre Schriften.* 2nd ed. Leipzig: Johann Ambrosius Barth.

Boltzmann, Ludwig. 1995 [1896–98]. *Lectures on Gas Theory.* New York: Dover Publications.

Brillouin, L. 1990 [1949]. Life, Thermodynamics, and Cybernetics. In *Maxwell's Demon. Entropy, Information, Computing,* ed. Harvey S. Leff and Andrew F. Rex, 89–103. Princeton: Princeton University Press.

Brown, G., et al. 2003. Os recursos físicos da Terra – Bloco 6 – O futuro dos recursos: previsão e influência. Campinas: The Open University and Editora da Universidade Estadual de Campinas. (Brazilian Edition of the Open University Course "S278 The Earth's Physical Resources: Origin, Use and Environmental Impact", 1984–1992).

Cabalzar, A., with collaboration of Ricardo, B., and L. Alberta (eds.). 2010. *Manejo do Mundo. Conhecimentos e Práticas dos Povos Indígenas do Rio Negro – Noroeste Amazonico.* São Paulo e São Gabriel da Cachoeira (Amazonas): FOIRN (Federation of Indigenous Organizations of Rio Negro)/ISA (Instituto Socioambiental).

Cápek, V., and D. Sheehan, eds. 2005. *Challenges to the Second Law of Thermodynamics.* Dordrecht: Springer.

Carnot, S. 1824. Réflexions sur la Puissance Motrice du Feu et sur les Machines proper a Développer cette Puissance. In *Carnot et la Machine a Vapeur*, ed. J.-P. Maury, 45–69. Paris: Presses Universitaires de France. 1986.

Clark, Colin. 1973. Profit Maximization and the Extinction of Animal Species. *The Journal of Political Economy* 81 (4): 950–961.

Danowski, D., and E. Viveiros de Castro. 2014. L'arrêt de monde. In *De l'univers clos au monde infini*, ed. E. Hache, 221–339. Paris: Éditions Dehors.

Dasgupta, P.S., and G.M. Heal. 1979. *Economic Theory and Exhaustible Resources.* Cambridge: Cambridge University Press.

de Almeida, M.W. Barbosa. 1990. Symmetry and Entropy: Mathematical Metaphors in the Work of Lévi-Strauss. *Current Anthropology* 31 (4): 367–385.

de Almeida, M.W. Barbosa. 1993. Rubber Tappers of the Upper Juruá River, Brazil: The Making of a Forest Peasant Economy (Doctoral Thesis). https://www.repository.cam.ac.uk/handle/1810/245084

de Almeida, M.W. Barbosa. 2013. Caipora e outros conflitos ontológicos. *R@U. Revista de Antropologia da Universidade Federal de São Carlos* 5 (1): 7–28.

de Almeida, M.W. Barbosa, and M.C. Pantoja. 2004. Justiça Local nas Reservas Extrativistas. *Raízes* 23 (1–2): 27–41. jan.-dez. 2004.

de Almeida, M.W. Barbosa, A.A. Postigo, R.C. Ramos, E. Costa, R.F. Ramos, and A.B. Melo. 2016. Usos tradicionais da floresta por seringueiros na Reserva Extrativista do Alto Juruá. In *Etnobotânica e Botânica Econômica do Acre*, ed. A. Siviero, L.C. Ming, M. Silveira, D. Daly, and R.H. Wallace, 14–37. Rio Branco: Universidade Federal do Acre.

Dietz, T., E. Ostrom, and P.C. Stern. 2003. The Struggle to Govern the Commons. *Science*, New Series 302(5652): 1907–1912.

Emperaire, L., and M. Barbosa de Almeida. 2002. Seringueiros e Seringas. In *A enciclopédia da floresta. O Alto Juruá: prática e conhecimentos das populações*, ed. M. Carneiro da Cunha and M.W. Barbosa de Almeida, 65–75. São Paulo: Companhia das Letras.

Emperaire, L., and M. Peroni. 2007. Traditional Management of Agrobiodiversity in Brazil: A Case Study of Manioc. *Human Ecology.* doi:10.1007/s10745-007-9121-x

Farage, N. 2013. No Collar, No Master. Workers and Animals in the Modernization of Rio de Janeiro 1903–04. In *Transcultural Modernism*, ed. F. Amir et al., 110–129. Berlin: Sternberg Press.

Foucault, M. 1976. *Histoire de la sexualité. 1. La volonté de savoir.* Paris: Éditions Gallimard.

Frank, G. 1966. The Development of Underdevelopment. *Monthly Review* 18 (4): 19–31.

Georgescu-Roegen, N. 1971. *The Entropy Law and the Economic Process.* Cambridge: Harvard University Press.

———. 1986. The Entropy Law and the Economic Process in Retrospect. *Eastern Economic Journal* 12 (1): 3–25.

Gibson, C., M. McKean, and E. Ostrom, eds. 2000. *People and Forests. Communities, Institutions, and Governance.* Cambridge: MIT Press.

Grandin, T., and C. Johnson. 2005. *Animals in Translation: Using the Mysteries of Autism to Decode Animal Behavior.* New York: Harcourt.

Hardin, G. 1968. The Tragedy of the Commons. *Science* 162 (3859): 1243–1248.

Heckler, S., and S. Zent. 2008. Piaora Manioc Varietals: Hyperdiversity or Social Currency? *Human Ecology.* doi:10.1007/s10745-008-9193-2

Hirschman, A.O. 1970. *Exit, Voice, and Loyalty: Responses to Decline in Firms, Organizations, and States.* Cambridge: Harvard University Press.

Hornborg, A. 1992. Machine Fetishism, Value, and the Image of Unlimited Good: Towards a Thermodynamics of Imperialism. *Journal of the Royal Anthropological Institute (Man, N.S.)* 27 (1): 1–18.

———. 2001. *The Power of the Machine. Global Inequalities of Economy, Technology and Environment.* Walnut Creed: Altamira Press.

Jaynes, E.T. 1957. Information Theory and Statistical Mechanics. *The Physical Review* 106 (4): 620–630.

Kohn, E. 2013. *How Forest Think. Towards an Anthropology Beyond the Human.* Berkeley: University of California Press.

Kopenawa, D., and B. Albert. 2013 [2010]. *The Falling Sky. Words of a Yanomami Shaman.* Trans. N. Elliot and A. Dund. Harvard: Harvard University Press.

Kümmel, R. 2011. *The Second Law of Economics. Energy, Entropy, and the Origins of Wealth.* New York: Springer.

Leff, H.S., and A.F. Rex, eds. 1990. *Maxwell's Demons. Entropy, Information, Computing.* Princeton: Princeton University Press.

———, eds. 2003. *Maxwell's Demons 2. Entropy, Classical and Quantum Information, Computing.* Bristol/Philadelphia: Institute of Physics Publishing.

Lemons, D.S. 2013. *A Student's Guide to Entropy.* Cambridge: Cambridge University Press.

Lévi-Strauss, C. 1952. 'Race et Histoire': La question raciale devant la science moderne. Paris: Unesco. In Anthropologie Structurale II, Paris: Plon, pp. 377–423.

———. 1973. Tristes Tropiques. English Translation by John and Doreen Weightman. New York: Atheneum.

———. 1973 [1952]. Race et Histoire. In Anthropologie Structurale Deux, 377–422. Paris: Plon.

———. 1973 [1955]. Tristes Tropiques. Trans. Doreen Weightman. New York: Penguin Books.

Luxemburg, R. 1951 [1913]. The Accumulation of Capital. With an Introduction by Joan Robinson. London: Routledge & Kegan Paul.

Martinez Alier, J., and K. Schlüpmann. 1990. Ecological Economics: Energy, Environment and Society. Oxford: Basil Blackwell.

McKay, B., and J.M. Acheson, eds. 1990. The Question of the Commons. The Culture and Ecology of Communal Resources. Tucson: The University of Arizona Press.

Meadows, D.H., D. Meadows, L. Randers, et al. 1972. Limits to Growth. New York: New American Library.

Mesquita, E. 2013. Ex-rubber Tappers and Small-Farmers' Views of Weather Changes in the Amazon. In World Social Science Report 2013: Changing Global Environments, 274–277. Paris: UNESCO, ISSC.

Ostrom, E., R. Gardner, and J. Walker. 1997. Rules, Games & Common-Pool Resources. Michigan: University of Michigan Press.

Pellegrino, E., H. Ghibaudi, and L. Cerruti. 2015. Clausius' Disgregation: A Conceptual Relic that Sheds Light on the Second Law. Entropy 17: 4500–4518. doi:10.3390/e17074500

Povinelli, E. 2001. Radical Worlds: The Anthropology of Incommensurability and Inconceivability. Annual Review of Anthropology 30: 319–334.

Quidel Lincoleo, J. 2012. La idea de "Dios" y "Diablo" en el discurso ritual Mapuche. Master Dissertation. State University of Campinas, Brazil, 2012.

Rival, L., and D. McKey. 2008. Domestication and Diversity in Manioc (Manihot esculenta Crantz ssp. esculenta, Euphorbiaceae). Current Anthropology 49 (6): 1119–1128.

Robinson, J.G., and K.H. Redford, eds. 1991. Neotropical Wildlife Use and Conservation. Chicago: University of Chicago Press.

Sahlins, M. 2014. On the Ontological Scheme of Beyond Nature and Culture. Hau. Journal of Ethnographic Theory 4 (1): 281–290.

Schmitz, J. 1965. Balanced Ecology. Analog. Astounding Science Fiction, March 1965, 31–38.

Schrödinger, E. 1967 [1944]. What is Life? The Physical Aspect of the Living Cell. Cambridge: Cambridge University Press.

Shannon, C. 1949 [1948]. The Mathematical Theory of Communication. In *The Mathematical Theory of Communication*, ed. C. Shannon and W. Weaver, 29–125. Chicago: University of Illinois Press.

Silveira, M., J. Torrezan, and D. Daly. 2002. Vegetação e Diversidade Arbórea da Região do Alto Juruá. In *A enciclopédia da floresta. O Alto Juruá: prática e conhecimentos das populações*, ed. M. Carneiro da Cunha and M. Barbosa de Almeida, 65–75. São Paulo: Companhia das Letras.

Solow, R. 1974. The Economics of Resources or the Resources of Economics. *American Economic Review* 64: 1–14.

Sraffa, P. 1960. *The Production of Commodities by Means of Commodities*. Cambridge: Cambridge University Press.

Tsing, A.L. 1994. From the Margins. *Cultural Anthropology* 9 (3): 279–297.

Van Wylen, G., R. Sonntag, and C. Borgnakke 2011 [1995]. *Fundamentos da Termodinâmica Clássica*. Trans. 4th US edition. São Paulo: Blucher.

Viveiros de Castro, E. 2005. *AND*. Manchester: ASA.

Wallace, D.F. 2007. *Consider the Lobster*. New York: Little, Brown and Company.

Wallerstein, I. 1974. *The Modern World-System I: Capitalist Agriculture and the Origins of the European World-Economy in the Sixteenth Century*. New York: Academic Press.

WCED (World Commission on Environment and Development). 1987. *Our Common Future*. Oxford: Oxford University Press.

White, L. 1949. *The Science of Culture*. New York: Farrar, Strauss.

———. 1959. *The Evolution of Culture. The Development of Civilization to the Fall of Rome*. New York: McGraw-Hill.

Wiener, N. 1948. *Cybernetics: Or Control and Communication in the Animal and the Machine*. Paris/Cambridge, MA: Hermann & Cie/MIT Press.

CHAPTER 17

Redesigning Money to Curb Globalization: Can We Domesticate the Root of All Evil?

Alf Hornborg

INTRODUCTION

As countless philosophers and social thinkers over the centuries have recognized, the phenomenon of money is recursively intertwined with central features of the human condition, from modes of cognition, religion, and morality to power, exploitation, warfare, and the nation state.[1] It is also foundational to the sociological condition of modernity, frequently characterized in terms of inclinations toward abstraction, interchangeability, individualism, and alienation. The very concept of money is thus a pivotal cultural phenomenon that ought to be at the center of anthropological deliberations on modernity, development, and sustainability.

In this chapter, I will discuss the notion of money as a historical and cultural construct that has been fetishized by the discipline of economics as a supreme measure of value, although detached from both material reality

---

This chapter overlaps with texts included in my book *Global Magic: Technologies of Appropriation from Ancient Rome to Wall Street* (Palgrave Macmillan 2016).

A. Hornborg (✉)
Human Ecology Division, Lund University, Lund, Sweden

© The Author(s) 2017
M. Brightman, J. Lewis (eds.), *The Anthropology of Sustainability*,
Palgrave Studies in Anthropology of Sustainability,
DOI 10.1057/978-1-137-56636-2_17

291

and human morality. The chapter begins by briefly reviewing the emergence of the mainstream concerns of economics and discussing the peculiarity of the money sign from a semiotic perspective. It then addresses the historical detachment of money from morality and from flows of matter and energy as interconnected components of mainstream, neoclassical economic doctrine, and proposes that the recent inclination toward financialization and financial crisis represents a continuation of these processes of detachment and fetishization. Finally, it argues that a sustainable and resilient economy will require the establishment of a complementary currency that distinguishes between values pertaining to local human survival, on the one hand, and the values in which financial institutions speculate, on the other. In order for such an alternative currency to accomplish a transformation of the economy, it concludes, we may learn from the mistakes of earlier experiments with "local money."

THE RELATION BETWEEN MONEY, SEMIOTICS, AND MORALITY

There is a wide consensus that modern economics has emerged as the understanding and explanation of capitalism (Heilbroner 1999[1953]: 37, 312, 319). Although money, market exchange, and price relations have existed for millennia, it was the conceptualization of abstract land, labor, and capital as quantifiable and commensurable categories that created the discipline of economics (ibid., 27). The emergence of economics has thus reflected and reinforced historical processes of commercialization and monetization. Although various schools of economics advocate different economic policies, they share the underlying assumption that (general-purpose) money is a valid metric for quantifying human transactions, and that statistics and mathematics offer methods for thinking and deliberating about them (ibid., 314). Significantly, a standard textbook on the history of economics that has shaped the minds of generations of economists, Heilbroner's (1999[1953]) classic *The Worldly Philosophers* thus devotes not a single word to reflecting on the phenomenon of money itself, without which economics as a discipline would not exist.[2]

For Karl Polanyi (1957[1944]), as for Marx, the emergence of the disembedded market economy is a tragic story of human suffering, while for Heilbroner and most of his colleagues, it is a story of emancipation: the very commoditization and abstraction of land, labor, and capital that Polanyi laments is for Heilbroner (1999[1953]: 24–29) what liberates economic logic from the fetters of social bonds, politics, religion, and culture. Polanyi was a leading proponent of the substantivist school in economic anthropology, as was Paul Bohannan (1955), who in the early 1950s identified the existence of separate spheres of exchange and special-purpose currencies among the Tiv of northern Nigeria. Although the ethnographic facts and explanation of such "multi-centric" economies have been disputed, the very idea of distinguishing between separate spheres of value is worthy of reflection and consideration. The fundamental problems of global sustainability may not be inherent in the market principle in itself as much as in the implications of general-purpose money and the globalized *scale* of the market. General-purpose money makes all values commensurable, regardless of whether they pertain to the reproduction of human organisms, communities, ecosystems, or the world-system. It was the exploitation of globalized price differences (i.e., arbitrage), particularly regarding land and labor, which provided the conditions for the turn to fossil fuels in eighteenth-century Britain, which in turn inaugurated anthropogenic climate change and the so-called Anthropocene. If slaves had been paid standard British wages, and depopulated American fields had fetched standard British land rent, there might not have been an Industrial Revolution.[3] A way of curbing the destructive consequences of economic globalization might be to rediscover the virtues of distinguishing local values (such as those concerned with food, shelter, energy, community, and place) from the values pertaining to global communication. Suffice it to say, at this point, that these virtues would be very difficult to grasp from the perspective of mainstream economics.

In view of the extent to which market economies, capitalism, and the conceptual framework of conventional economics are founded on the logic of money, it is appropriate to present some general reflections on this unique semiotic phenomenon. Semiotics (from Greek *semeion* = sign) is the study of sign systems. A semiotic perspective on money would thus approach it as a kind of sign, comparable to other systems of signs such as language, gestures, clothing, and so on. Signs are means of communication that presuppose subjects, meanings, codes, and interpretations. They are by no means restricted to the human species but seem to be pervasive in living systems at all levels of scale, from the internal biochemistry of individual organisms (Hoffmeyer 1996; Sebeok and Umiker-Sebeok 1992) to the various kinds of communication between the myriad organisms of an ecosystem (von Uexküll 1982[1940]; Nöth 1998; Hornborg 2001). The analytical study of sign systems was pioneered by Ferdinand de Saussure (1916) and Charles Sanders Peirce (1931–1958), but the strong linguistic focus of the former has not been conducive to wider comparative approaches such as those inspired by Peirce.

General-purpose money is a peculiar kind of sign. It seems impossible to classify as belonging to one of Peirce's three general categories of signs: index, icon, or symbol. The distinction between these three types of signs is based on differences between how they relate to their referents (i.e., what they refer to): an *index* relates to its referent through contiguity, an *icon* through similarity, and a *symbol* through convention. A money sign, whether a coin, a paper bill, a check, or an electronic digit, does not generally refer to a specific commodity or service in any of these three ways. A specific money object can, of course, contextually evoke, for example, the labor or sale that it represents, or its donor, or the monarch or nation whose imprint it bears, or even the purchase it is destined to perform, but its fundamental property is its capacity to assume any meaning at all that its owner bestows upon it. This is tantamount to saying that money is a sign without meaning, that is, without a referent (cf. Rotman 1987). This semiotic property of money is undoubtedly the feature that qualifies it as both the most celebrated and the most condemned of human inventions.

A second, related observation is that the code by which money communicates information only has one character. This is concomitant to the observation that the money sign can stand for anything at all, which means that there is nothing that it can be opposed to. Other kinds of codes (such as alphabets, genetic codes, musical scores) have more than one character, which is a basic requirement for transmitting information. It could be objected that the *absence* of money constitutes a binary opposite to its presence, so that a money payment can be interpreted as a message encouraging whatever activity is being paid for, while its absence would discourage it, but the undifferentiated character of money cannot convey messages more meaningful than a signal to continue whatever is being done. It can be argued that this limitation has important implications for sustainability. In principle, the parallel existence of two distinct currencies pertaining to separate kinds of exchanges would grant market actors the capacity to transmit messages about the limits of commensurability and thus about the range of possible repercussions that may result from their transactions.

A third observation is that even if money is conceded to signify nothing but abstract quantity, such signification will mean very different things to different people, depending on the amount of money they have at their disposal. This inherently "asymmetrical" aspect of commercial transactions completely contradicts the "liberal illusion" of the generalized and unregulated market as free, fair, and of universal benefit (Reddy 1987: 62–106). Asymmetrical exchange is certainly not specific to money-based economies, but money is a way of concealing such asymmetries by couching them in an idiom projecting the appearance of reciprocity and fairness. This intrinsic asymmetry between market actors, inherent in their divergent assets, applies regardless of whether there are asymmetries in the physical content of the exchange.

A fourth observation on the peculiarity of money is that "it is a form of social power that has no inherent limit" (Harvey 2010: 43). There is always a limit to the amount of physical assets a person can own, but there is no inherent limit to the amount of money he or she can command. Thus, there is no limit to the amount of money a human can desire. This is another way of phrasing the implications of the mainstream abandonment, within economics, of concerns with the finite, material aspects of the economy. As conceptualized by neoclassical economics, "the economy" can "expand without getting physically bigger" (Mitchell 2009: 417). The Gross National Product was invented to measure "the speed and frequency with which paper money changed hands," and it "could grow without any problem of physical or territorial limits" (ibid., 418).

The emergence of general-purpose money has been recursively connected to the emergence of modern forms of social life and thought (Simmel 1990[1907]). Through centuries of discussions about the social implications of these processes, a central theme has been the relationship between money and morality. Already in the fourth century BC, Aristotle denounced money-making for its own sake (i.e., "chrematistics"), and four centuries later, St. Paul warned that "the love of money is the root of all evil," but the sin of avarice seems to have been particularly condemned from the expansion of market trade in the eleventh to thirteenth centuries (Bloch and Parry 1989: 18). Aristotle's position was revived in the thirteenth century by Thomas Aquinas, who classified avarice as a cardinal sin, and up until the eighteenth century, the official condemnation of money-making in European civilization ran parallel to its increasing centrality in economic life (Macfarlane 1985: 71). As is reflected in several of Shakespeare's works, money blurs the moral distinction between good and evil (ibid., 69). From the late Middle Ages, avarice was viewed as less and less sinful (Hirschman 1977), and in 1714, Bernard Mandeville's *Fable of the Bees* finally equated "private vice" with "public benefit," which ever since Adam Smith's *The Wealth of Nations* has been the fundamental creed of economics (cf. Dumont 1977: 63). The five centuries between Aquinas and Smith saw an unprecedented expansion of commerce and ultimately the promotion of money-making from vice to virtue. As Maurice Bloch and Jonathan Parry (1989: 29) argue, in capitalist ideology, "the values of the short-term order have become elaborated into a theory of long-term reproduction." Another way of putting this is that "economics had to emancipate itself from morality" (Dumont 1977: 36). Economics has detached itself from ethical considerations, even though this has often entailed a distortion of Adam Smith's own views on ethics (Sen 1987). As David Graeber (2011) has shown, however, economic obligations generate their own varieties of rationality that paradoxically tend to be both imbued with and divorced from morality. The historical inclusion of human obligations in the sphere of "goods" exchanged through the medium of general-purpose money has generated pervasive ambiguities about how to draw boundaries between persons and (commoditized) things, as drastically illustrated by the phenomenon of slavery. Drawing on several millennia of human history, Graeber shows that societies in which economic indebtedness grows to the point where it more or less literally enslaves major parts of the population tend to reach thresholds where morality again intervenes in economics and there are large-scale cancellations of debt. In the normal operation of such economies, however, the mechanical rationality of managing money tends to be decoupled not only from considerations of face-to-face human morality, but also from the exigencies of living sustainably on planet Earth. Not least in the Marxian tradition, the logic of money, accumulation, and globalized market exchange is recognized as inherently opposed to sustainability (Foster et al. 2010; Klein 2014).

It is important to consider the connection between two kinds of detachment that mainstream economics has achieved over the past two centuries: the detachment from material processes and from morality. As Thomas Aquinas' condemnation of money-making was based on his conviction that merchants and money-lenders do not create value as laborers do, there is an interesting line of descent from Aquinas to the labor theory of value (Bloch and Parry 1989: 3, reference to Tawney). It is thus no coincidence that schools of economics that today have moral objections to what they identify as forms of "unequal exchange" that are invisible to mainstream economists—primarily Marxian and ecological economics—are precisely those schools which maintain a strong concern with material processes. It appears that arguments appealing to moral norms such as "justice" and "equality" need to be based on real asymmetries in the flows of embodied biophysical resources, whether labor time, hectares of land, or Joules of energy. It seems very significant that neoclassical economics is as impervious to moral arguments as it is to material metrics.

It is no coincidence that Aristotle's moral objections to money-making appeared in the first truly commercial civilization, established in the Aegean area several centuries BC (cf. Weatherford 1997: 28–45). The metal coinage that was invented in the region around 700 BC undermined the ancient agrarian, tributary empires and provided the foundations of the so-called Axial Age (700 BC.–AD 600). The transition from credit money, built on trust, to commodity money (precious metals) encouraged warfare, plunder, and slavery in this period (Graeber 2011). The Middle Ages (AD 600–1450) saw a return to credit money and tribute in kind accompanied by a cosmological emphasis on material production, rather than money itself, as the source of value, but the introduction of paper notes in Renaissance Italy in the fourteenth century initiated the transition from feudalism to modern banking and capitalism.[4] From the late fifteenth century, the early modern capitalist empires again focused on precious metals, epitomized by the doctrine of mercantilism. The worldview of the eighteenth-century Physiocrats retained a feudal emphasis on the material fecundity of land, but adopted an abstract analytical framework for understanding economic processes that was later to be conducive to conceptualizing the productivity of labor in early industrial Britain. As already noted, the labor theory of value thus traces its roots to medieval church doctrine and ultimately Aristotle, as opposed to the age-old inclination toward money fetishism, which has been particularly pronounced in periods emphasizing commodity money, such as the Axial Age as well as the period of capitalist empires since 1450.

The year 1971 marks the advent of electronic money and an electronic stock market (NASDAQ) as well as the abandonment of the Bretton Woods gold standard. Since then, there has certainly been a resurgence of credit money ("financialization"), as Graeber observes, but rather than an emphasis on material production (as in the Middle Ages), we have witnessed a further emancipation and fetishization of autonomous monetary value. It remains to be seen whether the events of 1971 were really another turning-point in the grand historical oscillations identified by Graeber, or a more temporary incident. The general historical trend toward a transition from metal through paper to electronic money has entailed a progressive separation of finance and monetary flows from "real" flows of matter and energy. Recurrent attempts to discipline banks and politicians, constraining them from issuing excessive amounts of new money by tying major currencies to a metal standard (e.g., by the Bank of England in 1844, the US Congress in 1900, and the agreement at Bretton Woods in 1944/1946) have all ended in a similar way. As the amount of paper currency in circulation has increased, diverging more and more from the value of a finite stock of bullion, the end result has repeatedly been devaluation and the severance of metal standards.[5] The volatility of trust as the sole foundation of economic value has led to recurrent financial breakdowns, from the banks of Florence in 1343 to the Wall Street stock markets in 1929 and 2008.

THE RATIONALE, HISTORY, AND PROSPECTS OF EXPERIMENTS WITH ALTERNATIVE CURRENCIES

Mainstream (neoclassical) and most heterodox (Marxian and ecological) economics remain confined within a worldview fundamentally shaped by general-purpose money. In not fully acknowledging the implications of Georgescu-Roegen's (1971) observations on the entropy-increasing character of economic processes, deliberations on economic policies, no matter how seemingly radical, that do not question the use of such money tend to promote increasing centralization, polarization, and environmental degradation. Although the many disadvantages of increasing scale and the obsession with economic growth were clearly articulated already in the 1970s (e.g., Schumacher 1973; Daly 1977), the conceptual lock-in of general-purpose money has continued to constrain the widespread aspiration, four decades ago, to envision an (alternative) emphasis on community, localized resource flows, and sustainability. Perspectives drawing on discourses of political ecology recognize that the inexorable tendencies toward globalized resource transfers, large-scale organizations, centralized power hierarchies, increasingly severe inequalities, local vulnerability, and ecological deterioration are inherent in the discourse on economics shared by mainstream and heterodox traditions (M'Gonigle 1999). But such insights from the wide spectrum of approaches here subsumed under the umbrella of "political ecology" only rarely identify the phenomenon of money itself as the root of all these undesirable tendencies (ibid., 23), and even more rarely suggest an alternative.

Perspectives from heterodox schools such as Marxian and ecological economics converge in observing that monetary exchange values tend to obscure the biophysical substance of the goods and services that are exchanged. Both schools recognize that money can thus conceal asymmetric transfers of embodied labor or resources, generating polarizations and inequalities between those who accumulate and those who are impoverished. A problem identified by both schools is the inclination of mainstream economists to exclusively focus on the internal cybernetics of systems of monetary market exchange, deliberately or unintentionally ignoring causal connections between the semiotic and material aspects of economies. As Heilbroner (1999[1953]) shows, mainstream economics has become concerned only with the logic of a monolithic market, and with the systemic consequences of various kinds of policies to regulate it. From the perspective of Marxian and ecological economics, this means that important determinants of economic processes are excluded from view, surfacing only in the form of unanticipated crises. Financialization represents a decisive disjunction of the logic of money from the physical conditions of production and human life. The metaphor of a "bursting bubble," frequently used in describing financial crises, illustrates that money in this form is ultimately a mere fantasy. Credit is not a matter of "borrowing money" in the sense of fetching it from a bank, but a promise to the bank to fulfill its fantasies of future debt service. Fantasies like these will work as long as people agree to subscribe to them, but, as financial crises have shown, when they no longer do so, money will dissolve into thin air. The volatility of cultural constructions such as the fantasy of money would not be a problem if it were not so inextricably intertwined with the material realities of human lives, from the tangible, physical metabolism of eating and working to housing, and environmental impacts. For many millions of people worldwide, the recent financial crisis has created severely difficult problems of a very material nature. Many heterodox economists would point out that the problems generated by the failure of mainstream economics to acknowledge material aspects of the economy are experienced by these millions of people precisely at this tangible level of reality which economics excludes from view.

It is no doubt unrealistic to hope for a fundamentally revised discipline of economics, which links monetary flows to flows of embodied labor, land, or energy, but it may be slightly more realistic to suggest means of insulating people's basic material needs from the vicissitudes of financial fantasies. The point of departure for the proposal to be presented here is that it is the semiotic vacuity of general-purpose money that accounts for its complete detachment from material referents and its encouragement of generalized commensurability. This universalized and increasingly globalized commensurability—the assumption that almost all values are interchangeable—is a cultural conception that ultimately jeopardizes not only human civilization but even the biological conditions for human life (cf. Klein 2014). To curb the destructive societal and ecological processes currently generated by the phenomenon of money, it will be necessary to redefine our cultural conception of commensurability. Such a shift means distinguishing values pertaining to basic human survival from the values in which financial institutions speculate. This would not need to be a matter of legislation, as it would suffice to provide people with other options for survival than to sell their labor and buy their food on the same market as is used by corporations as an arena for capital accumulation. If people would indeed tend to prefer the alternative option, a fundamental transformation of the global economy could conceivably occur without either legislation or coercion. *The idea is for national authorities to issue a complementary currency, which can only be used to purchase locally produced goods and services, and to distribute it as a basic income to all households in proportion to their size.* To define what is to be categorized as "locally produced," a reasonable procedure might be to restrict the use of this complementary currency (let us provisionally call it "Points") to purchases of goods and services originating within a given radius (say, 30 km) from the place of purchase. A practical way of distributing Points to households would be to provide them with plastic cards which are automatically charged with new, electronic Points each month, in the same way that credit cards give access to salaries. It will immediately be recognized that this proposal deviates in important respects from the many experiments that have been conducted with so-called local or community currencies in various parts of the world. Before discussing its advantages, we shall briefly review some recurrent features of these experiments.

The widespread recognition that the growing dependence of local communities on the global market economy has had a number of unfavorable repercussions—such as greater vulnerability and disempowerment, loss of social cohesion, and the exploitation of local labor and resources by distant centers—does not need to be reiterated. The idea of countering such processes by resorting to a local community currency has emerged in various places and at various times. It was widely discussed in nineteenth-century Europe and the United States, and several social movements attempted to implement it (North 2007: 41–61). The most well-known modern movement toward this goal is the ambition, beginning in Canada and the United Kingdom in the 1980s, to establish so-called Local Exchange (originally Employment) Trading Systems, that is, LETS (Dobson 1993; Douthwaite 1999; North 2007: 79–101), but similar initiatives have appeared in

Austria, Germany, Hungary, New Zealand, the United States, Australia, Argentina, Poland, Czech Republic, Slovakia, Sweden, Japan, Belgium, Greece, and several other countries. In some cases—most conspicuously Argentina at the turn of the millennium and more recently Greece—the idea of alternative currencies emerged as a survival strategy and an explicit response to severe financial crisis.[6] These movements have become a field of academic study with its own journal, the *International Journal of Community Currency Research*. A special issue (Blanc 2012) provides a recent overview of the history and prospects of such experiments with alternative currencies. Recurrent shortcomings include widespread dismissal, absence of a national governance system, inefficient promotion of local consumption, personal exhaustion of leaders, insignificant impact, accounting difficulties, risks of free riding, and unclear incentives on the part of shopkeepers (ibid., 1–4). The editor concludes that, "thirty years after their first emergence, [community currencies] still have to prove they can change the present state of things, while research agendas are increasingly considering them" (ibid.). LETS are now in "worldwide retreat" (Dittmer 2013: 6). However, the shortcomings revealed by systematic research on these movements provide a foundation for designing a complementary currency system that is fair, widely utilized, government-regulated, easily administrated, and efficient. A key challenge is to design this system in such a way as to provide all significant social actors—households and business as well as authorities—with strong incentives to participate.

The predominant justification for most complementary currency systems that have appeared so far is that they represent "forms of micropolitical resistance" from below (North 2007: 77). This means that they are generally grassroot initiatives largely contingent on the enthusiasm and ideological commitment of a restricted number of activists, with little or no support from authorities (Dittmer 2013). It also means that they are unlikely to reflect systematic analysis of the conditions under which they might succeed, including considerations of fairness, attractiveness, large-scale administration, efficiency, impact, and transparency. The system that is advocated here differs from most of these initiatives in the following respects: (1) It would be organized by the federal or municipal authorities. (2) The currency ("Points") would be distributed by the authorities as basic income to all households in the nation, in proportion to their size. (3) The Points would only be useful for purchases of local goods and services, that is, goods and services originating from within a specified radius from the place of purchase.[7] (4) All transactions with Points would be officially exempt from taxation. (5) To the extent that some individuals wish to save Points for later use, while others may temporarily want to borrow extra Points, special institutions would administrate such (electronic) transactions, but without offering or charging any interest. (6) Businesses would have the option of converting a portion of the Points they earn into regular currency, through the authorities, at adjustable rates calculated to compensate for the authorities' loss of tax revenue. (7) Parts of the authorities' expenditures for pensions and social security would be paid in the form of Points. Under these conditions, all significant social categories would benefit from the Point system.[8]

By systematically considering this arrangement from the perspectives of the social actors concerned, it is possible to avoid most, if not all, of the disadvantages and shortcomings of LETS and related community currency systems. *Households* would be able to liberate some of their regular income by utilizing Points, whenever possible; they would also be less dependent on salaried work and less vulnerable to unemployment; finally, they would experience more local interdependence, cooperation, and sense of community. *Businesses* would find opportunities for tax-free income, some of which could be used to purchase local resources, some to flexibly employ local labor, and some to convert into regular currency; there would also appear new opportunities for diversified local enterprise to satisfy the increasing demand for a wide range of local goods and services. *Authorities* would reduce their costs for pensions, social security, medical care, transport infrastructure, and environmental protection, thereby avoiding risks of fiscal deficits. Some of the many societal benefits of this system are: *lower demand for long-distance transports* (i.e., reduced greenhouse gas emissions, energy use, transport costs, and traffic accidents); *more local recycling of nutrients and packaging materials* (i.e., reduced eutrophication, solid waste, and resource depletion); *less mechanized agriculture* (i.e., reduced resource use and environmental degradation, more physical exercise for significant parts of the population); *lower demand for export production of food* (i.e., globally reduced vulnerability of rural populations, increased self-sufficiency and food security); *more localized food production* (i.e., less waste through overproduction, storage, and transport, fresher and healthier food with less preservatives, better transparency in relations between producers and consumers); *more diverse landscapes* (i.e., higher biological diversity and ecological resilience); *more diversified local business profile* (i.e., demand for a wide range of local goods and services); *greater financial resilience of federal governments* (i.e. lower costs for pensions, social security, and other major expenditures); and *more social cohesion* (i.e., less social marginalization, more sense of community, and better psychosocial health). All these benefits could be achieved by establishing a complementary currency thus designed, enhancing financial, social, and ecological resilience while not constraining the global market from encouraging vital industries (such as advanced medical equipment, pharmaceuticals, and information technology) that would continue to be in demand and that require global integration. The advent of electronic money in 1971 certainly unleashed an unprecedented fetishization of the global economy,[9] but it also opens completely new possibilities to design currencies that promote equality, democracy, and sustainability (Hart 2000). Two thousand years ago, St. Paul was no doubt right in that money is the root of all evil, but at this point in history, Bernhard Lietaer (2001: 7) is also right in that it is "the root of all possibilities."

Electronic money has a potential for making the economy more sustainable and equitable for the same reason that it has promoted financialization and financial crisis, viz., its *lack of material form*. Following the delimitation of its ideal use articulated by Aristotle, money should merely be a medium of exchange between socially connected producers and consumers. It should be a *means*, not an end in itself. But money inevitably becomes an end in itself when it is attributed with *intrinsic* value, as when precious metals or bills are hoarded or stolen, or when interest accrues on bank accounts. This is money fetishism. However, money that is both *electronic* and *interest-free* has no intrinsic value. In this form, it can finally serve its makers, rather than make them its servants.

The fundamental goal of a complementary currency system such as sketched here is to *relocalize* much of the material metabolism of human societies, essentially because such a strategy is both more equitable and more sustainable than current trends.[10] This is "the precise opposite of the modern trend of globalization" (Lipson 2011: 573; cf. Brennan 2003). In Marxian terms, it would mean an expansion of simple commodity circulation (C-M-C1) at the expense of capitalist circulation (M-C-M1) and financialization (M-M1). But it would not require violent revolution, merely the existence of an option that would be attractive and sensible to everybody. In fact, it would not even mean abandoning the insight of mainstream economics, from Adam Smith and onwards, that market exchange is an efficient way of allocating resources, because it does not challenge the market principle as such, only the *scale* of market organization. The chances of achieving the hypothetical "perfect information" imagined by economists inevitably diminish with increasing market scale. Nor could this proposal for a relocalization of the market be dismissed as regression, as it would be based on recently emerging, trans-disciplinary understandings of economic processes and on new digital technologies. History is not reversible, but we can take stock of millennia of historical experience in order to envisage our future.

NOTES

1. Cf. Simmel (1990)[1907], Parry and Bloch (1989), Corbridge et al. (1994), Graeber (2011), and McNally (2014).
2. Heilbroner (ibid., 109–115) does mention that the Utopian socialist Robert Owen in the early nineteenth century "naively" wanted to abolish money, but he never tells us why. There were, in fact, several movements to radically transform money in nineteenth-century England and the United States (North 2007: 41–61).
3. Cf. Inikori (1989, 2002) and Hornborg (2006).
4. The idea of paper money appears to have originated in China and was conveyed to Italy in the thirteenth century by Marco Polo (Weatherford 1997: 126).
5. Examples mentioned by Weatherford (1997) include the Banque Royale in 1720, the US Congress in 1780, the Bank of England in 1917, President Roosevelt in 1933, and President Nixon in 1971.
6. Although several different designations occur—for example, local, community, or alternative currencies—the concept of "complementary" currency seems most precise for the proposal presented here, as it does not aspire to replace normal currency with a geographically more restricted one, but to provide an option alongside it.
7. A convenient way of distinguishing the range of local goods would be to mark them as such, but such marking would of course vary between shops in different places. Rather than amount to a number of geographically distinct, local currencies, this system would mean *one* complementary currency for the whole nation, but with an in-built inclination to generate localized (but overlapping) circuits of exchange.
8. Of course, some people might consider looking for other jobs, for example, those who today profit from financial speculation or from industries such as the production of and international trade in foodstuffs or petroleum.
9. Following the introduction of digital money, the proportion of foreign exchange transactions that pertain to speculation in currencies now dwarfs the insignificant percentage pertaining to the purchase and sale of real goods and services.

10. For a recent and persuasive statement of this position, see Lietaer and Dunne (2013).

REFERENCES

Blanc, J., ed. 2012. Thirty Years of Community and Complementary Currencies: A Review of Impacts, Potential and Challenges. Special issue of *International Journal of Community Currency Research* 16.

Bloch, M., and J. Parry. 1989. Introduction: Money and the Morality of Exchange. In *Money and the Morality of Exchange*, ed. J. Parry and M. Bloch, 1–32. Cambridge: Cambridge University Press.

Bohannan, P. 1955. Some Principles of Exchange and Investment Among the Tiv. *American Anthropologist* 57: 60–70.

Brennan, T. 2003. *Globalization and its Terrors: Daily Life in the West*. London: Routledge.

Corbridge, S., R. Martin, and N. Thrift, eds. 1994. *Money, Power and Space*. Oxford: Blackwell.

Daly, H.E. 1977. *Steady-State Economics: The Economics of Biophysical Equilibrium and Moral Growth*. San Francisco: W.H. Freeman.

de Saussure, F. 1916. *Cours de linguistique générale*. Lausanne: Payot.

Dittmer, K. 2013. Local Currencies for Purposive Degrowth? A Quality Check of Some Proposals for Changing Money-as-usual. *Journal of Cleaner Production* 54: 3–13.

Dobson, R.V.G. 1993. *Bringing the Economy Home from the Market*. Montreal: Black Rose Books.

Douthwaite, R. 1999. *The Ecology of Money*. Cambridge: Green Books.

Dumont, L. 1977. *From Mandeville to Marx: The Genesis and Triumph of Economic Ideology*. Chicago: The University of Chicago Press.

Foster, J.B., B. Clark, and R. York. 2010. *The Ecological Rift: Capitalism's War on the Earth*. New York: Monthly Review Press.

Georgescu-Roegen, N. 1971. *The Entropy Law and the Economic Process*. Cambridge, MA: Harvard University Press.

Graeber, D. 2011. *Debt: The First 5,000 Years*. New York: Melville House.

Hart, K. 2000. *Money in an Unequal World*. New York: Texere.

Harvey, D. 2010. *The Enigma of Capital and the Crises of Capitalism*. Oxford: Oxford University Press.

Heilbroner, R. 1999[1953]. *The Worldly Philosophers: The Lives, Times and Ideas of the Great Economic Thinkers*. London: Penguin.

Hirschman, A.O. 1977. *The Passions and the Interests: Political Arguments for Capitalism Before its Triumph*. Princeton: Princeton University Press.

Hoffmeyer, J. 1996. *Signs of Meaning in the Universe*. Bloomington: Indiana University Press.

Hornborg, A. 2001. Vital Signs: An Ecosemiotic Perspective on the Human Ecology of Amazonia. *Sign Systems Studies* 29 (1): 121–152.

———. 2006. Footprints in the Cotton Fields: The Industrial Revolution as Time-Space Appropriation and Environmental Load Displacement. *Ecological Economics* 59 (1): 74–81.

Inikori, J.E. 1989. Slavery and the Revolution in Cotton Textile Production in England. *Social Science History* 13 (4): 343–379.

———. 2002. *Africans and the Industrial Revolution in England: A Study of International Trade and Economic Development*. Cambridge: Cambridge University Press.

Klein, N. 2014. *This Changes Everything: Capitalism vs. the Climate*. London: Allen Lane.

Lietaer, B. 2001. *The Future of Money: A New Way to Create Wealth, Work, and a Wiser World*. London: Century.

Lietaer, B., and J. Dunne. 2013. *Rethinking Money: How New Currencies Turn Scarcity into Prosperity*. San Francisco: Berrett-Koehler.

Lipson, D. 2011. Is the Great Recession only the beginning? Economic contraction in an age of fossil fuel depletion and ecological limits to growth. *New Political Science* 33 (4): 555–575.

M'Gonigle, R.M. 1999. Ecological Economics and Political Ecology: Towards a Necessary Synthesis. *Ecological Economics* 28: 11–26.

Macfarlane, A. 1985. The Root of all Evil. In *The Anthropology of Evil*, ed. D. Parkin, 57–76. Oxford: Blackwell.

McNally, D. 2014. The Blood of the Commonwealth: War, the State, and the Making of World Money. *Historical Materialism* 22 (2): 3–32.

Mitchell, T. 2009. Carbon Democracy. *Economy and Society* 38 (3): 399–432.

North, P. 2007. *Money and Liberation: The Micropolitics of Alternative Currency Movements*. Minneapolis: University of Minnesota Press.

Nöth, W. 1998. Ecosemiotics. *Sign Systems Studies* 26: 332–343.

Parry, J., and M. Bloch, eds. 1989. *Money and the Morality of Exchange*. Cambridge: Cambridge University Press.

Peirce, C.S. 1931–1958. *Collected Papers*. Cambridge, MA: Harvard University Press.

Polanyi, K. 1957[1944]. *The Great Transformation: The Political and Economic Origins of Our Time*. Boston: Beacon.

Reddy, W.R. 1987. *Money and Liberty in Modern Europe: A Critique of Historical Understanding*. Cambridge: Cambridge University Press.

Rotman, B. 1987. *Signifying Nothing: The Semiotics of Zero*. Stanford: Stanford University Press.

Schumacher, E.F. 1973. *Small is Beautiful: A Study of Economics as if People Mattered*. London: Abacus.

Sebeok, T.A., and J. Umiker-Sebeok, eds. 1992. *Biosemiotics*. Berlin: Mouton de Gruyter.

Sen, A. 1987. *On Ethics and Economics*. Oxford: Blackwell.

Simmel, G. 1990[1907]. *The Philosophy of Money*. London: Routledge.

von Uexküll, J. 1982[1940]. The Theory of Meaning. *Semiotica* 42: 25–82.

Weatherford, J. 1997. *The History of Money: From Sandstone to Cyberspace*. New York: Three Rivers Press.

INDEX

© The Author(s) 2017
M. Brightman, J. Lewis (eds.), *The Anthropology of Sustainability*,
Palgrave Studies in Anthropology of Sustainability,
DOI 10.1057/978-1-137-56636-2

proliferation, 15, 19, 28, 52, 53, 55, 57,
60–2, 97
protected areas, 4, 94, 113, 114, 120

R
race, 23, 39, 76, 152, 158
Rasmussen, K., 148, 149, 151, 152, 154
REDD
Free, Prior and Informed Consent,
132
Norway, 130, 135
policy makers, 8, 131–3
refugia, 15, 54
relationality, 10, 24, 75, 203, 214, 215,
243, 251
relational ontologies, 242
relocalization, 48, 250, 304
Renaissance, 48, 297
resilience, 2, 3, 10, 56, 65n2, 67, 159,
196, 302, 303
resurgence, 15, 19, 20, 51, 62, 65n1,
65n2, 65n9, 114, 297
Rio+20 summit, 193
Ross, J., 146–8, 151, 152
rules
rule enforcement, 100
rule-making, 118
rumour, 147, 171, 176, 178
rural development, 94

S
Sachs, J., 184, 203n1
St. Paul, 295, 303
São Paulo, Brazil, 10, 185, 187, 188,
191–3, 197, 198, 201, 202,
204n6, 204n7
Saussure, F. de, 293
scale, 2, 7, 8, 12, 14, 18, 21, 39, 72, 77,
105, 106, 112, 120, 146, 149, 160,

188, 196, 203, 216, 218, 223, 267,
293, 296, 298, 301, 303, 304
Schrödinger, E., 257–9, 268n3
science, 7, 12, 13, 16, 24, 25, 37, 40–2,
44, 75–8, 115, 118, 160, 166, 171,
184, 217, 220, 221, 229–32, 234,
240, 241, 250
SDG. *See* Sustainable Development
Goals (SDG)
sea-ice, 149, 156, 158
security
food security, 69, 100, 104, 167, 260,
267, 302
livelihoods security, 100, 104
semiotics, 61, 234, 292–4, 299
services, 7, 41, 101, 176, 251, 294,
298–302, 304n9
set aside, 98, 99, 104
Shakespeare, W., 231, 295
shifting cultivation, 18, 52, 56, 266. *See*
also slash and burn; swidden
horticulture
singularity
anti, 26
sink and source, 19
slash and burn, 18, 263
Smith, A., 53, 117, 120, 266, 295, 296,
303
social exclusion, 185, 193, 198
social housing, 187, 193, 196–8, 200,
203
socio-ecological projects, 10, 185, 202
social sustainability, 7, 68, 91, 105, 106,
146, 160, 221
spillover, 165–8, 171, 175, 177
Spinoza, B., 4
Stoermer, E., 12, 208
sustainability, 1–30, 53, 54, 61, 67–78,
91–6, 104–6, 125–40, 146, 150,
151, 153, 155, 158–61, 165–79,
183, 187, 208–10, 214–17, 220,